WE WERE BLACKWATER

BARRIE "BAZ" RICE

WE WERE BLACKWATER

Life, death and madness in the
killing fields of Iraq

AN SAS VETERAN'S EXPLOSIVE TRUE STORY

\B^b\
Biteback Publishing

First published in Great Britain in 2023 by
Biteback Publishing Ltd, London
Copyright © Barrie Rice 2023

This is a work of non-fiction, based on real events. Some names and details have been changed to protect the identity and privacy of individuals. Certain stories were told to the author by fellow security contractors; with their permission, he has incorporated their experiences into this story, changing the timelines to make the narrative easier to follow.

Every reasonable effort has been made to trace copyright holders of material reproduced in this book, but if any have been inadvertently overlooked the publisher would be glad to hear from them. The author is grateful to those who have sent their photographs for inclusion in this book. All other photos are taken from the author's collection.

ISBN 978-1-78590-814-9

10 9 8 7 6 5 4 3 2 1

A CIP catalogue record for this book is available from the British Library.

Set in Minion Pro and Trade Gothic

Printed and bound in Great Britain by
CPI Group (UK) Ltd, Croydon CR0 4YY

FSC
www.fsc.org
MIX
Paper | Supporting
responsible forestry
FSC® C171272

For the brothers we lost.
May you rest in peace.

For the people of Iraq.
May you find the peace you so deserve.

'The choice you make between hating and forgiving,
can be the story of your life.'
Gregory David Roberts
Shantaram

CONTENTS

AUTHOR'S NOTE

For reasons of national security, commercial sensitivity and/or confidentiality, it has been necessary to change some details of events, including names, places and dates, when writing this book. Mostly I have used first names and call signs only to identify individuals, at the request of those portrayed.

This book has been written from my memory and from conversations with those fellow operators who were with me at the time of the events portrayed. No one recorded the conversations that took place, and few written reports survive from that time, so I have therefore had to recreate conversations as accurately as I can and as I and my fellow operators remember them.

Not every event written involved me or my team directly; some of them were told to me by those who were there and personally involved but wanted their story told while remaining anonymous. Therefore, and with their consent, for ease of writing and to reduce the cast of characters I have moulded their experiences into the overall story.

I have been fortunate in that numerous other accounts of the 2003 war in Iraq have been published, and I have been able to cross-check many of the events portrayed. These include first-hand accounts of the activities of various military units, accounts of private security company operations, plus more general books giving a wider sense of the military campaigns in Iraq.

PREFACE

I started to write this book after much hesitation, and encouragement, from friends interested in hearing the non-media or tainted version of what it was like working for Blackwater USA in Iraq. Initially I didn't think I had much to write about that would be worth reading, plus there was a side of me that was resistant to revisit some of my experiences or those of my fellow contractor brothers.

There were also many times when I had to step away from the keyboard and clear my head, and eyes. But as I progressed, if anything, I have found the experience of writing this story extremely cathartic, and with the encouragement of some very special people I have what I hope is an honest account of my time with Blackwater Commercial (a branch of Blackwater USA). I also hope those who read it have an open mind and will realise we were not the heartless killers some people have tried to portray us as.

The people who were never there, never met us, never rode the streets with us, never walked in our boots. People who backed us and the invasion in the beginning then turned on us when they saw the tide of public opinion shift. People who didn't want to be the focus of attention themselves but wanted to stay with the cool crowd, the finger pointers.

But, if nothing else, it has brought into focus why the story of the security industry – the private war; Blackwater's war – in Iraq needs to be told, warts and all. It also served to clarify in my mind why I had to tell this tale, if for no other reason than to lay to rest the ghosts of the long years that I spent in Iraq and to set the record straight, once and for all.

PROLOGUE

'Oh my God!' The urgency in Rose's cry silenced the chatter in the team house. 'Baz, Mark come now, you must see this. Quick, come now! Oh Lord, no!'

I jumped up from my desk and ran into the TV room. It was mid-morning and there on the screen, in vivid colour, was a vehicle totally engulfed in orange flames, surrounded by a crazed mob. People were pushing each other out of the way to get to the red-hot hulk, surging forward then rushing back, forced away by the heat. Most were celebrating with a mix of hatred and joy, while others were hurling bricks, rocks or anything they could get their hands on at some black, charred shape in the passenger seat, all the while yelling at the TV camera like a pack of wild dogs that had just made a kill.

And to be honest, to them, that's exactly what it was.

As the camera crew moved around for a different angle, the profile of the burning vehicle became clearer. It was the shape of a 4x4, very much like one of our own Mitsubishi Pajeros, the type our boys had been using on their close protection run. But that run was hours ago.

As I watched, something shifted in the burning mass of flame. It looked sickeningly familiar, and I felt a cold shiver run up my spine.

'It can't be,' I said aloud. 'It can't be them.'

But even as I said it, more and more of what I was seeing brought on a gnawing sense of dread; the shape of the bowed head in the passenger's seat; the colour of the charred trim of the vehicle. A deep wave of revulsion mixed with an overwhelming sadness filled me, which I had to fight to keep under control. I hoped the glazing of my eyes hadn't been noticed by the others, who even now were hurrying into the room. I was their team leader, after all, and they looked to me for calm reassurance.

I feigned a cough to clear my throat. 'They were only going to deliver a client to Taji Airbase,' I muttered, so wanting it to be true. 'Nah, no way. This can't be them, can it?' I threw the question at no one in particular, trying to place our boys anywhere in Iraq but where I was watching this horrific scene unfold. 'Where exactly is this happening?'

'Fallujah,' Rose replied.

'Fallujah? Nah, it can't be them. What the hell would they be doing in Fallujah?'

But even as I denied it, I knew what it was. It was our team being burnt to death on the TV screen. *What the fuck were they doing in Fallujah?*

The more I watched the more there was no denying that these were our guys, our bros who had left the team house only the day before. The camera crew circled to capture the scene of carnage 360 degrees, moving further up the street to where a second fire raged, engulfing a vehicle of the same make. A blazing orange inferno, it was vomiting thick clouds of black smoke, and it too was surrounded by a frenzied mob. They were unleashing the same explosion of raw hatred, but this time it was directed towards something lying on the ground; something black and prone but with the arms bent up in the awful, twisted pose of a charred human corpse.

'Holy fuck, that's them all right,' I said, finally admitting out loud what I was seeing, a seething anger now replacing the feeling of sadness and building up inside me like a volcano.

I glanced around and saw all the others who'd been drawn here by Rose's frantic cries. We stood there in stunned silence staring at the TV, watching what we didn't want to believe playing out right in front of our eyes.

'Is this live?' someone asked.

'Yeah, I think so,' another answered. 'It's one of the Arabic news channels.'

'Holy fuck, this is happening right now...'

It was.

After this, nothing in Iraq would ever be the same again.

This was live footage of an event that would set into motion the death and destruction of thousands of people: Iraqis, Americans, and in fact everyone from every nation who was dumb enough to be in Iraq in the first place. This was the beginning of our war; the security contractor's war; our war against the insurgency; our descent into hell; our war against even ourselves.

Little did I realise that this also marked the beginning of the end for Blackwater itself. But the only thought that burnt through my mind on that bright sunlit morning, on 31 March 2004, as I watched the carnage unfolding on that TV screen, was this: *OK, you pricks, bring it on. You've crossed the line. If you want to do this to us, then we are going to do the same to you. The gloves are off.*

Little did I realise that beneath the burning rage and the bravado and the hurt, this was the beginning of my own descent into the bottomless pit; into the darkness of the nightmare that would affect me for years to come.

Maybe for ever.

CHAPTER 1

The 'bing!' of the seat belt sign alerted us to the imminent descent into Baghdad International Airport (BIAP). I glanced out at the wing flaps, felt the judder as the landing gear lowered and heard the clunk as it locked into place. The Air Serv flight from Amman, Jordan, was about to bank into the infamous corkscrew spiral we'd all heard about, a manoeuvre designed to lose altitude fast while staying safely inside the invisible protective cone of anti-missile systems stationed around the airport perimeter by US and Coalition forces.

That was the idea, anyway.

Formerly Saddam International, now Baghdad International Airport, BIAP was a vital hub these days, the first port of call for all air-transported logistics, including the mass of equipment and personnel necessary to run an invasion – like us, the private contractors. Consequently, it was becoming a favoured target for the burgeoning resistance movement whose fighters would take spray-and-pray shots with mortars, rockets or small arms in the hope of hitting anything or anyone. They weren't too fussed what or who: a hit was a hit.

To the budding insurgency, if it flew, drove or walked at BIAP it was worth shooting at, as the crew of a DHL cargo aircraft had found out just a few months earlier. Their plane was hit with a shoulder-launched surface to air missile (SAM), and it would have come down in a fiery heap if it hadn't been for the skill of the pilot and crew who nursed the crippled wreck back to the ground, flames spouting from its burning wing and licking rapidly towards the cockpit. Touching down just before the airframe became totally unviable, they skidded off the runway, the aircraft coming to a smoking halt. In the midst of a minefield. Talk about a shitty day.

Thereafter, the corkscrew had become the preferred take-off and landing method.

As our plane made its tight circles earthwards, I was able to look directly down at the sandy brown terrain. I fixed my gaze on the distinctive hexagonal terminal buildings, which were rapidly getting bigger. My eyes followed the big looping link road to a palace-like complex where it joined a major highway heading, I guessed, to Baghdad.

I felt a thrill of anticipation, but around me I noticed that the noisy chatter had died down, the sounds of bullshit and bravado replaced by the noise of screaming engines and the occasional nervous laugh. I sensed a lot of hard swallowing and seat belt tightening by guys still trying to look cool as the angle of descent verged on the vertical and they realised we had actually arrived; no more big talk, this was where the rubber met the road.

Whoever was bringing us in sure knew what they were doing. From the voice of the pilot and aircrew on the intercom, I guessed they were from South Africa and veterans from many a conflict, or just bloody good bush pilots, as 'Yarpies' tend to be. They were courageous men and women all right. I mean, who else would willingly fly commercial flights into the biggest shitstorm the US had started since the war in Afghanistan or Vietnam? You had to have some rock-solid kahunas to want to do that.

To think that just that morning we'd been having breakfast at the Bristol Hotel, in Amman, Jordan, the staging area for myself and around thirty other guys hired by a US security company with the name of… Custer Battles. Yeah, I know: you just gotta laugh. It sounds like a cowboy outfit, and for me the name conjured up images of General George Armstrong Custer getting his not-so-glorious ass-kicking at the Battle of the Little Bighorn. But a name's a name, right, and I guess it somehow seemed entirely appropriate to the company's two ex-military founders, Mr Custer and Mr Battles.

Once George W. Bush had declared an end to all armed conflict – 'Mission Accomplished' – in Iraq, Mr Custer and Mr Battles, like so many others, had seen an opportunity to make megabucks, and they'd formed their eponymous security company. They were ready and willing to assist in the 'reconstruction and democratisation process' of a newly liberated Iraq – well, one free of Saddam Hussein, at least – and to ease the load off the regular military who had bigger fish to fry, like trying to snuff out the rapidly growing Iraqi resistance.

Private contractors would do the 'little jobs' while the military cracked heads and searched for Saddam and his henchmen, who had understandably legged it.

At least, that was the theory…

I'd arrived in Amman on 16 October 2003 and discovered I was the only non-American in the whole Custer Battles contingent. No problem. I'd assumed we were all high-speed, low-drag former 'Tier 1 Operators', as we elite forces types tend to be known. I just presumed everyone would have a similar background and training to me – former special forces, unconventional warfare and close protection specialists, or something similar in US law enforcement like SWAT (Special Weapons and Tactics) or HRT (Hostage Rescue Team). After all, we were going to be working in the mother of all shitshows and would need all the skills of our trade. Only the top-tier guys need apply, right?

Wrong.

It seemed that in the hurry to find the manpower for the lucrative contracts the US State Department was doling out, every man, dog and time-serving former military gofer from the US, UK and other Coalition nations was getting in on the act. Those operators not immediately picked up by established companies, like DynCorp International, Triple Canopy or Blackwater, or Control Risks Group from the UK, had been scooped up by the newbies – like Custer Battles. That included me and the assortment of macho men that surrounded me right now. But hey, I needed the job and by hell I needed the money. Two hundred dollars per day was big bucks and it was, well, $200 a day more than I'd earned for a good while – so I wasn't complaining.

Not yet anyway.

Amman's Bristol Hotel had offered the typical three-star breakfast buffet with eggs cooked every which way, pork-free sausage, hash browns, oatmeal and soggy fruit. The food smelt OK, but there was a definite whiff of bullshit from the loudmouths talking up their credentials. While I was looking for a place to sit with my plate piled high, I was waved over to a table occupied by three guys. Chief among them was a burly 5ft 7in. rough-around-the-edges but friendly-seeming ox of a guy named Bobby. He wasn't overly muscular, but he was solid and shook my hand with the kind of grip that told me he was as strong as shit. He introduced me to the others – Chris, an older-looking guy in his early fifties, muscular, with thinning red hair and a matching moustache, then Bill, another burly dude around the same age with an infectious smile.

They looked like they were from a similar background and career path to me so I placed my plate down, knowing my New Zealand accent and Māori good looks would give me away in short order. It was all down to those strong Polynesian genes, and, hell, I didn't mind as long as they didn't think I was Australian, or there would be trouble...

After intros and a few laughs to break the ice, the chat turned to our military backgrounds. It turned out only Bill and I had been in our home country's respective armed forces. Bill's tattoos told me before he did that he had been in the US Marine Corps. Bobby, originally from Detroit, was a former personal security guy for some exiled Saudi Royal in Egypt. Chris, from Florida, seemed a solid-enough guy, and he'd been on the same protective detail as Bobby, in the land of the pyramids. He spoke slowly and quietly, but when I asked what he'd done prior to Egypt, he didn't answer directly.

Then, in a low conspiratorial whisper, he slipped in that his prior service was 'classified'. There was that warm smell of bullshit. In our line of work, everyone's been on 'classified' details. The point is, that's in the past and guys need to know who they're working with. I served seven years in the New Zealand Special Air Service (NZSAS), or 'the Unit' or 'Group' as it's known, and I put that right out there for the guys who needed to know. Classified is bullshit. Period. And it raises a huge red flag.

But now wasn't exactly the time or place to question 'Classified Chris'. These were the first guys I'd met – by default, my new amigos. They had welcomed me into the fold, and I felt I might need someone to have my back among the crowd of Yanks, so I pushed my doubts to the back of my mind and cracked on.

Over that first breakfast together, Chris, Bobby, Bill and I avoided talking about family or our views on the war. We all knew why we were there, and that was to do a job, earn as much money as we could and get the fuck back home in one piece, so we could give our loved ones a better life.

We each had our five-year plan, and this was the chance to finally provide a suitable living of the type we thought we deserved but had struggled to achieve on Civvy Street. Family or ethics didn't come into it. In any case, why would you want to get that close to someone, learning all about their wife and kids, when that person could be dead tomorrow? That was my view. At that moment and for all of us A-types we had balls to sniff, poles to piss on and territory to mark; the other shit could come later.

I found out from Bobby we would have to wait two more days in Amman before the entire Custer Battles contingent arrived. I didn't mind. Everyone in the military and security game knows there is always a lot of 'hurry up and wait'. As I met more guys and got a handle on their backgrounds, I felt increasingly confident in my own abilities. I reckoned my experience in the Unit would stand me in good stead, especially as a lot of the guys had never worked outside the good ol' US of A, let alone done anything particularly combat oriented. A good number were former law enforcement types, which was fine if we were going to be writing speeding tickets... but there wouldn't be much call for that in a full-on war zone.

The more I learnt, the more surprised I was at just who Custer Battles was sending into the cauldron of Iraq. So, I did what all 'grey men' do. In the world I hail from you're taught to be the grey man – the one nobody notices in a crowd. I sat back quietly and observed, categorising the guys into groups; who the big talkers were, who the born leaders were, who was capable and solid, and who was full of shit.

Worryingly, that last category sure looked a big one.

A contingent from the Australian Air Force was in control of air traffic for BIAP, and forty-eight hours after my sceptical appraisal of the Bristol Hotel crowd, our plane screamed into land, making full use of what felt like an entire twenty metres of runway. Talk about an emergency touchdown. As the plane taxied for cover, I craned my neck to see as much of our surroundings as I could through the porthole window.

The terminals would have looked dated and close to derelict even without the thick layers of dust and sand that seemed to cover everything. To the far right of what must have been the departure terminal were two faded green Iraqi Airways planes; they didn't look like they'd be going anywhere soon, or maybe ever again. One had its side door wedged open and I could only imagine the layers of dust and pigeon shit inside.

Our plane came to an abrupt halt and the door swung wide open. If the short take-off and landing hadn't emphasised how we had just landed in a war zone, the disembarkation certainly did. We were rushed out like spawning salmon at a waterfall with our feet hardly touching the ground. On the tarmac, a burly, distinctly worried-looking Scotsman yelled at everyone to get a move on, his accent so thick that none of the Americans seemed able to understand. He pointed and jabbered for everyone to get their asses inside the terminal with the upmost speed.

As I clambered down from the plane, I deliberately slowed the line behind me for a second, so I could soak in the atmosphere. There's a saying in our industry: 'You're not there until you're there,' and I was now 'there' – Baghdad, Iraq, 2003.

We gathered in a makeshift arrivals area to await luggage and instructions. The terminal looked as abandoned on the inside as it had from the outside. It was zombie-movie empty, like everyone had just got up and run the fuck out leaving everything behind: papers on tables; chairs pushed away from desks, half-empty teacups and just a few flickering fluorescent light tubes to appropriately light the horror-movie scene. The décor was so 1980s it was kind of cool, with yellows and greens that reminded me of a pair of *Partridge Family* pants I used to have as a kid. It was kind of nice, I thought, in that retro style – although I was probably the only one warped enough to think that.

It was the sheer size of the terminal, though, that really grabbed my attention; it was huge. Looking around, I would have bet the place could have processed thousands of travellers at a time, and yet today we were the only ones around.

I had to remind myself that beyond these walls Iraq was a free-for-all with a growing number of religious, tribal or plain-criminal factions wanting a slice of the spoils the country had to offer, now that Saddam was no longer running the show. It was obvious that when Bush had announced to the world that all combat missions were done and dusted, a lot of angry and increasingly well-armed Iraqis had begged to differ, having not appreciated being 'liberated' by the Coalition and having not got Bush's memo.

During passport processing I could hear a real commotion start up – there were raised voices from somewhere behind me. I turned to see that the source was one of the big talkers I had noticed back in Amman. Apparently, he had just decided this was as far as he was willing to go: he wanted back on the plane and out of there pronto. *Yep, thought so*, I said to myself. This caused a little commotion, but personally I thought it was kind of admirable that the guy realised this wasn't the place for him and wanted to get the hell out now rather than do it later and risk becoming a liability to himself and, more importantly, his team. The last thing you need when the shit hits the fan on an armed run is the one fuck who doesn't want to be there.

After a bit of hoopla, former Mr Big Mouth was separated from the rest of us to be shipped back to Amman faster than a fly finds shit on a hot Baghdad day. *Well, there's no turning back now*, I reminded myself. The work situation since leaving the military had been pretty good, but there was always that nagging feeling of what it would be like to be in an actual war zone; I guess every soldier has it. All the training in the world is great, but we all hope to get the opportunity to test ourselves operationally in full-on combat.

And now, here I was, not as a soldier but as a civilian security contractor – the new and 'politically correct' name for a mercenary or a soldier of fortune. I wondered for a moment what my father would have made of it. We had always had a complicated relationship. It seemed, to me, that no matter what I had done in life it seldom met his approval, which caused a lot of tension between us. Even when I'd passed selection for the SAS it didn't generate much, if any, praise. He just seemed a hard nut to crack emotionally. I put it down to him being a man of his time – what I like to call the John Wayne generation, where men didn't cry or show any feelings.

Well, this now was the new Wild West. *Yee ha! Let's get it on.*

We were herded together by a representative of the Custer Battles training wing who had been in the country for some time. He was a tall black guy, a former US Army Ranger, who seemed friendly enough and willing to answer most of the dumb questions being thrown his way.

We moved into a room he had set up with desks and chairs and a map taped to the wall and he showed us the layout of BIAP: the out-of-bounds areas, where the chow hall was, the accommodation blocks, and finally he laid out our schedule for the next ten days. It dawned on us then that we would not be immediately deploying to Baghdad but were to undergo training modules to assess our skills, prior to moving into the company's rented hotel headquarters in the city centre. It was a disappointment, but it seemed a sensible-enough move. Better to sort the shit out here at the airport, where it was quicker and easier to put any duds on a flight back home.

Our instructor told us that Custer Battles had been contracted to run convoy security teams: escorting trucks and supplies from Kuwait to Baghdad, using the civilian motorway that the military had call signed 'Tampa'. Route Tampa – also known as the main supply route (MSR) – had been the scene of many attacks by the Coalition forces during both Gulf Wars, but more recently, Iraqi insurgents had been hitting Coalition convoys there.

I can't remember our instructor's name, but about a year later he would be killed in a vehicle crash – right there, on Route Tampa.

But our role would not be escorting those convoys, he explained. We were to be the company's new close protection (CP) teams, tasked with running clients around Baghdad to the offices of government ministries, or to the newly formed International Zone (IZ), or the Green Zone as it became known, where the State Department and US military had set up shop.

First, we had to get familiar with working together as new CP teams and the drills. It was all pretty standard stuff as far as I was concerned – like primary and secondary road routes, the locations of the ministries and actions-on for contact and weapons use.

Just as important was learning the actions-on if we ran into the 'Big Army' – the US military, who roamed the streets in their big fuck-off Humvees, Abrams tanks and Bradley Fighting Vehicles (BFV), setting up checkpoints throughout the city. We were warned that we *really* needed to know how to approach those trigger-happy fuckers. As we were all to find out, dealing with the Big Army was just as scary as dealing with the bad guys.

Once we were done that first day, we were shown to our sleeping quarters – upstairs, in what would previously have been the airport's admin offices, four guys to a room just big enough for two. Bobby managed to claim a room for the 'four amigos', placing his big imposing frame in the doorway to deter anyone else from thinking about dumping their shit there. We marked out our territory by stacking our bags around our bunks. It was easy for me as I only had enough kit and clothing to fit into one large carry bag, and my new buddies did not have too much more.

By comparison, many of the guys had clearly made full use of America's buy-everything military shops and gung-ho websites, arriving with enough gear to fit out a small platoon. The place looked and smelt like a contractors' superstore, with all these lookalike, cloned operators – clean and identical, with the same gleaming equipment, clothing, weapon accessories, plus large-capacity magazines. You name it, they had it – everything you could ever imagine needing to fight a war.

Only, this was like no war any of us had ever served in before, if at all.

Some guys had brand new gun-rail systems, to be fitted to their M4 rifles, just as soon as they were issued with them, plus all the

Gucci accessories like optics, pistol grip assemblies, three-point slings, vests, Glock pistol holsters, go-bag backpacks, para-boots and even fucking ball caps with big-ass US flags on them against a desert-hued background. Not exactly blending in or low profile.

'Jesus,' I thought, looking at all this swinging-dick excess. Was all this just another indicator of those who had never really done this kind of work before? Or was I just jealous?

It sure as hell made my attire look pretty shitty: dirty battered sunglasses, two pairs of cargo pants, four pairs of socks and four pairs of boxers. Six T-shirts, one pair of former Unit-issue flight crew gloves, a black ball cap I picked up in the Dubai duty free, and some PT kit. Oh, and swimming goggles – why those, I really don't know. At least the physical training (PT) kit would get some use. But for sure, I was the worst-dressed fucker there.

Bill and Bobby had long since stopped giving a damn about middle-age spread, but each morning before breakfast Chris and I would do some PT, including a run around the perimeter of the car park within the BIAP boundary. It was good to get away from the gaggle of kit-comparing A-types and take in a lung-full of Iraqi dust.

I'd heard somewhere that the finer the dust, the older the civilisation. Baghdad dust was like fine talcum powder.

We would run for around three kilometres, and I never felt the desire to venture out much further or too far from something solid I could duck behind for cover. I always had the feeling we were being watched, not only by the Aussies in the twelve-storey control tower but by other, far less friendly eyes. The insurgents, it seemed, were getting very good at lobbing in mortars from outside the BIAP cordon, and there was plenty of concrete to help spread the shrapnel, effortlessly slicing a person to bits.

After a few days of basic CP training, we finally hit the firing range. This was where I'd see exactly who had the skills; who would stop talking the talk and start walking the walk. The range was the standard twenty-metre dirt berm with a tire wall at one end to shoot your bullets into. Ideal for zeroing-in weapons, plus run-of-the-mill instinctive shooting and mag change drills, but limited for doing anything other than static firing or turning-on-the-spot shooting drills. Without berms or walls down the sides, you can't conduct fire-and-manoeuvre or transition drills from long to short weapons for fear of someone cranking off a round in the wrong direction and hitting someone outside – so doing the insurgents' work for them. Still, at least it would give us a chance to get used to the latest shit-hot weaponry we were going to be issued with.

Then I got my first look at the equipment and… *Holy shit, Batman! You got to be joking, right?*

Those of us who hadn't come decked out with magazine webbing from Guns 'R' Us were given beige, sleeveless reporter's vests, which only had front pockets and hung to your knees if you actually put your mags in them. Custer Battles must have scored a bargain batch of XXXL size from somewhere because even Bobby, as big as he was, looked like he was wearing a tent when he slipped his on. As for any body armour or Kevlar vests, forget it. So, no actual protection from incoming bullets, then.

Plus, there were the weapons themselves. Fuck, they looked like they had been found in some ancient desert cave. They were the oldest, ugliest, most rattling Egyptian-knockoff AK-47s I had ever seen. So much for all the brand-new Gucci M4 assault rifle rail systems, fore-grips and other gleaming accessories the guys had brought with them; that shit wasn't going to fit these ugly pieces of crap.

To go with our decrepit bang-sticks, we were handed 3x30-round rusty-ass magazines that weren't in any better shape than the rifles. I was starting to have some serious doubts about Custer Battles' commitment to their guys, but surely these had to be the *training* weapons, right? Er, no. These were our *issue weapons*. Shit me, we hadn't even made it into Baghdad, and this was the second big red flag. Suddenly $200 a day didn't seem like a lot for what we were going to be asked to do. But I was here now and like all good soldiers, I signed for my equipment and just got on with the job.

I'll make it work. What other choice do I have?

Although it had been a few years since I had fired an AK, it was like falling off a log. The know-how stays in your brain until you need it again. It wasn't long before I was feeling the groove, cranking off controlled two-round bursts into the centre mass of the target. We had always practised 'double taps' in the Unit. Fired on auto or semi-auto, it was up to you. As long as both rounds impacted the kill zone on the target very close together – or, even better, touching and forming a nice little figure of eight – it didn't matter how they got there. As I was shooting away, I noticed a growing group of the guys behind me, watching what I was doing. After I had finished my first mag, one of them asked where I had learnt to shoot like that and what outfit I was from.

I glanced at him. It was one of the big talkers I had singled out in the Bristol Hotel. 'Nah, I'm not military,' I told him. 'I used to be a bus driver.'

With that I turned and walked over to chew the fat with Bobby, Bill and the boys.

'Wow, what the fuck sort of buses do you drive in New Zealand?' Bobby asked, with a chuckle.

It was clear some of the guys had never fired an AK before, or anything larger than the 5.56mm-calibre used in standard NATO military units. The spread of their bullets was proof of that. I would call it a 'grouping', but that would be insulting to groups. The AK fires a 7.62x39mm bullet, much larger than its US counterpart, and because of that it has a bit of a kick from the recoil. If you're not standing in a solid firing position, it will push you back and off balance, not to mention bruise your shoulder. There was more than one instance when those of us watching stepped back behind something a bit more solid, in case the dancing shooter on the mound lost control and spun around. Watching some of the guys reinforced my feeling that we did not all have the same calibre of training. As with the equipment, I wasn't impressed.

After two more days of shooting and more than a couple of the AKs self-destructing, including one that exploded in my own hands, we moved on to vehicle drills, walking drills, first aid and call signs. Call signs are a shortened name, nickname or number to make identification faster when on the radio. No two should be the same but, unlike in the military, where the call signs are given by the team commander, we were allowed to make up our own, usually with help from our buddies, whether we wanted it or not.

There was no way we could let Bill choose his call sign, having watched him devour his chow at the food hall, treating every meal like it was going to be his last and getting everything, including dessert, heaped on two meal trays in one pass, rather than going back for more. Bill got the call sign 'Two Trays', which he accepted like the big happy fuck he was. Bobby was 'G-Man', for no other reason than that his surname began with a G, and Classified Chris already called himself 'Yard Dog', so we stuck with that. Despite the guys trying to come up with something for me, I told them I'd be known simply as Baz, which is short for my real name and has been my moniker since I was a rugby-playing lad growing up in Gisborne.

Shortly afterwards, the Custer Battles chiefs decided those who'd proven themselves in training would move into the Baghdad hotel accommodation and integrate into the teams already based there. We were finally to start the close protection runs we were hired for. Yard Dog, G-Man, Two Trays, plus one other guy called Pappy and I were told to pack our gear and get ready for the move to where the action was: Baghdad City.

As we packed our meagre belongings and waited for the vehicles, I pointed out that none of the guys with the bulging bags of Gucci kit were with us. It reinforced my view about the difference between those who can walk the walk and those who just talk the talk. Chris's – Yard Dog – secrecy about his service was still the elephant in the room, of course, but we would have plenty of time to get around to that.

We were told the run into town would be done at last light as this was when most Iraqis were at evening prayers. Hopefully, there would be fewer people around and less chance of an attack. At this early post-war stage, it was still relatively safe to move around, but lately, there had been an increase in random shoot-and-scoot attacks and kidnappings in and around Baghdad, and not just against the regular military. Private contractors had been designated as fair game by the insurgency, we were warned.

Welcome to Iraq.

Just at last light, two soft-skin Chevy Suburbans pulled up in front of where we had staged our bags. To my surprise, each vehicle was driven by an Iraqi with an American riding shotgun in the front seat. So, just three, or even two, of us per vehicle. *Hell, that's risky.* There was no way you could keep a check on what was coming up behind you, and could you fully trust a local as your driver? I didn't want to distrust the Iraqis from the get-go, but I didn't know them or their background. For all I knew, they could be working for both sides, and what was to stop them from driving us into an ambush? Given the standard of some of the guys I had flown in with, I doubted whether Custer Battles had done much, if any, vetting of the Iraqi drivers either. We still hadn't left BIAP yet and there was another bloody great big red flag.

The ten-kilometre drive into Baghdad central proved breathtaking – finally seeing the city and its sprawling residential and commercial complexes. As we made our way down the busy stretch of road leading from BIAP to downtown, the lanes were separated by tall reed-beds and smart metal barriers. I thought Baghdad must have been a really nice place back in the day. Rumour was that Saddam had a tunnel system that ran beneath the length of this road, leading from one of his palaces direct to BIAP, so he could travel by golf cart and avoid being hassled by the locals.

'What's the name of this road?' I asked our escort.

'Irish,' he called back. 'Big Army have called it Route Irish.'

'Oh, nice road,' I enthused.

I wasn't joking; at least, back then I wasn't. Baghdad was steeped in history, and I loved being in the cradle of civilisation, a country so widely written about in the history books, even if the reasons for my being there weren't exactly the best. I soaked in everything I could see, while searching for any sign of an attack.

This was Baghdad, baby, and I was in it.

CHAPTER 2

Getting closer to the city centre, it was pretty much as I remembered it – that is, from the eerie-green-glow night-vision TV footage of smart bombs hitting targets during the air campaign of the war. I even recognised some of the buildings I had seen getting pulverised as anti-aircraft fire had arced into the night sky in a futile attempt to hit the incoming missiles and speeding warplanes. It brought home again exactly where I was.

I was surprised that the place still had the hustle and bustle of a major city, considering what it had gone through. *These are some tough and resilient people*, I told myself. The men seemed solid and stocky, and mostly they sported thick black moustaches. They say imitation is the sincerest form of flattery, but this was ridiculous: any number could have stood in as Saddam's body-double. The women were mostly covered from head to toe in black burkas, as they hurried to and fro dragging a child or two with them. In spite of any animosity they might have felt towards their foreign occupiers, the younger crowd were mostly wearing jeans and T-shirts sporting American brands and pictures of American sports stars.

Go figure. I guess it's the way of the modern world and an indication of America's reach and influence, good and bad.

Custer Battles had based themselves in two adjoining buildings of the Al-Aladdin Hotel Complex, set on the corner of a busy road within a row of four-metre-high blast-resistant concrete 'T' walls to separate them from the public. About thirty metres away down a side street was the entrance gate to the complex, manned by armed Nepalese guards. Separating the lanes in and out were metre-high concrete Jersey walls with barrier arms at each end to prevent any explosives-laden car or lorry – a 'Vehicle-Borne Improvised Explosive Device'; VBIED – from getting much closer.

VBIEDs were becoming more and more popular with the insurgency. They had been used with devastating effect against the UN, earlier in the year, so why give up on a good thing, they must have reasoned. Driving a truck packed to the gunnels with explosives was a simple, hard-to-stop, fear-inducing weapon, while the cost for the insurgency was minimal. They needed only one wannabe martyr to draw the short straw and drive the thing as far as they could, before blowing themselves and everyone else to hell.

Upon arrival at the Al-Aladdin Hotel, we were introduced to a few of the HQ team before being assigned our two-man hotel billets. As luck would have it, I was roomed with Yard Dog. Despite my reservations about his background, it was nice to be in a decent-sized room after the shoebox we had been housed in at BIAP. Each of the single beds had a bright-red polar fleece blanket that looked as if it had rarely seen the inside of a washing machine, but at least the sheets and pillowcases were clean. We were advised not to drink the water – duh! – although I had a long-lived habit of cleaning my teeth with local tap water, as a means of building up some resistance to the local bugs. It didn't always work, but as long as I didn't unexpectedly shit myself driving over a speed bump, it was good enough for me.

Although we were roomed together, me and Yard Dog were assigned to different CP teams. My team leader (TL) turned out to be a former Canadian SF guy in his early fifties, who seemed to know his onions. A typical Canadian, he was polite and friendly to anyone who crossed his path, whether he knew them or not, but I could see in his eyes that his kindly demeanour could change at a moment's notice, if need be. He told me our first run on an actual CP job was to be the next day. We were to take a client to the Elections Ministry somewhere within Baghdad and would meet the rest of the team at the morning mission brief.

That decided, Yard Dog and I wandered downstairs to the hotel restaurant for a beer or two and some chicken and rice. The next morning, I gathered my battle kit, such as it was, and headed downstairs to the operations room (ops room), where I was pleased to find the team leader giving the brief in the manner I was used to. We call it SMEAC: Situation, Mission, Execution, Administration and Command and Communication. It's a simple, effective and proven technique for getting across what needs to be said in an indepth and precise manner, formulated over time through countless wars.

Different countries have slight variations, but the SMEAC method is basically the same for all of them. Hey, if it ain't broke, don't fix it. The orders started with the usual update on the ground situation, recent attacks and when, where and how. For me, as a new guy, I was keen to know if all the stories I had heard were just hype or actually true. The Elections Ministry, I learnt, was situated on the edge of an area known as Sadr City, which was proving to be a real pain in the ass for the US military. Named after Mohammad

Mohammad Sadiq al-Sadr, a Grand Ayatollah who had been assassinated most likely at the orders of Saddam Hussein in 1999, the city was now run by his son, Muqtada al-Sadr, who, with his many followers – the 'Mahdi Army' – had decided that negotiations with the US administration in Iraq, run by American diplomat Paul Bremer, were not to his liking. Al-Sadr's preferred way of exerting influence these days was to launch gun and bomb attacks from within Sadr City.

As the orders continued, I liked what I was hearing, but when the Canadian TL read out the seating positions and vehicle allocation, I started to get a serious attack of the 'oh, fucks' again. The driver would be the same local Iraqi who had picked us up from BIAP the previous evening. Apparently, the soft-skin Chevy was his vehicle, and he wouldn't allow anyone else to drive it. (Soft-skin vehicles are unarmoured; hard-skin vehicles are armoured. You can guess which I would have preferred to have.)

Wait, what? It's his vehicle? We don't even have our own vehicles?!

As I tried to digest it all, I wondered what the make-up of the second vehicle would be and, yep, you guessed it, *there wasn't one.* This was to be a single-vehicle move. *WTF.* I figured I couldn't stay quiet any longer. I glanced up from my notebook to see if anyone else was concerned, but it sure didn't look that way.

'Uh, excuse me, mate,' I ventured. 'Did you say one vehicle?'

'Yes, one vehicle,' he replied.

'OK, then excuse me for my ignorance, but how's that safe? I mean, what happens if we break down, run out of gas, get hit? Where's the support, back-up, quick reaction force (QRF)?'

I could see the TL knew I was asking all the right questions. 'We only have enough vehicles for one per team,' he remarked, trying to hide his own embarrassment. 'That's all we've got.'

I approached him for a quiet word at the end of the briefing. 'Shit me, mate, have you guys been running single vehicle on all your runs so far?'

He nodded. 'All of them. I know, mate,' he added, 'it's not ideal, but it's all the company can afford right now.'

Custer Battles was gathering more red flags than you'd find at a get-together for the Chinese and Russian Communist Parties, and we hadn't even got started yet. At least I had managed to swap my rusty, antique AK for an ageing but infinitely preferable HK MP5, plus a few thirty-round mags of 9mm. The Heckler & Koch brand is German and, like most German products, it's famous for quality and reliability. There are a few knockoffs, but this one was stamped with US/German markings, so I was pretty confident it was genuine.

The MP5, which is considered the gold standard for submachine guns, is used by most, if not all, of the world's elite special forces outfits. In the Unit, I was brought up on the MP5A3 and MP5SD (suppressed) variants, and I can operate them in my sleep. They seldom have problems and are accurate up to about 100 metres with an extendable butt and a choice of 30 or 15x9mm-round mags, which can be fired on full or semi-automatic with very little recoil. Admittedly, the 9mm-calibre is small compared to the bigger AK-47 bullet and the 100-metre range isn't so great, but that wasn't going to be a problem here in Baghdad, I figured. We were going to be inside a vehicle in an urban setting, and with the MP5 being far more compact it would be quicker to bring on to target. Besides, everyone else had their Custer Battles-issue AK-47s, so I guessed we were plenty covered for any longer-range stuff.

Our team make-up was the local Iraqi driver, the team leader in the front passenger seat and me in the back seat, along with a guy

I didn't recognise but who turned out to be a Nepalese gate guard dragged in to make up the numbers and another guy to ride as the 'trunk monkey' (TM), whose job is to face backwards riding in the trunk or rear of the vehicle, like a tail gunner on an old Second World War bomber. From there he has to cover our six (ass), calling out anything potentially hostile coming up from the rear. Usually, one of the smaller guys gets this honour, due to the lack of space, and given we were going to be a one-vehicle move, his role was especially important.

Operating as a single vehicle meant we didn't have the benefit of mutual support, extra eyes, extra guns, or the ability to block other vehicles or lanes of traffic, but at least we wouldn't stick out as much as a multi-vehicle convoy and could use the beat-up and dirty Chevy to try to blend in. Going 'low profile' isn't the ideal option, but it was the only course of action open to us right then.

I naturally shoot left-handed, so I prefer to sit on the right-hand side of the vehicle, behind the TL, where my arcs of responsibility are from the driver's front 180 degrees around to my rear. If needed, I can swap hands and fire just as well right-handed, if a little less accurately, but when you're travelling at 50mph, it's not about sniper rounds on target; it's about getting maximum rounds down range, as long as they are in the right direction and keeping the other fucker's mind off shooting you.

Prior to moving out, we readied our weapons then headed for the vehicle. In the cold light of day, the Chevy looked like it had more miles on the clock than the Space Shuttle *Discovery*. It turned out the wagons Custer Battles were using were hired from some local outfit, which also provided security at the hotel. *That's safe. NOT. Yep, another red fuckin' flag.*

The client squeezed himself between me and the Nepalese gate guard guy, and as we pulled out onto the main road and turned right towards the city centre, I felt like I was in a scene from the black-and-white movie farce series, *The Keystone Cops*.

This was my first experience of seeing downtown Baghdad in daylight, and it was even busier than I could have imagined. Despite all the conflict and unrest, the Baghdad locals were out and about trying to make a living. The roads were packed with vehicles, and any pedestrian who spied a gap in the traffic took it as an invitation to dive across. The place was like a circus, and it made keeping an eye out for threats somewhat challenging. I had to keep my head on a permanent swivel to see everything going on and to cover my arcs.

Fixated on doing my job, I naturally assumed the Nepalese guy on the other side would be doing the same, until I glanced across at him. To my surprise, I saw his head slumped down in the familiar snooze position. Yep, the fucker was asleep. As soon as I'd laid eyes on him it had struck me that he looked as if he'd spent the entire night in the hotel bar, necking the vodkas. But even so, I hadn't for one moment thought he'd be napping on the job.

I stared at him, laser eyes trying to communicate my disquiet. *Hey, wake the fuck up.*

I would have verbalised it, had the client not been sitting between us. Instead, I slowly turned and got the attention of the trunk monkey, gave him a nudge, then nodded towards the comatose idiot on the far side. The TM turned to look and was just as shocked as I was, so he gave Sleeping Beauty an elbow to the back of the head to wake him the fuck up. For a moment it seemed to work, as he yawned and rubbed his eyes, but then he slumped back down in his seat staring at his feet, and I could only imagine he was nursing the hangover from hell.

I could feel my anger starting to boil.

After a thirty-minute drive through busy streets and a few military checkpoints, we finally approached the ministry, only to be met by a crowd of locals thronging the sidewalks. This was nerve-racking as hell, but finally we pulled into the ministry and parked up outside the main entrance. As we dismounted, the TL and I escorted the client into the building, leaving the TM and Sleeping Beauty to cover the entrance and the driver to turn the vehicle around and stage it for our exit.

Once we were inside, I noticed a lot of people in office attire, and what looked like Iraqi military uniforms, bustling from room to room. More than a few of the looks I got were not exactly friendly, but kind of just accepting that I was there. Whatever the locals thought about foreign gun-toting guards being part of the occupying force I couldn't tell, but the males in uniform seemed to glance at me as if they were just tolerating our presence, for now; as if we were going to be a temporary imposition, whether we knew it or not.

The meeting went on for about an hour and I kept my back to the wall, on high alert. As sweat trickled down my neck and my pants started to climb up my ass, I did my best smile and wave, showing a face of calm confidence, while never letting my finger leave the MP5's trigger guard and with my thumb resting on the safety, just in case I had to flick it down and let rip.

Finally, I spied movement from the office that the client was in, which indicated to me he was finished. I would have radioed the guys in the vehicle to stand by as we would be coming out soon, but, guess what, *we didn't have any radios.* Another major point of concern; another red flag.

Once the client was back in the vehicle, we headed out through the maze of barriers and steely-eyed sentries then onto the main road and into the chaos, taking the route back to the hotel. The trip was quick compared to going there, and I used the time to hone my observation skills, looking for target and threat indicators, getting a sense of the lie of the land and memorising features and landmarks to use as navigation aids, while looking for possible safe routes or buildings we could use as cover in case we had to make a go of it on foot. Needless to say, we didn't have a GPS.

I was tired now, partly due to the stress of it being my first CP role in Iraq and partly due to all the quick learning I'd had to do. It had been great on-the-job training, but I was keen to use the mission debrief to raise a growing list of concerns. I escorted the client inside the hotel then moved into the briefing room. Unsurprisingly, the debrief was as informal as I hoped it wouldn't be, but when I got the chance I raised the main point of contention – our colleague, Sleeping Beauty.

The more the Nepalese guy tried to deny it all, the more riled I seemed to be getting. Seeing my growing anger, the TL cut in. 'OK guys, good points. Baz, thanks very much.' He then looked directly at Sleeping Beauty and told him no more napping. 'Tomorrow's run, same place, same time, see you then.'

Are you shitting me? That's it? No repercussions?

I left to meet up with the amigos and vent my frustrations. It seemed I wasn't the only one who had had a bit of a shitty day. G-Man, Yard Dog and Two Trays had had similarly unsettling experiences on their runs. This could be vented only over another dinner of chicken and rice – all the hotel menu offered – and several beers.

The next few CP runs proved an exact replay of the first, with Sleeping fucking Beauty continuing to nap on the job, showing little interest in watching his arcs and almost seeming to take pride in pissing me off.

At the end of the week, I finally confronted the TL, demanding to know if he was going to do anything about it. 'Unfortunately, we're short of manpower, so we just gotta make do,' was his response. He promised to raise it with the Custer Battles chiefs, but I figured I'd give that a go myself, 'cause if Sleeping Beauty's antics went on a lot longer it could very easily get all of us killed.

Within the HQ staff of Custer Battles there were one or two decent guys. I'd noticed one in particular – a former Tier 1 Delta Force operator called Matt. To the unwise, Matt might have seemed a bit seasoned to be still kicking down doors, given he was in his mid-fifties. But he was a true professional, like all the delta guys I have ever met, and his experience made up for any lack of youth. Besides, age is irrelevant to guys who have been around the SF block, and Matt still had the look of being very capable; a guy who could fuck you up if he wanted to.

I approached Matt and asked for a quiet word, and he was more than happy to oblige. I told him what had been happening on the runs and that I had had enough. I asked if there was someone else who we could use in place of the Nepalese guy. He understood completely and promised to find a solution. He knew about my SAS background. We drank a few beers together while chatting about our respective units and their histories. We got on well and I felt I had finally found someone within Custer Battles who I could trust and had my back. Matt said I was to leave it with him, which I was very happy to do.

I left Matt feeling cheered, as something was finally going to get done about our problem, and caught up with the amigos at the hotel bar, only to discover that none other than Sleeping Beauty was there as well, sinking vodkas with one of his countrymen. He gave me an arrogant grin, as he raised yet another shot in mock salutation, all designed to wind me up, of course.

'What's all that about?' Yard Dog asked, as he eyed the little fuck.

'Nothing to worry about,' I reassured him. 'I just had a good chat with Matt about it. He's assured me he'll deal with that fuck and fix the issues I've been having with him sleeping on the runs.'

'Well, that's good,' Two Trays agreed, sliding me over a beer.

'Yes, it is,' I said. I glanced across at Sleeping Beauty, who was lining up the vodkas like a condemned man's last drink. Which gave me an idea. 'But you know what, guys, I still have to do something about it.'

I told the amigos I would wait until the little fuck went to the toilet, follow him in and lay him out. They listened to my plan and nodded their approval. Well, I don't know what he had for a bladder, but he didn't go for a piss the whole evening, so we decided to call it a night and wait for another opportunity.

We paid our bill and made our way out of the bar.

'Hey, has anyone tried the elevator in this place?' Two Trays asked.

'No' was the collective answer, as we had always opted to use the stairs, not fully trusting the electricity supply in Baghdad.

'Fuck it,' Two Trays said, 'I can't be assed walking three flights of stairs.' Not wanting to leave a man behind, we all joined him in the elevator, but just as the doors started to close a hand reached in and forced them to reopen.

We were all a little pissed off that some jackass had delayed our departure, until we saw who it was... My friend from the Himalayan Mountains had just stepped in with his familiar sozzled 'head down not paying attention to his surroundings' attitude. The guy hadn't even realised who was in there with him. It was typical of the lack of awareness that he exhibited on a CP job, which could get us all killed. Just as the doors started to close again, Yard Dog put his hand out forcing them to stop. Without a word being said, he, Two Trays and G-Man quietly stepped out, leaving only Sleeping Beauty and me.

As the doors closed for the third time, I could feel my adrenaline starting to kick in and it felt good. The elevator started on its journey, and I cleared my throat loud enough for Sleeping Beauty to glance up. A look of horror swept over his face as he realised he was trapped in a little tin box with a pissed-off Māori.

I love elbow strikes and have a lump of built-up skin and gristle on my right elbow to prove it. There's just no fucking around or ambiguity with elbow strikes and this one was no different. I had chosen his forehead as the point of impact so as not to cause any serious bleeding, like if I hit him on the nose.

The elevator reached the third floor and stopped. I turned to face the door, and as it opened who should be standing there but the amigos. They showed no sign of surprise at seeing the only one left standing was me, as they looked past me at the figure laid out cold on the floor.

The next morning, I paid particular notice to those coming in and out at breakfast but didn't see my buddy from the snow-capped mountains anywhere. I got my kit ready for what I was sure was going to be a better day. The runs had got so lax by now that even the mission briefs had gone out the window, but as we mounted up, I was happy to see there was a new guy on our team – one of the guys from BIAP. He'd been called in to replace Sleeping, or should I say, Unconscious Beauty, who had still not made an appearance.

I gave him a quick run-down on what to expect and where we

were going. It was a nice sunny day and I felt good as we rolled out of the gate, and then I saw him, my sleepy old friend slumped in the hotel lobby, sporting an ice pack bandaged to his head looking very much the worse for wear. Sometimes you just gotta fix the problems yourself.

A few days later, we received a surprise visit from Big Army. They screamed up in their Humvee, pulling over right at the entrance of the hotel where their driver was having a shit time trying to turn the big fucking thing around so they could get into position. Apparently, they had been tipped off that an attack on the hotel was imminent. *Holy shitstorm, Batman.* Word spread, and the place suddenly turned into complete chaos with guys running around looking for places to hide and hunker down.

Some were busy pushing their mattresses up against the windows and looking for places where the ceiling wouldn't fall on them if there was an explosion big enough to drop the hotel, like that would save them. I approached my delta buddy, Matt, and asked him what the actions-on were for this kind of attack, because as far as I could remember we had not practised any. Matt was busy securing the clients, but he told me there were some heavy weapons in a spare room. He had the keys for it, if I'd like to grab a couple of guys, load up, head for the roof and find some suitable overwatch positions.

Yard Dog, G-Man, Two Trays and I set out to grab some firepower, along with a guy I hadn't met before named Tom. Tom and I shook hands and man-bumped and I felt an instant connection with the dude. I unlocked the door to Matt's spare room and stepped into what can only be described as man-paradise. To our surprise, we had stumbled upon a mini-arsenal the likes of which I had only seen in movies. Shit me, there were Soviet guns of every model and calibre, with a few European weapons thrown in for good measure, all nicely laid out with tins of ammo stacked neatly beside each.

We looked at each other with shit-eating grins; we were like fat kids in a candy store. Tom and I grabbed a PK each and a couple of boxes of ammo and spare barrels. The PK is a large-calibre 7.62x54mm Russian belt-fed machine gun that weighs a shit-ton; roughly 1.5 metres long, it's a big mother of a gun and just what you need to keep someone or something hostile from getting anywhere near close. G-Man and Yard Dog grabbed a couple of Belgian FN SLRs, an excellent self-loading rifle that can deliver an almighty punch, thanks to the big-ass NATO 7.62mm bullets they fire. The SLRs were the weapon of choice for the Argentinian and British militaries during the Falklands War, back in 1982, and proved very effective over the mostly open ground.

So, with guns, magazines and as many boxes of ammo as we could carry, and with a few stops to catch our breath along the way, we slogged up the three levels of stairs to the hotel roof. We were greeted by a dozen or so of the other guys, searching in the distance for any enemy to shoot at. Tom and I positioned the big PKs to face up and down the main roads running to the hotel, as these, we assumed, would be the likely paths of approach for any hostile vehicle or mass foot assault.

Meanwhile, Two Trays, Yard Dog and G-Man found locations looking down some of the side streets and alleys in case of a sneaky approach that way. It was clear to me that Tom knew what he was doing, and he soon took charge of the rooftop gaggle, organising the others into teams, assigning arcs of fire and duties like water and food details in case we were in for a long siege. That done, we settled in for whatever was coming, like a bunch of excited kids about to take their first ride in the haunted house at the fair.

Well, for about three hours, we did. As the light started to fade, we noticed the numbers on the roof started to thin out, rapidly. It was getting dark and as the attack hadn't happened yet, most deserted their posts, deciding that dinner and a beer was more important than the defence of our rock. Tom, Yard Dog, Two Trays, G-Man and I glanced at each other from our respective vantage points, and we all had the same expression of vexed exasperation on our faces. Everyone knows that the most likely time to suffer an attack is either last light or first light: that's basic military doctrine. If we needed men at their posts at any time, now was it. *But beer and chow called!*

Luckily for us the bad dudes didn't show up, so the intel was most probably faulty, but the rot had definitely set in with Custer Battles. But what to do? By 23:00 we were the only ones on the roof, so we decided to pull the pin ourselves and head down to one of our rooms for a beer. The five of us sat on whatever we could, cracked a ring-pull, clanked the cans, then slammed the golden liquid down our throats, dousing all the Iraqi dust we had collected on the roof.

'You know what?' I said. 'One good beer deserves another.'

I passed out another can to each of us. The first was good, but the second was better, though I have to admit nowhere near as good as the third, fourth or fifth. Soon enough, Yard Dog pulled out his guitar and before long we were banging out a few tunes where only the chorus mattered. Tom, as it turned out, was a former SEAL Team Six (ST6) guy, the cream of the US SEAL Teams. He, like us, was fed up with all the bullshit from Custer Battles. He told us he had good contacts with a US company called Blackwater, which maybe was an option to get us away from all this crap.

We all drank to that.

Blackwater was primarily a security training company, formed by a former SEAL officer based in Moyock, North Carolina. It was already in Iraq, providing CP for the State Department and Paul Bremer and team, in the International Zone (IZ). To be on that detail you had to be a US citizen and to have high-level security clearance. After several calls to Moyock over the following days, Tom was given the green light and a very basic budget to stand up 'Blackwater Commercial', which would be a stand-alone entity in Iraq. The team would be manned by whoever Tom could find. Now, all he needed were men who were willing to ditch Custer Battles and take a punt with him.

G-Man, Two Trays and Yard Dog were the first to be asked to join, then a few other US guys. This, of course, all had to be done under the noses of the Custer Battles HQ guys, who would have kicked Tom out if they had known. I knew my chances of being asked to join were slim, due to me being non-American, but I asked G-Man to put in a good word and ask for a meeting with Tom as I'd had it up to my balls with the Custer Battles crowd. My background and experience as the only other former Tier 1 operator spoke for itself.

At a meeting in Tom's room, I put forward my case and he outlined what he could offer. First, we would have to be more-or-less self-sufficient until Blackwater could see we were worth putting money behind, and that meant we would need to secure a contract basically immediately. Second, we would have to live in the Red Zone, an area lying outside the walled-off and heavily protected Green Zone, which meant minimal security. Third, we would have to scrounge equipment, weapons, ammo and vehicles.

'And, after all that, if it goes pear-shaped and we all get wiped out by the insurgency, we will have no fall-back, insurance or assistance,' Tom added. 'How about them apples?'

I looked at him unfazed. 'I'm still interested, mate,' I told him.

'If, and I mean if, this works and we prove we are a risk worth taking,' Tom continued, 'and if Moyock likes what they see, we stand to get paid, wait for it...' he paused for dramatic effect, '$600 per day.'

I did my best to stop my balls from jumping into my mouth. *Six hundred dollars per day? Fuck me, now that was a day-rate I could get to like, compared to the $200 I was currently on in a set-up that was out-and-out suicidal.*

'You still keen?' Tom asked.

'Yeah mate, I'm in.'

Keeping my voice as calm as possible.

'Welcome aboard,' he said offering me his hand.

'Glad to be. Thanks a lot, mate.'

To be honest, I would have joined for a lot less than six hundred bucks a day, as I just wanted to get the fuck away from Custer Battles. Don't get me wrong – I was very grateful to the CB guys for getting me to Iraq, but I believed my skills and level of professionalism, versus their commitment to their contractors, just wasn't a good match. Plus, I didn't want to leave Iraq in a wooden box, which I felt there was every possibility of doing if I stayed with Custer Battles's set-up.

As Tom and I shook on the deal, I felt ballsy enough to add that there was just one condition – *like I was in any position to make conditions.*

'Sure. What's that?' he asked.

'I would like to be the Command One (C1),' I said, which is an American term for team leader. 'Like I said, my background speaks for itself, and I am used to, and like, leading men. Apart from you, Tom, I'm the only other Tier 1 guy here. If anyone's going to be making critical decisions that can spell the difference between my life and death, I'd like that to be me.'

He nodded, pensively, knowing what I meant. He thought it over for a few seconds longer, then gave a smile. 'I'm down with that.'

We shook on it some more. Deal sorted.

Exactly one month after arriving in Baghdad, I and eight other guys handed in our notice to Custer Battles. Tom had covertly arranged transport and accommodation a few days earlier, and we packed our meagre belongings and loaded everything into three rented Chevy Suburbans. Just before we left, I found Matt – the former delta guy – and thanked him for being the one stable fucker in the company.

He appreciated it and let me know he understood my reasons for leaving. He wasn't really surprised so many of the others were going as well. As another night fell on war-torn Iraq and the curtain fell on my time with Custer Battles, I climbed into the vehicles, along with the other newly recruited Blackwater Commercial guys. Turning left, we made our way onto River Road, towards our new base. It felt good to get some distance between me and a place that had made me feel uneasy right from the start.

Without weapons, armour or any guarantee of success, we were driven through the dark streets of Baghdad to the Al-Hamra Hotel, set in the district of Karrada, about twenty-five minutes away. Karrada is a thin strip of land sandwiched between tight bends in the Tigris River, Baghdad's central artery. Look on the map and it's easy to find as it looks like a penis. You know it does, go check.

It was once the barracks area for Saddam's Republican guards, plus it housed the residences of various senior government ministers, and it lies only a stone's throw from what was, until recently, Saddam's main hang-out, the Iraqi Republican Palace, which is adjacent to the 14th of July Bridge, a major Baghdad landmark. That whole area was now being used as a base of operations for the occupying US forces, and it was rapidly being turned into the highly protected IZ.

The Al-Hamra Hotel turned out to be a tall, white building lying well outside the IZ, but at least it had its own external security post... of sorts. It was manned by a couple of burly, moustachioed Iraqi guys, who were carrying their AKs in a very relaxed manner – one dangling by the sling and the other by the foresight. There was only one streetlamp, and its limited glow threw the guards into these eerie silhouettes, which struck me as being like the poster for the movie *The Exorcist*. After a few minutes' chat with our lead driver, they finally raised the checkpoint's barrier. We pulled into the hotel's rear, unloaded our belongings and followed Tom inside.

As we passed the reception, I noticed the restaurant, a large open area paved in white marble and a swimming pool that was full and seemed to be working. Great. Now I didn't feel quite so stupid for dragging a pair of swimming goggles halfway around the world.

Tom wasn't able to secure enough rooms in the one hotel for everyone, so he had to split the team, with some of us in the Al-Hamra and the rest in another hotel about fifty metres down the road. This was OK, as the whole compound had been blocked off by concrete 'T' and Jersey walls, with access in and out by only two checkpoints: the one we had come in through and another on the far side. Tom instructed the driver to take the group I was in to our rooms, while he and his gang checked in to the other hotel. He told me to gather all the guys in my room, as we'd meet there for a briefing in twenty minutes.

My room was on the fifth floor, and it was pretty damn nice, all things considered. It turned out to be a suite, with a small lounge furnished with an old-ass couch and loungers, plus a small kitch-enette with a glass-topped table and four chairs. There was a stove and a fridge big enough to hold about forty cans of beer. The two bedrooms had clean sheets and the customary red-and-brown polar fleece blanket. The bathroom looked clean enough, the water was hot, and the pressure was good.

Unfortunately, for now, the amigos would be split, but we figured it would only be temporary. Yard Dog, G-Man and I were in the one suite, along with some guy I hadn't previously met named Randy. He was a goofy-looking fuck, who'd been a team leader at Custer Battles, and by the way he was acting it seemed as if he figured that would carry some weight here. My vibe from him was not good, so I decided to keep a close eye while being nice in a very fake kind of a way. I didn't know what it was, but my gut told me not to trust him, and I trust my gut.

Once everyone had been allocated a room and dropped off their shit, they gathered in our suite. Ten minutes later, Tom and his group squeezed in and, voila, there we all were: the first nine members of Blackwater Commercial; a group of guys brave/dumb enough to throw our cards into the air to see where they would land. We had little idea of what we were about to take on, in a country that was becoming more and more hostile to the 'Western invaders' – those who, in the average Iraqi's eyes, had broken so many of their promises.

One thing was for sure, though – we were all as happy as shit to be away from Custer Battles. At least our destiny in Iraq was now entirely in our own hands.

One of our Iraqi drivers also happened to be our chief fixer at Blackwater Commercial. His name was Mohamoud, so we called him Mo, which he didn't seem to mind; he was good-humoured and spoke pretty decent English. To underplay Mo's role as a fixer and key contact in those early weeks of Blackwater Commercial would be to do him a total disservice. Mo would prove crucial to our survival. If we needed something, anything, we just asked Mo. Give him a day or two and he would find it, tell you the price, haggle for you, strike a deal and deliver it. It never paid to ask too many questions as to how or where he got what he got. That was best left unsaid.

Being the forward-thinking man he was, Mo had secured six cases of warm Amstel beer ahead of that first meeting. As the cans were passed out among the group, Tom brought things to order.

'Listen up, guys,' he began. The room fell silent. 'Welcome to a new beginning and a whole new opportunity. I want to thank you for trusting me to do this. This is not going to be easy, but if it was easy everyone would be doing it. For all we know, the last pay cheque from Custer Battles could really be our last pay day in Iraq.'

There was a ripple of nervous laughter.

'Better not be,' someone commented, a little too loudly.

Tom gave him a look that said, *you dick*. 'That's pretty obvious, but even so we definitely have a tough job ahead. I'm sure as hell we can succeed and show Moyock we are worth the risk. We'll aim to start operations as soon as we secure proper kit and equipment. That will be a job for me and Mo for the next few days. We are hitting the ground running and I want to get guys orientated with the roads as quickly as possible, as we will be driving ourselves.'

Some of the guys glanced around nervously, but as far as I was concerned this was good news. Yes, it would have been less tiring to be chauffeured everywhere by a local guy who knew the routes, but I preferred it this way. Not only is it the best way to learn the roads and how to get around, but there were just too many things that could go wrong having someone whose country you had just invaded driving you from A to B.

'Our first run will be to Basra,' Tom announced.

Wherever the fuck 'Basra' was, I thought.

'I will get back to you on who will be on it. Again, support items are low to non-existent, but I will be making a trip to the Blackwater State guys in the IZ to see what I can scrounge from them: maps, plus anything not nailed down. Mo has arranged a visit tomorrow night from someone who can get us weapons and ammo. I have a little bit of money for AKs, but if you want something a bit more exotic, you'll have to buy it yourself. We will use the vehicles we drove over in, and Mo will arrange fuel until we can get into Blackwater's supply line in the IZ.'

We sat sipping on our beers, soaking it all in.

I'd kind of been there before: setting out on a road with no idea where it led. Growing up in Gisborne, I'd had few options – commercial fishing, work at the meat-freezing works, or try to be a pro-surfer. So, at twenty I just disappeared. I was down at the wharf one day, saw some mates who were working on a Japanese fishing boat, jumped on and was off for two months. When I got back, I joined the New Zealand military, like my sister before me. I wanted to travel and I sure as hell couldn't afford to do it myself, so the military was the only way. Right from the beginning I wanted to be in the SAS, but even when I'd made it into the Unit, my experience in the NZ military was a damn-good lesson in making things work with bugger-all resources, so in many ways my insecure and under-resourced new Blackwater Commercial career felt like familiar territory.

As we drained the last of the amber nectar, Tom instructed everyone to 'dead marine' their old can and grab a new one. Empty cans of beer clunked to the ground and fresh warm ones were handed out, but, before anyone could take a sip, Tom cut in.

'One more thing: command.' I saw Randy sit up a bit more in his comfy chair, obviously believing his TL rank at Custer Battles was going to carry on through. 'I've given this a lot of thought, so this will be short and sweet,' Tom continued. 'The C1 is Baz.' I got to my feet to show who the fuck I was to those who did not yet know me. 'You report to him, he reports to me, comprendo?' Tom added.

There were no obvious objections, but I noticed that Randy was slumped down in his comfy chair looking far from happy. Yard Dog, Two Trays and G-Man raised their cans in salute, and everyone else toasted my appointment, or maybe they just wanted to get the beer into them as quickly as possible. So, there we were – Al-Hamra Hotel, Baghdad, December 2003, the birthplace of Blackwater Commercial in Iraq.

Unleash the Kraken.

It's not what you know but who you know, and this was never truer than for us in those early days in Iraq. Like Tom had said, in order for us to succeed we needed to hit the ground running, and while he was busy finding contracts, one of the other guys, Frank, was ready to put his self-proclaimed bargaining skills to good use, with the assistance of Mo. Frank claimed that he could haggle with the best of them and the Arabs, in my opinion, are the best of the best. Through a friend of a friend, Mo was able to secure a line of weapons and other essential support items, and the next night in the back corner of the hotel car park they brought us a vehicle loaded with goodies.

We gathered around the trunk for what was literally a midnight boot-sale. With flashlights and headlamps set on dim, we did our best to look like seasoned arms dealers checking out the wares. Where the booty came from didn't need to be known; we were just grateful to have a line of goods available. The weapons on offer were mostly clunky old AKs, with the occasional Scorpion machine pistol thrown in. The Scorpions are ultra-compact 9mm weapons with a rapid rate of fire, but they were pretty useless for our needs. There were also a few Iraqi-made Tariq pistols, Kevlar vests, minus the plates, a good line on contaminated fuel and some Iraqna mobile phones, which used scratch-card, pre-paid credit.

Frank did seem a natural at bargaining, but that didn't make him a real haggler, at least not by Iraqi standards. As the purchases were mostly coming out of our own pockets, it was important that we didn't get fleeced. Mo's arms dealer buddy didn't seem to speak a word of English, but he told us through Mo that, because we were Mo's friends, he would do us a one-time deal: we could buy the AKs for as little as $75 to $125 apiece, depending on quality and country of manufacture; the Scorpions for a one-time price of $150, and the Tariq pistols for $50.

No doubt, these were bargain-basement prices.

We grabbed what we liked and put in orders for some extra stuff that was a little more exotic, like the AKS-74U – the same type that the Republican Guard used, which we were assured he could get. One or two pistols were bought by some of the guys and soon we were tooled up, happy and ready to roll. Now all we needed was the means to keep the bullets in the weapons; a gun is no good without bullets, and bullets need magazines to stop them falling out all over the ground. So far, we'd paid for only the guns.

Frank had seemed totally in his element when buying the guns, waving his hands all over the place in the Italian style, and exclaiming, 'Get out of here,' and, 'You gotta be kidding me.' Then he'd walked away, before suddenly turning back to renegotiate. Yep, he'd really thought he was a match for the Iraqi dealer who, through Mo, now reassured us once again that these were 'friend' prices. And then he announced he was asking for the magazines and the bullets.

Mo's arms-dealer buddy had definitely not come down in the last shower, and, believe me, there aren't a lot of showers in Baghdad. He calmly spelled out the price in Arabic to Mo, who passed it on in English to Frank. The look on his face, for those of us not quite within earshot, indicated things had just taken a turn for the worse.

The AK magazines would cost $40 each, so not a great deal less than the guns; Iraqi AK ammo was $120 per can of 200 rounds, or $200 per can for the more reliable Ukrainian bullets; Iraqi 9mm would be $75 per box of fifty – 'very hard to find, you see'; vests minus the plates $60; slings and bits and bobs thrown in for a bargain price, 'because you're my friends'. These prices, the dealer informed Mo, were not open for negotiation.

Shit me dead, Frank had been well and truly snookered.

Everyone knows that without magazines and bullets, guns are just trendy lamp stands, unless you're happy to run around yelling 'bang bang, you're dead', like we used to do during our army basic training days in NZ. With the number of insurgent attacks in Iraq, we just needed to get in the game and pay these prices or get the fuck out of town. Tom was simply going to have to hit up Blackwater for more cash to make up the difference in what we couldn't afford out of our own pockets. We needed the equipment and the seller had plenty of other buyers he could just as easily go to.

Under the glow of headlamps, in the back corner of the Al-Hamra Hotel car park, the cash-for-gun exchange was sealed. After all was done and dusted, the dealer shook Mo and Frank's hands and, *in perfectly good English*, proceeded to tell us to let him know if we ever needed anything else. Then he drove off in his orange and white taxi, no doubt laughing his smelly balls off all the way back to the insurgency.

To be honest, we didn't really care about the prices that much; at least now we were kitted out and armed. Plus, the whole incident gave us plenty of 'ammo', as it were, to give Frank shit for many days to come.

So, when all was said and done, everyone was happy.

CHAPTER 3

We now had weapons, but what we also needed was intelligence. We needed to know what the hell was going on around the country, particularly if we were to be hitting the roads outside Baghdad any time soon.

It was essential to know things like which direction and the best roads to take to get us to MSR Tampa and south to Basra; where attacks were known to be taking place; what districts and towns to avoid like the plague; basically, anything that could make our job safer and thereby easier. Also, maps were as rare as rocking horse shit and those who had them weren't about to part with them. All the security contractors were in the same boat, so it was mutually beneficial to trade information, which we did.

Tom spent the next few days pounding hallways over in the IZ and writing business proposals. Top of our wish-list was to provide security for the new satellite headquarters compounds for the Coalition Provisional Authority (CPA), which were to be dotted around the major cities and provinces of Iraq, constituting the US State Department's boots on the ground. The proposed sites needed to be recced and surveyed before we could even consider tendering, and we weren't alone. All the US security contractors were in a frenzy to be the first to get recces done and proposals submitted before the deadline.

In fact, there was a manic bidding process going on for all the new contracts that the Bush administration had opened to tender – but only for those companies hailing from the countries that had supported the invasion. That principally meant America. Even Britain, after all of Tony Blair's brown-nosing, got only the scraps. The plum contracts had been earmarked well before the invasion, for favoured US companies. These 'no-bid contracts' were given to them to provide everything needed for running a war: logistical support to the military, drinking water, catering, convoy drivers and laundry services, among many others.

War was business and business was good; just like the military in Iraq, the big security and logistic companies were making a killing.

Of course, Blackwater HQ at Moyock wanted the State Department Blackwater guys to conduct the CPA site surveys, for they were on-the-books and reliable. But they just didn't have enough boots on the ground in Iraq. So, Moyock asked Tom to fill a couple of slots with his guys, and he, of course, jumped at the chance to show that we were more than capable. It was also a great way for us to learn the ropes.

Each city survey would involve leaving Baghdad early in the morning to be back by nightfall. No one wanted to be out of the protective walls of our quarters after dark. The insurgency had already taken on boogeyman status; it was said if you were outside the walls after last light, you were as good as dead. I didn't give this too much credence, but I also wasn't keen to test it out. While situated in the Red Zone, at least our hotel-HQ lay within its own security walls and was close to the IZ.

Tom asked if G-Man – Bobby – and I would front-up our side with the recce missions, riding shotgun with some of the State Department Blackwater contractors we had christened 'the Bremer Boys'. Naturally we jumped at the opportunity to get out and see the country. We knew the significance of this in terms of proving the viability of Blackwater Commercial, so we were chuffed as all hell that Tom had asked us. Besides, the only other opportunity for getting out of the hotel had been a few recce runs around Baghdad City and we had seen nothing of the Iraqi countryside.

We were told to meet the Bremer Boys inside Saddam's former Republican Palace, within the IZ, the following day. How we would get in without any proper identification cards was a concern, and we didn't look forward to being left waiting in line. Not only would we be exposed to any watching insurgents, but the young American soldiers who manned the checkpoint were known to be shit-scared, trigger-happy fuckers who would shoot the shit out of anyone they suspected could kill them, and I was acutely aware of my brown, permanently sun-tanned Māori complexion.

To be fair, those soldiers had a genuine concern, as there had been a growing number of attacks at the checkpoints. The poor fuckers were getting hit by everything from improvised explosive devices (IEDs) to suicide bombers mingling with the crowds and drive-by shootings. Because of this, the IZ was quickly growing into one hell of a fortified compound, surrounded by kilometres of concrete 'T' and Jersey walls.

Tom decided to drive us up to the checkpoint. We joined the military-only lane, where we were no doubt lined up in the middle of some young fuck's M240 Bravo machine gun's sights well before we got within fifty metres of the barrier arm. I sat in the back seat, so it was clearly two Americans up front, and it was they who would be seen by the poor uniformed fucker who had drawn the short straw and was sent to wave us forward, as his buddies crouched below the barrier walls. In the next lane to us, some poor Iraqi family was being screamed at to do a whole host of things they obviously couldn't understand, while having guns pointed at their heads. The usual tactic of speaking loudly and slowly in English was proving as ineffective as ever, but the look of sheer terror on the Iraqis' faces needed no translation.

'Fuck me, so that's how you win over the local population,' I muttered.

Tom opted to seize the moment, pulling up to the guard, cracking his window and asking him how his day was going. The cheerful salutation threw him just a little.

'Um good, thank you, sir. How about you?' he stuttered.

'Good,' Tom grinned.

'Who are you with, sir?' the young soldier asked.

'Blackwater,' Tom announced, and apparently that was all that was needed.

The guard stepped back and signalled the gate guard to raise the barrier.

'Fuck me, that's impressive,' G-Man enthused.

Tom grinned. 'As easy as that, boys.'

While crossing the 14th of July Bridge leading into the IZ, I gazed down at the mighty Tigris River and marvelled at the thousands of years of human history it must have witnessed. All those advancements in the arts, sciences and culture, medicine and astronomy, and then the lunacy it had witnessed as man seemed determined to destroy it all over greed and barbarism. *Fuck, people are dumb.* We seem destined, no, programmed to destroy this planet and ourselves. Once all humans were dead and buried, Mother Nature would breathe a sigh of relief and be as thankful as fuck we were all gone.

We reached the far side, turned right at a roundabout, and on the left I could see a few Black Hawk helicopters taking off and landing. This, Tom informed us, was LZ – landing zone – Washington, and it was also where the Blackwater MD-530F Little Bird special operations helicopters were based. Parking up outside the Republican Palace, I took a moment to take in the sheer size and grandeur of the place. It was one impressive building and, having read a little about its history, I tried to visualise what these grounds must have seen under Saddam's rule. At the front four points of the roof were four massive green busts of Saddam's head, demonstrating the cult of personality he had enjoyed.

We were early, so Tom showed us around the place. Now, I had been in some pretty ornate palaces working close protection around the world, but this blew them all out of the water. The rooms were huge, the walls and ceilings were beautifully painted and the marble and woodwork were first class. We took the obligatory selfies, including one of us on Saddam's throne, apparently, then after a few wrong turns, we finally found the Blackwater State office hidden out back of the main building. About twenty jacked-up, high-speed, tobacco-chewing motherfuckers were busy in a room that reminded me a lot of our special forces team house when I was in the Unit, with guns, energy drinks and calendars with half-naked girls everywhere.

Hell, yeah. This is my kind of place.

G-Man and I stood at the door in our hand-me-down dollar store clothes, with ugly street vests and shitty-looking AKs, and they all momentarily stopped what they were doing and stared at us, before it must have dawned on them who we were, and they got back to what they were doing.

Tom introduced us to the ops manager, a fit-looking, red-haired guy called Frank; not our Frank, another one, who seemed genuinely glad to see us. Apparently, word had got around that a new commercial arm had been formed, so Frank and the rest of his guys were intrigued to meet the dumbasses stupid enough to volunteer to live outside the safety of the IZ walls. After a bit of a chat, he introduced us to the two guys we would be riding with on the surveys: Larry and Mike.

Larry and Mike were friendly enough, and we hit it off immediately. I have always liked working with Americans. They're generally polite and willing to help you out, unless they're invading your country. Even then they have a smile on their faces and call you 'sir', while they bomb the shit out of your village. Yep, real friendly fuckers.

Larry and Mike led us over to a whiteboard and taped up a map of Iraq for us to see. Being such a rarity, it was a welcome sight, and I took a mental snapshot of it to file for future use. On the map were marked all the proposed CPA locations.

'OK guys,' Larry began. 'I've numbered them from one to eight and from north to south on the map: one being the closest to the IZ and eight the furthest. We have Al-Kut, Al-Hillah, Karbala, Najaf, Tikrit, Diwaniyah, Samawah and Basra. Tomorrow, we will start. It's a bit too late in the day to head out now; besides, you two have a bit of admin to get done first.'

We nodded. We were good with that.

'First site will be Kut. We'll head out at 08:00, so if you guys can be here before then we can get motoring. If you want to be here by 07:00, you can have breakfast with us first.'

That was music to our ears. US military food is not to be missed.

Tom took us into Frank's office, where he flicked the switch on an identification card-making machine, to give it time to heat up while he took our photos. Minutes later, we were done.

An official identification card was the most useful bit of kit we could ever have asked for, apart from a gun, in those early days. It meant that the world was our oyster, with regards to getting anywhere controlled by the State Department. This was the equivalent of a backstage pass at your favourite rock band's concert, with booze, groupies and blow.

The next morning, after what can only be described as the mother of all breakfasts, we rendezvoused with Larry and Mike in the car park and, to our delight, found that we were going to be using one of their B6 – armoured – SUVs. After zipping about in our battered, soft-skin Chevy Suburbans, it was like going from flying economy on a shitty airline to moving up to first class on a good one.

But in a place like Iraq, you can never quite shake off the feeling of vulnerability. The problem with an armoured vehicle is that it tends to give you a false sense of security. Basically, you're locked inside a toughened glass, Kevlar and metal box, with no way of defending yourself apart from the skill of the driver using the vehicle as a ramrod. But it sure as hell felt comfortable.

Our first recce was Kut, lying around 100 kilometres south-east of Baghdad. The proposed site for the CPA was situated in a very tight bend in the Tigris River, similar to the way the IZ was located in Baghdad but very much smaller in scale. Like the IZ, it was a very exposed location, with the river running directly along one side. This would need some serious T wall installations to make it safer from an attack across the river, we reckoned.

For the next nine days, we thundered all over Iraq surveying the locations of interest to us. As we went about our work, we would bump into other security company staff vying for the same contracts, and, although we were competitors, we made some good contacts for the future. Mike was ex-Delta Force, and he managed to catch up with some of his old unit buddies who'd formed a security company called Triple Canopy. Great guys and rock-solid operators.

Basra was the only city where we had to hole up for the night, as it's located as far south as you can go in Iraq, so only a short distance from Kuwait. To get there meant a six-hour drive down the MSR, and there was no way we could safely make it there and back in daylight. As the British military had a base there, we figured we could ask to doss down with them for the night. Unfortunately, there was no room at the inn, so to speak, but the Fijian guards, as friendly as always, allowed us in to refuel, before directing us to an Iraqi-Christian-run hotel on the edge of the city.

The people of Basra were certainly no friends of Saddam, but the Brits had faced some major battles in order to capture the city's Port of Umm Qasr, and we were warned there were still plenty of bad guys around spoiling for a fight. After about thirty anxious minutes following the Fijians' directions, we eventually found the hotel and parked the vehicle in its walled-off car park.

We knew our gleaming bulletproof SUV would advertise our presence, so, before checking in, we had a quick word with the ancient-looking night watchman, who proudly stood guard armed with a Second World War-era Russian drum-fed PPSh-41 Papasha – 'Daddy' – submachine gun. There was an extra $50 for him in the morning if he didn't put a bomb under the vehicle while we slept and made sure others didn't either.

There was no way of knowing if the owners of the hotel were genuinely friendly or if they were passing on details of our presence to the insurgents, but we got rooms next to each other and slept lightly with our guns close by. The next day, we made sure we were up in time to move out at first light. We quietly made our way downstairs, past the sleeping hotel staff, and Larry left the money for the rooms with a note on the check-in desk. After giving the vehicle an extensive check, we handed the promised $50 to the watchman and headed back to Baghdad along MSR Tampa. Job done.

As comfortable and secure as we felt in the armoured SUV, there was one more thing that made them less desirable than their soft-skin counterparts: their thirst. All that extra weight meant we needed to fuel up a lot more than with a lighter soft-skin, which meant we needed to make a stop at the refuelling outpost set up by the US military halfway along Tampa. A quick flash of our Blackwater credentials got us a full tank and we were on our way again thundering down Tampa back to Baghdad.

By the end of the CPA surveys, G-Man and I had become good friends with Larry and Mike, and we'd got to know the roads pretty well, I thought, but now it was back to the Al-Hamra and Blackwater Commercial; back out into the Red Zone where we were on our own. To be honest, I was very comfortable with that.

A few days later I was tasked to head back to Basra. I was to self-drive on another recce, this time of the Umm Qasr port area, and taking the amigos – Two Trays, G-Man and Yard Dog – as my team. Plus goofy-looking Randy, the guy who had believed he should be team leader. We headed out early morning in another shitty soft-skin Suburban acquired by Mo. We were a single vehicle with no comms and no maps, a very large bag of pistachio nuts, a packet of Reese's Peanut Butter Cups (chocolate and peanut butter cupcakes), plus a twelve-pack of bottled water. What could possibly go wrong?

Moving out of Baghdad was always ass-puckering and required 100 per cent alertness from all. One wrong turn, roadblock or unexpected obstacle could force you into a part of the city you really didn't want to be in. G-Man and I used our collective memory to navigate our way to a series of elevated roads that we'd nicknamed 'the spaghetti loop'. If you got it correct, it looped south, down MSR Tampa to Basra. If you got it wrong, it led north, to Fallujah, where, in Monopoly terms, we wouldn't pass go or collect $200 ever again.

Fallujah was turning into a definite no-go destination for anyone other than the very well-armed US military. A lot of pissed-off Iraqis and Muslim foreign fighters were flocking into the country and gathering in Fallujah, keen to have a go at killing the 'foreign invaders'. Us.

The roads weren't a great deal safer, and driving on MSR Tampa had become known as 'running the gauntlet'. Every five to ten kilometres there was a vehicle overpass. Some were legitimate on/off ramps, while others were unfinished roads going nowhere, but each offered the insurgents an excellent observation point – a place from which to launch an attack. So we always scanned them thoroughly as we made our approach.

Due to their prominence and the great views they offered of the surrounding area, I thought they could work for us too, so I designated each new overpass we zipped under as an emergency rendezvous point (ERV) – somewhere we would all meet up, if we were hit hard and had to leg it on foot, which was always the biggest danger.

Tampa was a well-made highway with three lanes in each

direction separated by a metal barrier down the middle. Its surface and width allowed us to get up a pretty good head of steam and generally, in our industry, speed is your friend. Cruising at over 100mph makes you a harder target to hit, but at night the insurgents had taken to burying IEDs or tying explosives to the central barrier in the hope of hitting a vehicle as it flashed by. The roadside was still littered with the burnt-out carcasses of Iraqi armoured personnel carriers (APCs) from both Gulf Wars, but this was now being added to by a growing number of SUVs and civilian flatbed trucks, which had fallen victim to insurgency ambushes and IEDs. Most of the supplies for the war effort were driven by 'third country nationals', or American truckers, who risked their lives for peanuts. I had to admire these men and women, the Americans in particular, because I'm sure none had ever been shot at or had their vehicles blown up back in the States. Here, they were getting the snot kicked out of them yet getting on with the job at hand.

The convoys, some thirty to fifty vehicles long, moved at a snail's pace, and despite Big Army providing mounted protection in Humvees, there was no way in hell they could adequately protect anything that big. The truckers were sitting ducks, making the convoys a 'target-rich environment', as we call it in the military.

The Big Army escorts were also a real danger to the likes of us. Those fuckers weren't the sharpest at target identification and tended to open up on anything they deemed 'dangerous', including private security operators like us, who drove civilian vehicles. In fact, it was becoming all too common for them to 'confuse' us with insurgents.

To help them distinguish friend from foe, we'd made up these large colourful cardboard flags. Whenever we saw the military, we would quickly place one on the inside of the windscreen, hopefully before they opened up with their big guns. It was soon obvious that most of the troops could only reliably identify two flags: the Stars and Stripes for the US and the Union Jack for the British, and even then only sometimes.

Speeding down Tampa for hours on end, white line fever was another danger – falling asleep at the wheel – so I implemented a power nap rotation system. None of us would need any help staying awake this morning, however, when, out of the clear blue sky, a big-ass Apache Longbow attack helicopter came thundering over no more than twenty metres above us, and my asshole bit a big chunk out of my boxers.

'What the fuck?' we all yelled in unison.

Either the Apache crew were bored shitless and out for some fun scaring a bunch of security contractors, or they thought we were insurgents and had come in for a closer look at who was driving a beat-up Suburban at 100mph.

It was scary, crazy and awesome all at the same time, but it was about to get a whole lot more frightening. Having roared ahead of us, it pulled up 500 metres in front, rolled over and came back, this time facing us, either to get a better look at us from the front... or to shoot the living shit out of us.

'Flash the lights! Flash the lights!' I yelled at Yard Dog, who promptly hammered back on the light switch like he was sending Morse Code, while I made sure the makeshift Star-Spangled Banner was flapping like it was Independence Day. Seconds later, they roared over the top of us once more and disappeared into the heat haze, but it took a long few minutes for us all to begin to relax again.

After a few nervous kilometres we slipped back into our routine: watching ahead and behind, calling out possible threats and looking for roadside bombs – dead dogs, fake rocks or people stuffed with explosives. As we scanned for attackers in the distance, we checked all the overpasses and made sure we zig-zagged as we flashed past under them.

At the speed we were going I calculated the drive should take about five to six hours. The only thing that would slow us down, apart from the obvious – a breakdown, getting blown up or running into Big Army – was about three-quarters of the way south to Basra, where the tarmac road suddenly ended and you dropped about two feet into thin air before coming to rest on an unsealed dirt nightmare. If you weren't ready for it, that could spell the end, and more than one vehicle had suffered a horrific fate, dropping off into space at speed and rolling to a mangled stop.

Although I knew it was coming, I couldn't remember exactly where it was. I must have missed it on the CPA recce when we last encountered it, although G-Man wasn't much more helpful than me. We found it by flying off the main seal and sailing into thin air, just like you do not want to do, but Yard Dog, being a very good driver, managed to keep us sandy side up and oily side down. Apart from hitting our heads on the roof when we landed, we were all none the worse for wear. But no sooner were we over that when we ran into a Big Army convoy, causing everyone's heart rate to go up a beat or twelve.

The dust it threw up reduced our visibility to as little as three metres, so we had to slow down in one hell of a hurry. Then we had the problem of getting past. More often than not, the communication between the lead Humvees and tail Humvees was non-existent. Often, we would have to wait to attract a soldier's attention before being waved through, only to be shot at or run off the road by the next fuckers down the line. Even our makeshift flags didn't seem to mean shit. Sometimes, it just seemed like they were deliberately trying to run us off the road. In fact, it was happening so often I had started to think it might be jealousy on their part. In their minds, we were getting paid the big bucks and living the fast life with better rotations than theirs, and we could pull the pin and go home any time we liked, so why should they give a damn about us?

Getting past that convoy was another big relief, and as we continued south, we were able to pick up an English-speaking commercial radio station, broadcasting from Kuwait. As we tuned in, we all thought about how good it would be to be south of the border, sipping a chilled beer. As we imagined sitting on a sun-drenched Kuwaiti beach, Dido's 'White Flag' came on the radio, and we must each have drifted off to the same kind of place with thoughts of love and of home: someone or something that we normally kept locked firmly away when out here. As the song finished, my watery eyes refocused on where I was and what was in front of me, and I realised I had been temporarily blind to my surroundings. I reached to wipe away whatever grit was *obviously* making my eyes moisten, while trying to make sure the others didn't see, before I heard G-Man clear his throat behind me, snapping himself back to reality too.

'Fuck me,' he said. 'That song nearly killed me.'

I looked around the vehicle, and sure enough we were all misty as hell. Well, no point hiding it, I guess. We let out a nervous, embarrassed laugh, then cleared our throats as the radio was snapped off.

'Hey, how about those Raiders, eh?' someone piped up.

'Yeah, love the Super Bowl,' another voice responded.

Anything to re-establish our masculinity before it was back to looking for people wanting to kill us.

By my time and distance calculations and the look of the ground, I figured Basra was close now. Shortly, Tampa came to an end and split into two directions. I recognised the T intersection from the CPA surveys we had been on the week before and confirmed it with G-Man.

'OK, eyes peeled boys,' I told everyone. 'We are close, around forty minutes out, so we can expect a lot more traffic and a lot more eyes on us.'

As I scanned the horizon in the direction of Basra City, I could suddenly see what I thought was a lot of automatic bullet tracer arcing into the sky. The ground down south is pretty flat and open, so visibility was good. I told Yard Dog to pull over so we could have a roadside piss and assess the gunfire. It was around 15:00, so there was still plenty of daylight. Still, the tracer was very visible, while the sound of the firing wasn't reaching us. Weird.

'What d'you think is going on?' Two Trays ventured.

'Not sure bro, but with all that gunfire it must be a goodie,' I replied.

I figured that it couldn't be a two-way battle, for the tracer was mostly arching skyward and there weren't any aircraft to shoot at, or not that I could see. If it were a full-on contact or a big-ass shootout, the arcs would be flatter and ricocheting off at weird angles as they bounced off solid objects, like armoured vehicles, concrete or steel.

Either way, we couldn't wait there all day, exposing ourselves as a sitting target. I asked the others what they thought, and we all agreed that we needed to mount up and push into the city limits on full alert. As we got closer to Basra, the roads were more and more congested, with hundreds of vehicles careering about, burning rubber and generally having a wild time. Most were crammed with ecstatic-looking locals shooting their AKs, pistols and whatever else they could find up into the air, like a bad rap music video.

They might have been having fun, but I was still nervous as hell.

'Hey, why don't you turn the radio back on and see if there's any info?' Two Trays suggested.

'Good idea brother.' I turned the dial and we were soon enlightened.

The breaking news, and the cause for all this crazed expenditure of ammunition, was that the big kahuna himself, Saddam Hussein, had finally been captured. It was 13 December 2003, and a special ops team had found him hiding in a camouflaged hole in the ground on a farm in Ad-Dawr, near his home town of Tikrit. This was especially good news for the people of southern Iraq who, on the promise of support from the US that never materialised, had launched an uprising against Saddam after the first Gulf War, only to be on the receiving end of a brutal crackdown that left tens of thousands buried in shallow mass graves.

Not that the people of the south were unique in this regard. The Kurds in the north fell for the same false promise of US military assistance if they toppled Saddam and, of course, they suffered the same fate. And we wondered why we weren't being welcomed with open arms by the Iraqis.

We continued into town with more than a little caution, considering the number of guns out on the streets. The celebrations meant some of the roads were blocked, so we had to divert off the route I knew, which only added another level of ass-pucker to the situation. At least it was a good opportunity to gauge the alertness and temperament of my guys, this being our first proper run together. I needed to know how each handled stress and conducted his drills and responsibilities.

It was while we were heading down a crowded dirt road that I noticed a red sedan coming towards us. It was driven by an Iraqi, but something about it struck me as being different, and, as the gap between us closed, I noticed that those in the rear looked to be European. Something in my gut, and the hairs on the back of my neck, gave me reason to think they weren't security contractors like us, and, as we passed each other, they noticed us as well. The looks on their faces as we eyeballed each other were none too friendly.

I called them out to the guys. 'Fuck me, keep an eye on that red sedan, boys; I think we have just seen our first pair of foreign fighters. Step on it a bit, Yard Dog.'

The atmosphere in the Chevy was now electric, but the sedan seemed to have been swallowed into the celebrating crowds.

'Boys, we are going to have to be 100 per cent alert here because where's there two, there's bound to be more,' I announced. 'Eyes out on stalks, OK.'

We drove on, taking a zig-zag route through the streets until I found the hotel G-Man and I had stayed in during the earlier recce. I quietly let out a sigh of relief, but internally I was still concerned about the two European-looking guys in the red sedan. As we pulled up, Two Trays opened the door to get out and provide security in the normal fashion, while Yard Dog backed the vehicle into a parking slot, facing out.

'Hey, bro, stay in the vehicle will you,' I told him. 'I don't want anyone in the street to see us. I'm a bit worried about those two fuckers I saw.'

We gave a wave to the same old gate guard as before, who closed the big metal gates and shut us off from the outside world like he was throwing some kind of cloak of invisibility around us.

I was glad to get us all into the hotel, out of sight of prying eyes and out of danger of falling bullets. I checked us in at the reception, securing rooms to the rear, away from the main road and the threat of a VBIED attack to the front of the hotel. We were also one level up, so we could secure the stairwell and control anyone trying to attack from the ground. Crucially, this could be done without trapping ourselves on a level too high to evacuate from if the building was on fire. It's always good to secure a high point like the roof if your attackers are a few blocks away, but if the building is burning and the bad guys are beneath you, your evacuation options are pretty limited.

Once we'd settled in, I tried to place a call on the mobile to Tom in Baghdad to let him know we had arrived safely, but the usual lack of signal made it impossible. Instead, I told the lads the actions-on in case we were attacked that night, before we made our way down for dinner.

The hotel menu offered a mouth-watering selection of local dishes. Yard Dog was put in charge of ordering for us all, since he spoke a lot more Arabic than the rest of us, which was none, but since each menu choice was met with the same response, we all soon understood that 'lah' meant 'no' and, for the umpteenth time since arriving in the country, we had to settle for chicken and rice.

Outside, but attached to the hotel, was a little two-seater barber shop. It had been a while since I had had a haircut, so I buddied up with Yard Dog to go get one. The drill is to never go anywhere alone. Always take a buddy and always tell someone where you're going. After our meal we told Randy, G-Man and Two Trays our plan, then we ventured next door for a bit of a tidy up. Due to his noticeable lack of hair, I encouraged Yard Dog to go before me. My job was to provide security, with a pistol held out of sight, as the barber trimmed and combed the small number of strands on his dome.

As expected, Yard Dog was done in no time, so I made my ass comfortable in the chair, but, just as the barber got to work, I noticed Yard Dog get up and walk outside. I watched his reflection in the mirror, anxious that he should stay within view, but he turned back towards the hotel entrance and disappeared.

He'll be back in a minute, I told myself, but the prick didn't come back, and this was the point at which the barber produced his very new, very shiny straight razor to trim the back of my neck, and my throat felt suddenly very exposed.

By far the most logical option would have been to just get up, pay and calmly walk out, popping nervous farts as I escaped with my life. But I just kept on sitting there as I didn't want to be rude and insult the man. How stupid is that?

The barber stood behind me, razor in hand, looking at me looking at him in the mirror. He placed his other hand on my head, gently pushed it forward and steadied himself. *Here it comes.* Just as he brought the razor up into view, he very gently placed his hand on my shoulder and leant in towards my ear, whispering in broken English, 'You are safe here, my friend. You are safe. Relax, we are Christian.'

Relaxed was certainly not how I was feeling, and I guessed it wasn't the time to tell him, 'Yeah, I'm an atheist.'

Finally, the barber declared he was done, and I paid him his $10 fee and tipped him an extra five bucks for not killing me when he had the chance. I then hunted down Yard Dog to chew him out big time for leaving me alone. Yard Dog's initial stupid grin soon left his face as he apologised, but I wasn't in the mood to forgive straight away. Yard Dog was the guy whose service was supposedly 'classified' – the one I'd initially nicknamed 'Classified Chris'. He'd already raised a big red flag due to all that, and now this. I just stood there looking at him, holding my stare long enough to make him break eye contact and realise he was in the shit.

We gathered in G-Man's room for me to go over the plan for the next day, after which I told them to call it a night. As I finished the brief, I reiterated the importance of teamwork and explained what had happened in the barber shop as an example. Everyone looked at Yard Dog with the 'WTF dude' look. I was still pissed off, so I sent him out to check the vehicle once more for bombs, dust, tyre pressure, in fact anything, to teach him a lesson. And I made him go alone. Fuck him.

At first light the next morning, we quietly packed up. While the guys loaded the vehicle, I woke the hotel's night manager, who slept on the floor behind the reception desk, and paid for our stay.

'I thought you were staying two nights,' he said, rubbing his eyes.

'Yeah, but something's come up and we need to head out,' I answered, while peeling off a couple of $100 bills.

'Oh, OK, and you're going to Baghdad?' he asked.

'No, we are going to Kuwait and out for Christmas.' This was a lie, but I didn't want him to know where we were heading, just in case that information got passed on.

By the time I got out to the vehicle the boys had loaded our bags and cleaned out the mess of empty water bottles, Reese's Peanut Butter Cup wrappers and the million or so pistachio shells that littered the floor.

Our task was to recce the Port of Umm Qasr and the crossing point into Kuwait. I didn't really understand why, but, as anyone in the military will tell you, you don't ask, you just do, so we did, and I was happy as all hell to be out on the road with the guys. We were learning the lie of the land first hand and getting to know each other a lot better.

The first problem was that none of us knew where the hell the Port of Umm Qasr was, but given it had 'Port' in the name, we guessed it was by the water. I figured all we had to do was head out to the road we'd come in on, hang a left and hug the coast. The second problem, which was also part of the first problem, was that we didn't have any maps. Nada, none, not one, nothing. The State Department and the military were keeping those things all for themselves.

I'm very confident in my built-in, homing pigeon-like navigation skills, perfected during my time in the Unit, but going off into the Iraqi Badlands on a pigeon-wing and a prayer was not... ideal. But Yard Dog, G-Man, Two Trays and I didn't really have any other options, so we got going regardless. But Randy did appear to be shitting himself somewhat. Heading out into the great unknown with no maps or route-plan didn't seem to sit well with the guy, and he was beginning to whinge.

Before he could say a great deal more, I told him the time for moaning was over: 'Just get your ass in the vehicle and shut the fuck up.'

Two Trays, meanwhile, had been digging into his go bag, and partly to prevent Randy from saying anything more to incur my wrath, he announced, with not a small note of triumph, 'Hey, what about this?'

Two Trays pulled something out of his go bag that looked a bit like the Shroud of Turin but which to me was actually far more valuable right now. It was an old tea towel, and printed on it was a map of Iraq. No bullshit – the same type of souvenir tea towel my grandmother always brought back from her holidays overseas when I was a young kid. Just like my grandmother's had, Two Trays's tea towel showed the major cities and the roads connecting them, with cutesy pictures of the key tourist sites printed around the border.

I looked it over with amazement. 'You're a gift from the heavens, you little beauty,' I murmured. Yard Dog, G-Man and even Randy seemed equally impressed, realising we might not be as far up shit creek as we first thought, and now we had a paddle.

'Where the hell did you get that from?' Yard Dog asked.

'It was given me by an aunt when I was a kid. She had a vacation in Iraq back in the 1970s, when it was known as the "Jewel of the Middle East" and was a tourist destination.'

For some reason Two Trays had packed the tea towel, never for one moment thinking he would actually need it, but there we were, in 2003, in the era of GPS, laser-guided stealth bombs and satellites that could see you from space, and we had a $2 antique tourist tea towel from the 1970s to guide us around a war-ravaged and insurgent-infested country.

Well done Aunty Two Trays. Top job.

I looked over our new map closely. Although it was old and rudimentary, it showed the main road we called 'Tampa' and a few others to the west that were not as prominent, revealing a network of highways connecting towns here and there across the country, all the way to Kurdistan.

'Holy nut, man,' I said, 'I think we can make this work.'

I passed the tea towel to the others, so they could memorise as much as possible, before we mounted up like happy campers and paid the watchman $20 for not putting a bomb on the vehicle.

One of the good things about the Chevy Suburban is that it comes equipped with a digital compass in the rear-view mirror. It, like the tea towel, is rudimentary but more than adequate if you have good map-to-ground navigation skills, which I did. Back in the SAS, it would be nothing to fly into a foreign country and be dropped off in pairs somewhere unknown, then be told to find your way to a given finish point many clicks away, through thick jungle, open country or whatever lay before you. And like everything we did in the Unit, it became a competition. You couldn't do a shit without someone trying to do it better, bigger and faster, navigation included. I felt fairly confident we would be OK with the tea towel and the rear-view mirror compass, providing the vehicle didn't get a flat battery, break down or get blown up.

And so, with Two Tray's tea towel to the fore we headed out of Basra into the great expanse of southern Iraq. Shortly, all around lay rolling sand, vast open flat terrain and herds of camels and, of course, the burnt-out remnants of Saddam's once mighty military machine.

After about an hour, we found Umm Qasr. The British had stationed a company of Nepalese Gurkhas to secure the port, and the Gurkhas, as they tend to, were not letting anyone near the place. We recced as much of the port as we were able to and crossed it off the list, before deciding to have a look at the border crossing into Kuwait.

The US military had set up a checkpoint and camp on the border with Kuwait, called 'Nav Star'. They'd just finished digging a deep trench system all the way around the Iraqi side and were in the process of erecting fencing. We approached slowly and carefully, so as not to be shot at, after which we chewed the fat with some of the US military engineers who were operating the heavy equipment. They told us that Kuwait City was only a two-hour drive from there and, at night, you could see its bright lights, which conjured up images of its American fast-food joints, slick five-star hotels and the gleaming international airport. Oh, to be there, we thought.

Once I was happy that we'd seen enough of the border cross-ing, the engineers pointed out the main route leading back into Iraq, the one that most US military convoys were taking. There was an alternative road leading north from the checkpoint, but it passed through a small town that was already known to be ripe for ambushes; it was a place where insurgents would gather intel on passing vehicles so that an ambush could be set up ahead. One half-kilometre stretch of that road was lined on both sides with forty-foot-long shipping containers, stacked two or three high, and huge heaps of scrap metal filled any open spaces. It was a dead man's alley, with no gaps to escape through if you got hit there.

I crossed that off the list – a real no-go area.

With all tasks completed, we had been out for around five hours and I figured we wouldn't make it safely back to Baghdad in day-light. We had no 'fudge time', in case of any hold-ups or unsched-uled stops along the way. I talked it over with the boys and we decided the best plan was to go back to the hotel in Basra and stay another night.

First, we had to refuel the vehicle, which we did at the Brit camp that G-Man and I had visited during our CPA surveys. The Fijian guards checked my Blackwater ID while I engaged them in the uni-versal Polynesian/New Zealand language – rugby talk. By the time we were done, we had only about two hours of light left, but I was becoming familiar with this part of Basra, and we soon found the hotel. As we reversed into the walled parking area, I felt pretty good about the day's work, but, when I went to check us in, I realised that my gamble about not wanting to give the hotel too much intel by booking two nights had backfired big time. The hotel was full.

There was no room at the inn, and we were fucked.

As I stood there in the lobby feeling just a little annoyed at myself, I contemplated our options: go back and ask the British if we could crash the night with them; drive out into the desert and pull sentry in a wadi; kip in the vehicle in the hotel car park until daylight. Fuck. None of them was anywhere near ideal. Plus what was I going to tell the boys, who were ready to move their shit inside?

A few words from the hotel manager snapped me back to the present. 'No problem, my friend, let me make a call to another hotel and see if they have rooms.'

I was grateful for his help but in two minds about whether to take it. It was getting dark by now, so maybe this was the least-worse option. I thanked him for his offer, while kicking myself in the ass for not having added enough 'fudge time' for the recces.

After jabbering away in Arabic the hotel manager put down his phone and, with a big smile on his face, announced that the other hotel had spare rooms and was waiting for us. The guy assured me it was a safe hotel for Westerners, but – and there's always a 'but' – it lay further into the centre of Basra. While that was far from ideal, it was almost completely dark by now, which should serve to camouflage us as we got on the move. It was also our only real option.

I called Yard Dog, explained our predicament, then had him listen to the directions the hotel manager gave him. I left him doing his best Arabic translation act, hands waving this way and that – 'left, right, no, no, right left, straight on, on and on' – while I went outside and explained the plan to the rest of the boys. Yard Dog rejoined us and we set off, a wee bit nervous and guns at the ready, heading for the city centre.

Even at night, Basra is a bustling place and there didn't really seem to be anyone paying too much attention to us, or to the rules of the road for that matter. After a few anxious wrong turns and more than a few 'fucks', we finally found the new hotel. We heaved a collective sigh of relief but discovered there was no off-street parking – so nowhere to stash the vehicle.

No dramas, I told myself. We had a dirty old civilian Suburban, which should fit in really well. I got Yard Dog to park like a local, at an angle and with one wheel on the sidewalk. I then instructed G-Man to climb over and take the wheel, while Two Trays and Randy stayed in the vehicle, guns at the ready, and Yard Dog and I went inside to check on the rooms.

As the previous hotel manager had promised, they were expecting us, and they had two rooms on the second level good to go. But the atmosphere here was very different. The manager urged us to get the fuck off the road and into those rooms as quickly as possible, for it was as dangerous for them to be seen harbouring us, as it was for us to be seen here. I paid up front, plus a bit extra to keep them all sweet, and we moved ourselves and everything inside as quickly as our asses could take us.

The plan was to secure ourselves in the rooms and stay there all night, no matter what. We'd have to stave off our hunger with any leftover peanut butter cups and pistachios – Two Trays included. Far better that than be spotted by any of the hotel guests, who might not like the fact that we were there and decide to make a few phone calls.

I did a quick brief of actions-on in the case of an attack, before Yard Dog and I locked ourselves in one room and G-Man, Two Trays and Randy did their best to squeeze into the one across the hall. Getting to sleep after a long day under the hot Iraqi sun was not difficult, but, as I dreamt of death and horror, as I typically did, I was woken by a distinctive burst of AK-47 fire, which sounded very close. It was so close, in fact, that the lumpy old walls in our room rattled and the whole place seemed to vibrate.

Without even opening my eyes I quickly rolled onto the floor, on my back, with my AK between my knees aimed at the door. Unfortunately, Yard Dog had had the same kind of reaction, and he came rolling on top of me in the dark, pinning me to the ground in a tangle of limbs and asses.

'Get the fuck off me,' I hissed, as he struggled back off the floor.

Still in complete darkness, we took up more comfortable firing positions on our beds, ready to engage straight through the door and the walls if necessary. The other guys weren't directly opposite us, which was just as well, as they would have been shot to pieces if we were forced to open fire, as bullets pass through doors and walls like a hot knife through butter.

'Keep facing the door, bro,' I whispered to Yard Dog. 'I'm gonna take a peek outside. That's where I figure it's coming from.'

'Roger that,' he replied.

Spinning around on my bed, I slowly pulled the curtain slightly aside, which let in a sliver of night light. As I moved my face towards the dirty glass, the AK kicked off again directly below us on the street, pretty much where the Suburban was parked on the pavement.

Each muzzle flash lit up our room like a strobe light; each burst of sound was deafening. But the weirdest thing of all was that the noise of the firing was immediately followed by a strange siren-type wailing. It kept going on and on: *bang-bang-bang* went the AK; *howl-howl-howl* went the high-pitched siren. Eventually, I figured out the siren noise was actually of human origin. It sounded as if we had a group of wailing women who were not only inside the hotel but on the same floor as us.

'What the fuck is going on?' I asked Yard Dog.

Yard Dog figured the high-pitched caterwauling was a good sign.

'It's what Arabic women do when they celebrate something,' he whispered. 'They wiggle their tongue about and cover their mouths at the same time, to make that God-awful sound, just like a siren.' There was some sort of celebration going on, and since we were in a hotel, there was most likely a wedding, he suspected.

I got off the bed and told Yard Dog to cover me, as I was going to take a peek out of the door. I put my pants and boots on and waited until there was a lull in the noise of the ululating women. Then, I slowly cracked the door and poked my head out. The other boys' door was still closed, so I opened ours wide enough to take a proper look. A little further down the corridor I spied a group of six women, all clad in their full-black body robes, waving their arms in the air, in between making that wailing noise with their tongues. They were holding up a bed sheet with a red smear on it, which I assumed was blood.

The sheet could only be from the bed of a newly married couple. The group of women must have been waiting outside their room until the marriage had been consummated, the blood being proof that the bride was still a virgin. I'd heard of such rituals, and it was the only thing that made any sense.

It's lucky they don't do that in New Zealand, I thought to myself, *or there would be a lot of white sheets and disappointed mothers, unless the newlyweds stole some tomato sauce sachets from the buffet beforehand.*

I told Yard Dog to go get a look. It was a standard Arabic practice, he confirmed, adding that it can turn ugly very fast if the sheet stays white.

Once the commotion had died down a little, I checked with the guys in the other room, letting them know what was what. Two Trays and G-Man appeared pretty cool with it, but Randy seemed more than a little freaked out. In fact, G-Man had to pull me to one side to let me know that they'd had to hold Randy back from storming out into the corridor with his weapon and opening up on the women.

Fuck me. Not good.

Just before daybreak we were woken again, this time by morning prayers. We waited for thirty minutes or so to allow the streets to clear of worshippers, then I gathered the guys, and we headed out to repack the vehicle and get moving. After a quick flashlight vehicle inspection for any bombs or bullet holes, we loaded up and made our way at top speed towards MSR Tampa.

It felt good to be heading back to Baghdad, but, twenty minutes out of Basra, just before the turn onto Tampa and not far from that small town with the dead man's alley of shipping containers, we came across a group of Iraqi Police (IP) in the middle of the road, with guns and flashlights waving for us to slow down. We gripped our AKs ready for action. The IP had something of a dodgy reputation, to put it mildly, and many were suspected of working for both sides.

'What the fuck's all this?' I remarked. 'Keep your eyes peeled, boys.'

We scanned our arcs in the pre-dawn half-light, as I raised my weapon to just below the level of the glass, safety catch off, a round racked into the chamber and ready to let rip in a split second.

Yard Dog pulled up about twenty metres short and slightly off to one side of the IPs. 'Keep it in drive, ready to blast out of here,' I told him.

The IPs motioned us to come a bit closer. I ignored that and waved for them to come to us. After a minute's standoff, one of them drew the short straw – the youngest by the looks of him – and cautiously walked towards us. I gave him a wave, in an effort to appear friendly, and motioned him to my side of the vehicle. I rolled my window down with my AK sideways on my lap, my left hand on the trigger and the barrel pointed right at his stomach.

Once he was within earshot, I looked directly into his eyes, smiled and waved with my right hand. 'Hola, beautiful morning, isn't it? How are you?'

If he didn't reciprocate the friendly greeting, I would assume he was not one of the good guys and get ready to light him up, if need be. But he waved back and smiled, though he was clearly a bit unsure of what I had said or why there were five gringos driving a beat-up-looking SUV.

'What's the problem?' Yard Dog asked in Arabic.

The policeman explained that there had been an ambush on a convoy coming out of Kuwait, about ten kilometres ahead of us on Tampa, and that the military had closed it to all traffic.

'How long's it closed for?' Yard Dog asked.

The young policeman had not the slightest idea, but he suggested that we could wait until it reopened, if we liked.

I didn't like, and for any number of reasons. We had two choices, as far as I saw it. We could either wait for who knew how long, stuck on the side of the road with the traffic building up, or turn back towards Basra and find another way through. I imagined those two dodgy-looking European fuckers hearing reports that we were sitting here hemmed in with traffic – an easy target. *Fuck that.*

I remembered spying another road and a sign reading 'Nasiriyah', a city lying to the north-west of Basra, which, according to my built-in homing sense, would take us in the direction of Baghdad. After a quick explanation to the boys, we said a hearty 'shukran' to the young officer, Yard Dog turned the vehicle around and we headed back into town.

When we'd got about a click away from the IPs, I told Yard Dog to pull over. I needed to take a piss and get a look at the tea towel. Basic though the map was, it confirmed my thinking, so I gathered the guys and told them the plan. Everyone but Randy was keen to give it a go. Randy argued that we should wait for the road to clear and head back up Tampa. He seemed convinced that 'the Iraqis knew that the US had come in peace to free them from Saddam', and that 'no one was out to harm us', which I thought was somewhat at odds with his desire to start shooting up the Iraqi women in the hotel when they'd put the shits up him the previous night.

I wasn't the only one who thought he was wrong and a fucking idiot, but I listened to what he had to say before I told him to shut the fuck up and get in the vehicle because we were going the way I had outlined.

The sun was definitely up by now, and the roads back into town were packed with cars and pedestrians reducing our progress at some points to a crawl, which massively increased the tension in the car. I reminded everyone to be on extra-high alert and to report anything they saw that could raise suspicions or be thought of as a threat. We were in the perfect environment to be ambushed. There were masses of people swarming all around the vehicle, and it was easy enough for them to tell that we weren't locals.

The chatter within the vehicle picked up as Yard Dog, Two Trays, G-Man and I called out potential targets and their locations according to the time-honoured hands-of-the-clock method.

'Suspicious male at two o'clock.'

'Woman taking an excessive interest at eight o'clock.'

'Vehicle coming in fast from four o'clock.'

Only Randy was noticeably quiet.

To me, it was better to shoot and be wrong than to not shoot and be dead, but that meant our discipline had to be of the highest standard, since any wrong call could lead to one hell of a shitstorm.

While he was driving, I noticed Yard Dog trying to fumble for his AK. He'd placed it down at his side by the door.

'Leave it alone bro and focus on the driving,' I told him. He glanced at me, his expression a little wide-eyed and helpless. 'Your weapon weighs about 5,000lbs and has a fuckin' big engine,' I added.

His expression seemed to relax a little, as he understood what I was telling him.

'Look for gaps, try to blend in as much as possible,' I continued, 'but, if the shit hits the fan, your job is to get us the fuck out of here, and I don't care who you flatten to do it, OK? Drive it like you stole it, bro.'

We nosed along for another five blocks at a dead crawl before the crowd thinned out to where we could finally get above 25mph. Suddenly, out of our rear left – so our seven o'clock – something slammed against our vehicle, the heavy Suburban juddering with the impact. It was the side Randy was on. Yard Dog swerved to the right to break off from the impact, swearing his ass off as he did.

'What the fuck was that?' I yelled, without turning around, so as not to neglect my arcs.

'Oh, just some guys trying to get past,' Randy replied.

'What the hell does that mean?' I demanded.

'No threat. Don't worry.'

'You sure there's no threat?' I demanded, but Randy didn't reply. 'Two Trays, what the fuck is happening back there, bro?' I yelled.

'We got a couple of young fucks trying to get themselves shot back here,' Two Trays yelled back.

'Your call,' I told him. 'Deal with it.'

Two Trays wound down his window and pushed the barrel of his AK out, taking aim at the occupants. As soon as they saw the gun and the unsmiling eyes behind it, they hit the brakes, disappearing into the throng of cars behind.

'Yeah, you better fuck off,' Two Trays yelled after them. Then he turned to Randy. 'Fuck me, man, why the hell didn't you call it out?'

'They weren't a problem,' Randy insisted.

'Well, how the fuck do you know?' I yelled. 'And how come you didn't see them coming, and why the fuck didn't you tell us?'

'Yeah, you dumb fuck. You must have seen them coming,' G-Man shouted.

By this time, I was feeling severely pissed off. 'Fucking call everything out, OK, and I mean everything.' Randy stayed silent. 'OK?!' I yelled, even louder.

'Yeah, OK,' he finally answered.

I knew I wasn't alone in thinking that there was no way that vehicle could have come up on us like that without Randy seeing it. The last thing we needed was a broken-down vehicle in the middle of nowhere. This little castle-on-wheels was our only means of protection, disguise and transportation right now. It was our number one means of life support and Randy had nearly allowed it to be taken down. For all I knew the wheels could have been whacked, we could have a slow puncture or there might be some damage we would only find out about in a few hours, when we were further into the bad-lands. I was not at all happy with the goofy-looking fuck who was now staring out of the window like a sulky child. I would need to get to the bottom of this, but right now I had a far more important task to focus on, which was getting us back to Baghdad.

I put the tea towel on the dashboard, orientating it to the mirror compass. While I knew we needed to push north, this was all new territory to me. I felt the tension ease a little when we passed a sign for Nasiriyah, which at least meant we were on the right path. Even so, I instinctively glanced at the base of the sign to check the ground didn't look disturbed, just in case some fucker had spun it around. I kept checking and rechecking compass, tea towel and time, until after about an hour my gut feeling started to tell me we weren't going where we wanted to go any more.

I figured we were moving too far north-east, when in fact we needed to head more directly north or even north-west. I'd hoped to encounter a tarmac road leading directly west, which would have taken us back onto Tampa and ground that we knew, but there was nothing like that anywhere in sight. The drive time from Basra to Baghdad is normally five to six hours at 100mph. We were averaging about 80 to 90mph, so I calculated a drive time of around seven to eight hours with stops, after which Baghdad should be on our left.

My head was constantly bobbing between the tea towel, compass, my watch and the road ahead, looking for any signs of the bad guys or anywhere where roadside bombs might have been hidden. The sealed road we were following seemed to be taking us further off course, but there was no way I was taking us onto some shitty dirt track. By my calculations we should be getting close to Nasiriyah, and I was desperately searching for any small indication that we were – like a store or school sign with the word 'Nasiriyah' in it.

Three hours after leaving Basra, we hit the outskirts of what looked like a town, or definitely a populated area. The mud-brown houses began to look a bit more modern. As much as I wanted to, I didn't think it would be a good idea to stop and ask for directions, for obvious reasons. Plus, it would have made me look bad in front of the boys, so I held onto the hope that the build-up was a good sign. Then, finally, I saw it: *Nasiriyah*. A lovely, blue sign, pockmarked with bullet holes. *You little beauty.*

All of us – Randy included – felt the tension lift a little within the vehicle. We carefully made our way into the city, still alert for danger, when I spied in the distance two white Toyota 4x4s parked up on the roadside. Even from a distance, it was obviously a group of security contractors working around a flat tyre. Getting closer, I noticed one of the guys standing over and offering some unneeded advice to the poor bugger working the tyre iron, and I couldn't help but grin.

Fuck me. Not only had I found Nasiriyah, but I had found someone I knew and who could direct us to Baghdad. It didn't matter that I couldn't see his face. I recognised the way he was standing, from many years of working together in the Unit. As we approached, I told Yard Dog to slow to a stop. Of course, the other security team were suspicious of the shitty-looking Suburban crawling towards them, and more than a couple lifted their guns.

From about thirty metres out, I wound down my window and yelled out, 'Hey, black ass!'

The figure offering advice turned to see who had just insulted him, before realising it was me. His look of surprise at seeing me was matched only by my look of gratitude at seeing him.

'Hey, Baz, you cunt,' came his reply. 'What the fuck are you doing here?'

His guys lowered their weapons, and I instructed Yard Dog to park up close to the 4x4s. We all got out for a well-needed stretch of the legs. My guys took it in turns to take a piss, while I strolled over to my mate.

'Hey, bro, how's it going?' I said.

We approached, shook hands, shoulder bumped, then greeted each other with a traditional Māori Hongi, which involves pressing noses together twice then giving a man-hug, which I could see left my guys looking more than a bit perplexed.

'T' and I had served together in the New Zealand infantry and then the SAS. He was a good, solid guy: strong as an ox and one hell of a rugby player.

'What the fuck are you doing here?' he asked again.

'Lost as fuck, bro,' I replied. 'Trying to get back to Baggers, but Tampa was closed by Big Army. Some assholes ambushed a fucking convoy early this morning. What about you?'

'We're based at the fucking CPA in town.'

'T explained he was here with the British security company Control Risks Group (CRG), who had won the bid to protect the State Department's interest in Nasiriyah. He and about ten other New Zealand guys worked for CRG, and most were back at their camp, if I wanted to follow him there for lunch, once they got their tyre changed. Never being one to turn down a meal and a chance to refuel, I gladly accepted.

We headed for CRG's camp, and it was great to see a bunch of familiar faces, a lot of whom I hadn't seen since leaving the New Zealand military. Most were former Unit guys, with a few from assorted other NZ corps. I introduced my guys to everyone before sending Yard Dog with T's driver to refuel the Suburban.

You always refuel your vehicle before refuelling your body.

Having gone without dinner and breakfast, we were starving, and it was good to get something other than chicken and rice,

Reese's Peanut Butter Cups and pistachio nuts. We shared a few stories about good and not-so-good-old days, before I decided we needed to head on, as we still had a fair distance to travel. I asked if they had any maps but, like us, resources were slim, and as their area of operations (AO) was southern Iraq, they didn't have any maps that covered as far north as Baghdad.

'So, what the fuck are you guys using to get around?' T asked.

By way of answer I pulled the tea towel out of my vest. T and the rest of the New Zealand contingent stared at it, as if I was taking the piss.

'You're kidding, right,' T said, holding out his hand for a closer look. 'Is that a tourist tea towel? Fuck. I haven't seen one of those things since I was a kid.'

He handed it around to the others on his team.

'Fuck me, that's awesome,' was the general consensus. Followed closely by, 'You guys are totally fucked.'

We said our goodbyes, and I went around all the Kiwis repeating the Hongi, each of whom then proceeded to do the same to a very confused-looking G-Man, Yard Dog, Two Trays and Randy.

With the vehicle refuelled and a belly-full of decent food on-board, we loaded up the Suburban and, with our tea towel and mirror compass, headed back out into the abyss.

The road exiting Nasiriyah pushed us due north, and I knew we really needed to head more west to hit Baghdad, so after three and a half hours driving, and with the knots in my stomach really starting to twist, I decided, *fuck it, we'll take the next left*. We'd been heading north for long enough and, besides, it was getting close to dusk.

I consulted the tea towel, which revealed a black wiggly line branching off left and leading directly to Baghdad. Of course, the tea towel wasn't to scale, and the roads could have changed since the 1970s, when lovely Aunty Two Trays had purchased it, but that was the road we needed to take and I just had to hope and pray that it was there. By my time and distance calculations, we should be bloody close, but where the hell was it?

Twenty minutes later I spotted a vehicle turning left about 400 metres ahead. *Surely, that was a good sign.*

'Hey, Yard Dog, see that car? That must be the road we want,' I announced, confidently.

'You sure, bro?'

'Fuck, no,' I answered, truthfully, 'but we're taking it anyway, 'cause no way do we want to go any further north.'

So, Yard Dog turned onto this little ribbon of tarmac, while I hoped like fuck it was the road we needed. We drove down our new road with the sun setting to our front, so that at least confirmed we were heading west, as I willed the Gods of Navigation for a sign. Any sign. After what seemed like a painfully long time, I started to notice a few more vehicles on the road and pedestrians on the pavements, and shortly a mosque hove into view. That had to mean we were moving into a built-up area. Maybe even the outskirts of Baghdad.

It was getting darker with each passing minute, and I still had no confirmation of exactly where we were, but still I was feeling happier. My gut was telling me this was right. As full darkness hit, the stress level in the vehicle went right back up to boiling point, but we all stayed outwardly calm – working together to call out the threats. All of us that is except for Randy, who was shitting himself and unable to hide it any more.

'This isn't good,' he muttered. 'Fuck this, we're lost. Fucking not good at all.'

Eventually, I'd had enough. This fucker was about as useful as tits on a bull. 'Hey back there, watch your arcs and shut the fuck up, or I'll shut you the fuck up,' I told him. The tone in my voice left no room for misinterpretation, and I'm sure I heard a chuckle from Two Trays.

Admittedly, it was now completely dark and spooky as fuck, and a lone Suburban full of males-of-fighting-age out driving at night could just as easily be mistaken for the bad guys by Big Army as it could be pinged by the insurgents. We needed to get off the streets, pronto, but panicking wasn't going to help.

My gut was telling me we were close. 'Hey, bro, let's take the next road left,' I told Yard Dog. 'I got a feeling we need to go left.'

'A feeling…' I heard a voice mutter from behind me, and I knew exactly who the fuck it was.

We took the next left, which turned out to be a very dark residential street, and drove slowly along it, eyes peeled and willing for a sign, when something big, grey, glorious and beautiful hove into sight. It was the unmistakable outline of a four-metre concrete T wall extending right across our front. It could only mean one thing: we were in Baghdad, and this was one of the walls of the IZ.

Now we just had to find a checkpoint or an entrance.

'OK, dudes, left or right?' I asked. The silence was not very enlightening. 'OK then, left it is.'

Yard Dog flipped the vehicle around, we drove back up the street, took the first left, and kept leap-frogging to the left as much as possible, while always trying to keep the T wall within view.

After another twenty agonising minutes, I was thinking we might have to turn back around, when I spied the unmistakable glow of spotlights up ahead.

'Lookie there, boys, a way in,' I announced.

But now we had a new problem. How did we approach the checkpoint and not get shot to shit by some frightened, trigger-happy teenage soldier on the business end of a fucking big gun?

About 100 metres out, I placed our DIY US flag on the dashboard and instructed Yard Dog to slow to a dead crawl. Plus, he was to turn the hazard lights on and flash the headlights every few metres, to doubly attract their attention. He needed to make it look as if the flashing was deliberate, to draw their gaze, at which point I hoped to hell they would spy the flag through their night-vison scopes and recognise us as friendlies. We crawled closer, moving at just about walking pace, hazard lights blinking, flag up and headlamps flashing like a lighthouse on speed.

Come on you fucks; can't you see the light show? And can you please not blast us to fuck with a burst from your .50-calibre HMG?

As each metre passed beneath the wheels, we held our breaths, expecting to get blasted at any second. I told the guys to be ready to get the hell out of the vehicle if they opened up on us. We crawled ever closer to the checkpoint: seventy metres, sixty, then at around fifty metres out the unmistakable sound of small-arms fire erupted out of the darkness, as spurts of angry dirt kicked off the road just to our right. Clearly, we were being kindly asked to stop or face obliteration, which we did very gently, for at this stage any erratic move would almost certainly be our last.

We rolled to a halt and sat there, not moving, just staring into this big blinding light.

After a short pause, so everyone with a gun aimed at us could take a good few breaths, I slowly started to open my door.

'What the fuck are you doing?' Two Trays asked.

'I'm going to get out, bro, let them know we're friendlies and that we want in,' I replied.

With that, I very slowly stepped out of the vehicle, leaving my gun inside and holding my hands open and above my head. Then with one hand I slowly started to remove my vest, while at the same time yelling out, 'Friendlies.' Everything was very slow and deliberate. I wanted them to see it wasn't a suicide vest. I did this until all my kit had been removed, and I then slowly turned a full 360 degrees, to show I was now unarmed.

No sooner had I made it around to face the lights again, when a gunshot erupted from the darkness and went pinging by my feet. *Are you shitting me?* What was needed now was even better proof of our status as friendlies, something even they would understand.

'Hey, you fucks, are you totally retarded?!' I yelled, in my clearest English. 'Stop fucking shooting at me.'

I didn't give a shit that I might be blowing our cover for any bad guys who might also be out there. The real danger was obvious right now.

My angry outburst seemed to work, for I heard someone in the darkness to my front yell, 'Hold your fire! Hold your fire.'

I was then yelled at to move forward with my arms outstretched, which I was more than happy to do. From out of the darkness emerged two silhouettes, moving very cautiously. I could tell they were carrying weapons by the way they walked, and they were no doubt as nervous as I was, considering their guns turned out to be pointed right at me.

From about five metres out, they commanded me to slowly turn around 360 degrees again. Happy to oblige.

'Who the fuck are you?' one asked once I'd finished twirling.

'Blackwater. Friendlies.'

The two guys looked at each other for several long seconds, before approaching to within a couple of metres. One lowered his weapon while the other kept his gun trained on me.

'Hey, guys, what's happening?' I announced, in my friendliest possible tones.

The guy who'd lowered his gun reached for my ID, which was hanging around my neck, and I could see that his hands were trembling. He shone his flashlight on the front, which showed my picture in one corner, with 'BLACKWATER' stamped in red beneath it and a big bear's paw in the other corner – the company logo. He scrutinised the card for a few more seconds, then glanced up at my face, before he eventually seemed to relax just a little.

He took the card from me and began to walk back towards the light.

'Can I lower my arms now, mate?' I asked.

'Sure, sir,' he replied.

It's really weird how a few minutes can seem like an entire lifetime in circumstances like these. Despite my getting across who we were, I didn't want to make any unnecessary moves, no matter how non-threatening, just in case someone in the dark mistook it as an aggressive gesture and unleashed hell. What seemed like an age went by before the soldier returned and handed me back my ID, with something approaching a smile.

'Get in the vehicle and slowly bring it forward will you, sir.'

'Sure mate, no problem.' *Thank fuck for that.*

Most of the boys waited for me to get my head back in the vehicle before asking what was going on. Randy was the exception. He was so wound up he couldn't contain himself.

'I should have gone out – I'm an American,' he blurted out. 'We're fucked now, I bet.'

I looked at him like he was a piece of total shit, before calmly saying, 'Good to go, boys.'

I climbed back in, not bothering to kit up again. I felt a trickle of sweat flow down my back and pool in the place no one wants a trickle of sweat to be.

Yard Dog got us rolling and we crawled towards the gate. There we halted, so the underside of the Suburban could be searched for bombs, using a mirror mounted on a wheeled trolley, plus a sniffer dog, and then finally we were waved inside. The tension and stress of the day started to dissipate as we slowly passed from one side of the big grey 'keep the fuck out or we will kill your ass' barrier to the other, into the place of safety, sanctuary, unicorns and big soft titties.

Once inside we let out a collective sigh and executed a bit of a fist-thrust, like in all the movies wherein America saves the day, the planet and the universe. All we had to do now was find our way through the IZ to the 14th of July Bridge and back into our neck of the woods – the Red Zone and our cosy hotel in Karrada.

We made it with no further dramas, and while we unloaded the vehicle, I noticed a figure standing in the doorway of one of the adjacent hotels, smoking a cigarette. He seemed strangely familiar, though the person he reminded me of was highly unlikely to be in an Iraqi war zone, I thought. Besides, I had a beer to crack and a debrief to conduct, so I didn't want to dwell on it for too long. Then he stepped out of the shadows, and I could clearly see it was the actor Sean Penn.

Sean Penn had been one of the first Hollywood celebrities to come out against the war in Iraq and, fuck me, he had received one hell of a lot of flak for doing so. I pride myself on not being starry-eyed about celebrities, but Two Trays and G-Man were unable to resist their inner groupie, and they wandered over to talk to him and ask if he needed any help. He thanked them for their concern but said he was waiting for his driver. He seemed friendly enough, though he would probably have seen us – private security contractors – as part of the problem.

I finished up and made my way to our room for the debrief. Even though we were civilians, I still treated all security operations as if I was in the military. No matter the task, I always tried to meticulously plan every aspect. This was something that had been drilled into us in the Unit. In Iraq, it didn't matter how many times we might do the same run, we had to remember that any time we went outside the relative safety of the hotel complex we were in enemy territory and on ground of their choosing. I had to assume the insurgents were just as professional as us and just as determined to kill us as we were to avoid getting killed.

We gathered in the lounge area of our Al-Hamra suite, cracked open a beer and I began. I had the guys sit in the order we were in when in the vehicle. I placed the tea towel in the centre of the table and found something that would make a suitable pointer, then went over everything from the time we'd left Basra. I explained my reasoning for turning round rather than waiting for Tampa to be cleared, and I offered Randy the chance to say why he thought waiting would have been a better option. But as it happened, he had nothing to say.

Then we got to the incident that everyone wanted to hear about: the vehicle collision in Basra.

'What exactly happened?' I asked Randy. 'Wasn't that on your side of the vehicle, the side you were meant to be covering?'

He shifted in his chair, looking awkward, as everyone eyeballed him. Finally, he said, 'I decided not to say anything because I thought you guys would have shot them. They were just young guys trying to get through. I didn't think they were a threat.'

This was unexpected, and I could see the rest of the guys were as surprised as I was.

'So, Randy,' I announced, 'you decided two males of fighting age were not a threat because you had somehow determined we were going to shoot them? So, their lives were more important than ours? And what about when they crashed into us? Did you still think they weren't a threat then? By any chance, did they have guns?'

I was dumbfounded when Randy admitted that one of them at least was armed with an assault rifle. I could feel the tension in the room ratchet up several notches, but Randy continued digging his own grave, grinning stupidly, as all the guys glared at him, hoping for some explanation as to why he had put all of us in danger.

'Yeah, I saw them and made the choice,' he continued. 'I think you all ride too hard – not everyone is here to kill us. The Iraqis know we have come to help them rebuild their country. They know we're the good guys. So, yes, I saw them and didn't call it, and I'd do it all again.'

I'd heard more than enough. For him to say he would do it all again was the final straw.

'Hey, motherfucker,' I announced, looking straight at him. 'You're fired. Pack your shit right now and get the fuck out of here.'

He looked at the other three for support but got nothing.

'Don't look at us, you fucker,' Two Trays kicked in. 'You heard Baz – get the fuck out of here.'

A couple of tense seconds ticked by before Randy finally got up and left the room.

Unsurprisingly, he went directly to the other hotel, where Tom and the rest of the crew were billeted. There, he cried his version of the story and bunked with that lot for the night, before catching a lift to BIAP and the first plane out of Iraq.

As for us, we cracked open another beer and decided to get stuck into one of the three boxset TV shows we'd brought with us. One beer followed another and soon enough we were regaling each other with stories of times gone by, before Yard Dog brought out his guitar and we had a jolly old singalong. Only when we had finished a shit-ton of beers and many a piratical song, did we decide that we'd had enough.

Songs and laughter. That was the medicine we would turn to during my time in Iraq, sometimes much to the annoyance of the poor fuckers in the room next to us. It was a little bit of escapism, in a place that, in terms of deadly insurgency attacks, was only just getting warmed up. I had already been in Iraq for long enough to know that if you wanted to have any chance of surviving, you couldn't rely on fucks like Randy. Now with Randy gone, there was room for Two Trays to move in with the rest of us, reuniting the four amigos once more.

The following day there was no sign of Randy, or of Sean Penn for that matter, but I did spot an altogether contrasting figure, one that I would see several more times when we returned from recces. For me, this tortured individual would become a symbol of all that was wrong with the war – *with our war* – in Iraq.

It was a young Iraqi boy. He must have been no more than ten years old, though it was hard to be sure because he was covered from head to toe in dirt and, from my first sighting of him, he didn't seem right in the head somehow. I spied him hiding out among the collapsed ruins of a multi-storey car park, which lay opposite our hotel, and which I guessed must have been the recipient of a very large bomb dropped during the air campaign.

Smart bombs my ass, I told myself, ruefully. *They hit a car park. Fucking idiots.*

Little did I know.

The young boy wouldn't come any closer no matter what I did to try to coax him out of his shadowed place of hiding. I asked Yard Dog to try to communicate with him in Arabic, but he just stared blankly back at us, his dirty young face expressionless, his brown eyes gazing into the distance with the 'thousand-yard stare' – the look everyone gets after seeing too much horror, hell and combat. Finally, he ducked back inside the rubble, and I couldn't help but think he was like the sad, tortured, possessed figure of Gollum from *Lord of the Rings*. We decided to leave him some food and water in the hope he might take it, but I would never see him do so.

One evening, I spied him again. I was finishing up unpacking the Suburban and gagging for a beer when, out of the corner of my eye, I saw him watching me. He was picking at something and eating it, and I assumed it was a loaf of bread. I managed to get a little closer without scaring him away, but as I did so I was horrified to realise that his meal wasn't a piece of bread at all, but a dead pigeon. He'd torn away the feathers and piled them in a heap, and the poor kid was peeling off strips of dried meat and chewing on them like jerky. As I watched, aghast, he flitted once more into the darkness of the ruins.

I felt shocked, deeply saddened and angered at what I had seen, plus I was confused. I didn't understand why he was always hanging around these ruins. Surely there was somewhere better he could go, I reasoned, so I asked one of the night security guards, an Iraqi who spoke decent English.

'That kid,' I nodded at the ruins. 'D'you know him? Why's he always here?'

The guard shook his head. 'He's just this crazy kid. He's always there.'

When I asked why, the guard stared at me for a second, before raising his arm towards the pile of concrete in the way Saddam had always pointed: arm held at shoulder height, hand turned palm in, fingers together and flat.

'His parents are there,' he replied, pointing at the rubble.

'Where?' I asked, unsure of what he meant.

'There,' he repeated, pointing at the ruins.

I pointed in the same direction, to confirm we were talking about the same thing. 'There? In the car park?'

The guard shook his head again. 'No, no, that's not a car park. That was his home. It was an apartment block with many families, his family. It was hit by a bomb many months ago, in the air-attack. That was his home,' he said again. 'His family are still in there – dead, all dead.'

I gazed at the ruins as a horrible understanding dawned on me. I could feel the hair on my head tingle and my blood start to boil with anger, as I realised that this poor child was ruined for life, and no one, not one soul, seemed to give a damn. *What the fuck!*

It made me think of my own kids back at home in NZ, who were about the same age, safe, warm, well-fed and secure. I felt a complete fool for having thought the Iraqi kid wasn't 'right in the head'. No doubt the poor little fucker was suffering from a full-on case of post-traumatic stress disorder (PTSD). And he was by no means the only one. This war had made a lot of orphans and screwed generations to come. I couldn't help but think that such actions would come back to bite the US in the ass one day, and one day soon.

I had some water, peanut butter cups and other food, and I left them where I had seen the kid dart back into the ruins, clutching his rotten pigeon carcass. Whether I was really trying to help him, or simply easing my own sense of guilt, I wasn't sure, but his family were dead, and it broke my heart that he seemed to be just waiting for them to emerge, unable to accept that that was never going to happen. What would become of him, I wondered. This was war at its worst. This would explain why the insurgency was steadily attracting more followers hell-bent on vengeance. I couldn't blame them one bit. Fuck, I'd join too if this ever happened to my country, *to my family*. Who could honestly say they wouldn't?

I was overcome with a feeling of utter contempt for those who had sold the lie about weapons of mass destruction and the bullshit that this war was somehow revenge for 9/11, and nothing to do with getting our hands on Iraq's oil or securing the plum 're-construction' and 'security' contracts, just like the ones we at Blackwater Commercial were working hard to land right now.

It was obvious to me that the insurgency would have no trouble recruiting kids like this one to their cause. With the huge number of young Iraqis who had been orphaned, and the vast swathes of parents made childless, it was only natural to want to avenge their deaths, even if that meant making the ultimate sacrifice to do so.

The guys who drove the VBIEDs or strapped kilos of high explosive (HE) to their bodies must have had a bloody good reason to sacrifice themselves, and I was sure it had nothing to do with the promise of seventy-two virgins. I truly hoped a different fate awaited the kid in the rubble. It wasn't his war. He wasn't anybody's enemy, and he didn't deserve to have this situation dropped on him from 10,000ft, destroying his life entirely. In truth, he would have been far better off dying with his family.

The more I thought about it, the sadder and angrier it made me feel. If the insurgents did recruit him and persuade him to carry a bomb, at the point of ignition I hoped only that he would feel he had got his revenge and that he would go to his parents and his God with a smile on his young face.

I was lucky. I could go home. The kid in the ruins – he had no-where left to go.

As 22 December 2003 arrived, that's just what I did – I set out for home. All of us did on my team, heading out for a much-needed Christmas break. We were going to fly out of Kuwait, which meant another drive down MSR Tampa. We packed up the Suburban, before fuelling up, grabbing some take-out food, and we hit the road south, and with not one fucking peanut butter cup between us. En route, I briefed everyone as normal, reminding them that we weren't there yet, so not to slacken off.

You ain't there until you're there.

It had been only a week since we'd last driven the route, but the increased evidence of insurgency attacks was clear for all to see, with bomb craters every few kilometres, and especially near the Al-Hillah and Najaf turn-offs. If only Randy was still with us, maybe he'd finally get to see just how happy the locals were with being 'lib-erated'. At camp Nav Star, on the Kuwait border, there was an old buddy of Tom's, who bagged and tagged our weapons for us, ready to be picked up in the New Year.

That was if we came back in the New Year.

Tom's vision for Blackwater Commercial had begun taking real shape in the past few weeks. The concept of bidding on more than just State Department contracts had proved viable, and, as long as Blackwater HQ could see there were big bucks to be made, the future looked bright. But over Christmas we would have to wait anxiously for Tom to let us know if we were coming back. It had been a big gamble for all who had jumped ship from Custer Battles.

But we'd known what we were getting into, and as we'd driven around Baghdad and across southern Iraq in our soft-skin vehicles, with no armour or maps and shitty guns, we'd prayed that the gamble would pay off.

The next couple of weeks should prove it, one way or the other.

I boarded my flight to New Zealand with only $300 in my pocket to show for the weeks I'd spent in Iraq. All of us had been burning through the cash, using whatever we had just to survive. I had only a one-way ticket, which is never a good sign.

But now, it was all in the hands of the Gods and Tom's ability to sell us to Moyock. *Inshallah.*

CHAPTER 4

Hallelujah! February 2004, and I was back in Kuwait, the stepping-stone to Iraq. *Yee-hah!* The weeks in New Zealand had been tough on $300, but I wasn't going to complain, and who the fuck would listen anyway. I was back in the heat and the desert and the sun on my skin felt good.

Tom was there ahead of me, and it was great to see him at the airport. It meant a lot to me that he was there to pick me up. We had bonded over the past few weeks in Iraq and become pretty close. We grinned and man-hugged: a hug of success.

'You did it mate,' I announced, stating the obvious. Neither of us would be here if Tom hadn't managed to sell us to the guys in Moyock. 'How did you bring them around?'

'The owner isn't silly,' Tom replied. 'Once he saw the numbers and the potential, it was a no-brainer, but they want to run the show now pretty much from there and control everything.'

So, we had gone out on a limb with very little support to prove it was viable, and now the BW (Blackwater) big chiefs wanted to come in and grab the glory. Isn't it always the way?

'So, what d'you think of that?' I asked.

Tom shrugged. 'It is what it is, mate. Between you and me, there are a few people back there who are only interested in looking after their own asses. The owner is a decent guy, but there are others you got to watch out for.'

'Yeah. I get it bro. I get it.' Tom steered me towards a red Mitsubishi Pajero 4x4 and told me to bung my bags aboard. 'This one of ours?' I asked.

'Yeah, plus we have a blue one just like it, and we'll be picking up a few more. It's soft-skin, but that's all we need at the moment.'

Well, OK, this is a start, I guessed. *And presumably we'll get hard-skin vehicles as we prove ourselves more and more.*

During the drive into Kuwait City, Tom explained how BW HQ recognised BW Commercial could be a right little gold mine, not just generating more business but giving them the ability to train more guys in-country while they awaited their security clearance to join BW's State Department teams. It was a win-win situation.

'We will be using Kuwait as a base,' Tom explained. 'We've scored a new catering supply contract, taking it over from Control Risks Group, so the plan is to set up a team house here, to cover the southern regions of Iraq, and another main team house, where you'll be going, in Baghdad.'

Cool. Sounded like we were hitting the ground running.

'It's much easier and cheaper to fly the guys into Kuwait than to go via Jordan, which has become a ridiculously expensive place to conduct business,' Tom continued.

We will be here for two days, he explained, and he had three new guys for me to meet, since Yard Dog and G-Man had left to take up new contracts with DynCorp, a rival security company, and Two Trays was still to arrive.

I'd been in constant contact with the amigos, so I knew all about their jump to DynCorp. So now the four amigos were down to two – Two Trays and yours truly. It was a pity to lose Yard Dog and G-Man so soon, but in our game it's all about making money when and wherever you can. I didn't blame them for jumping ship, rather than going through all the waiting and uncertainty. My meagre funds had barely seen me out, but I'd gambled on the big one. Blackwater was paying an average of $200 more per day than any other company, so to me it was worth the wait.

Arriving at the hotel, we parked up next to the blue Mitsubishi – our other vehicle. They were mid-size, moderately powerful 4x4s: a more modern model than the Suburbans, so they should be far more reliable. One concern, however, was that they had a spare jerry can for fuel clamped high on the back door.

Nice target. That goes up and you're toast.

I grabbed my bag and we moved into a hotel suite that had been converted into our operations (ops) room. It had whiteboards, office desks, chairs and printers: the works. I dropped my bag and we strolled to the restaurant. Gathered around a single table in the vast empty dining room were four unmistakable Americans, chowing down on pasta, hotdogs, burgers, fries and cola. Tom introduced me as 'Baz the Kiwi', then went round the table. He started with John, or JP, who would be our ops officer based in Kuwait with responsibility for the new contract we had with the catering firm Eurest Support Services (ESS). Next was White Boy, then Ben and finally Jerry.

'You guys are the new team,' Tom announced.

There's a lot you can tell about a person by the way they shake your hand, and these were four good, solid handshakes. Tom had let them know about my SAS background, which cut out any of the ass-sniffing that would normally accompany such introductions.

'Guys, we'll meet for an ops brief at 14:00, OK?' said Tom, as he got up to leave.

I grabbed myself some chow from the buffet and sat down with my new teammates. JP, White Boy and Ben were former SEALs, and Jerry was a former US ranger. The rangers are a solid outfit and normally the stepping stone into Delta Force. Jerry had worked for a security company called Cochise, in northern Iraq, and he had some basic Arabic language skills. He was roughly 6ft 2in. and solid as a brick shithouse with dark, deep-set eyes. He wore sleeveless shirts to show off his muscular arms and spoke about 100 decibels louder than anybody else. Maybe he was a bit deaf, but listening to him for any length of time was hard on the hearing.

JP stood around 5ft 7in. and looked to be in his early fifties. He was one of those guys that you could tell had been there and done it all and was a friendly bugger to boot.

White Boy was about 6ft 2in., with very little body fat on his honed, wiry frame. He sported a droopy handlebar moustache, and his eyes had a definite intensity about them; I could tell right away that he was used to being a leader.

Ben was 5ft 5in., maximum, standing on a box. He was stocky and thickset with teeth that looked far too big for his mouth and friendly as hell.

We chatted for around an hour, after which I figured I had a good take on all at the table. I hadn't spoken much. I was more interested in listening right then. Besides, Jerry had done enough talking for everyone and my jet lag was starting to kick in.

Ten minutes before 14:00, we assembled in the ops room. Tom gestured to a whiteboard, on which he had drawn up responsibilities for the next few days. 'OK, guys, here's the plan,' he announced. 'We head out to Baghdad in two days. BW has rented and is fitting out a house inside the IZ, which will be our new HQ.' *Now that sounded real good.*

'Transport will be the two vehicles parked up outside: one red and one blue Pajero. Yes, I know they're soft-skin, but hard cars are as rare as rocking-horse shit right now. Everyone wants them and any order will take six months to arrive. So, they'll have to do for now.'

'Tomorrow we've got a lot of running around, picking up equipment and office supplies for the house in Baggers. That will be done by me and Baz in the blue. White Boy and Ben will take the red and head over to the Kellogg Brown and Root (KBR) HQ. They have a massive compound – it's obscene really. See what you can scrounge from there. Maps in particular would be nice and whatever else you can carry. Don't come back empty-handed, OK?'

'Jerry, you will help JP make up the new ID badges for us all and print the paperwork BW wants us to fill out before heading in – your bank account and tax details, next of kin, medical stuff, the works. Get it all done, guys, or you can't deploy.'

'OK, the move in,' Tom continued. 'We will move out on Friday at 07:00 to the border, pick up the weapons we left at Nav Star, refuel and make our way to Baghdad up Tampa. Order of travel: Baz, because you know the way better than any of us, you will lead in the blue, with me and with Jerry riding in the back seat. White Boy and Ben will follow in the red. Oh, and one other thing: we have these.'

JP swivelled around in his chair, reached into a box and pulled out a brown bulletproof vest, minus the business part – the plates.

'Yeah, I know there aren't any plates,' he remarked, 'but we'll get some as we move up north. Take one each and don't lose it.'

Early Friday as planned, we set off north heading for Baghdad.

The drive from Kuwait City to the Iraq border takes about two hours. With White Boy taking the wheel of the other vehicle, I figured he really only trusted himself to be in control, and I figured if Tom hadn't been there, he would have tried to grab the team leader's position. I had no problem with that. He seemed like a very capable guy, and he had Tom's trust.

In our vehicle, though, we were having a bit of an issue. Jerry, it soon became clear, thought he was in charge, and rather than concentrate on his arcs he was trying to tell me how to drive.

Fuck me, Jerry, we haven't even entered Iraq yet and you're starting to piss me off.

I glanced over at Tom, who rolled his eyes. Sod it, now was as good a time as any to set the ground rules.

'Hey, bro,' I said, eyeballing Jerry. 'Tell you what – why don't you do your job and I'll do mine, and if you have a problem, we can sort it later, OK?'

Jerry started out the window, pretending he didn't hear me. I was starting to sense it was going to be a long day.

Arriving at camp Nav Star, I made sure I was reunited with the same ratty old Ukrainian-made AK as before. 'Hello, my precious,' I greeted her. 'So, did you miss me?'

The Ukrainian-manufactured AKs were ten times better than the Iraqi or Chinese knockoffs. I certainly didn't want one of those fuckers exploding in my face again when fired on full auto for too long burning through some crappy ammo. The other guys grabbed what remained. It was a bit sad seeing the amigos' guns going to other guys, but they were needed. We piled the rest of the guns in the vehicles, refuelled and set off once more.

We didn't have plates for the vests; we'd be picking those up in Baghdad. We drove about a kilometre into the desert before pulling over, so we could test-fire our weapons. There is no point driving around a war zone with a gun you're not sure is serviceable because you didn't take the time to check it. Happily, all the guns worked just fine, so, after changing the mag out to have a full load, we set them at whatever state of readiness we preferred and moved out.

An hour into the drive up Tampa, we came across a long convoy of flatbeds parked on the roadside, as the drivers grabbed a break. They looked mostly American and Filipino, and they were busy making tea or sleeping wherever there was a slice of shade. Beside them, providing cover and slightly out in our lane were the gun-truck escorts. All of a sudden, Jerry leant out of his passenger window and started yelling at the nearest gun-truck to move over, waving his AK like a mad-man.

Tom spun around in his chair and yelled at Jerry, 'Get the fuck back in the vehicle!'

But Jerry just ignored him, or didn't hear him, and kept leaning out yelling for the escort to pull over.

'What the fuck are you doing?' I yelled. Not only were the flatbeds immobile on the side of the road, but the gun-truck was obviously part of their team and no threat to us.

'No man, this is how you got to do it,' Jerry yelled back at Tom and me. 'You got to move them over. This is how we did it in Cochise.'

Tom told me to pull over. I did as requested, with White Boy pulling up behind me. Tom and White Boy got out and converged on Jerry.

'What the fuck are you doing?' White Boy yelled at him, getting right in his grill. 'Don't you ever wave your fucking gun at friendlies.'

At the same time, the gun-truck Jerry had just been yelling at came roaring over with its top-mounted, belt-fed PK heavy machine gun pointed right at us. *Nice work, Captain Dumb Fuck!*

The team leader in charge (TL) of the escort was a British guy, and he was rightly pissed off. His anger was tempered a little when he saw Tom and White Boy giving Jerry a verbal ass-kicking, threatening to take him back to Kuwait if he didn't sort his shit out, pronto. As Jerry skulked back into the rear of the vehicle, Tom apologised to the Brit TL for Jerry's actions. We set off again for more long hours of hot, dry driving, coming across new evidence of insurgent attacks and their growing effectiveness.

Eventually, I could tell by the change in terrain when we were getting close to Baghdad, so I told Tom that I wanted to pull over to the side of the road.

'Sure,' he said. 'You've done this more than me, so do what you need to do.'

It was getting close to dusk and the sun would soon be directly in our faces, making forward visibility an issue. Learning from the experience of my previous drives to and from Basra, I'd decided this was a good time and place to clean our windscreens of the hundreds of bugs we had splattered along the way. White Boy came over and asked why we had stopped, with so little distance still to go.

I explained why.

'We should push on while we can,' he argued, but I wasn't budging.

'No mate, clean your windscreen. You'll thank me for it later.'

If the sun was hitting a dirty windscreen, there would be little chance of seeing anything to our front, and in an attack the difference between seeing and not seeing can often be the difference between life and death. We made it safely to the border of the IZ, where our new Blackwater IDs got us whisked through. We arrived just on last light at the new team house, which lay on the far side of the Four Soldiers roundabout and close to the 14th of July Bridge. I was pretty happy with myself for getting us there with zero navigational problems, and Tom thanked me for a job well done.

We unloaded the vehicles of all the shit we had brought up from Kuwait and traipsed inside, sore, dusty, tired and hungry. The house was a large six-room multi-level property with a sizeable flat roof and a great view of the surrounding area. There was a fine and roomy front yard that was completely walled in, with two large date trees for shade, and a car port that could hold two vehicles.

Apparently, Blackwater had rented the property for about $90,000 per year from its Iraqi owner, who was more than happy to receive the large cash payment. Plenty of other Iraqis had seized the chance of a lifetime and were charging a fortune to companies desperate to be within the IZ.

The house was a hive of activity, considering the hour. For the past couple of weeks, a group of guys – all American – had been working their asses off getting the place up and running: fitting bunk beds; removing old fixtures and furniture; and preparing the ground for the generator that would be arriving from Turkey and was essential, given the frequency of the power cuts Baghdad was experiencing.

The Coalition air campaign had deliberately targeted Baghdad's electricity and clean water supplies, and now the insurgency had started targeting the infrastructure services too. So not only was electricity in short supply but so was clean drinking water, and not just for us, but for the Iraqi people too, of course. Many would die from simple illnesses and diseases and, you guessed it, the result would be further animosity and anger towards the Coalition. *Nice work, guys.*

The biggest and most impressive purchase, apart from the generator, was laid out in the front yard. The entire grassed area was covered by row upon row of AK-47 assault rifles, plus RPK and PK machine guns, all varying in condition, country of origin and year. There must have been about 300 weapons lined up like soldiers on parade. Over the coming few days, I would get to know them intimately as we were tasked to clean, inspect and swap parts from one gun to another to make the maximum number of serviceable weapons. We'd log them all and lock them in the new armoury.

Tom introduced us to the people he knew on site who mattered. Moyock had decided that, to justify the expense of a set-up like this one, Tom had to go get more contracts, so he would have little role to play in the day-to-day running of operations. That would be down to the chief here, Brian, a gnarled-looking former frogman – SEAL – who was more senior in age and rank than Tom and had the weathered look to prove it. Brian was a whiteboard wizard who would meticulously plan every detail of any task. He was tall and thin with a friendly, caring manner, and he and I would become good friends. I would look to him for advice and guidance in the months ahead. In return, he would look to me as someone who could get the job done.

Next was Mark, a guy who had formerly run the FedEx depot at BIAP before joining the Blackwater Commercial set-up. He was about 5ft 2in., had no military experience and was tasked with overseeing the finances and administration. He was another genuinely top-class guy who'd been hired for his brain not his brawn, despite being a tough little fucker.

Then there was Dave, another old navy guy. He was big in stature and personality, with a ponytail and a decidedly cool manner. Finally, there was Rich, another former SEAL and a really knowledgeable operator. If this was the standard of the guys who I'd be working with in the leadership team, then I was as happy as a pig in shit.

The rest of the operators were a mishmash of former marines, US Army, police or whoever else was hanging around Moyock waiting to be deployed. Brian had also hired two local Iraqi fixers, Omar and Mohammad, or Mo. Not the old Mo from before but a new Mo. These guys would be essential to securing all our local purchases, and they were risking their lives and the lives of their families to be working with us.

The insurgents had started kidnapping anyone who was helping the US military, plus anyone who was involved in the rebuilding effort, who they had branded as 'traitors'. I could only admire Mo and Omar, who only wanted a better future for Iraq, now that Saddam was behind bars, and to make some money for their families.

One day while out buying stuff for the house, Mo, Mark and I decided to make a run to a pizza joint he knew, one that was still operating and apparently selling great pizza. As risky as this seemed, it had to be better than more chicken and rice. The restaurant was full of young students who must have just finished their school day. Though our arrival didn't draw too much attention, I knew it was not safe for us to be seen there for too long.

I told Mo to order takeaway and Mark to use his lack of height to hide in the crowd. Even though Mark wasn't ex-military he was tooled up to the nines. The little fucker looked like a one-man wrecking machine, with his MP5K, pistol, grenades, vest with plates and all the holsters and slings to go with it, and I did not doubt his ability to use all his firepower if he had to.

I opted to step outside and keep a lookout, so I positioned myself where I could keep one eye on our vehicle and one on the restaurant. There had been an increase in sniper attacks against the military and contractors alike, and since I didn't want to be another notch on someone's Dragunov sniper rifle, I backed into an alleyway, making use of whatever cover I could find.

After about twenty minutes, I was feeling increasingly exposed and wondering what the hell was taking Mark and Mo so long. I was about to set out to investigate when I suddenly felt a whack to my shoulder and a splatter of fluid against the side of my face. *Fuck me, I've been shot*, was my first thought. Must have been a silenced Dragunov, for there was no crack of the gun firing.

I waited for the searing pain, but it didn't hurt like I had imagined it might. I'd dropped to one knee and was frantically scanning around to see where the round might have come from. Safety off and weapon at the ready, I could feel warm fluid dripping down the side of my face and neck.

Oddly, I still seemed to have complete use of my shoulder and neck, and to my surprise, everyone in the street was continuing with their business seemingly as if nothing had happened. Then I heard the cooing of birds directly above me. *Are you shitting me, you dirty fuckers?* Yep, to my disgust they were. I had been sniped by a group of Baghdad's killer-ninja pigeons. With nothing to wipe off the fresh, white pigeon shit, I just had to stay there until Mark and Mo came strolling out with the pizzas, like they were on a date.

As soon as they saw me, they burst into laughter, as did some of the students who were gazing out of the window. We climbed aboard the vehicle and made our way back to the team house as the goo slowly dried and stank the crap out of our wheels. Once we were back, I cleaned up and enjoyed a slice of Iraq's finest takeaway pizza.

Shortly after our visit, someone would walk right into the same crowded pizza joint wearing an explosive vest and blow themselves to pieces, along with fifty bright young students.

It would be a while before we had pizza again.

A few days later, White Boy and Ben – the two former SEALs with whom I'd made the drive up from Kuwait – plus Jerry, the gung-ho former ranger, and I were called to the ops room for a briefing with Brian. Blackwater Commercial needed to raise a protective services detail (PSD), putting together our best team to escort the State Department's representative in and around Karbala, a city lying around 100 kilometres south-west of Baghdad.

The chosen team was us four, and we would have to stay out there the whole time. We'd done the odd run around Baghdad, so we were reasonably familiar with how each one of us operated by now. As I'd predicted, White Boy had taken on the team leader role, which was fine by me. Ben was a solid operator and definitely White Boy's sidekick. Batman has Robin; the Lone Ranger has Tonto; White Boy has Ben. But that of course left me stuck with Jerry. As a group, we were already starting to question Jerry's abilities. I feared he was a rush-hire – here to fill a hole but with very little due diligence having been done to assess his ability to do the job.

Brian rounded off the briefing by telling us to saddle up and report to the temporary CPA base in Karbala the next day.

'Er, where might that be?' Ben asked.

I was the only one who had been to Karbala before. It was during my CPA recce days with G-Man, Larry and Mike. But the military base that we had surveyed was now considered too dangerous for anyone to stay in overnight, and with good reason. The insurgents had driven a truck packed full of explosives into the outer barrier, blasting a hole big enough for the car behind it, also packed with explosives, to barrel on through. The driver of the sedan made it right into the camp, before blowing the shit out of himself and a barracks full of sleeping Ukrainian soldiers.

The safest place to stay now was apparently the Polish military camp, Brian explained, which lay on the Western outskirts of Karbala. Luckily, someone in our team house had secured 100 large-scale maps of Iraq, covering nearly every major town and road we should ever need to use. So, no more relying on the tea towel it seemed. We'd each have a set of maps for the upcoming run, which should make finding the Polish base child's play.

But now came the kicker. Brian explained that our client, the State Department representative, was known to be a 'difficult woman', one not inclined to listen to the advice of her security detail.

'Fuck me,' I announced, 'not only does she sound like a problem, but she, is a she.' In such a male-dominated society as Iraq, was it really a good idea for the CPA representative to be a woman, I asked?

'Oh, I'm sure that won't ruffle any feathers,' White Boy remarked sarcastically, rolling his eyes.

Brian assured us that he had raised exactly the same concerns, but no one was listening. Their argument seemed to be that she was ideal for the job because she was fluent in Arabic. *Well, that's OK then. Not.*

After an evening spent poring over the maps, we found the location of the Polish base and worked out it would take us about an hour and a half at maximum speed to reach it. That done, I packed up all my kit, plus anything that was not nailed down that might make our life a little easier where we were headed. We would be on our own out there, at least until BW could stand up proper teams in rotation, using more guys brought in from the US. Ideally, this was at least a ten-man job, and we were just the four. We were clearly being sent before Blackwater was ready, but it was either that or lose a juicy contract, so guess what?

Despite the lack of ready cash over recent weeks, I'd splashed out on a Thuraya satellite phone, one that finally gave me the ability to make international calls. It ran on a pre-pay scratch-card credit system, and while it didn't have total global coverage like some of the more expensive options, it sure as shit covered Iraq, which was good enough for me.

The Thuraya came with a built-in GPS capability, so the user's latitude and longitude could be transmitted at set time intervals to another Thuraya, so acting like a tracking beacon, which would be great for plotting our out-of-town road moves. I figured as my life was on the line here in Iraq, the money invested was more than worth it.

We left for Karbala with Jerry and I leading in the red Pajero and White Boy and Ben following in the blue; four men in two soft-skin vehicles heading into one of the shittiest parts of central Iraq. It was far from ideal. On top of that, and in spite of my Thuraya, radio comms were a major issue. All we had were Motorola hand-held radios, which enabled line-of-sight comms between vehicles but over no greater distance than 200 metres, tops. Despite our repeated requests for something better, Moyock simply ignored the problem.

I made sure that everything I might need sat nicely around my driving seat and within easy reach: I had recently acquired a fine new MP5, plus an RPK and even an M72 rocket launcher – because you never know when you might need one, right? The M72 is a 66mm rocket launcher weapon; a one-shot throwaway deal. With all that at hand, I felt pretty much ready to take on anything. I had also acquired a new Rhodesian-style recon rig that fitted over my bulletproof vest now that we had Kevlar plates. It was perfect for my thirteen spare mags, high-explosive grenades and white-phosphorus (WP) grenades, which were to be used to lay down smoke if we had to ditch the vehicle. The intense exothermic reaction of the WP making contact with air would set anything in the vicinity aflame and, as a bonus, would likely melt the vehicle to nothing remotely worth stealing.

I had stopped wearing my Glock pistol strapped to my leg, like I did in the Unit, and moved it up to my cargo belt on my waist. I still couldn't draw and shoot someone when I was driving, but, like I'd told Yard Dog back in Basra, *that's what the vehicle is for, dumbass.*

We drove through Baghdad's Karrada district, past the Al-Hamra Hotel where it all began – where we deserted Custer Battles and founded BW Commercial – alongside the Tigris and up to a road junction where we turned left onto the spaghetti loop, heading south on Tampa out of Baghdad until the Al-Hillha turn-off.

I was growing to really like Iraq and I looked forward to seeing some of the historic parts of the country, rather than being a one-town warrior like so many guys would become. I love history and Iraq has plenty of it, but you won't see it any of it sitting behind the twelve-foot concrete T walls in the IZ.

As we were driving, I noticed Jerry had a new piece of kit for his Bushmaster AR-15 assault rifle, the weapon he'd selected from the BW armoury.

'What the fuck is that?' I asked. I knew what it was, but I'd decided to ask anyway.

'It's one of the new suppressors someone brought over from

Moyock,' he answered. Suppressor – mil-speak for silencer. 'For the silent kill,' he added with a grin, and I wasn't sure if he was joking or not.

'So how silent is it?' I asked, coaxing him to shoot it.

Mind trick successful, Jerry screwed the long black cylindrical contraption to the end of his bang-stick, making the long gun even longer. Awkwardly, he manoeuvred it around, trying to get the dangerous end out of the open window without poking us both in the face. Finally, with it now positioned out of the vehicle by about two feet, he aimed at nothing in particular and fired off a round: CRACK.

'Fuck me,' I yelled, an intense ringing in my ear, a dollop of shit in my pants and the smell of cordite wafting through the vehicle. 'That's loud as fuck, bro.'

Admittedly, it was somewhat quieter than if the weapon had been fired without one, but, as he unscrewed it and tucked it back into his go bag, giggling like a schoolgirl, I added, 'Wow, that's fucking awesome. If your target is two miles away, and deaf, they'll never hear it!'

It's one of the few times I can remember Jerry and myself laughing together.

But I wondered if he'd even got my point – that his chosen weapon was completely unsuitable for riding in a cramped vehicle, even without the added bulk of the silencer. Somehow, I doubted it.

Once through Al-Hillah, it was a straight run to Karbala, apart from one more little town we'd spotted on the map. As we approached, the streets were bustling with locals going about their business, but as we got deeper into the centre, I noticed people seemed to be paying a little more attention to us than I was comfortable with.

'Keep your eyes peeled,' I barked at Jerry. 'This just isn't feeling right.'

As I reached down to check on my MP5, I radioed back to White Boy and asked if he had noticed anything odd. They too had seen the looks we were getting, which were none too friendly. The further we drove into the town, the fewer people there were on the streets. All I needed now was to see one of those fuckers running, which is right up there in the attack-indicator sequence. On full alert, we drove through streets that were definitely emptying. And then I saw it – a middle-aged, potbellied, sandal-wearing fucker doing his best Usain Bolt impersonation.

'OK, that's it,' I yelled. 'Stand by, Jerry, 'cause we are about to get hit.'

I radioed White Boy and gave him a heads-up, but he was fully aware of it and told me to punch it hard to get the fuck out of there. The road had narrowed to almost a single lane, preventing us from turning around and going back, and to stop here would be suicide. I hit the accelerator as far into the floor as it would go and waited as the Pajero took a painfully long time to get up a head of steam.

My chief thought now was this: *If you're on the street, you're a baddy. And if you step out in front of me to try to get me to slow down, I'll run you the fuck over.*

Then it happened.

We were going at balls-out speed as I roared around a left-hand bend and there was a loud pop. A wave of fine brown sand erupted from the ground just forward and to the left of my side of the vehicle, and instinctively I screwed my eyes to nearly shut and hunched my body into the smallest shape possible, hoping like fuck that the hot shards of shrapnel would somehow miss me.

The vehicle shot through the cloud, dust covering the windscreen and spraying through the open windows, and I waited, shitting myself, for the whirlwind of shrapnel, which I expected to be the last thing I'd ever hear, see or feel. But still we roared onwards at break-neck speed. I glanced in my rear-view mirror, only to see White Boy and Ben thundering through the cloud of sand, bang on our tail.

Holy crap, it looked as if they had got through safely, too.

Then I heard the distinctive *crack-crack-crack* of AK rounds firing off, followed by a couple of bangs, but nothing seemed to hit us, and eventually the sound drifted away on our slipstream as we sped on.

'What the fuck was that?' I asked Jerry, who had just radioed White Boy to check they were all right.

As the dust in the air mixed with the sweat covering my face, arms and neck, I concentrated on putting more distance between us and whatever had just happened. Eventually I figured we were safe enough to have a proper chat with those on the other vehicle.

'Was that an IED?' I asked, via the radio.

'Looks like it might have been a dud,' Ben responded. 'If that was an IED then the main charge can't have gone off.'

'Just the dets, I think,' added White Boy, with an unmistakable note of stress in his voice. 'Dets' equals detonators.

'What about the cracks and pops?' I asked.

'They had a go at us with AKs,' White Boy replied, 'but Ben laid down some cover fire and threw a couple of flash-bangs.'

Flash-bangs – stun grenades. They produce a massive bang and a blinding flash of light. *Where the hell did Ben get those from*, I wondered? Right now, I didn't really care.

'No doubt someone will be getting their hairy insurgent ass right royally kicked with a dirty pair of sandals for screwing up that ambush,' I volunteered.

'Yeah, roger that,' White Boy affirmed. 'Let's keep punching it until we get to the outskirts of Karbala, OK?'

'Roger that,' I replied. *Roger fucking that.*

'We might have been too much of a surprise,' Ben added. 'Too fast. Whoever was waiting for us didn't set the IED properly.'

I agreed.

As the driver, I wouldn't normally be doing the comms as well, but Jerry, for whatever reason, just wasn't getting his shit together right now. Turned ninety degrees away from me, all I could see was his back, as he faced out of the right-hand window. He was hunched over wiping dust off himself with his shemagh – his Arab-style headscarf – and his pose just seemed all wrong.

'Hey, bro, you good?' I asked.

'Yeah, Baz, all good.'

I wasn't convinced. It was like he hadn't even registered what had just happened. If that IED had been properly armed, we would all now be toast – Jerry included. But it just didn't seem to have hit home. It was like he was in denial, pretending it hadn't happened and that we hadn't just been that close to meeting our maker. I told myself to keep a close eye on Jerry, from here on in, again. His actions ever since we had met hadn't exactly filled me with confidence, and now this was just fucking weird.

The last major chokepoint before hitting the outskirts of Karbala was a narrow bridge over a deep ravine. There was no other way to get across it, which made it the ideal place for a follow-up attack.

'Another great place for an ambush,' I pointed out to Jerry.

'Roger that,' he replied. I didn't expect much of an answer, but this was just more of the same: Jerry not engaging.

As luck would have it, we made it across the bridge into Karbala without incident, but even so I stored the bridge in my memory as a place to be very wary of in future.

Karbala is considered a very holy city for Shia Muslims, on a par with Mecca for Sunnis. There are two giant golden-domed mosques – in honour of Imam Husayn and Imam Al-Abbas – which Shias make pilgrimages to in their millions at a certain time each year. Very holy-moly indeed.

We entered the city, and I spied the familiar defences of stacked, sand-filled Hesco bags and Jersey walls.

'This must be the Thai base,' I remarked to Jerry. Other than the Polish camp, the Thai military also had a base here.

Jerry radioed White Boy, who instructed us to pull over when we could. The Thai base looked well-fortified, but it also seemed as if it had been on the receiving end of a few major attacks. I wasn't entirely surprised. Its front wall was set back only about twenty metres from the main road, and close to the former Ukrainian base that was hit, which meant they were asking for trouble.

I spotted the camp entrance just up the road ahead. I wasn't keen to barrel through the centre of Karbala and attract more unwanted attention, so I radioed that we were going to stop and ask the Thais if they knew an alternative route to get us to the Polish base. We threw the flag on the dashboard and gently rolled up next to a Humvee parked by the barrier arm.

Jerry and White Boy got out and were joined by Ben, but all the waving, headshaking and pointing in different directions from the Thai guards didn't look particularly promising to me. Then, as luck would have it, out of the base gates rolled two white, jerry-rigged, Dodge Ram double-crew-cab trucks, with a seriously impressive amount of armour plating welded to their bodies.

These 'Hate Wagons', as they were affectionately known, were crewed by a bunch of guys who looked as if they were spoiling for a fight. They wore a mismatch of anything they wanted – most had green bandanas wrapped around their shaven heads – carried very modern-looking AKs with optics and drum magazines, and all had cigarettes jammed in their mouths.

These guys just had to be the Polish GROM, I thought to myself. The GROM (in English: Group Operational Manoeuvring Response) are that nation's special forces, and from my experience they were very capable guys. I had had the pleasure of training with them back in the day.

White Boy waved them down, words were exchanged, and shortly we were following the Hate Wagons back to the Polish base, at what seemed like 100mph. We roared down some back roads, took a bypass that skirted around the outskirts of the city, cut through a few residential areas on dirt tracks, thundered through the middle of a soccer field, on past a cemetery and into the gate of their base.

The entire trip had taken about twenty minutes. The entrance lay at the end of a long road, which they had blocked off, so there was only one way in and out. At the end of the road, and right in the middle of both lanes, they had placed a multi-barrelled 40mm anti-aircraft gun levelled at vehicle height. It stayed pointing that way until they were happy you were a friendly. *Fuck, I loved it.*

We followed the guys into the base and were shown to the sectioned-off State Department area at the rear of the camp. Six Conex shipping containers had been stacked together to provide offices and sleeping quarters for the handful of state personnel on site. We were told to park up a short distance away. It seemed we security types were to be kept at arm's length from the state personnel, which was fine by me. We would be living two guys to a four-man Conex container. There was a bedroom at each end, with a flushing toilet and shower unit in the middle, and they had aircon and hot water, so I was as happy as a pig in shit.

White Boy and Ben would be in one; Jerry and I in the other. It looked like I was going to be roped to him for the entirety of the gig. *Hey, how bad could it get?* I just hoped we wouldn't be calling this Conex container home for too long.

We dropped our gear and were taken to meet the CPA representative, or GC (Governing Council) as we were told to call her. The GC looked to be in her early forties, and it soon became clear she was one of those career State Department people, who believed they could really make a difference. She was going to help these poor primitive people receive all that America had to offer, including democracy, women's rights, schools for their kids, Burger King and monthly subscriptions to *Vogue* magazine, no doubt.

I was tempted to remind her that one of the oldest civilisations in the world originated in Iraq. Thousands of years ago, the people of this country had raised one of the earliest civilisations, inventing, among many things, written language, mathematics, astronomy, the wheel and no doubt a shitload more things than the good ol' US of A had ever contributed to the advancement of mankind.

When she had finally finished gabbing on about how great she and her mission here were, how we worked for her and how we would do exactly what she told us to do, we nodded our heads in agreement and mumbled 'fuck you' under our collective breaths. So, with introductions done, we decided to recce the rest of the camp.

The Poles had based themselves in an old multi-storey barracks, most likely a former Iraqi military or police camp. A friendly State Department guy showed us around – taking us to where the Poles had set up their ops room, meeting room and chow hall. But he was hardly able to hide his embarrassment when he told us we were to eat with the Poles, as if we weren't good enough to eat with the state fuckers.

He showed us the fuel point and a makeshift gym, which got Jerry's interest right away, but my attention was drawn by a small, corrugated iron shed, no more than two metres square, surrounded by razor wire, which lay smack bang in the middle of the camp. It had to be the prisoner holding cell, I reckoned. At present it was occupied by two local-looking men, who were sitting cross-legged with their hands plasticuffed behind their backs and brown sacking hoods thrown over their heads.

It was a hot day, and the poor buggers were sitting in the open sun, roasting. The more I stared, the more I really felt for them.

'What's the story with those guys?' I asked the Polish guard standing watch over them.

'We caught them last night,' he said. 'They were acting suspicious, so we took them in.'

'Oh, right,' I said. 'Were they actually doing anything, like digging in IEDs or criminal stuff?'

'No, but they looked suspicious.'

Although I hadn't been in Iraq for that long, with each passing day I was growing ever more sympathetic to the locals and the reasons why they had formed an insurgency. Hell, who wouldn't raise a resistance, if this is what the 'liberators' did when they got hold of your country?

'Hey, Jerry, what's that movie with Patrick Swayze in it?' I asked. He looked at me puzzled. 'You know, the one where the Russians invade the US, and he and his football buddies form a resistance group and fight back. What's it called?'

Of course, I knew full well what it was called, but I just wanted to see if Jerry would pick up on my sarcasm and the whole hypocrisy of the situation. After a minute of thinking, he correctly answered *Red Dawn* – which in the ultimate irony of ironies also happened to be the name of the operation to capture Saddam Hussein. And no, Jerry most definitely did not pick up on the sarcasm.

The next day I noticed that the holding cell was empty. I didn't know what had happened to the two guys I saw in there, or where they had been taken, but during my time in that camp I would see the cells fill and empty about a dozen times.

Our job was to transport the GC around Karbala to various meetings with the local big-wigs. Naturally, we sometimes got a bit geographically challenged, despite having the maps, but we soon got our bearings. The main problem was that there were no street signs or street numbers, nor any detailed street maps to assist with navigating to a specific building in the city. All we had were key reference points and the two major landmarks – the great big golden domes of the mosques.

We tried to encourage the GC to have her meetings in the safe confines of the base as much as possible, but she was having none of it. One of her earliest 'gatherings' involved hosting a large gaggle of various tribal leaders in the bombed-out ruins of a former military camp, which meant there were a lot of people that we had no chance of vetting or of searching, and there was no way to control ingress points.

Each tribal leader would arrive with his entourage, travelling in a convoy of Toyota Land Cruisers. It seemed that the more vehicles, the more important the leader. Each boasted his own militia, and the militiamen were armed to the teeth, and some seemingly had their numbers bolstered by members of the Iraqi Police (IP). Go figure.

No one trusted the Iraqi Police, as the insurgents had taken to buying or stealing their uniforms – or simply getting jobs as policemen – as the perfect cover. They would mingle with the crowd before either shooting the shit out of the entire gathering or blowing themselves to bits, taking as many people as possible with them. Consequently, the presence of the IP always put me on edge.

I was relieved as hell when that first meeting was over, but then we had to get out, which turned into another clusterfuck. Every tribal leader wanted to show that he was the most important, so he and his entourage would rush to be the first to leave, guaranteeing traffic chaos. It turned into a total pissing match, one watched by crowds of locals and providing the perfect time for insurgents to attack. We waited until the coast was clear, eyes out on stalks the entire time, before rushing out of there like a robber's dog and straight back to the camp.

When manoeuvring through the chaotic traffic, we employed the 'pyramid' hand signal, one that the locals use to get cars to stop or wait. This was something we'd got accustomed to in Baghdad. First, we'd wave our hands and point to the offending vehicle, so they could see we meant them. Then, we'd hold out our hands with the palms vertical, bringing our fingertips together to form a pyramid shape. It meant, 'Hold on, brother. Wait.'

If the pyramid gesture didn't get the desired response, we would show our weapons, or sometimes throw a water bottle. Lastly, you might fire a round at or close to the vehicle, but only when all else had failed. This was the commonly accepted way to ask for a bit of space or request that others wait. However, it seemed that no one had told the Arabic-speaking expert on Iraqi culture – the GC.

One day, we'd just returned to camp when her puffed-up assistant came over and asked to speak to us about a 'very grave matter'. She informed us that the GC was unhappy having us as her close protection team and would prefer to use a local driver and helper: someone who wouldn't make insulting hand gestures at the locals, whose confidence she was trying to gain. We finally worked out she was referring to the pyramid signal.

We were dumbfounded and tried to explain that the gesture was in no way rude. The assistant wouldn't have it, insisting that her boss, the GC, knew otherwise. It was then that I called over a local fixer, and together we demonstrated that he understood the sign just as we had described it. Needless to say, there was no apology, and I took it as another warning sign.

As we made our way towards our accommodation, I remarked to the guys. 'Hey, dudes, what did that little episode tell you?'

Ben and Jerry looked a little puzzled, but White Boy knew exactly what I was driving at. 'That GC is going to get herself killed and us with her,' he growled. 'You got it,' I confirmed. 'You just heard what her assistant said. She doesn't want us as her close protection team and would prefer locals instead. That's downright suicidal.

'Plus, there's this,' I continued. 'I don't think she's going to be entirely open with us as to what's going on. She's going to start holding shit back, so we're going to have to watch our backs for unscheduled meetings at unknown locations and expect even more resistance to our suggestions. But when all's said and done, we can't keep her safe if she doesn't want us to.'

Sure enough, the relationship between the GC and us deteriorated pretty fast. In her eyes we were impediments to her ideas for educating and 'freeing' the Iraqi people – especially the women – and I felt sure that there was collusion between her and her assistant to keep us in the dark regarding upcoming meetings. We wouldn't find out where she wanted to go until the last possible moment, which made our job even more difficult.

Truth be told, it was a real problem. If she wanted to get herself kidnapped, raped and killed once we were gone, that was up to her, but our job, while we were with her, was to provide security, transport and close protection, and that's what we were determined to do.

One evening we were chilling in our rooms when we got word that the GC wanted to go to a meeting at an undisclosed location, pretty much right away. White Boy explained to her assistant that it would soon be dark and that it was extremely risky to be heading out at night to somewhere we had not had the chance to recce first. I could also tell by the reaction of the assistant that she was unhappy about going outside the wire at night, but she was too gutless to stand up to the GC.

White Boy decided to argue our case to the GC directly, but she was having none of it. She'd arranged for whoever had set up the meeting to wait for us just outside the camp perimeter, and we were supposed to follow them to the venue. She gave White Boy an ultimatum: she was going with or without us. Like it or lump it.

White Boy put a call through to Brian, our boss back in Baghdad, but while he shared our frustration, he pointed out there would be no one from the State Department available at that time of the day to put a call through to the GC to try to get her to see sense. In other words, we had no choice but to take her. Brian said he'd write it up in the morning and try to get it sorted, so there would be no repeat performance.

As for us, we just had to hope we would still be alive come morning.

Reluctantly, we kitted up and, given that it was going to be a night run and that the weather looked like it was changing for the worse, with a sandstorm threatening to roll in, we had to adjust our rigs. We threw on some cold weather gear, after which I made sure

I had my shemagh and desert goggles handy and gave my MP5 a careful wipe-down, removing any excess oil that could clog it up if the expected sandstorm did roll in.

I'd just finished kitting up when Ben strolled over, grinning from ear to ear. 'Check this out buddy,' he announced.

From somewhere he had scored a set of night-vision goggles (NVG) and a small AN/PEQ sight. This was an awesome little unit that attached to the rail system of his AR-15 assault rifle. It emitted an infra-red (IR) laser, which could be seen only by someone wearing IR googles. You'd use it only during the hours of darkness, of course, but as ours was a night mission in the utter unknown, it might well prove useful.

'Fuck me, bro, where did you get those?' I asked.

'Some SEAL Team buddies out at BIAP. Cost me a few slabs of beer and a couple of bottles of bourbon.'

'Excellent. Won't they miss them?'

'Fuck no, bro. No one knows who has what and where the fuck anything is over there.'

'Hey, you should get the suppressor from Jerry too, bro,' I suggested. 'That will complement the whole ensemble.'

'Good idea,' Ben said, and he ran off to find Jerry.

Shortly, we loaded up our guns and go bags and gathered around the hood of the red vehicle for a quick brief and actions-on. We agreed that White Boy and Ben would lead out in their vehicle. With Ben having the night optics, he could scope ahead once we reached the venue, in case there were any shitheads lying in wait. Jerry and I would have the GC in our vehicle, as we normally did, and, to keep comms open between us, we would wear Nokia mobile phone earpieces that plugged into the Motorola radios.

I suggested that when we got to the mystery venue, White Boy and Jerry would escort the GC inside, while Ben and I provided perimeter security. I reasoned that Ben with his night-vision optics and suppressor, plus me with my MP5 9mm loaded with hollow-point rounds, would make far less noise than the unsuppressed AR-15 and AK the others carried, in case we needed to open up on any fucker.

Looking skyward, there were now all the signs that a bloody great sandstorm was heading in, so I grabbed a thick jacket and stuffed it into the top of my go bag for good measure because I hate being cold. Just then the GC rolled out and got straight into the back of our wagon, looking for all the world like Lorraine of Arabia. We bundled aboard, followed by her very spooked-looking assistant, did one final comms check and fired up the vehicles.

It felt very unnerving heading out at last light. The sky was start-ing to dim a lot earlier than usual, due to the increase in the amount of red dust in the air, and the whole atmosphere seemed eerie.

As we drove by the baffled Polish guards manning their multi-barrelled Bringer of Death, I told Jerry to tell them to expect us back in a few hours. They needed to inform the next sentry shift, so they wouldn't blow the shit out of us. About 100 metres beyond the 40mm Bringer of Death, around the street corner, sat a Toyota 4x4. This, we assumed correctly, was who we were meant to link up with and follow to our mystery rendezvous.

With all the cloak and dagger bullshit, I figured this meeting had to be with tribal leaders, ones who for whatever reason did not want their rivals to know what they were up to. With the sandstorm almost upon us, I just hoped we reached our destination pretty damn quick.

The Toyota set off with us following. The driver seemed to de-liberately keep to the unpopulated outskirts of Karbala. I tried my best to look for recognisable landmarks, but, as visibility was low, the best I could do was make a mental note of the left and right turns. We did this for about twenty-five minutes in total, before finally we pulled up outside what looked like some kind of decrepit old town hall.

As we rolled in, I gave it the once-over for anything obviously hostile but could see nothing. White Boy veered off to one side to drop Ben, before pulling back in behind me. Already parked up were two more Land Cruisers, but we couldn't see anyone anywhere at all. This struck me as being very suspicious, and I could tell that even the GC was starting to get nervous.

Good stuff. In truth, I hoped she was bricking it.

White Boy radioed me with instructions to pull up next to the entrance but keep the GC inside the vehicle until he had executed a quick recce himself. I slowed down, relaying the instructions to those in the rear, but then, and with zero warning, the GC jumped out. Fortunately, Jerry seemed ready for this, and he jumped out on her heels, moving into position right behind her. The GC's assistant and White Boy slotted in behind them, and so the four figures disappeared into the building without having had any time for any security checks at all.

What an absolute cunt. That's exactly how you get yourself killed.

I parked up close to the door with the vehicle facing out. I walked over to Ben, while in my earpiece I could hear White Boy sending us a SITREP (Situation Report) from inside the building. Apparently, the meeting was starting. There were five people in attendance, with half a dozen armed local security guys/drivers who were smoking and making tea in a room to the left of the entrance. White Boy outlined the internal layout of the hall, in case we had to bust our way inside. He said he would position himself outside the doorway where the meeting was taking place, but that the GC didn't want him in there with her. Jerry, the big burly fuck, would keep an eye on the tea-drinking crew, moving between there, White Boy's static position and the route back to the vehicles.

Ben and I took up a position lost in the shadows, on the perimeter of the building's parking area. For ten minutes we stood there in total silence, making sure there weren't any unexpected arrivals or hostile forces stationed around the place. It was pretty-well dark and, with everyone in the hall, now was the perfect time for dudes with bad intentions to surround and attack the place. Anyone who hadn't already shown themselves had to be regarded as a threat.

Once we'd completed our silent 'listening watch', Ben suggested we go and check around the back of the hall.

'Yeah, roger that,' I replied.

Stealthily, we made our way down the side and around to the back of the hall, deliberately keeping the pace very slow. We kept to the shadows, stopping every so often and straining to listen for anything in the darkness up ahead. I was far from happy that we had been forced to enter potentially hostile territory, at night, with zero time to prepare, but, still, it felt good to put some of my military skills into practice.

As we reached the corner of the building, Ben indicated he wanted to move slightly further ahead of me to do a scan of the rear with his night-vision goggles. I slowly dropped to one knee and took up the 'six' position, bringing my MP5 to my shoulder, safety off and on full-auto mode and with my finger outside the trigger guard, but ready to engage. After a few seconds covering Ben and listening intently, I'd heard nothing but the barking of some dogs nearby, plus the breeze rustling through the trees.

'Clear,' Ben whispered, having completed his scan.

I moved up to join him. 'Hold it, mate,' I whispered, right on his ear. 'See that bunch of trees, about ten metres away?'

'Yeah.'

'There's a good bit of high ground there, so why don't you set up over there and cover me, while I make my way down to the far corner, then I'll signal you down.'

Ben looked where I was indicating and agreed it was a good place for him to provide some overwatch. If any insurgent was out there, I reckoned Ben would spot him. That agreed, I reached up and pressed my radio transmit switch.

'White Boy, Baz.'

'Roger.'

'We are securing the rear of the hall, over.'

'Yeah, roger that.'

'Jerry, you got that?' I queried.

'Roger,' Jerry replied.

I stayed in position until Ben had reached the high clump of trees, whereupon he pressed the squelch switch on his radio, to indicate he was in position without the need to talk.

I gave my pistol one final pat for reassurance, then brought my MP5 up to my shoulder again, but not under my cheek – lower, and pointing forward. If I tried to carry it in the aim-ready position, my vision to the left would be obstructed, and if I needed to open fire, it was already pointing forward and would hit whatever it was pointed at. Besides, the MP5 is so light you can literally fire it one-handed if need be.

As I stood up, I could feel the cold breeze stiffening as the wind started to pick up, which meant the sandstorm was coming in. It was all the more reason for there to be no one anywhere around about, unless they were up to no good.

Already, I could feel the first gusts of sand hitting my back, and I knew I would have to move a bit quicker now, so Ben wouldn't lose sight of me in the coming storm. I reached for my shemagh and pulled it up, wrapping it around my mouth and nose, then pulled on my Oakley ski goggles. The reddish lens made everything look brighter, increasing my ability to see in the dark.

I set off, moving lightly on my feet over dirt and sand so there was very little noise, stopping every so often to listen. The deeper I stole into the darkness at the rear of the building, the less sure I was that Ben could still see me. I was getting close to the far corner, before the ground opened up into what looked like a soccer pitch, lying on the far side. I couldn't see around the corner, but that could wait until I got there.

The sandstorm was coming in thick and fast now, the whole area turning a burnished orange colour and getting eerily dark. With my goggles on, it felt like being on the inside of a vehicle, looking out through the windscreen as this massive wall of sand came rolling in, like a big tumbling brown-orange wave. Visibility had dropped to just a few metres and the temperature was downright cold. Glancing beyond the corner, the footie field faded from view, the sand engulfing it like some giant's cloak.

I reached the corner of the building, went down on one knee and signalled for Ben to join me, making three clicks on my radio's send button. A few seconds later I felt his hand squeeze my shoulder. He looked like some long-beaked alien, with his night-vision optics strapped over the front of his goggles. He scanned the terrain ahead of us for a few long seconds.

Then, 'Clear.'

I gave him a thumbs-up, then leant in to tell him that we would move around the corner together, him leading, me on six again. But as I did so, I suddenly got a faint whiff of cigarette smoke. The wind was at our backs, so it must have come from behind us. I grabbed Ben by the shoulder, to stop him going any further.

'Cigarette smoke, behind us,' I whispered. We were still in the shadows, and I sure as shit didn't want us moving anywhere until we'd checked this out. 'Bro, someone is behind us,' I added.

It might sound like stating the obvious, but the problem was we had just cleared that area, so where exactly were they? On the roof? In among the trees? It stood to reason they had to be somewhere deep in hiding, or our checks would have found them.

Ben turned and scanned the darkness from where we had just come, before slowly lifting his AR to his shoulder and using its AN/PEQ infra-red sight to sweep the treeline. The beauty of the IR device was that it picked up heat – so even when a person was hidden from view by trees, it should still detect their thermal signature: a warm body against the freezing cold of the sand-whipped darkness.

The wind was blowing directly into our faces now. Thankfully, the shemagh covering my mouth and nose kept the sand out, making breathing possible, and the goggles were doing a great job of shielding my eyes as I strained to see into the darkness.

'There you are,' Ben whispered, just loud enough for me to hear. He'd picked up the glow of the cigarette as it was being inhaled. I knelt close behind him.

'What is it?' I asked.

'Two people, about ten metres back, up in the treeline.'

Fuck. How did we miss them?

Either they had just got there, or they were very well hidden. But had they seen us? We had to assume not, or they'd have challenged us, or very possibly opened up on us. So, who might it be lurking in the dark, smoking, in the midst of a sandstorm? It was just possible that they were one of the mystery tribal chief's security teams, sat out on some kind of a security cordon. But somehow, I doubted it.

I cupped my hand by Ben's ear. 'Here's the plan: you stay here, I'll cross over into the shadow of the treeline. Once there I'll give you a thumbs-up to move, then we'll move parallel together until we get close to them, OK?'

Ben signalled he was good with that, and I set off. I moved at a dead slow pace, creeping softly across the gap between us and the trees. I hoped the combination of the dark and the swirling sand would serve as some kind of 'invisibility cloak', but I was taking no chances. I made sure each step was slow and deliberate, until finally I reached the edge of the trees.

I gave the signal to Ben, not knowing if he had seen it. My heart rate was starting to really pump now, and the sweat was running down my back. I was nervous as hell as I stepped out with extreme caution, moving closer to the mystery smoker. I kept just inside the fringe of darker shadow given off by the trees but just outside the treeline, to avoid any fallen branches or twigs. I had to assume that Ben was doing likewise, just a few yards to my right, his form lost in the sandstorm.

Then I caught another, stronger blast of smoke, which had to mean we were drawing close. As I strained my ears, I heard muffled voices, followed by the metallic creak of an ungreased vehicle door being slowly opened.

Fuck me, they must be just in front of me, a bit to my left and higher up on the bank.

Listening for any further clues, suddenly my body froze completely. Every part of me was hyper-alert now, as I heard the unmistakable sound of an AK assault rifle being racked. I knew that sound so well, as I had done it myself a thousand times: a round was being ratcheted into the breach. But did that mean they had seen us?

I slid my thumb over the selector switch on my MP5, just to make sure it was down in full-auto mode. It was. Just then my earpiece crackled.

'I heard that too, bud.' It was Ben. 'Hold it there.' I heard him whisper again into his radio. 'White Boy, Ben here, we have two suspect males with AKs back here.'

I pressed my earpiece as far into my ear as it would go, cupping my hand over it to kill any noise that might be audible to any watchers and listeners.

'Roger that,' White Boy responded. 'Act accordingly and keep me posted.'

Act accordingly meant – if you need to, take them out.

I returned my hand to my weapon, readying myself for whatever was next. Should we back off and get the GC the fuck out of there, or should we confront the threat? I figured I'd move back to Ben, to get his opinion, but at that exact moment the sledgehammer-crack of a round exploded through the darkness. It was so close I felt the wind whip past my head. I froze as still as a statue. *What the fuck?*

Then, in the darkness slightly up and to my left, I heard a groan and the thump of something heavy hitting the dirt, followed by a soft high-pitched sound like air escaping from a pinched balloon. I then heard what sounded like someone in shock suddenly becoming aware that the person they had been sharing a cigarette with had just been shot and was now a bloodied heap lying on the ground.

I swivelled to the left, raised my MP5 in the direction of the startled noise, and turned into a perfect firing position, pivoting on my front leg to face the new direction. With my elbows tucked into my body like a boxer protecting his flanks, I was ready to attack or defend.

Then, through my earpiece, I heard, 'Directly in front of you, twelve o'clock high. Get him.'

I instinctively dropped my finger to the trigger and squeezed off three, quick double-tap bursts. I counted each round as it sprang forth: *bi-bang, bi-bang, bi-bang*, each squeeze of the trigger releasing two rounds of 9mm hollow-point towards what was for me an unseen target. Six rounds fired off in less than two seconds, my muzzle spewing bright flame and sparks of burning cordite, completely destroying my night vision and kick-starting my tinnitus.

Knowing I was exposed by the muzzle flash, I took one big step to the right and dropped to a kneeling position, keeping my MP5 pointed to where I had just fired. The smell of sand, cordite and rifle oil was wafting into my shemagh, as I stayed where I was, but still there was no reaction. My heart was surprisingly calm, and I felt completely in control of my body.

Suddenly my earpiece crackled again. 'Good hit, buddy.'

From his vantage point, Ben had seen that I had hit the figure in complete darkness.

As the seconds ticked by, my hand started to tremble slightly, and I could feel the adrenaline starting to work its dirty magic. I took three deep breaths of sandy air, to calm myself. *Keep your ears open, stay still, say nothing, but be ready to do it all again*, I reminded myself. *There could be more of them up there.*

Taking in more deliberate, deep breaths, I thought I could hear a soft groaning and gurgling noise. It was coming from where I had fired. I knew what it was: a human was fighting for his last gasps of breath, each intake sounding shorter and faster before they slowed to nothing, and I could no longer hear anything but the wind.

Ben moved up alongside me, and we quickly and quietly slipped along the treeline for about five metres before kneeling back down and waiting, ears straining for the slightest noise. Still nothing, only the sounds of the wind in the branches. A further thirty seconds went by. Still nothing.

'OK, fuck this,' I announced. 'Let's go check it out.'

The noise of the sandstorm was really intense now. It was howling all around us. We moved up to where we had engaged the figures. As we came to the top of the rise there was a clearing, and I could make out the shape of a vehicle. Unsure if the scene was clear, I signalled I would move around the vehicle, checking it out 360, while Ben covered me. He tapped my shoulder to confirm, and I slowly moved off, keeping my weapon up, finger outside the trigger guard, ready to do it all over again.

Shuffling forward, I moved towards the vehicle with my weapon poised and slowly looked inside. I was hoping to all hell I wouldn't spy someone lying on the back seat with his AK in the aim and waiting for me to show my head. To my relief, there was no one.

While holding my MP5 in one hand, like a pistol, I opened the door, moving to the side so as not to expose myself. I was committed to 'clearing' the vehicle now and there was no turning back. I drew my Glock, so I had one weapon in each hand as I stretched out my left arm and poked the MP5 in, barrel first. If anyone was lurking in there, they would hopefully grab the MP5's barrel, not expecting me to blast them with my Glock. No bites. That done, I eased open the front door and repeated the performance. Again, nothing.

Reaching the front corner of the hood I holstered my Glock and checked down the side of the vehicle. On the ground was a large dark shape. There was no movement. Ben came around the back of the vehicle with his weapon pointing down at the lumps on the ground. 'Thwack,' he blasted a round into one of the bodies. *Fair enough; can't be too sure, I guess.* Then he walked over to the side where I was, and 'thwack' into the figure by my side.

I told Ben to remove his night-vision goggles, before I switched on my flashlight, cupping my right hand over the lens to reduce the glare. The muted light revealed two figures, crumpled almost on top of each other. Their blood had pooled and was being soaked up by the sand; bits of white bone and pinkish red brain matter had merged with the blood and a tart, tangy smell tainted the air.

I shone my light over the mess that had once been their faces. The first had two holes in it: one in the left eye, and one just under it, on the left cheek. That must have been the guy who I shot, for it was a classic double tap. I looked for any other signs of the six rounds I'd fired and found two more holes: one in the chest and one in the stomach, plus another that looked to have scraped the top of his head, leaving a parting in the hairline like a canoe.

Ben's shot was larger and very obvious. The guy had a crack right through his skull, running from his forehead to the top of his head. It looked like he had been hit with an axe, and bright pink and clear gel had congealed on his face. He still had one eye open, looking right at us, or so it seemed, but lifeless none the less. The dirt had mingled with the ooze and there was dark blood and snot coming out of his nose.

To their sides were two AKs. 'You better call White Boy and tell him what we have here,' I whispered.

'Roger that, bro.' Ben radioed it in. 'White Boy, we have just engaged two guys with AKs back here, over.'

'Really? Ah, roger that.' White Boy said. 'I didn't hear a thing.'

I guessed the sound of the sandstorm must have covered the noise of the shooting, plus the effect of using the suppressor and my small-calibre rounds. Stepping over the bodies, I felt under the vehicle trunk for a latch. Just as I found it, I stopped and glanced at Ben.

'Do we really need to look in here?'

'Yeah, why not?' he asked.

'Well, because it may be rigged with something.'

Unlikely though it was, it was still a possibility, but we decided to risk it.

'OK.' I said. 'Hold your ears.'

I gestured to Ben to move off to one side, while I moved to the other and slowly unlatched the trunk, holding it under pressure so as not to let it spring up. Finally, gently, I let the lid come all the way up.

We looked inside. Laying on the floor, wrapped in a brown and red polar fleece blanket, was an American AT4 anti-tank weapon, a pile of M4 mags of US military issue, a bunch of loose M4 5.56mm rounds, several grenades, plus a blood-stained US military-issue bulletproof vest. The AT4 especially was a very serious piece of kit. Made in Sweden, by Saab Bofors Dynamics, it was an 84mm recoilless smoothbore anti-armour weapon, in common usage with US and allied forces.

'Fuck me,' we both said, gazing down at the ordnance, and the evidence.

The more we studied the contents, the more we realised the trunk contained a mini war-in-a-box. Seeing the bloodied vest especially killed any feeling of guilt or remorse that I may have felt for what we had just done. These fuckers were definitely bad boys, for how else would they have got their hands on that equipment? And most importantly, what the hell had they been intending to do with it all?

'White Boy, Ben. We have weapons in the vehicle, a US military-issue vest, some M4 mags and an AT4. What do we do? Over.'

There were a few moments of silence before White Boy replied. 'Umm, I don't think we have much choice – bring the vest and AT4 and leave the rest. We're getting close to moving out. Wrap it up quick, get back here and stage the vehicles, over.'

'And the mess we've made here?' Ben queried.

'Leave it and let's go. Over.'

'Roger that,' Ben replied.

We did as we were instructed, and we managed to get the GC and all of us out of the building and back into the vehicles without further incident. We arrived back at the camp some thirty minutes later, by which time the sandstorm had moved off a bit and visibility had improved. That meant that the Polish guards manning the Bringer of Death could actually see us, and they let us enter without too much kerfuffle. It's always nice not to be shot to ribbons by a multi-barrelled anti-aircraft gun.

Once we'd delivered the GC safe and sound to her Conex cabin, we set about debriefing the night's activities. We each explained what we had done, how and why. White Boy's sense of the meeting had left him with some very serious suspicions about what exactly the GC was playing at. Why she had agreed to a rendezvous at night in the middle of nowhere with a mystery tribal leader was anyone's guess. But the biggest question was why the hell those two fuckers had been lurking in the trees, armed with everything up to an AT4 anti-tank weapon?

White Boy summed up what we were all thinking. 'I'm going to say it clear as shit: they were there to blow us all the fuck up.'

If it hadn't been for the sandstorm, the two guys could just as well have seen Ben and I before we spied them and opened up with their AKs, meaning the whole dark saga might have had a very different ending. If they'd sprung an ambush on us as we left the complex, which is exactly what we figured they were there to do, the AT4 would have made mincemeat out of our soft-skin vehicles, not to mention the grenades as back-up.

Even so, that night I lay in bed going over the shootings time and time again. I was in two minds about the whole thing. Ever since arriving in Iraq, I had grown increasingly sympathetic to the plight of the Iraqi people. They had been unwillingly thrust into yet another war that they didn't want. Even before that they had been forced to live under inhumane sanctions for nearly a decade, arising from the 1991 Gulf War. Those sanctions were still being enforced right up to the 2003 invasion, and because of them many ordinary citizens had suffered needlessly.

Hospitals had been unable to get the medical supplies and equipment required to treat basic everyday diseases, causing the infant mortality rate to skyrocket. Food and essentials for living were scarce. They'd also had to endure the crazed rule of a power-mad dictator and his family, who had ruthlessly plundered and stolen from the country while remaining utterly unaffected by the punitive regime of sanctions.

But those two guys tonight had been different, I told myself. They were out to kill us. What had really changed it for me was seeing that blood-stained vest. That's what had brought it home. It would have belonged to some young American soldier who most probably joined up seeking a better life for himself and his family.

Most likely, somewhere back in the States a family was grieving and broken and, quite possibly, a brother or sister was thinking of joining the US military, to seek revenge.

But at the same time, I had just killed someone who was quite possibly a father, definitely a son, and because of that a member of his family might even now be thinking of joining the insurgency to seek vengeance. It was a never-ending spiral of grief, anger, death and more grieving. The more I thought it over, the more I realised that I didn't feel all that good about what had transpired that night. In a way, I had got to him before he had got to me, but what if we had not found those items in the trunk? How would we then have justified taking those lives?

Had I contributed to all the bullshit and the unfolding nightmare of the Iraqi occupation, something that I was turning against? And no matter how tortured I might feel, there was no getting away from the fact that I was here profiting out of the messed-up situation. No matter how torn or conflicted, I was here to make money – pure and simple.

For now, I resolved the dilemma like this. While I still felt a ready sympathy for the Iraqi people, while I was here working for Blackwater it would have to be reserved for those members of the population who didn't carry guns and weren't out to kill us. Even so, I would play and replay tonight's killings over and over in my sleep for many years to come.

Two days later, we had to take the GC for a meeting with her fellow GC in Al-Hillah, about forty minutes' drive south, so back towards Baghdad. We departed in the usual two vehicle convoy, with Her Highness riding with me and Jerry, White Boy and Ben following. This level of protection really wasn't sufficient for securing such a high-value target (HVT), but there was sod all we could do about it.

We arrived unharmed and used the time to chew the shit with the Al-Hillah Blackwater team, while Jerry went to the gym to pump iron as usual. The guys here were facing very similar problems to us; maybe even worse. Their GC was an all-American feminist in her mid-thirties who had ruffled a few local feathers by bringing copies of *Vogue* and other Western fashion magazines to meetings and handing them around to the women's groups she had set up.

This had been about as well received as a dose of herpes at a kissing competition. Once the Iraqi males found out, sadly some of the women received a severe beating and were banned from attending any more meetings. It had also resulted in death threats to the GC. But what had she expected? Women's rights weren't that high on the agenda in the Middle East, and never had been. To make matters worse, from what they told us it seemed that the Hillah GC had taken to using a local driver and translator and trying to sneak out from the camp to conduct meetings, all without telling the Blackwater guys.

Watch out boys, we warned them, *this won't end well, and you'll be the scapegoats.*

After grabbing some lunch, we headed back to Karbala, thundering like a Road Runner cartoon through the town where we had escaped the failed IED blast. Then all that lay before us was the narrow bridge with only the single-lane access each way. As usual there was a lot of foot and vehicle traffic, forcing us to slow to a crawl and mingle with the riff-raff. If anything, today the congestion was even worse than normal, and I was forced to slow to a walking pace.

After attracting a few stares and scowls, I reached down to feel for my MP5 and gave it a reassuring pat. I wasn't feeling the slightest bit safe, constantly swivelling my neck to look forward, then checking the wing mirrors, and the rear-view; my eyes were basically roaming all over the place, scanning for the threat. Just as we were ground to a stop for the umpteenth time, Jerry suddenly sprang out of the passenger door and disappeared into the crowd.

He'd done so without breathing a word, leaving me alone with the GC sitting in the rear of the vehicle.

My mind was doing back-flips: *What the fuck, dude? What are you doing, you fuck? Get back in here!*

White Boy immediately came up on the radio. 'Jerry, get back in the vehicle, for fuck's sake!' There was no response. I didn't have an earpiece in, so the GC could hear what was happening via the radio's speaker and looked as unimpressed as I was.

If my head had been swivelling at 100mph before, it was doing so at warp speed now. I scanned everywhere looking for the big fuck. *Where was he?* The crowd was so thick I couldn't see shit. Then I spotted him, about four vehicle lengths to my front – sleeveless T-shirt, body armour and newly pumped biceps looking like GI fuckin' Joe. He was waving his AR at everyone, yelling in Arabic, 'Ameraki! Ameraki!' (Arabic for American) and 'Yalla! Yalla!' (Hurry up! Hurry up!). He began slapping the trunks of the vehicles, to the surprise and annoyance of the owners, who were just as stuck as we were.

You stupid fuck! Not only did you just abandon me, but you have now announced who exactly we are to the whole town. Why not just stand on the roof of the vehicle spinning a baton, waving the Stars and Stripes and singing 'Yankee Doodle Dandy'?

To say I felt vulnerable is the understatement of the century. I felt like this was where I was destined to die: a gunshot in the back of the head by someone walking up behind our vehicles.

My head spun from side mirror to side mirror; rear-view mirror to my front and back again, like a fucking bobblehead doll. Thanks to Jerry's antics I had little choice now but to push my way through the traffic to get us the hell away from here. Fuck being polite any more – I nudged vehicles, pushed others out of the way and generally made a real prick of myself as we gradually cleared a path through the mass.

Then, just as quickly as he'd jumped out of the vehicle, the big prick jumped back in again. Not only that, but he had a big shit-eating grin on his face, as if he had just done good and it was no big deal. I was extremely pissed off, but with the GC seated in the rear there was fuck all I could do about it, apart from the death stares thrown in Jerry's direction.

Without breathing another word to Jerry, I hightailed it back to the camp, dropped off the GC and went to refuel. You always take care of your wheels, even before taking care of a big useless fuck like Jerry. That done, White Boy and I pulled Jerry aside and began to tear strips off his ass. I had had more than enough of this kind of behaviour. He was a total liability and a danger to me, to the others, to the client and to himself. As far as I was concerned, he had to go.

Back in my Conex, I wrote a long email to Brian telling him exactly what had happened and listing the other times Jerry had done something that defied CP logic. I concluded that I had absolutely no doubt that 'Jerry WILL get someone killed, sooner rather than later'. I sent the email and followed it up with a Thuraya call, as I wanted some form of immediate response to my protests.

Brian took my call, confirmed he'd got the email and assured me he would look into it. But almost in the same breath he told me that, unfortunately, there just weren't enough BW guys to replace Jerry, or not just yet. There had been a big recruitment drive back in the States, but even so the new guys wouldn't be in-country for another couple of weeks. They were all in Moyock undergoing training.

It was the first of many emails I would send about Jerry. All I ever got back was the same line: 'Just make it work' or 'We are looking into it.' Nothing ever happened, not until it was way too late.

To make matters worse, I learnt from Brian that White Boy and Ben were being immediately retasked to stand up the CPA team in Najaf, leaving just Jerry and me to conduct two-man – yep, you read it right – *two-man*, close protection missions from our Karbala base. *Fuck me.* I had really thought that Blackwater would be better than Custer Battles, but it sure as shit wasn't turning out that way. What would it take before someone took any of this shit seriously? How many people had to die?

The only good news was that our stint here would soon be over, as the full replacement BW CP team was arriving shortly. All I had to do was stay sane and alive for a few more days, keep the GC safe, and not end up killing Jerry with my bare hands.

I began counting down the days like some inmate waiting to be released from prison.

CHAPTER 5

Reduced to two men, we continued with the mission to the best of our – severely limited – ability, but it turned out we were not the only ones dicing with death. A few days after Jerry had done his batshit-crazy walkabout, I noticed a tall white guy on his own among a crowd of locals and wandered over to introduce myself. We'd taken the GC to yet another meeting downtown, and I had not the slightest clue who the lone white guy might be.

'Hey, mate, how's it going?' I asked, extending my hand.

'Yeah, good mate, no worries,' he replied, in that tell-tale, nasal accent, which to me is instantly recognisable. *Fuck me, he's a bloody Aussie.* There is probably no other inter-nation rivalry greater than that between an Aussie and a Kiwi. Somewhat surprised, I asked what the fuck he was doing there and *on his own.*

'Yeah, mate, I don't have a team,' he told me. 'Just me and my local driver. My client's in there.'

It took me a few seconds to realise what exactly he was telling me. Turned out this poor fucker had been sent on a *one-man* CP mission to Karbala. And I had thought my situation was bad. This guy was operating out of a house just around the street from our camp, in what could be called the 'Red Zone' of Karbala, and he had been doing so for the past three weeks.

'Three weeks?' I repeated. 'How come I haven't seen you around before?'

He shrugged. 'This is our first time away from the house. Got a bit lost finding this place, too.' *Don't tell me: no maps.*

'Really?' I said, shaking my head in disbelief. 'So, who do you work for, mate?'

'An American company,' he replied. 'Custer Battles. You heard of them?'

I choked back the laughter. 'Yeah, mate, I know them. I worked for them when I first got here. Fucking useless, so I quit.'

'Who are you with now?' he asked.

'Blackwater,' I said. 'But I have to confess, right now they're not much better than your lot. It's only me and that big muscly fuck over there,' I said, pointing to Jerry. 'But at least we stay in the Polish camp and have a slightly better degree of kit and equipment. What's your name, mate?'

'It's Pete, but you can call me Goodie.'

'Nice to meet you Goodie, I'm Baz.'

'Hey, you guys fancy to coming over to my place tonight, for a beer?' he asked.

Having been stuck in the dry Polish camp for several weeks, with just the occasional sneaky beer or two, and more recently with only Jerry left to talk to, I leapt at the offer.

That evening, Jerry and I found our way across to Goodie's pad. There was no security barrier or any other protection but, given that he was there by himself with just his local driver, it probably didn't make a lot of difference anyway. If the bad guys wanted to kidnap or attack him, they wouldn't have a problem. I cringed at the recklessness of Custer Battles, sending a single operator into such a dangerous and hostile location. *It's all about the bucks with you fucks, isn't it?*

But hell, it was good to enjoy someone other than Jerry's company. We drank a shit-ton of beers and chewed the fat about our respective companies and their failings and, of course, slagged the shit out of each other's countries. I told Goodie that if he ever wanted to jump ship and come over to Blackwater, I would get the wheels moving for him. He thought about it for one good swig of his beer, looked around at his dire surroundings then asked me how much we got paid.

He was getting $200 a day, he announced, with a satisfied look.

'Fuck me,' I said. 'The fuckers still haven't increased the rate from when I was there. Well, my drunken Aussie friend, how does $600 a day sound?'

'Fuck me. Yes please mate. I'm in – get me over.'

Jerry and I drove back to camp, both as drunk as hell and laughing fit to burst. There were no other cars on the road, so we figured it wasn't a problem. Well, not until we reached the road leading to the base and found that big-ass, four-barrelled anti-aircraft gun levelled right at us. We had forgotten to tell the guards we were heading out and would be back later in the night. Seeing the head-lights of a lone civilian vehicle at the far end of the street had put them on high alert.

I decided to rely on a drunk's diplomacy. 'Hey, you fucks, it's us!'

After a few more such yells, but with very little obvious effect, Jerry stumbled out to try where I had failed and, fuck me, the big dopey fuck knew a lot more Polish than he had previously let on. We were soon waved through.

A short time later, I finally got the news I had been waiting for:

Jerry and I were being recalled to Baghdad. Our GC was rotating out, which just happened to coincide with the Al-Hillah team's GC being murdered. She'd driven out with her press officer, a former marine colonel, and their translator, with zero security. Not far down the road they were stopped by a force who they believed to be IP. After ID checks, they were waved through, but shortly after, a second group of IP opened fire on them as they sat in their vehicle, killing them all.

We had no way of knowing if it was an opportunist ambush by the insurgency posing as Iraqi Police, or a planned hit by a corrupt Iraqi Police unit, or an attack orchestrated by locals upset at the Western ideals the GC had been trying to introduce among the local female population, but it sure reinforced my distrust of Iraqi Police checkpoints.

I used our imminent return to Baghdad as an excuse to raise with Brian the possibility of Goodie's recruitment. Brian was all for it, so we got the paperwork rolling. On the day of our departure, we threw our shit into the back of the Pajero, said goodbye to the few state people we liked and tore our way back to Baghdad like it was the Gumball Rally. Rarely had I been happier to leave a place. Through skill, luck, ignorance and a good dollop of teamwork, we had managed to survive Karbala. As much as I didn't like the corner-cutting or working with someone I considered to be more of a liability than a help, we'd got through it unscathed. I put a lot of that down to my training and my experiences with the Unit.

Even so, it had been a busy and stressful beginning to 2004, and I still had six long weeks before I would be rotating out on my first leave of the year. The standard rotation was three months on, one month off, which was about right.

Upon my return to Baghdad, I was told by Brian that I was to lead a new team of guys, so I wouldn't have to work with Jerry any more. He would be staying with the company but used for other jobs around our Baggers HQ. As long as he wasn't running any teams, I could live with that, but I couldn't help thinking that the guys in Moyock would still try to charge him out like the rest of us. It seemed like it was all about the money. Team or individual welfare just didn't feel like a priority.

After getting briefed by Brian, I went to find Two Trays and Yard Dog, who were back in the BW Commercial fold. A couple of weeks ago, while I was in Karbala, they'd got themselves back in. Plus, there was another new guy I'd get to really like called Cash. With Yard Dog and Two Trays back in the fold, that only left G-Man, who for some reason had sought employment with a new British company called Edinburgh Risk and Security Management.

It was really good to be back in Baghdad. The night air was warm and dusty, the smell of human sewage wafted on the breeze, and the familiar noise of distant mortar and machine-gun fire added a comforting sense of being... home. Hailing from a coastal town in New Zealand, I have always loved the hypnotic sound of waves breaking on the beach, but now the thumping of machine guns, mortars and artillery and the throb of helicopter rotor blades was becoming my new bedtime lullaby, easing me into a night of terrible dreams and sweats.

I had really missed the place, I told the guys, as we settled ourselves around a white plastic table, for a long night of beer drinking and puffing on a hookah – a traditional Arabic pipe, which bubbles the aromatic smoke via water, to cool it. G-Man had come over for a visit and reunion, and I got talking to the guys about all that had happened in Karbala, my concerns about Jerry, and the new Aussie fuck who was working a one-man team for Custer Battles, but we kept to the unwritten rule of never talking about family, religion or politics. Those three topics can turn any traditional family roast lunch into a murder Sunday. We might share the same views, but then again, we might not, and it just wasn't worth the risk, particularly when tonight's drinks were all about celebrating being alive and making it through another day.

In any case, I didn't figure it would be particularly smart to confess all my concerns about the invasion of Iraq to a bunch of US dudes, and especially ones I had to work with and lead. Plus, I was deeply conflicted within myself. I despised what it was all about, yet at the same time, I was happy to keep banking my $600 per day. *Nah, better keep my views quiet.* If there was an issue you had to talk about, it was better done one-on-one, not in a beer-fuelled group, and deep family stuff was just out of bounds – why would you want to share that kind of stuff with someone who might be dead in a day or two?

Because business was good and Blackwater was expanding, Brian was no longer based at the team house. He'd moved to a new team house in the Mansour district of the city, working a contract under a new arm of Blackwater called 'Greystone'. He'd recruited yet another gnarled SEAL dog – George, a crusty good-humoured old fuck. George was straight out of the Wild West, with a chiselled face, pair of cowboy boots, long white handlebar moustache and the kind of gruff, gravelly voice that had been honed over many years of chewing rocks and kicking ass.

Under George was his deputy, Phil, a former British officer, but not the red corduroy pants and Pimm's drink kind that I can't stand. Phil was the reverse: he didn't take being from the officer class too seriously, which was just as well, because, if he had, he'd have been treated with the distain those fucks deserve. No, Phil was a good fuck, and for sure we needed good guys right now, for the insurgency had really started to up its game.

There had been around twenty private contractors killed in Iraq in 2003. There had been almost as many killed already in 2004, and we weren't even a quarter of the way through. Things were really heating up, and attacks in Baghdad had increased to at least three VBIEDs per day. There were frequent hits on Route Irish, mortars were constantly being lobbed into BIAP, and there seemed to be all-night battles raging on the fringes of Sadr City. Hand-in-hand with that, the insurgency was starting to use social media to spread their propaganda, so we were able to follow the kidnappings and attacks on our laptops.

There was also a new administrator in the team house, who went by the name of John. Now, I don't know what retirement village Moyock was digging these old dogs up from, but Iraq was for sharp bodies and sharper minds. I feared a lot of these guys were like a former heavy-weight boxer coming out of retirement for one last payday, only to get smashed, humiliated and see their reputations trashed. They deserved better than that, but more to the point, so did we.

John might have been a good operator once, but those days were long gone. Sadly, some of the guys started humming the Bruce Springsteen song 'Glory Days' whenever he started banging on about his time in the Teams. I'm not sure what he was on, medicine or alcohol-wise, but within two hours of closing up the team house office he would turn from a semi-functional guy into a completely incoherent, rambling idiot. It became embarrassing and sad to see.

I hadn't been back in Baggers long when I received a call on my radio. John was causing trouble in the team house kitchen. Apparently, he had grabbed one of my new guys, Peanut, who was a former marine and maybe a quarter of John's age but double his strength, and was forcibly restraining him while babbling on about Peanut being 'one of the bad guys'. Of course, Peanut could have muscled John off him in a flash, but he was worried about hurting the old codger. It was only out of respect for his age that he hadn't broken the hold, broken John's arm and fucked him up.

I hurried downstairs to the kitchen, where I found Peanut looking to me for help. I stepped in between them and told John to let Peanut go and get to fucking bed. To the surprise of all present, he did just that without any fuss. I followed the incident up with a call to Brian, explaining that John needed to go before he became a real liability. An environment where all of us, John included, carried guns was not a safe one for him to be in. This time someone in Moyock seemed to listen: John was put on the next Blackwater flight out of there.

A couple of nights later, I got an invite for a quiet drink with a new guy in the company who was one of Jerry's mates at the team house. Wes was a former ranger and Cochise contractor, just like Jerry, so you might wonder why I accepted. I didn't know Wes well, but I had clocked two things about him. One, he had this odd habit of wearing the bottom of his T-shirt tied into a knot, exposing his flat brown stomach and belly button. Two, we shared a connection that the others didn't: we were both from Polynesian backgrounds. Wes hailed from Hawaii and was as proud of his culture, heritage and family as I was of mine, being part Māori from Aotearoa (New Zealand).

Over a few glasses of fine Glenfiddich whisky we talked about the similarities in customs, language and traditions, before he showed me some photos of his wife and kids. The Polynesian gene is strong, and like my kids, they were a damn good-looking bunch, of which he was understandably very proud. Right now, I was in full-on Iraq-mode, and I could have done without the reminder of my four kids back home. Normally, 'family' was a subject we all did our utmost to avoid, but Wes was new, and I didn't want to put a downer on him at our first meeting.

As the evening wore on, I felt comfortable enough with Wes to tell him some of my own plans and dreams, as I figured we had a deeper connection than just being hired guns from a military background, which was all that united the rest of the boys. In Māori tradition a person with *Mana* is spiritually powerful, courageous and influential, yet has humility too. I could sense Wes's *Mana* and I think he could feel mine also. Our traditions, and our belief in the spirits of our ancestors, of the earth and of the sky, were pretty much identical.

Wes told me that he was heading out shortly to escort a client from the catering company, Eurest Support Services (ESS), moving north from Baghdad to Taji Airbase. This was the ESS contract that Tom had been gearing up for when I'd transited through Kuwait. Wes said he expected to be back at the team house within 24–48 hours, depending on how it went, and we should catch up some more then.

'That's cool, bro,' I told him.

But then, he hit me with the real kicker. To my gut-churning horror and dismay, Wes told me that Jerry was to be the team leader and that their numbers would be made up with new guys who were driving up from Kuwait and would be arriving later tonight. Fuck, this didn't sound right to me at all. If they were making the five or six-hour drive from Kuwait, when would the 'newbies' get any time do any in-country training and orientation?

I asked Wes as much.

'Not sure,' he replied. 'I think they've been doing runs down south around Basra. All I know is we were told by Tom that we were going on the run and that we should be ready by the morning.'

Shit, this wasn't good. If Jerry was to be team leader, then, surely, he had to be the guy with the most experience in-country. Which meant we had a total loose cannon leading a bunch of absolute newcomers on a long run into one of the worst parts of Iraq.

Earlier in the day Tom had asked me if I, or any of my guys, were free to go on a run. I didn't bother to ask what it was 'cause I had to decline anyway, since we were due to take our own client out. Now that I'd discovered who would be the C1 – team leader: Jerry – I was glad I had declined. I'd had more than enough of working with him in Karbala, and, to make matters worse, Jerry was hardly flavour of the month at the team house, having kicked in a load of bedroom doors supposedly searching for something he had misplaced, only to find it later in his go bag. *Fucking idiot.*

But something else was bothering me.

'Hang on, isn't the ESS contract still going through a handover period?' I asked Wes. 'Surely Blackwater aren't due to be manning it for a couple of weeks?'

'Not sure, bro. Like I said, I just do as I'm told.'

I'd understood that Control Risks Group (CRG) had wanted to do some proper handover stuff, including route briefings for the regular runs in Iraq, before officially passing on the contract to BW. That was good standard practice. Although I'm not a big fan of British security companies, CRG were one of the best. They had been around long enough and had earned a good reputation for doing things by the book.

Apparently, they'd found out the hard way that some of the places where they were contracted to escort convoys of catering supplies were in Iraqi provinces deemed far too dangerous to enter, unless you had a shit-ton of armour and the firepower to match. They wanted to alert their successors – us – to the problems, which was why the run planned for tomorrow didn't make a great deal of sense.

I told Wes what I was thinking: this didn't add up.

He took another sip of his single malt and repeated, 'I'm just doing as I'm told, bro.'

Anyone who's spent any time in the military will relate to what Wes was saying. A lot of Big Army is like that, and truth be told, it wasn't a great deal different in the private security contractor's world.

'I see you're going to be using those soft-skin Pajeros, bro,' I remarked. 'Jerry and I used them on the Karbala job. Just be careful of those strap-on petrol cans on the back. Toss them in the rear, or better still leave them behind, 'cause you won't be needing them.'

I had been to the Taji base myself a while back, and the return trip could easily be done in one morning and on one tank of gas. But there had been an increase in insurgency action out there of late. Hell, there had been an increase in insurgency action everywhere. The last thing Wes needed was a big-ass fuel can strapped to the vehicle's rear. We clinked glasses a final time, downed the last dregs of whisky and scraped back our chairs.

'You better get to bed, bro,' I said, 'long day tomorrow.'

We shook hands, followed by the traditional Pacific Islands Hongi, then man-hugged and parted as brothers.

The guys driving up from Kuwait would arrive later that night.

Once they gathered at the team house early in the morning, their team leader, Jason, was told by Tom that they would be going on their first mission right away. There were two tasks, and they would be broken into two separate teams: Team November 1 (N1) and Bravo 2 (B2). N1 was to drive to Taji Airbase and deliver their client, then wait to see if they were to be retasked. That would be Jerry's team, including Wes. Jason's team, B2, was to drive west to the Jordanian border, where they would pick up an ESS principal and escort him back to Baghdad.

I watched a good bit of the briefing from the side-lines. It seemed to me that it was building up to a perfect shitstorm, but Tom was one of the senior people delivering the contract, and he was sure to know a lot more about it than I did, so who was I to say anything? Unsurprisingly, the new guys were not at all happy and they gave voice to their disquiet. They had little in-country experience, apart from a few runs in the south, they were exhausted from the long drive, plus they'd had no time to rest or orientate to their new surroundings. On top of all that, there must have been a bloody good reason why CRG would want to show them the ropes and brief them on the no-go areas before they fully took over.

For some inexplicable reason, a decision had been made to reduce the manning of Jerry's team from four people per vehicle to only two, which eliminated any effective all-round scrutiny and protection. That meant that Jerry now had only Wes with him, plus two of the new guys, Scott and Mike, riding in the rear Pajero. Oddly, Jerry seemed almost comfortable with the set-up. Admittedly, it was how we'd been running in Karbala, but that was out of sheer desperation.

By contrast, the other team leader, Jason, sure as hell wasn't happy, and he went as far as lodging his concerns by sat-phone higher up the BW chain of command. Unfortunately, there was no change, and like true professionals the teams set out as tasked, but Jason especially was vowing to see that their complaints were properly addressed once they had returned.

The next morning as Jerry, Wes, Scott and Mike went to load up, I grabbed a quick intro handshake with the two new guys.

The Pajeros rolled out, and I waved out to Wes. 'Later, brother,' I called.

He waved back, smiled, and I grinned at seeing his T-shirt tied in his trademark knot, right beneath his body armour.

CHAPTER 6

It was Rose's anguished cry that got me running into the TV room. Rose was the team house cleaner, cook and maid and Mother, all rolled into one. A Kurd hailing from the north of Iraq, she was in her early thirties and married with kids. But that hadn't stopped her getting soft on one of the guys, and, as sod's law would have it, it was Jerry. She had taken him under her wing while the rest of us tried to avoid him as much as possible.

That made the events unfolding on the TV screen even more traumatic for her. The sight of a baying mob surrounding the two burning vehicles on screen was nauseating, but there was something worryingly familiar about the shape of the blackened figures, something that made my blood run cold and caused me to take a closer look at the outline of the 4x4s as they were consumed by the flames.

I didn't want to believe what I was seeing, but the longer the camera dwelled on the unfolding horror, the more undeniable it became.

'It's in Fallujah,' Rose answered, when I asked where on earth this carnage was happening.

I allowed myself a flicker of hope. In recent weeks Fallujah had become the biggest no-go area in Iraq: the graveyard for Americans, the locals would rightly declare. Even Big Army tried to avoid going anywhere near Fallujah unless absolutely necessary. As for our guys, they had no reason to be anywhere near Fallujah. But the longer I watched that utterly chilling TV footage, the more I knew that I was kidding myself.

'Holy fuck, that's them all right,' I admitted at last.

I glanced around and saw that I had been joined by others from the BW teams, who had heard Rose's frantic call. We stood there in stunned silence, just staring, not wanting to see what we were seeing but unable to tear ourselves away.

The news spread quickly throughout the team house, and the TV room became packed with shocked, sickened and angry men. I could tell they were having a similar kind of reaction to the one that I had. They too could not believe what they were witnessing; they too wanted revenge for our boys and were grasping desperately for someone – anyone – to blame.

'Who the fuck is reporting this?' someone demanded.

'Yeah, how fucking convenient is that?'

'They must either have been very lucky to be in the right place at the right time, or they were forewarned of the attack, or they're embedded in the insurgency, the fuckers.'

'Couldn't they have warned our guys and stopped this, or was the chance to film this shit just too tempting for those arseholes?'

Maybe we were wrong to feel animosity towards the TV crew, but at that moment, mired deep in the horror, all we could think about was that someone – hell, everyone – was going to have to pay for this.

Brian, Dave, Mark, Tom and I left the guys in the TV room and headed for the ops room. They made calls to the State Department and Moyock, followed by all the BW outstations. We needed to let our people know that something terrible had happened, but there was another equally urgent consideration. We had another team out there, unaccounted for. If B2, unaware of the unfolding horror, took a shortcut through Fallujah on the way back from Jordan, they too would be driving into a death trap.

Tom made a frantic call to JP, in Kuwait, hoping for any information or updates regarding B2's location; he was desperate to place them anywhere but the town where Jerry's team had been so brutally murdered. It wasn't just B2 that was a concern. We needed to account for all our Blackwater teams and get them off the streets. The massacre being played live on TV could well embolden the insurgency all across Iraq, encouraging them to hunt down any Westerners and to try to outdo their comrades.

Brian and Tom were summoned to the Coalition Provisional Authority, and they roared off hoping there would be some good news regarding B2. The State Department and military heads had seen the TV footage and recognised the seriousness of what had just happened and the possible ramifications. On the one hand, our guys were civilians and not the military's problem. But equally, those boys whose bodies were being so publicly desecrated were American, and they knew that the footage was being beamed all over the world.

In the team house, the atmosphere was becoming frenzied, with guys wanting to launch a quick reaction force (QRF). They were rightly refused permission; there was no way of knowing the doomed team's location, and driving into Fallujah to try to bring out the bodies of the boys would only result in more deaths. Right now, they were being strung up from a bridge in a triumphant display by the insurgents of their murderous power. We all felt as helpless as fuck.

After several hours of this, some of the guys decided that the best plan of action was to drink copious quantities of alcohol. Huddled outside in the front yard, each new beer added further fuel to their anger; each can helped shape a new but equally implausible plan for rescue and revenge.

I couldn't blame them, and nor was I going to stop them, but I knew the situation had the potential to get well out of hand. Guys with guns don't mix well with alcohol. I hoped their team leaders would keep it under control while we focused on trying to find B2 and piecing together what had happened to Jerry's team.

Sure enough, a short time later, Mark came into the office looking visibly distressed. He told me he was having trouble with one of the guys hassling him for the keys to the armoury. The scenario I had hoped wouldn't happen now looked like it was threatening to.

The troublesome guy was Oscar, a former marine. He was a good operator and I liked him, but he was not the sharpest pencil in the case. I sent Mark to tell Oscar to come to see me, then sat down at a desk and drew my pistol, laying it on top of my leg under the desk so it wasn't visible. I didn't want to risk being last to the draw if I failed to persuade Oscar to stand down. As he and Mark came in, I told Mark to close the door. I didn't want anyone else joining us, giving Oscar more numbers or added courage.

'What's the problem, Oscar?' I asked.

'Hey, Baz,' he started, the slur in his voice an indication of the amount of alcohol he'd consumed. 'There's the PKs, AT4s and all the ammo up there in the armoury, bro.'

'Yeah, so?' I replied, keeping my voice calm, so he knew I was in control and in charge.

'Well,' he continued, 'we want to get them.' He raised his arm and loosely pointed in the direction of his drinking buddies outside. 'We want to go to Fallujah and kill those motherfuckers for what they did to the boys.'

'No bro, that's not happening,' I answered, gently but firmly.

I moved my finger a little closer to the trigger of the Glock on my knee, but as Oscar looked at me with his glazed eyes, I could tell that there was no real fight in them.

'But Baz...'

'No, Oscar, there's no way you're getting those keys to make a bad situation even worse, bro. And stop hassling Mark; he's not going to give them to you. The best thing you and the boys can do is forget about revenge for now and chill out. We are waiting for Brian and the others to get back and give us the plan, OK?'

I deliberately avoided any of the swearing I normally use in my everyday speech. I didn't want him to think I was being confrontational, but his face now wore a look of resignation. He looked at Mark and told him he was sorry. I'm sure there were a few tears welling in his eyes as he left the room, and I couldn't say that I blamed him. It was a dark, dire, fucked-up situation and everyone was emotional.

I headed outside and gathered together the team leaders, telling them to get their guys to put away all their weapons immediately and gather up their teams' vehicle keys before we had any more Oscar-type situations. Rose was sent home. The poor woman was distraught after seeing what they had done to 'her boys', as she called us all. She had got very close to Jerry in particular over the past couple of weeks, and she was going to take this very hard indeed.

Mark, Dave and I sat alone in the ops room, trying to figure out how the hell they had ended up in Fallujah. Eventually, Brian and

Tom returned from the CPA. They had been told that Jerry's team had made the drop-off as planned at Taji Airbase, but then they had been retasked to escort three empty flatbed trucks, which were going to pick up some kitchen equipment from the marine camp on the outskirts of Fallujah. The killers who had ambushed the convoy had apparently let the drivers of the flatbeds go.

'I'll continue coordinating with the military and let you know what's going on,' Brian told us. 'They are trying to find the flatbed drivers to interview them, but there's nothing more we can do tonight.'

'Fair enough, but what about the other team?' I asked.

'No one knows where they are,' admitted Tom. He looked devastated, like the weight of the world had fallen on his shoulders. His eyes were red and veined, his face pale.

The next few hours proved edgy and anxious as fuck. The last thing we wanted to hear was that the insurgents had scored another big kill. Tension was high and the lack of comms wasn't helping one little bit. Close to 21:00, one of the guys came running into the ops room.

'We've made contact with them, the missing team!' he announced. 'One of their vehicles had an engine problem and they had to resort to towing it, but they should be here soon.'

The tension in the room dropped just a notch. 'That's good news,' Brian said. 'Did you tell them about Jerry and to avoid going anywhere near Fallujah?'

'Yes, I told them,' the guy said, 'but they knew already.'

It was good to hear they had been accounted for, but until they were back safely, there wasn't going to be much sleep tonight.

The waiting got more difficult as each minute passed. The thought of Jerry, Wes, Scott and Mike hanging burnt and disfigured from a bridge over the Euphrates fuelled our anger and kept us awake. My only hope was that they had died quickly. I had to remind myself it was only their bodies hanging from that bridge, not their spirits or their souls. Whatever they had done to his corpse, Wes still had his *Mana*, of that I felt sure.

Tom especially was emotionally finished. Not only did he have a key role in the ESS contract, but Blackwater Commercial was his brain-child. He had convinced the bosses in Moyock to back it and now, so soon out of the starting gates, it had suffered a catastrophic loss. Had the need to prove our worth been so great that safety and equipment had been sacrificed? Was there a belief that because we had been able to get away with cutting corners before, we could continue to do so until the kit and personnel arrived to do the job properly?

Tom knew that heads would roll, and he must have known that his would be first on the block, but more immediately he had another team to find and bring home. I was torn. I felt sorry for my buddy but knew that nothing I could say would make him feel better. At the same time, I didn't want him to think I was deliberately not offering any support, making him feel even worse, like an outcast. Whatever turmoil he was feeling internally, he stayed at the helm, but I knew it must be killing him emotionally.

Tom and Brian started going over the mission plan and trying to pinpoint where it had all gone wrong. I offered everything I knew from what Wes had told me. The big unknown was this: what had happened so that they ended up escorting those empty flatbed trucks into the centre of Fallujah?

Back in the US, the blame game and ass-covering had already begun. The calls from Moyock were coming in thick and fast, with Tom and Brian having to duck out to speak, away from anyone else's earshot. Copies of the ESS contract were pulled out and many more calls to JP and the staff in Kuwait were made.

I had plenty of questions myself. The soft-skin cars were a problem, but they were all we had ever known, and hard-skins were in desperately short supply. It was the jerry cans of fuel on the back of each vehicle that bothered me most. If they'd failed to remove them and the cans were hit and ignited, they would block a key means of escape. Plus, the flames would quickly spread to the rest of the vehicle.

Looking at the footage of the ambush, I figured that was exactly what had happened. I was unhappy, too, about the issue of the Bushmaster AR-15s for use in vehicles. I'd argued all along that they were too long to be manoeuvrable in the enclosed space of a 4x4, they were semi-automatic only and, most worryingly, they were prone to jamming after sustained firing, or when the rifle got hot, which it did if left in a car in the heat of Iraq.

But the biggest question, and it was not only me asking it, was why there were only two guys per vehicle, with only one shooter in each? And why, when the manning was cut, were the inexperienced new guys, Scott and Mike, not split between Jerry and Wes's vehicles? Scott and Mike were together in one vehicle, which meant it was woefully lacking in any experience or street nous. Plus, they would both have been tired as hell from the long drive up from Kuwait.

Had Tom tried to give the newbies some downtime? Was that why he had asked me if I was interested in going on the run with my guys? We already had a client, but we could probably have changed plans, if only someone had explained. And if we had loaded up the full complement of men and guns, could we have changed the outcome of the ambush, or would we have ended up hanging from the bridge over the Euphrates as well?

As we tortured ourselves with the 'what ifs', the agonising wait for news of team B2 just seemed to drag on and on. Eventually, around

23:30 Jason and his guys rolled back through the team house gates. There were more than a few misty eyes and extra-long man-hugs as they were greeted like brothers brought back from the dead. It was a moment that reduced the level of tension and anger, just a little. We'd all ridden a rollercoaster of emotions, and with the missing team back safe and sound, a lot of the guys downed the last of their beers and headed off to bed.

Meanwhile I got the newly arrived team into the ops room to debrief on what had happened. None of them deigned to take a seat, when invited to by Brian. Instead, they stood side by side, with Jason a few feet in front of his crew. They were obviously deeply unhappy, and as their eyes fell on Tom it was clear he was in for a shitstorm of anger and accusations. But first we needed to know their story.

Jason reminded us that they had only arrived in Baghdad late the previous night and hadn't had time to recover from the journey or even zero-in their weapons before they were told that they would be going out on a mission the very next day. As he stared angrily at Tom, he pointed out that he and his second in charge had lodged their objections to this. Brian looked shocked when he learnt that they had been told they risked being fired if they refused to carry out the task.

'Who told you that?' Brian demanded.

By way of answer, Jason gestured towards Tom, like he was pointing to an accused in a courtroom. 'He did.'

By now you could cut the atmosphere with a knife. Jason explained that the brief was to go to the Jordanian border and then pick up an ESS client and escort him in his vehicle back to Baghdad. They weren't given any maps, because they were wrongly told there were none, and had therefore tried to follow the route dictated by their GPS. Jason explained that they had headed out on a major highway until they made it to the turn-off to Fallujah and a checkpoint manned by the Iraqi Civil Defence Corps (ICDC).

That road can be used as a shortcut to the border and can save about an hour of driving, but it takes you right through the heart of Fallujah, so I felt a shiver at the very mention if it.

Jason said he had a gut feeling that that would be a bad move, so they made a U-turn, back onto the main highway, looping around Fallujah altogether. Holy fuck! Had they not turned back, they might well have suffered the same fate as Jerry and his team. By their estimation they were at the Fallujah turn-off around 10:20, less than thirty minutes after Jerry and his team had gone down that road and ridden into the heart of hell.

As they had approached the Jordanian border to pick up their client, unaware of all that was happening in Fallujah, one of the team had spotted a European-looking man standing at a petrol station, so they pulled in to see if this was their guy, and it was. Jason remarked that not only were the pick-up instructions they'd been given wrong, but the name they were given for the client and his phone number were also incorrect. He had been waiting at the petrol station for several hours.

While they were refuelling, Jason received a call from BW Ops in Kuwait, who told him of the incident in Fallujah. It was recommended that they seek safe harbour somewhere until the situation had died down, so Jason had decided to travel back into Iraq, making for a US military installation they had passed about five clicks back. They made their way to the camp and were given shelter; however, because it was full, they had to leave their vehicles outside and hand their weapons into the armoury before finding a space to wait it out.

Jason spoke to the base's intel staff sergeant, who told him that, due to the incident in Fallujah, there was now a massive increase of US military vehicles out on the roads, meaning they could likely duck in behind one of their convoys if they decided they wanted to continue on to Baghdad. With nightfall, Jason decided it should be safe enough to push on to Baghdad, with the approval of the Kuwait ops team.

Then, somewhere between there and the outskirts of Fallujah, one of his two vehicles had engine problems, so they had to cross-load everything from the stricken vehicle into the one that remained driveable and continue towards Baghdad. Jason called Kuwait again and was told that a QRF would be launched from the team house in Baghdad, which, as we knew, never happened. Even so, they'd made it back safely to Baghdad and the team house.

With Jason done speaking we sat there in stunned silence. What a clusterfuck. All eyes were back on Tom, but Brian stepped in to defuse things, thanking Jason and his guys and telling them to get some rest. They would be needed the next morning for after-action reports (AAR) while everything was still fresh in their minds – as if it was the kind of thing they could ever forget.

The whole mission could be read only as a complete fucking disaster and one that should never have been allowed to go ahead. The guys had been left woefully unprepared and the list of red flags just went on and on, not least the absence of any proper comms. It was only by luck, professionalism and an ability to adapt and overcome that Jason and his guys had not suffered the same fate as Jerry's team. But what was done was done, and I knew Tom would have given his life to have Jerry and the boys back in the team house, downing a beer right now.

With Jason and his guys having told their side of the story, we knew we hadn't finished piecing this sickening puzzle together, and the only source of reliable information about Jerry and his team was the drivers of the flatbed trucks, wherever they might be. Their lives had been spared by the attackers and now we would have to find and interview them. It was not going to happen that night, so one by one we wandered off to our rooms, leaving Tom alone, still figuring out what had happened and how we would recover the bodies.

I was the only BW guy to have spent much time with Jerry. I had got to know him well, on an operational level at least. He had started to call me 'Bear', instead of Baz, but given our times drinking together, it could have been 'Beer'. I didn't dislike Jerry, far from it, but watching and working with him my gut had told me that, in spite of his military background and his Arabic language skills, he wasn't cut out to run high-risk close protection missions here in Iraq. That was not to say that he wasn't a good soldier, brother or son, but it takes a certain skill to do this kind of job, and frankly I didn't think he had it. To me, Jerry was not a leader, and on several occasions his judgement had been found lacking.

Maybe a bit of honesty about that from the start might have saved his life.

Of course, this was no time for 'I told you so', but I felt strongly that, if my warnings had been heeded, all this could have been avoided. Jerry never feared a mission, but he never appeared to show any caution, either. Leading his guys into Fallujah was not a smart move, but what we had to focus on now was what had happened and why, so as to avoid making the same mistake again.

Over the next few days, my team and I became the main transport for Brian and Tom, who had been thrown into a whirlwind of crisis meetings, such as the brief at Camp Victory by Lt General

Ricardo Sanchez, the man in charge of the overall military mission and security of the CPA in Iraq. Commanders like Sanchez could see how this event could embolden the insurgency and escalate an already volatile situation. Although Blackwater wanted to retrieve the bodies from Fallujah, the US military had been brought in to handle the negotiations. This was knife-edge stuff and a problem the military neither needed nor wanted but would now have to sort out.

Under Lt General Sanchez's watch, the insurgency had taken root, especially in Fallujah, and he was taking the flak for it back in the US. He knew going into Fallujah to retrieve the bodies was going to be far from easy, but he also knew the eyes of the world were upon him, and that the insurgency were now waiting for him to make the next move. They had fortified themselves deep within the city and were waiting for the inevitable battle, *a battle they wanted*. And for sure Lt Gen. Sanchez knew a lot of people were going to get killed over this, both Iraqis and Americans.

Of course, in the US this was headline news, putting Blackwater firmly in the spotlight, and for all the wrong reasons. The TV news channels had no end of fat-bellied 'security experts' lining up to give their bullshit views on how they would deal with the situation, knowing damn well they wouldn't have the cojones to come within 1,000 kilometres of Iraq, and the poor families of the dead had to put up with reporters camped in their front yards, hungry for any scrap of news or a teary-eyed comment.

Blackwater HQ was desperate for answers, so when the drivers of the flatbed trucks were finally found we immediately drove Brian and Tom out to Taji Airbase to speak with them. What emerged over many hours of interviews was that the boys had been deliberately led into the ambush by members of the Iraqi Civil Defence

Corps. The ICDC had been formed post-invasion as a way of using former Iraqi military personnel and tribal militias to bolster the Coalition presence in Iraq. At least, that was the theory. In practice they were renowned for being in bed with, or part of, the Iraqi insurgency.

Jerry and Wes in the lead vehicle had pulled up to the ICDC checkpoint on the outskirts of Fallujah, followed by the three empty flatbed trucks, then Scott and Mike bringing up the rear. A distance of more than forty metres from the front to the back of the convoy, they were spread too far apart for two soft-skin vehicles, with only two people per vehicle, to be able to provide even the most basic security.

According to one of the flatbed drivers, there was confusion over which side of Fallujah the marine's base was situated on, and the ICDC convinced Jerry that they could get to where they had to go by driving directly through central Fallujah. Once they had pulled away, the ICDC relayed the numbers of vehicles, men and weapon types to the waiting insurgents, who doubtless could hardly have believed that such a soft target had landed in their laps.

Forewarned, the insurgents had made a hasty plan to allow the long convoy to make its way into the narrow streets of the city centre, where they'd be hemmed in by the barriers separating the road lanes from the shops. Turning around there was next to impossible. To close the trap and prevent any forward escape, the insurgents had blocked off the roundabout at the end of the street.

As Jerry's team, with its convoy of three flatbed trucks, made its way into the kill zone, they would have been watched the entire way. When the narrow streets and roadblock to their front had caused the boys to slow to a standstill, there was no way Scott and Mike in the rear vehicle could have seen what was happening up front, and nor could Jerry and Wes have kept an eye on what was happening behind.

Reportedly, half a dozen insurgents armed with AKs split into two groups. One group crept up behind Mike and Scott's vehicle, hiding in its blind spot and using other vehicles for cover, while the second group made their way to the front, stalking Jerry and Wes. They opened up on Scott and Mike first, firing automatic bursts into the back of their heads and bodies, killing them instantly, before stripping them of their vests and weapons.

Jerry and Wes must have heard the gunfire and immediately tried to turn their vehicle around, to go to the aid of their teammates. Wes was driving and, in attempting a hasty U-turn, hit the barrier, bursting the tyres of the vehicle. It was around now that the other group of insurgents attacked, firing their AKs directly into the boys, killing them instantly and again stripping their bodies of their vests and weapons.

Having watched in stunned fear, and expecting to be killed next, the truck drivers explained that the insurgents ran off, leaving them to escape. It was the civilian population of Fallujah, and not the attackers, who had swarmed on the bodies and started the desecration that had followed. The mob had torched the vehicles, dragged out the bodies and hung them from a bridge for the TV cameras.

When we returned to Baghdad, my team was tasked with sorting the dead guys' personal effects and bags, sanitising them of any ammunition or ordnance before they were shipped back to the US. We also had to drive out to the military morgue each day in the hope that their bodies, or parts of their bodies, had been retrieved.

Every afternoon we would make the run to the morgue, roaring down Route Irish to its location near BIAP, keeping alert and trying our best to avoid ending up there in body bags ourselves. Leaving the rest of the boys with the vehicles, I'd usually take Yard Dog in with me, walking past the dozen or so large shipping containers that were being used as refrigerators for the daily allotment of bodies to be shipped back to the States.

It was a morbid task, but the mortuary officer we liaised with was always calm and respectful. I didn't envy him his job one bit. The bodies of our four guys, or what was recovered of them, did not come back to BIAP. Or maybe they did, and the mortuary officer wanted to spare us the pain of seeing them, knowing there was little we could possibly identify.

So, I never got to see what remained of Jerry or of my new brother Wes, or the others. After a few days of going there, I was told the bodies had already been flown to Dover Air Force Base in the US.

Thank fuck.

I had been so distracted by everything that was going on that it wasn't until several days after the attack that I finally called my family in New Zealand, only to discover that the news media there reporting the incident had incorrectly reported that the victims of the attack had been three American contractors plus one non-American. Whether they had misread Wes's Hawaiian background or whatever, I don't know, but my family naturally feared that I was the non-American and when I had failed to call for days, my poor mother had been in hysterics. When I finally spoke to her, she rightly tore me off a strip.

The insurgency, realising the propaganda value, made maximum use of the video of the attack and, in later interviews, their leader claimed they had killed a member of the Central Intelligence Agency (CIA). For some reason they believed that all contractors like us were CIA. *No wonder we were targets.*

Nothing would be the same again for a very long time in

Fallujah, and the repercussions of the killing of our boys will be felt for generations to come, but at that moment I was struggling to feel any sympathy for the Iraqis. Seeing young children, old men and women celebrating the murder of my BW brothers the way they had been doing shocked me, and my natural empathy evaporated. Now I was just shocked, sad and angry.

War has rules, and while not everyone was going to play by the rules, what they had done to the guys, even after they were dead, was simply unacceptable. It didn't matter much when I tried telling myself the Iraqis were reacting to the failure of the US to play by the rules themselves, and the complicity of gutless world leaders who supported and legitimised the invasion. I felt stuck in a grey area, torn over where my allegiances lay and who to call my enemy. Were my enemies only those Iraqis who took up arms against me, or was every Iraqi my enemy after what had happened?

Did the people who had committed such an act know or care that our guys were there to help with the rebuilding of Iraq and to get the nation back on its feet? Did they know or care that we weren't the military, and we weren't the ones who had invaded their country? Did they care that we weren't the ones ripping Iraqi families apart, sending them to Abu Ghraib to be tortured and abused?

We were civilian contractors providing security for those trying to help repair and rebuild the Iraqi nation. We knew the risks and didn't expect that our presence would be welcomed by everyone. It would be naive to think that we would not become targets or possibly be viewed as fellow invaders. We expected to have to defend ourselves with deadly force, if need be, but to me there are still rules and those rules had been violated.

This was no longer the military's war, Big Army's war; it was our war too now. That was the conclusion I reached. *If you shoot at us, we will shoot at you. If you kill us, we will kill you. Those are the new rules.* And from that day on, we were no longer security contractors, we were mercenaries.

In the years since leaving Iraq, this is the only incident that still causes my stomach to knot up and my eyes to mist. It was so brutal and so barbaric. I strongly believe to this day that it could well have been prevented if only the warnings had been heeded.

But in Blackwater HQ, in Moyock, it seemed to me that no one had been listening.

CHAPTER 7

D ue to the internal BW investigation into what happened in Fallujah, the company's senior staff descended on Baghdad like the plague. The company's owner, Erik Prince, had had a vision when he set up Blackwater USA, and he'd had the nuts to go for it. My first impressions of him were that he seemed open and friendly and like he took a real interest in our concerns. He would listen to our gripes, like any good commanding officer, and then order his top dogs, never far from his ass, to sort it all out.

Unfortunately, not every instruction he gave to his entourage seemed to be acted on. Did he say things just to appease us, knowing that his lieutenants would understand what not to follow up on? He had a number of deputies who, to me, appeared like sled dogs, each nipping at the heels of the dog in front, hoping to take their place and end up as top dog and most favoured by their master.

While they busied themselves looking for the evidence to land all the blame on Tom and promote themselves in the process, I was given a bunch of new guys to train as my new team. That wasn't all. Finally, we received two hard-skin vehicles and brand-new armoured Nissan flatbed trucks: two per team. The flatbeds came

181

complete with a crew cab that could just about seat four people,
so long as that didn't include armour, vests, guns, rocket launchers or go bags. They had that nice new-car smell, but fuck me they
were small. Fitting the cab's armour plating had taken up a lot of
the door space, so to get in or out was like a lesson in yoga. You had
to lead with your inside leg first, swinging it up to get it inside the
high cab, haul yourself up then contort your neck and slide your ass
onto the seat at the same time. After that you had to slide the rest of
your body in with your head shoved as far down into your armour
as possible, effectively choking yourself in the process. Finally, you
had to lift your outside leg in before jiggling your ass across far
enough so the heavy door would shut without breaking your hip.
It was hard enough for average-sized guys like me, but it was a real
treat to watch the bigger guys like Two Trays try the manoeuvre.

We were starting to pick up a few more contracts. Never mind
the fuck-ups that had led to the deaths of our guys, it seemed tragedy and horror were good for business. The Fallujah killings had
had the effect of advertising just how dangerous the country was
and the need for security. *Kerching!*

My new eight-man team were a great bunch of guys. We gelled
fast and trained hard. Not only did I have Yard Dog and Two Trays,
who'd both returned to the BW fold, plus Peanut, the former US
marine, but I got a former SEAL, call-signed Bullfrog. He had a
barrel of a frame, and he loved his Harleys and the Sturgis Motorcycle Rally. But Bullfrog's chief characteristic was that he was
always grumpy, and I loved him for it. He was also funny as fuck
when he was on the beers, and after Fallujah, the drinking nights
were becoming more and more frequent.

Then there was a short, stocky, former Chicago policeman who
I christened Stumpy, for obvious reasons. He was another crazy

fucker and he always seemed proud as punch to show off his 'Prince Albert': his penis piercing. Because of his short stature he got the job of trunk monkey, sat at the rear of the vehicle facing backwards, cradling a SAW (Squad Automatic Weapon) light machine gun and with a stash of high-explosive grenades. Stumpy was always on the go and busy doing something. He wasn't always doing it that well, but he was always funny as fuck to watch. My policy was that whoever fucked up the most each day was punished by having to make sure the plastic table and chairs were set out on the front yard, the beers were chilled and the hookah pipe primed and ready to go for the evening. Stumpy got pretty good at loading a hookah pipe and chilling beers.

Next there was Tank. He was a former marine and, like all the marines I have ever met, he was a very solid operator. A young guy in his mid-twenties, he was short and solid as... well, a tank. Because of his lack of elevation, he was the second trunk monkey. Often, when we would drive the five-hour journey to Basra, in two vehicles, it was easy to forget the two little fuckers, Stumpy and Tank, sat there facing backwards and feeling car sick, but they never, ever complained.

I had another ex-SEAL on the team called Lish, who claimed he could trace his heritage as far back as the famous pirate Captain Morgan. He had a great belly laugh and loved sipping a glass of whisky after the day's run. His main passion, though, was stones and gems, so he was often called Rockman. He would often talk about heading over to Tora Bora, in Afghanistan, where the US Air Force had bombed the shit out of the place with bunker busters trying to hit Bin Laden. They missed him, but they did apparently manage to unearth a shitload of precious rocks and stones that Lish wanted to go and collect one day.

Finally, there was Brownie, a tall, wiry guy who was pretty reserved, compared to the rest of us unruly rabble. His weapon of choice was the Dragunov sniper rifle, and he had the perfect temperament to spend hour upon hour, alone, in a high place, in silence, watching unsuspecting targets through a scope.

So, there we were: Me as C1, Yard Dog as my 2IC, Two Trays, Peanut, Stumpy, Tank, Bullfrog, Lish and Brownie. We would, on occasion, have to borrow or steal an extra body for different runs, like Cash, or Randy, not that Randy, another, better one, but this was my core team now. It was now time to get everyone up to my standard and speed.

Every Friday, we would book a day at one of the ranges that had popped up around the IZ. Any good soldier takes pride in keeping his equipment in tiptop condition and your weapon is priority number one. We private contractors were no different. The first thing to do was rezero our weapons, so we knew they were firing true, having been bumped around inside the vehicles for a good few days.

One Friday not long after the Fallujah killings, Tom chose to join us on the ranges. He had been on the receiving end of some tough interrogation by the Blackwater HQ sled dogs. The poor guy was just a shell of the man I knew, having taken the deaths very personally. He desperately needed some fresh air.

I was running the range and in the midst of things James, one of the Moyock sled dogs, turned up. Another former SEAL, James pulled Tom to one side so they could talk away from the noise of our guns. I was keeping one eye on them, knowing this had the potential to turn decidedly unfriendly. It wasn't long before the talking turned into finger pointing; the finger pointing turned into arm waving; and finally, even with all the noise of the weapons, I could hear them screaming at each other.

It all ended when James turned and left abruptly, leaving Tom standing there, his hands on his hips and head bowed. It turned out that the axe had finally fallen, and Tom had been removed from all BW contracts. He'd been unceremoniously fired.

We returned to the team house in a sombre mood. I had started cleaning our kit, as usual after a range session, when I was called into the ops room to have a chat with the BW high-ups: the boss, Erik Prince, James – the guy who had fired Tom – plus Erik Prince's top sled dog, a guy called Alex.

The impression I'd gained of Alex was that he wanted to know everything about all the contracts and that everything had to go through him before reaching Erik, but whenever I or one of the other team leaders raised the issue of why we didn't have any long-range, reliable radio communications system, like every other security company making a shit-ton of money in Iraq had, it seemed that wasn't something he had any control of. We were convinced he was doing his best to downplay our concerns to Erik, no matter how hard we pressed him on it.

His response was always the same: *Yeah, we're working on it. It's in the pipeline. It's one of my top priorities, as soon as I get back to the US.*

As soon as I entered the ops room, I found that all eyes were on me.

'Hey, Baz,' Alex greeted me, with an oily smile.

I glanced around the faces: all were smiling. *OK, that's not a good start. They're all grinning at me, and when they start using your first name, you know you're in the shit.*

'There's been a change in a few things,' Alex went on. 'We know you worked closely and well with Jerry.'

There was no way to know for sure, but it seemed to me that my emails raising serious concerns about Jerry had either not been passed forward or were just ignored. I would have put money on it being the latter.

'So, we want Tom to work with you, on your team now,' Alex announced.

He smiled again, as did Erik and James. Brian and Dave were there too, the two guys who ran the team house, but just hung their heads in embarrassment and shame. We all knew what was happening here. Tom had been hung out to dry, but, at such a sensitive juncture for BW, rather than have him outside the tent pissing in they wanted him inside and pissing out. In other words, they wanted me to keep an eye on him, so he didn't leave the company and give testimony to some lawyer on what had happened with the ESS contract.

But demoting Tom to one of my team could only be seen as publicly humiliating him by all the guys. That was all the guys who were earning $600 per day, thanks to Tom; all the guys who regarded Tom as the man responsible for Blackwater Commercial happening, many of whom he had hired in the first place.

Wow. Do you think I came down in the last Iraqi shower?
Fuck me, you guys are ruthless.

'Sure,' I said, acting as if it was no big deal. 'No problem. What exactly do you want me to do with him?'

'Well, we know he's your buddy, and you guys were together at the inception of Blackwater Commercial. So just slot him in as a shooter, if you're good with that.'

Wow, again. That's brutal.

'OK. No problem. Is that it?'

It was, so, with their thanks ringing in my ears, I walked out.

There was no way I was going to insult Tom by slotting him in as one of my shooters. I went to his room and found him sitting on his bed staring into space. He didn't look much better than when I'd seen him earlier in the day at the range.

'Hey, bro,' I greeted him.

'Hey, Baz, how's it going?'

'Bro, I've been asked to include you in my team on my runs.'

'Oh,' he said. 'No problem.'

'I can't do that, bro,' I told him. 'I have too much respect for you. You're the reason why I'm here. Those fuckers will be gone soon, so what I suggest is we drop you off somewhere in the IZ each day, or you can chill in your room, until you figure out what you want to do.'

Tom gave me a weak smile. 'Thanks, Baz.'

He didn't say anything more and we shook hands and left it at that.

Something had gone terribly wrong with the ESS contract, which Tom had a key role in. If there was negligence on his part, then it was proper that his head should roll. Being an honourable guy, he knew he would have to take the rap. I was sure there wasn't a day gone by since the Fallujah killings when Tom didn't wish he could have traded places with Jerry, Wes, Scott and Mike. No one had been harder on Tom than himself. He was my buddy, and he had my support. I gave him the room to make some decisions while I got on with knocking my new team into shape.

By the time I was happy with my team, Tom was gone. He'd quietly walked out on BW, or at least on those who had put the knife in his back and hung him out to dry. For a short time, he'd take up work with Edinburgh Risks, the same British security company that G-Man was with, but his heart wasn't in it. Within the month he would be gone from Iraq. After that he dropped completely off any of our radars, and I never heard from him again.

I have no idea what happened to the guy who had the initial inspiration, back in the Custer Battles days, who had then taken all the risks and made the first steps to found BW Commercial and set us all on this path.

Brutal.

If you're out there, brother, I hope you're OK, and thanks.

But for now, it was time to put my new team to the test by going out into the city and getting among it. I planned a route that would take us out of one gate and through town, then make a big loop around the city, crossing over one of the bridges and back into the IZ. It should take about two hours, unhindered.

I briefed the guys, using the SMEAC format, and then we mounted up into our vehicles and assembled at the 14th of July Bridge exit. We carried out radio checks and ensured our weapons were loaded and made ready, and then away we went.

Whenever we moved into the Red Zone, I would radio everyone with the same message as we passed the last bastion of safety – the gates out of the IZ: 'All call signs, this is Baz. Safeties off, eyes open, here we go.'

It was my way of letting them know that all the fun and games were over; that it was time to switch on to the task and do their jobs. It also helped me to switch from casual to combat mode. The streets of Baghdad were not the place to joke around. We were targets from the moment we arrived in the country to the moment we left, but especially outside the relative security of the IZ.

We made one run in the morning and one in the afternoon for four days in a row. I mixed it up by travelling out to key areas and places that we needed to be familiar with, learning multiple routes, if possible. We would run out to BIAP, the main government ministries, to spaghetti junction for MSR Tampa, and the routes leading north towards Mosul, Kirkuk and Erbil. Once I was happy the guys were good to go, I eased up on the practice runs. I felt we were a great team and we worked well together.

The new flatbed trucks I wasn't so sure about. The one nagging issue was that the armour, coupled with the vehicles' height, made them very top heavy. I was grateful to finally be riding in an armoured vehicle, but it always felt like we were going to tip over when taking a corner any faster than a slow jog. One day, while we were doing some training near Baghdad's Victory Arch, which is made up of a huge pair of crossed swords, I thought I'd try a J-turn, a driving manoeuvre in which you spin a reversing vehicle 180 degrees to face forward without changing the direction of travel. I kind of knew that I shouldn't, but I wanted to know for sure whether, if push came to shove and we needed to turn around and get the fuck out of Dodge, we could do so without executing a nine-point turn.

As I prepared to do it, Lish wanted to sit in the cab with me, which I agreed to, and Peanut asked if he could sit in the open back of the truck. After a little thought I told him I didn't think that was such a good idea.

I squeezed my ass into the cab, started her up, put her in reverse then shot off backwards. Now, I have done many J-turns in my time and never once had a problem, but these were all done in large SUV or sedan-type vehicles, not a narrow, top-heavy truck. Once I thought I had enough speed up, I spun the steering wheel around as fast as I could and jammed it out of reverse and into first gear.

Now, I was expecting a bit of sway and wobble, but I just didn't seem able to wrestle it back onto an even keel. I tried to counter but it was too late. The crossed swords of the Victory Arch monument to the front of Lish and me suddenly went from the bottom of the windscreen to the top, and finally off to the side. Yep, I'd rolled the fucker good and proper, and I was now staring straight at the ground through the driver's side window with my legs around my chin.

Lish was holding on for dear life to his door handle. He eventually managed to get his feet under him, standing up inside the cab with me beneath him. Thank fuck Peanut had not been in the back. The boys came running over and, it has to be said, the fuckers were laughing a little. Peanut jumped up on the side and, with a lot of grunting, managed to open the very heavy passenger door like the hatch on a submarine.

Lish climbed out with a few cuts to his shoulder. I turned the key off and managed to stand up and climb out with only bruises to my ego and a slight cut on my arm from the cracked armoured side window.

'Well, there's your problem,' Peanut announced, with a snigger, as I climbed out.

The real problem was how we were going to get it back on its wheels. As luck would have it, or not, there was a group of US military guys taking pictures of themselves at the crossed swords. It was lucky, because I figured they could help; it was unlucky because they had seen what had happened and had swapped from taking photographs of the monument to taking photographs of the monumental driving cock-up, which only added to my embarrassment.

'Hey, any chance you guys can help us right the ship?' I asked, swallowing my pride.

'Sure, no problem,' their staff sergeant replied.

He instructed his driver to bring their Humvee up to the exposed underside of the truck. They linked a hook and chain from the front of their Humvee to the side of our beached whale and hit reverse. And boy did they hit it. The Humvee shot backwards, and the hook dug into the truck's side panel, bending the living shit out of it. The truck slammed back on its wheels looking a lot worse for wear.

'Ah, thanks guys, much appreciated,' I told them, as they drove off, still smirking at the dumbass contractors.

To everyone's surprise, the truck started, so I had Stumpy drive it slowly back to the house while we followed in the other vehicle. As we did, I went over how I was going to have to tell Brian that one of the new armoured vehicles had just been written off, due to driver error. It would definitely be my job to chill the beers and set up the hookah for the evening, if I still had a job with the company, that was.

Brian took the news pretty well, all things considered. He wasn't overly happy, of course, and would have preferred I hadn't tried a J-turn in a brand-new truck, but he didn't dwell on it. That Nissan became the most rat-fucked vehicle in the entire BW fleet, stripped apart by every team for the next two years, for everything – from the armour and engine parts to the mirrors and even the fuckin' floor mats, the fuckin' floor mats I tell you.

To replace the wrecked Nissan, Yard Dog contacted a local mechanic, somewhere in the IZ, who had a couple of Chevy Trailblazers: one green and one blue. These were good, powerful SUVs with plenty of interior room. Yes, they came at a ridiculously high rental price, but we were assured we could do whatever we wanted with them. After we got Brian's approval to rent them, Yard Dog and Stumpy disappeared with them for two days and, to everyone's amazement, they returned with them kitted out with 10mm-thick, homemade steel armour plates that hung by hooks from the windowsills inside the vehicle. They'd also made plates that fitted inside the door jambs to protect our heads from side fire, and there was even a plate fitted behind the back seat to stop any rounds that came in from the rear.

Unfortunately for Stumpy and Tank, who would still be sitting in the back facing rearwards, there was no protection from incoming bullets. On the bright side, if the bullets came in higher than the steel plates, we would all get it in the back of the head anyway.

The combination of the steel plates and our fully kitted-up asses must have weighed a shit-ton, but the Trailblazer is a powerful work horse, so it didn't seem to slow either vehicle down much.

As good as they were, there were two minor problems with the up-armour jobs. First, the plates that hung over the doors meant you couldn't wind the windows up, but, hey, it didn't rain a lot in Baghdad. Second, in summer the temperatures easily reached over fifty degrees centigrade, and the plates became as hot as frying pans. Any touch by exposed skin meant burns, so long sleeves and gloves were the order of the day. Or you could tape a towel over the plate, so you could still wear a T-shirt and look cool.

Blackwater had also shipped in four ancient Mamba armoured personnel carriers, like those used by the police in South Africa during the fucked-up apartheid days. Designed to be mine-and-blast-proof, the Mambas were big growling monsters that could carry about eight passengers inside, plus a team of shooters positioned around the roof facing every arc of the clock through armoured portholes. Big and slow as fuck, they were surprisingly manoeuvrable for such a beast, although I wasn't about to attempt a J-turn with one any time soon.

The Mamba team was under the control of a guy called Harry, yet another ancient SEAL, who insisted his four-man Mamba crews be known as 'The Regulators', a reference to that stupid-ass movie,

Young Guns. Prior to any runs to BIAP, or wherever the fuck they were going, Harry would come over the open radio and announce, 'Regulators, mount up', to the acute embarrassment of his teams and endless amusement of the rest of us.

To the relief of his guys, Harry moved on, and the new Mamba chief took over, a former cop with an Asian look who was quickly dubbed Miyagi, after the Japanese mentor in the *Karate Kid* movies. Hey, if you had thin skin about your call sign, then Iraq wasn't the place for you. Miyagi proved an excellent operator and would hone the Mamba guys into a solid team, aided by his deputy, T-Boy.

At long last we were getting better vehicles and there was a massive influx of new guns heading into the country. These included American close protection operators, Chilean static security guards, medics and new project managers (PMs) and CIs to run the expanding teams. Apparently, finding the numbers wasn't a problem any more, for, perversely, there had been a massive surge of interest after the Fallujah incident. But that left me more than a little dubious about some of the newcomers' chief motivation. I just hoped it wasn't revenge.

While we were bumping up the numbers like this, I put in a request to Dave at the team house and Moyock to see if they would hire an ex-military buddy of mine from New Zealand. Lionel and I had worked on several contracts in the past, so I knew he had the skills and the temperament. He was, however, also my good mate. My only worry therefore was that if I got him over and something bad were to happen, it would be down to me, and I'd have to face his wife and kids.

Moyock gave their approval and Lionel was given an arrival date, but I got his start delayed for a few weeks. The situation in Baghdad had become very violent, and I kind of hoped it would calm down a bit before he got there. Of course, it was wishful thinking on my part. If anything, the situation only got worse. There were now at least three or four attacks a day on Route Irish. The US military wasn't too keen on policing the world's most dangerous stretch of road, and who could blame them?

Eventually, I ran out of excuses to hold Lionel back. Before he deployed, I called him on my Thuraya phone. All credit to the fucker, he understood that I was experiencing a bit of 'pre-death guilt', but like a true warrior he said that this was his call, so I told him to get his ass on the plane, pronto. Three days later I was due to pick him up, along with a larger group of twenty-odd newbies who were arriving at BIAP from Amman.

I decided we needed two minibuses to transport the personnel and one flatbed 'bongo' truck for their bags and extra kit. I wanted to use the Mambas, but they had been tasked with a slow and dangerous run to Al-Hillah. So, my plan was to have the up-armoured blue Chevy truck, operated by Two Trays and crew, up front, leading the minibuses. I would follow some three minutes behind in the green Chevy, as tail-end Charlie and the QRF. I also planned to take extra AR-15s and AK-47s, plus mags, for the new guys, so they could arm themselves for the drive back. If we were hit (and had to go to ground), that extra firepower would be needed.

The buses would be driven by a couple of guys from around the team house who had IDs enabling them to join the military queue – the fast lane leading into BIAP. But the 'bongo' truck would have our local guy, Mo, at the wheel, and although he had a Blackwater ID card, he would still have to join the non-military line and face extra delays and searches.

Blackwater operated a CASA-212-CC turboprop transport aircraft, capable of seating twenty-six passengers, so we didn't have to rely on commercial flights, but we still had to run the gauntlet of Route Irish to BIAP to meet the new arrivals.

We reached BIAP without too much fuss, and when I heard the sound of the CASA coming in very fast and very low, I ran out just in time to see the plane banking left with its tail ramp down, so I was looking directly into the belly of the beast, and more than a few startled faces were lined up on either side staring back at me. The pilots of those birds were real characters, and they sure knew how to make an entrance so as to put the shits up the new guys.

After getting processed, the newbies came out from the arrivals building. As I'd expected, most were looking as white as sheets, but I noticed a couple trying to appear cool and unfazed. I knew it was a cover. Everyone is a bit overwhelmed, shell-shocked and excited on their first day arriving in Baghdad. It's only natural.

One of the CASA pilots escorted them out to me and we shook hands and chewed the fat for a bit.

'Any pukers?' I asked.

'Only one, but a lot of pants are still clutched up their asses,' he replied. 'You got anything for me to take back?'

'No bro, just waiting for these guys.' I said.

With that we man-hugged and he disappeared back into the terminal ready to load up the guys who were rotating out.

Once the new guys had gathered around, I started the brief. 'OK guys, listen in. My name is Baz. Welcome to Baghdad. The insurgents will have seen the CASA coming in, so they know we will be rolling back to the International Zone (IZ) pretty soon. Here's the plan. Listen closely so there's no fucking around and we can get out of here pronto.'

I pointed to the vehicles. 'Over there we have a flatbed truck and two minibuses.' They glanced over and I happily noted their 'fuck yeah, I'm cool' smiles change to looks of horror. I loved it. No doubt they'd thought they were going to be chauffeured into Baghdad like VIPs in armoured vehicles. Think again.

'I want you to drop all of your luggage and everything you brought with you on the back of the flatbed, then evenly divide yourselves between the two buses.'

'What about weapons?' one asked.

'Slow down, cowboy. Listen in, not talk in.' I paused. 'As for weapons, you'll get those when you mount up, now off you go.'

They loaded their gear onto the 'bongo' and lined up beside whichever bus they had chosen. While they were doing this, I searched out Lionel. He, like the rest of them, looked to be only just getting the blood back to his face.

'Hey, brother,' I announced, with a dirty great smile on my face. 'What the fuck are you doing here?' I shook his hand and we man-hugged. I was genuinely happy to see him.

'Friggin' hell, bro, I'm actually here,' he replied, with a note of disbelief.

The use of 'friggin' instead of 'fucking' should tell you who achieved more at school and had the parents who enforced man-ners. He looked towards his fellow arrivals, then back at me and at my crew of dirty pirates.

'You want me over there too, bro?' he asked.

'No, mate, you're over there with us,' I told him, pointing to the green Chevy.

Yard Dog walked Lionel over to the vehicle while I turned back to the new guys. 'OK, everyone grab a weapon and two mags. Face the wall and load up.'

At this there was a rush to get hands on an AR-15 and mags. The slow ones got an AK and looked at them like they had missed the last seat in musical chairs. It just went to show how brainwashed they all were about the superiority of the US-made AR-15 over what was actually the more reliable assault rifle, the AK. 'OK, load up and get on the buses. I'll come and brief you onboard about the move back to the house.'

As they did this, I headed over to Lionel and introduced him to the rest of the team. I reached into the back of the Chevy, took out a weapon and a set of armour and handed them to him. 'It's been a while since you've had a fucking gun in your hand, bro, so I've taken the liberty—'

'Oh no you friggin' didn't!' he complained, rightly guessing that I'd already loaded it for him, just to rub salt in the wounds. 'I'm not that much of a fuckin' invalid.'

I grinned. 'I just don't want you shooting anyone by accident on your first day, bro,' I said.

'Fuck you,' he fired back.

Second naughty swear word. If only your mother could hear you now.

I stepped back to the buses, which were now fully loaded. I climbed aboard the first and surveyed the new faces.

'OK,' I began, 'we are about to drive down what has been named the most dangerous road in the world: Route Irish.' Pause for effect. 'There is an average of three attacks a day, the last being this morning.' It was a wee lie, but I didn't want them feeling complacent. In fact, it had been the previous night. A bit of a slow start for the bad guys.

'One of my vehicles, the blue Chevy Trailblazer over there, will lead all the way. The IC's call sign in that vehicle is Bullfrog. The vehicle you are in will be call sign B1: B for bus, OK?'

They all nodded.

'I'll have comms with your driver, who will have his comms open and on loudspeaker, so you can hear what's going on. You will hear a bit of chatter, as possible threats are called out from the front Trailblazer as we go. Listen as best you can. We have about a three-click drive before we get to Checkpoint 1, and out of the safety of BIAP and on to Irish proper. Once we pass Checkpoint 1, we will be in enemy territory and it's all-on from there.'

There were nervous glances back and forth, as they all knew exactly what I meant. They were new but mostly they got the idea.

'We will drive as fast as we safely can and I want you guys to keep a lookout as we go, but do not, I say again, do *not* under any circumstances shoot at anything unless you hear instructions to do so from Bullfrog's vehicle or from me. If you are shot at and you can see where it came from, let the driver know and he will let me know.'

I left a few seconds for the reality of what I was saying to sink in: *Lots of chances to get shot at where we're going. Be alert.*

'No offence, guys, but everything is going to seem like a threat to you today,' I added. 'So, unless it is an all-out shit fight, keep those safeties on and barrels pointed firmly at the floor.'

That part was very important, as the last thing I needed was for some trigger-happy new fuck thinking he saw something and shooting up a bunch of civilians on his first day, which would make it his last day too.

'If we run into traffic, things might slow down a bit so just keep calm and listen to the radio comms. We'll have it under control. If we have a vehicle breakdown, then we will all debus and go into all-round defence until we can get it sorted. Does everybody understand?'

Heads nodded.

'Good. Apart from that, sit back, ensure your tray table is folded away and your seat back is upright and enjoy the ride. Any questions?'

There were none.

I then moved on to the next bus and repeated the spiel to them but, obviously, with call sign B2 for their bus. Once that was all done, I left them to it and told Mo to make his own way back to the IZ. By having him keep away from us, the only problem he should face would be Big Army and, like all of us, he was used to them by now. He was far safer keeping as much distance as possible between us and him, for we were the bullet-magnets.

I returned to my Chevy and we mounted up, with Lionel squeezed between Two Trays and Peanut in the back seat. Stumpy slid into his trunk monkey position and cocked his 5.56mm belt-fed SAW machine gun, loading a belt of 200 rounds from the box mag. I glanced in the rear-view mirror at the expression on Lionel's face – it was of someone facing a crazed, rollercoaster ride: full of anticipation and dread but raring to go.

I jumped into my seat, reached in and slid the CD into the player. All the boys gave a *'hell yeah!'*

'OK,' I said. 'Let's get going.'

I radio-checked all the drivers one last time and with Bullfrog commanding the front Blazer, away we went.

The plan was for my Blazer to hang back so that if we were being watched, the bad buggers would hopefully think it was a three-vehicle move: one Blazer and the two buses. If they attacked, then we would come screaming up and surprise the shit out of them while laying down some heavy fire.

We reached Checkpoint 1, the exit from BIAP, and I radioed to everyone. 'OK guys, safeties off, eyes open, here we go.'

The three vehicles accelerated away and as we waited for them to get a bit ahead of us, I turned to Yard Dog and told him to hit 'play'. With that he turned up the volume of the stereo. Most teams had adopted a tune they would play as a means of gearing themselves up for battle. The military were well known for choosing hard, death-metal tracks. Our battle anthem was a lovely little number by the UK psycho-punk group The Prodigy, called 'Breathe'. The beginning is a series of beats that slowly build up to heavy thumping drum and bass before the vocals kick in. It was a track that summed up the crazed, fucked-up, evil, heady and addictive mix that was Iraq in 2004.

We all picked up the beat and nodded our heads in unison, as Yard Dog hit the accelerator and the Blazer heaved forward, gathering speed.

I brought my MP5 to bear with the short barrel poking slightly out of the window, as did Peanut, who had taken to carrying a Beowulf .50-calibre assault rifle, plus Two Trays, with his folding-butt short-barrelled AK-47. Stumpy in the back had his SAW poking slightly out of the open rear, so he wouldn't shoot up the tail gate if he had to open fire.

Soon enough, the first calls in from Bullfrog came over the radio.

'Figures on overpasses.'

'Slow vehicles up ahead.'

'Kids on house rooftops and a flock of pigeons just been let go.'

'Hear that?' I yelled to the guys. 'Pigeons!'

'Roger that,' they all yelled back.

Lionel looked around confusedly, not knowing why we were so interested in pigeons at a time like this (they were used as an early warning for waiting attackers that a target was leaving BIAP and would soon be coming down the road to attack). Bullfrog and the buses were about 500 metres ahead of us, and I could see them clearly above the traffic, which made me happy. Good to be visual.

The calls continued from Bullfrog. 'Two people on the next overpass.'

'Roger that,' I replied.

'White Toyota nine o'clock. Stopped vehicle 200 metres, three o'clock; hood up. Watch it.'

'Roger that,' I replied.

The two buses were rumbling down the road as fast as they safely could. Although I couldn't see what was going on inside them, I was damn sure there were a lot of very wide eyes desperately scanning for the boogeymen.

'Hey, Lionel, how's it going, bro?' I asked.

'Holy frig,' he yelled back over the music. 'This is insane, bro.'

I, like the rest of the guys in the Blazer, couldn't help grinning.

Then Bullfrog came up on the radio, his voice tense and tight: 'Shots fired! Shots fired! That stationary vehicle, three o'clock. He's got a gun.'

'Roger that,' I replied.

I could hear the familiar 'crack-crack' of weapons being fired, the noise coming from in front of us.

'He's got a gun, he's got a gun,' Bullfrog repeated, keeping his voice calm. He knew you should never scream over the comms, as there is a good chance the words will get distorted.

The boys in the lead Blazer laid down some covering shots as they thundered past. That forced the guy with the gun to keep his head down, stopping him from getting off a good long burst and hopefully keeping him occupied, at least until the buses were past. The guys in the buses would have heard everything, but happily they were doing as I had briefed and hadn't shot back. So far, so good.

I radioed the bus directly in front of us. 'B2, Baz here, move to the centre of the lane a bit will you, we are coming up on your right.'

'Roger,' he replied, and the driver carefully pulled the bus out to the left, giving us the space that we needed.

Yard Dog pushed the pedal to the floor then moved the Blazer close to the right shoulder of the road, matching the speed of the second bus and using our vehicle as cover. If there was a shooter using the old 'broken-down-vehicle' ruse as a decoy, he would likely, hopefully, wait until his target was close before stepping out and unloading a full mag into its side and rear.

Our plan was to get as close to him as possible. If he did step out, we could run him over or at least reduce his time on target, since we'd force him to dive out the way to avoid getting flattened by our vehicle.

We were roughly 100 metres from the 'broken-down' vehicle when I saw the shooter step out and raise his AK in the direction of the first bus. He hadn't seen us, because he was too focused on the big target. I leant out of my window and squirted off a burst from my MP5, shooting at an angle to my front and right. I kept firing three to four-round bursts as my angle on him was almost ninety degrees. Peanut, who was sitting behind me, let him have a few semi-auto bursts from his .50-cal Beowulf as well. *Thump, thump, thump.*

Our rounds tore into the near side of his vehicle, punching through the raised hood, tearing apart the back windscreen and the side windows. The shooter spun around in complete shock, momentarily forgetting about the minibus, as he stared at our big green Chevy Trailblazer barrelling straight at him. He leapt backwards to avoid getting hit and, just for a split second, Peanut's angle opened up. He unleashed a thunderous burst with the Beowulf: *thump, thump, thump.*

The roar of the guns inside the Blazer was deafening, the hot brass was pinging off the steel armour plates, and the smell of cordite filled the vehicle as we flashed past the gunman by barely a metre. We were too close and too fast for him to respond.

We roared onwards, with Yard Dog just keeping the right-side wheels on the road, kicking up a shitload of dirt and dust as our would-be assassin tried to raise his weapon again. But now it was Stumpy's turn to come to the party, and fuck me did he come bearing gifts. If we thought the noise of my 9mm and Peanut's .50-cal was loud within the confines of a vehicle, then we hadn't heard anything yet.

Despite the cloud of dust, our very own trunk monkey unloaded with a series of well-aimed bursts. A series of five to ten rounds of angry 5.56mm belt-fed spoilers hammered into the ground all around the shooter, impacting dirt, metal, tyres and human flesh. I looked in my side rear-view mirror and, through the clearing dust I saw him down on the ground. Our gunfire had caused the traffic to come to a screaming halt. No one wanted to get caught up in this kind of shit, or to be hit by any of the stray rounds that were pinging all over the place.

Then, just like that, it was over. The firing stopped and the music filled the vehicle once more. Yard Dog slowed the vehicle down to get back behind B2, while I focused on our front and reached for my radio mike.

'All vehicles, this is Baz. Everyone all right?'

'Good to go, over,' Bullfrog replied.

'B1 all good, over.'

'B2 all good,' the driver came back.

'Good work and thanks,' I said.

Through the radio I could hear a lot of noise from inside the two buses. The new guys had just received a grandstand introduction to the realities of Iraq. It would certainly be something to tell their folks back home, and all on day one.

Putting some distance between us and the carnage we had left behind, I reached forward and turned the music down a little. My guys, like true professionals, had returned to watching their arcs, and the vehicle became quieter, with just the noise of the engine and the tyres on the road.

'Hey, bro, you OK?' I said, searching for Lionel through the mirror in my sun visor and noticing the last wisps of cordite hanging in the air back there. There was no reply. 'Hey, bro, you OK?' I asked again.

I moved the visor, but all I could see were his shoulders and the top of his head. Two Trays glanced over at me and started to laugh. 'Hey, Baz, looks like we have a human turtle back here.'

Lionel had slid so far down the seat between Peanut and Two Trays that his head had almost disappeared inside his vest.

'Holy fuck,' he said, as he reappeared, his face pale and covered in sweat.

There was no time for anything more, as Bullfrog came up on the comms again. 'Checkpoint 11.'

'Roger,' I replied.

We pulled up behind B2 as the convoy slowly made its way into the IZ. When it was our turn to enter, one of the soldiers on guard leant in on my side of the Blazer.

'Hey, was that you guys back there?' he asked. 'What happened?'

'Roadside ambush, mate. Lone shooter with an AK. Sorry, attempted ambush.'

'Oh,' he said casually. 'You got him.'

'Stumpy back there took care of him; he won't be doing that again.'

The young soldier glanced at Stumpy, who was unloading his SAW. 'Good shit,' he remarked. 'I'll let my staff sergeant know there's a mess on the side of the road back there.'

With that we drove into the IZ and, from there, back to the team house.

As we pulled up outside, the new guys were all facing the wall. Bullfrog had got them to unload their weapons and relinquish both guns and mags. He knew I'd want to debrief the run, so he had told them all to move into the house and TV/briefing room.

We parked up the Blazers and waited. Unlike the new guys, we did not unload our guns fully; mags and safety-on was good enough for me. Our practice was to always have our weapons in a ready state, as long as the safety was on. By always treating our guns as live, it made the guys completely confident in their handling and use of them.

I always conducted a debrief after each run, even if it was just a quick verbal one about the vehicle positions. Because this one was a little out of the ordinary, I also asked Bullfrog and Stumpy to write a short after-action report (AAR). We would talk more about it over evening beers, where, just like a fishing story about the one that got away, we'd embellish the fuck out of it.

Yard Dog led Lionel into the house, showed him where to drop his stuff and explained the layout of the place, while the rest of the boys readied the white plastic table, chairs, beers and hookah.

I had known Lionel for a number of years. We'd met when I hired a bunch of guys for a close protection job, looking after a member of some bullshit royal family who was hiding out in New Zealand.

It was the measure of the man how he reacted to our unhappy first introduction.

I was living overseas at the time, which meant I had to return to New Zealand to get everything in place before the client arrived. At least that gave me a chance to pay a visit to my father. We had a difficult relationship and, true to form, we'd had a phone call a couple of weeks earlier that had ended up with us having an argument and one hanging up on the other. I was looking forward to seeing him and making things up, but, rather than let him know I was coming, I'd planned to surprise him.

Once I could grab a spare moment from readying the job, I cut away to give my dad a call. Lionel was manning our ops room, and we chewed the fat for a bit as I told him I was planning to get the drop on my dad with news of my sudden arrival back in NZ. I dialled the number and was a little surprised to hear my sister, Carol, answer. She was just as surprised to hear me and told me she had been repeatedly trying to call me on my overseas number.

'I'm back in New Zealand with work, so I can come and visit,' I told her. 'Is Dad there?'

There was a long pause, and when she came back on her voice sounded choked up. 'Dad's dead, bro. He died last night.' My whole body suddenly felt like it had doubled in weight, like I had been shocked by a thousand volts. 'We got here today,' my sister continued, but I was barely hearing.

I could feel the tears welling up in my eyes and I couldn't hide them. 'When? How?' I asked, my voice breaking.

Lionel, who was sitting off to one side, could hear my distress and, though he didn't know what had happened, he recognised that the call had not gone the way I had planned. He quietly placed a chair behind me, so I could sit, then got up and left me in the ops room, gently touching my shoulder as he went.

My father had died of an aneurysm – a ruptured artery. I felt utterly helpless, and so upset that I hadn't called Dad before to let him know I was coming home. At least my sister, the rock of the family, was now taking control. I asked her to let me know what was going to happen with the funeral, told her that I loved her, and then we hung up.

I sat in the ops room for a few more minutes trying to compose myself. *Good one, Dad. You got the drop on me. You couldn't even let me get the last surprise in without you beating me to it, you bugger.*

Lionel came back in, handed me a glass of water and just let me sit there in silence. After a while I went to splash water on my face, thanked him, then went back to organising the arrival of the client.

Ever since then we had been great mates. We shared a love of cigars and a million drinking stories we can't remember. In fact, out of all the people I knew, I really only had three close friends: Lionel, plus two of my old SAS buddies, Bomber and Pug. We all have the same stupid, dark sense of humour. Though, when we drink, I'm always the one in the group to have the dumbest idea, or so I'm told. My mates are the ones who, through their calm patient manner, invariably talk me out of doing something incredibly stupid. I affectionately called them my Prozac.

After the shock of Fallujah, it was good to have one of them, Lionel, with me here in Iraq.

CHAPTER 8

After I'd finished the debrief, and while we waited for Lionel to freshen up, Brian came to check we were all good after the incident on Route Irish. Then he turned to introduce two of the new guys, Steve and Jim. We shook hands as I looked them both over, somewhat sceptically.

Let's just say Steve and Jim were not your typical high-speed, low-drag, former military swinging-dick types, like the rest of us. These fuckers were large, and by large, I mean fat. They must have weighed about 250lbs apiece, bone dry. This wasn't big-boned with bubbly personalities. These fuckers were Krispy Kreme, too much aioli on the fried chicken, fat.

I looked back at Brian, slightly bewildered. 'Yeah mate, so... how can I help?'

He looked at me then back at the two man-mountains. 'I want to put these guys with you. They're going to be on your team.'

I turned to look at the sun-blockers, then at my boys, who were just as shocked as I was. 'You're shitting me, right? I have a full team already.'

'I know,' Brian replied. 'But I want them to run with you to boost your numbers and to give them some valuable experience.'

What, my kilogram numbers?

'Sorry mate, but no can do,' I told Brian, as Steve and Jim looked at Brian, at each other, then back at me, a little confused. Fat and confused, actually.

'No offence, Brian,' I said, as I was about to offend Steve and Jim big time, 'but I don't think they would be suitable for what we're about.'

'How's that?' Brian asked, missing my failing attempt at diplomacy.

'Well, look at them, mate. I'm going to go out on a limb here and say I don't think either of them could get in or out of the vehicles even as they are, let alone fully kitted-up.' Steve and Jim looked like the kind of guys who would never say 'no' to sugar-coating, but they weren't about to get it from me. 'If we get hit and the vehicle goes down, there is no way they could react quickly enough. Could they even move on foot for any period of time without having a heart attack? Besides, if they got hit, none of us could carry them any distance without busting our backs or shitting our pants. They would just be a hindrance, mate, no offence.'

'What d'you mean?' Brian asked, knowing full well what I meant but trying to put up some small justification for the shit that Moyock had given him to sell.

I'd had a long day and the cigars and beers were calling. 'Well look at them, mate, they're fucking huge.' Steve and Jim looked shocked, as if they had never noticed how fat they were or, more likely, as if no one had ever told them to their faces before. 'I bet you $50 they wouldn't be able to get into the Nissan over there, fully kitted, in under twenty seconds.'

Yes, I knew we also had the bigger Trailblazers, but there was

ABOVE The guns on the lawn of the Baghdad team house. We were like kids in a candy store.

My good friend T, who I worked with back in the Unit. A formidable rugby player and a sight for sore eyes when I ran into him in Iraq.

Bullfrog, who sadly passed away after a motorcycle accident once he left Iraq. A good soldier and friend whose permanently grumpy demeanour is sadly missed.

Noodle about to embark on a puke-inducing Little Bird flight, nursing a monstrous hangover on just his second day in-country. Priceless.

Rock, a solid-as-fuck leader in my Karrada team. He was someone I could always rely on.

Haggis, Gabby and Miyagi. I didn't work much with Gabby; Miyagi ran the Mambas, and, as for Haggis, fuck knows how a Scotsman made it to Iraq.

Shadow and Dodger with, believe it or not, a Porsche that had belonged to Uday Hussein, son of Saddam.

An informal brief. In those team houses, an M72 rocket launcher didn't really look out of place beside the cutlery.

Mark and Brian, two of the administrators in the Baghdad team house. Don't let the lack of height fool you.

Peanut with his trusty M203. As a former marine, he was the calibre of guy you wanted providing overwatch.

This Colombian soldier was a hero of the Battle of Najaf. You don't want to know what he did with that knife.

Nightly beers at the team house. This ritual fostered a real sense of togetherness and gratitude that we'd made it through another day, and we kept it disciplined, always packing up by 22:00.

Me, minus the war goatee, when I got dragged on a Mamba run.

Me and Tool on a Mamba pick-up, Baghdad International Airport. Those ball caps looked cool, but on reflection they perhaps weren't the safest choice of headwear.

Me, Noodle and Two Trays, featuring bottled water, cigars and my trusty Thuraya phone. Good times.

My four beautiful kids: Keely, Arden, Chaz and Zel. Just look at those strong Māori genes!

One of the armoured Nissans we used. Grateful as we were for the protection, all that armour really did limit the space inside the cab. It also got cooked by the Iraqi sun. Still, it was better than a bullet in the eye.

My happy place. It's been tough finding peace after Iraq, the SAS and all my military work, but moments like this come close.

Me in Kurdistan. Growing up I always wanted to travel, and I'm grateful that my military work allowed me to do just that, but it's a shame to think that humans have brought violence to such beautiful parts of the world.

Rooftop protection. Just try me.

My good mate Yogi, the big friendly bear, featuring two of his favourite things: the good ol' American flag and a big-ass gun.

Stumpy, the former Chicago policeman, one of the best operators and coolers of the beers I ever had.

Lish, who claims he's descended from the pirate Captain Morgan, and like a pirate, he loved whiskey and precious stones.

My later years. I'm grateful to have come through many struggles both in and out of the military and to have the chance to scrub up and enjoy life.

no way I was going to make this easy on them. Steve and Jim were starting to fidget. They clearly hoped that Brian wouldn't insist that a test of their unworthiness was necessary. I could see from their red faces that anger and embarrassment were raising their blood pressure, or maybe it was just the effort of breathing while carrying that much weight.

'OK,' I continued, as Brian hadn't intervened. 'Come over here, guys.' I walked them across to the armoured Nissan. 'Peanut, bring me over two sets of armour and two ARs, will you. Give one set each to these guys.'

Because he was fit, not fat, Peanut was back with vests and guns in hand faster than greased lightning.

Steve and Jim looked again at Brian for support, but, getting none, they reluctantly took the vests and weapons. As they struggled, huffing and puffing, to squeeze their blubber under the Velcro and plates, they looked utterly sad and ridiculous. The front plates were resting high on their bellies, literally facing straight up to the sky.

Brian stared at the both of them, feeling just as embarrassed as they must have felt, his plan to dump them on my team melting like lard in the hot Iraqi sun.

'Now get to the front of the Nissan, one on each side,' I announced, Steve and Jim selecting their preferred sides. 'OK, on my go, you have twenty seconds to get all the way in and the doors closed. Ready. Three, two, one, go!'

Both Humpty to my left and Dumpty to my right struggled to lift their legs high enough to reach the cab door sill then, while on one leg, to jump-roll their asses onto the seats, which sat higher than the length of their legs. This move put them off balance, causing them to start hopping backwards like fat, one-legged kangaroos.

Once they did manage to reach the sill, they then had to squeeze their heads down as far as they could onto the top of the vest plates, to try to get through the door opening. Their leg inside the cab was now pushing the armour plates upwards, forcing it under their 'chinny chin chins', cutting off their air supply and slowly choking them. The harder they tried to force themselves in the truck the closer they got to unconsciousness. They were both turning an odd shade of blood-pressure-red mixed with asphyxia-blue, and sweat was pouring down their faces.

As I counted out loud towards twenty, and the boys laughed just as loud at the free entertainment, Brian opted to throw in the towel.

'OK, OK, that'll do. Get out, you two,' he commanded. 'I've seen enough.'

Relieved it was over, Steve and Jim rolled out of the vehicle just as unceremoniously as they had tried to get in, gasping and panting for air.

'Get that shit off and get inside,' Brian told them.

He turned to me and the team, unable to hide the smirk on his face. 'Well, that was embarrassing, and I get your point.'

Steve and Jim would be shipped out the following day. Brian promised he would make some stern calls to Moyock, reminding them that Iraq was the real deal, and it was completely unacceptable to send us guys who were so unfit and overweight that to even get in an armoured vehicle was downright dangerous, for them and for us. Admittedly, this was a problem almost all companies were starting to face, as the lack of available top-notch operators really began to show. Companies were lowering their standards, hiring anyone they could just to fill a contract, in a race to the bottom.

But that didn't mean we had to accept whoever they sent, for lives literally depended on it – in this case, Steve and Jim's, and our own.

But at that moment I had other things on my mind, as I prepared to formally welcome Lionel to the team. The evening drinks routine was there so we could unwind from a full day's operations and celebrate making it through another twenty-four hours alive. The job of cooling the beers and preparing the hookah had gone to Two Trays, not because he had performed badly, but because he'd been seated on the opposite side of the vehicle to the would-be assassin, so had taken no part in the action.

In truth, his role had been equally important. I always stressed that I didn't want everyone involved in a firefight unless it was absolutely essential. There is no wrong side to be sitting on in a vehicle. Wherever you were seated, you had to watch your arcs and be on the lookout in case of an attack from multiple directions. The same went for shooting. Our tactic was to shoot alternately, not altogether. That way, we reduced the chance of everyone having to change magazines at the same time, causing a break in the line of fire and an opportunity for a counterattack.

As Two Trays set up the table under the date trees, iced the beers and fired up the coals for the large communal hookah, Bullfrog and Stumpy came to join us. Double apple tobacco was the flavour of choice for the hookah, but I always had a ready stock of cigars that I kept in a plastic cooler box, with a little bowl of water and wet toilet paper as a makeshift humidor. That seemed to work fine in keeping them in a perfect state of readiness, and now Lionel had brought in a new supply as well.

Lionel grabbed a seat between Yard Dog and Two Trays as I stood up and addressed the gathering, raising a lovely can of iced Heineken to surviving another day.

'Well done at BIAP and well done on Irish. Well done everyone. Get it in ya.' All stood and raised their cans and we clanked them together, downing a good gulp. 'I'd also like to welcome Lionel to the group. He's a bloody good man and a buddy of mine and now, a buddy of yours. Welcome to Iraq, you fuck.'

Another clank and another big swig.

Lionel remained standing while the rest of us sat down. 'Thank you, guys, it's a pleasure to be here, and that's one hell of a way to get picked up from the airport.'

We laughed, clanked and gulped back again.

'Well then, boys, without further fucking around, let's get fucked up,' I commanded.

Another clunk and we emptied our cans. Despite the unwritten rule of no talk of politics, religion or family affairs or home, I thought a bit of chit-chat would be good, so the guys could get to know Lionel some more.

'Well, bro, how's home?' I asked.

'Same old, same old, bro. Everyone's still doing the same shit, complaining about this and that. You know how it is.'

'And the family?' I asked.

'Yeah, all good, thanks, bro.'

'And the wife?'

Lionel was warming to the assembled company. 'Well, between you, me and everyone sitting here, I can honestly say I gave her a serious "goodbye" rogering before I left.'

'Well done, buddy. She must have been pleased,' Stumpy remarked, with just a hint of sarcasm.

'Yeah. Bloody typical, though, she complained I was too fast.'

'Too fast? Is there another way?' Bullfrog demanded.

'I know, mate!' said Lionel, with mock indignation. 'She only bloody well compared me to those packs of instant noodles – all done in two minutes.'

Suddenly the table went quiet. We all looked at Lionel, then each other, then back at Lionel with shit-eating grins.

'What?' he said, not appreciating what had just happened.

I stood and announced, 'We all heard that, didn't we?'

'Yep,' came back a loud chorus.

'OK then, let's get it formalised.' Lionel still looked utterly confused. 'From this day forth, your official call sign is...' I paused for effect. 'Noodle.'

'Noodle,' the rest of the boys repeated, standing with their cans raised in the air, to Lionel's horror.

That night, like many more to come, we sent many dead marines to Valhalla, and by many, I mean enough to get well and truly fucked up. The end-of-day drinking had become our way of coping with the dangers and, being a good C1, I was usually the one who instigated this ritual, which, for the boys, gave it some legitimacy. In truth it made us a very tight team, cementing a definite brotherhood.

Drinking had been a very big part of my upbringing. In New Zealand, I was not the only one to treat consuming alcohol as a personal challenge. If you didn't blank out and get fucked up, you weren't trying hard enough. In my circles, and particularly the military, there were no social drinkers – one or two beers then off to bed. For us it was all or nothing, and I always chose all. I can't say for certain if that made me an alcoholic. I didn't know or want to know what level of drinking earned you that title, but I certainly had a drink problem.

I didn't drink every day; far from it. Before Iraq, I drank only one night a week, but that night was always a big one and made up for those when I didn't drink. It was like I was scared there wasn't enough booze in the world, so I had to drink as much as I could, as fast as I could, before it ran out.

'Go ugly early' was our motto, and I sure as hell did that.

It wasn't just a case of getting shit-faced. I would often get the blanks and have no idea what foolishness I had got up to the night before. The hangovers were horrendous, often taking two days or more to pass. I could still wake up early and be functional, but I would be in a nasty mood all morning, or at least until I had drunk an ocean of water and could finally feel the fog lift.

With the hangovers, I would also take unnecessary risks, which, in Iraq, meant going out in Baghdad actually looking for trouble, feeling invincible and bitter.

When I was sober, I felt empathy for the insurgents and their cause. I still got knotted up and angry at what had happened in Fallujah, but then I would feel sorry for that poor idiot on Route Irish. For all I knew, he could have suffered some terrible tragedy at the hands of the military or another security company. Maybe he'd lost his family and was hell-bent on revenge, just like I'd have felt in his place. I wasn't rooting for the insurgency; I didn't want to join them; but I felt I understood what they were doing and why.

The post-war standard of living in Iraq was arguably worse than it had been under Saddam. Infrastructure had collapsed, power was always cutting out, food, drinking water and fuel were scarce, making the price of everyday living skyrocket. The black market thrived, education was in freefall, and there were armed gangs roaming the streets. Yes, Saddam had been a dictator, but he was an American-made dictator and was 'good to go' while it suited them, as far as I understood it. The propaganda the public were being fed bore little resemblance to what I was seeing on the ground. The whole invasion was sold as a 'liberation', when it didn't take a rocket scientist to realise it was all about greed and profit.

The real galactic fuck-up was that, after the removal of Saddam, the US administration had the opportunity to keep the Iraqi people, the police and the military onside, and to work with them to stabilise the country, but they had spurned it, which made me think that keeping control was always their plan. If they had imagined there would be no resistance, or a half-hearted attempt that could easily be stomped out, they'd got it badly wrong. With little regard for the lives of the Iraqi people or the men and women in uniform from the US and other allied nations, they blundered on regardless with seemingly no end in sight.

I would never forget the orphaned kid in the bombed-out apartment block who ate rotten pigeons and had lost his mind.

Yep, that's how I felt when I was sober. But when I was drunk, or hungover, I just wanted to get into a shootout and actually went looking for trouble. It was not only dangerous but stupid and irresponsible. I would unnecessarily put my team at risk, just so I could get my kicks. Unfortunately, this habit would gradually get worse as the situation in Iraq continued to deteriorate. Maybe it was to mask my own fears, but it was not something I could sustain for long.

The morning after christening Lionel 'Noodle', we were all nursing monster hangovers, but I had one more surprise in store for him. We loaded up the vehicles and headed over to Landing Zone (LZ) Washington, where Hacksaw, the lead pilot of Blackwater's flight of Little Bird helicopters, was waiting. Hacksaw was a slow-walking, slow-talking, blond-haired air warrior from Texas and a great guy.

'Everyone here?' he asked.

'Yeah, bro.'

'And the new guy?'

'That's him,' I said, nodding in Noodle's direction. 'The real pale fucker not looking too hot.'

'Understood, Baz. Glad to be of service.'

I got everyone kitted up – everyone but me, that is – and loaded onto the helicopters. The look of sheer terror on Noodle's face was priceless. The thing with the Little Birds is that you can only put your ass cheeks inside, perched on the floor, with your legs dangling outside. The Little Bird crews were some of the best former special forces pilots the US had to offer, and their helos were fantastic machines that would prove invaluable in Iraq, though they had a very limited load threshold. But today's mission was all about giving Noodle his baptism of fire.

With startled faces and vomit brewing, the boys headed up, up and away, as Hacksaw and one other Little Bird took them on a crazy whirlwind flight around Baghdad, swooping up and over the IZ then banking steeply and generating as many puke-inducing Gs as possible. Just when the boys thought it was all over, he took them for the ultimate low-level buzz – a pass beneath the crossed swords monument. What a ride. I'm sorry I missed it. NOT. I'd been on enough rides across Baghdad and central Iraq in those things already.

When they finally landed, everyone was as sick as a dog, and Noodle was even whiter than he had been on Route Irish right after the shootout. Fuck me, even Bullfrog wasn't rocking on all cylinders. I thanked Hacksaw and crew very much and handed him the Leupold scope I had managed to acquire for one of his pilots, who had been trying to find one for his Colt Commando rifle for ages. *Nice doing business with you, guys.*

We drove back to the team house and, as the client was away for forty-eight hours, there was time to relax and clean our kit. Some went for a gentle workout, before almost everyone, still not feeling 100 per cent, headed for a nap. Noodle and I made to the roof to get a selfie with the dirty-great Dushka – DShK 12.7mm heavy machine gun – we had mounted up there, which stood about five foot high on its tripod and weighed a shit-ton.

But there was something I wanted to talk to Noodle about, and up there was about as private as we could get. 'Hey, bro, just so you know, there are a few dos and do nots, conversation-wise, that I have implemented for end-of-night beers and hookah time. You know that time is for relaxing, giving each other shit and celebrating making it through another day, right?'

'Yeah, sure, I get that, bro,' Noodle answered. 'So what things are left off the table?'

I reiterated that we didn't have deep conversations about family, we didn't discuss religion, and we didn't air our views about the invasion.

'Oh, I get that for sure, bro,' Noodle remarked. 'I bet it would be a touchy subject with this crowd.'

I told him that I had flip-flopped on the issue many times over, but I didn't want to risk getting into any arguments about it with our American colleagues.

'Yeah, I get it,' Noodle agreed. 'Shit like that could cause a lot of aggro in the team, and no doubt cause you to be on the next flight home. So, you've been having doubts?'

'No, bro,' I answered. 'Not so much *doubts*. Don't get me wrong, I love being here, I love the guys and I particularly love making $600 per day, considering what we were making back in New Zealand.'

'Amen to that. Oh frig, sorry, bro, no religion.'

I looked at him grinning. 'Fucking dick! But I don't know, bro, as you stay here longer, you'll get to see all the trauma the local population are living under because of all this.'

I went on to tell him about the one thing that epitomised for me the unholy mess that was Iraq: the young boy I used to see opposite the Al-Hamra Hotel, and how I thought he was living in a bombed-out car park until I found out it was all that was left of his home and his family; how the sight and the thought of it still haunted me, and how he was definitely not an isolated case.

'But you know what, after our guys got killed in Fallujah, I just fucking hated every Iraqi and wanted to do to them what they had done to the guys,' I concluded, lamely.

Noodle is a very bright fucker and knows me well. He could see how conflicted I was. 'What do you plan to do then?' he asked.

'I'm not sure. But what I definitely won't be doing is telling anyone other than you. I'm sure I'll find a way to bury it and get on with the job.'

'Yeah, but that's a recipe for disaster down the road, bro,' Noodle remarked, quietly.

'I know. In the meantime, I'll just take it one day at a time and burn that bridge when I get to it. I just want you to be aware of it, bro. I know you've only just got here, but you'll maybe see things that don't necessarily flow in the direction of your moral compass.'

'I get it,' he said. 'Thanks for the heads-up.'

Looking back, the months had flown by really quick. A lot had changed since December 2003. Despite the Fallujah killings, Blackwater Commercial had kept pulling in the security contracts, teams were almost fully manned and the team house had a great HQ staff running it, under Brian. But the dark cloud that cast a very long shadow was the death of our guys in Fallujah, and that one incident influenced everything we did. Every Iraqi male was now regarded as an insurgent just waiting to kill us. As a result, we rolled harder, fired a lot more warning shots and smiled and waved a whole lot less.

The insurgents saw the Fallujah killings as a great victory and were doing everything they could to capitalise on it. There were daily attacks all over Iraq, while in Baghdad, there were more mortars fired into the IZ and BIAP, and even more VBIEDs on Route Irish, with sometimes up to six per day.

The insurgency had used the Fallujah killings as a recruitment tool, attracting more and more Muslim extremists from Iran, Syria, Saudi Arabia and Chechnya, all drawn to the opportunity to come to Iraq to kill Americans. Many attacks were videoed before being edited and uploaded to the internet for propaganda purposes. It was even said that there was a $250,000 'kill or kidnap' bounty on the heads of anyone from Blackwater. Fuck me, I'd have turned Stumpy in for that amount.

Then there was Muqtada al-Sadr's cult-like Mahdi Army, based in Sadr City, on the outskirts of Baghdad.

In early April 2004 I got a call out of the blue from Ben, who was still with White Boy, working a BW team at the CPA in Najaf. Unfortunately, it wasn't a 'Hi, how you doin'?' kind of a call. Ben told me that they were under attack from hundreds of supporters of al-Sadr, who had taken exception to their presence in the Shia's holy city of Najaf, ordering his Mahdi Army to take it back by all means. Ben, White Boy and their guys were getting hit with AK-47 and machine-gun fire, rocket-propelled grenades (RPGs), plus a human wave of attackers bent on killing everyone there.

Ben and White Boy – plus two other BW guys I knew, Hollywood and Goldberg – and the rest of the team were trying to help the small group of US marines defend the CPA compound, aided by a force of Colombian perimeter guards. There was also a Spanish military unit there, but they were medics only, not fighters, and they had withdrawn to the bunkers set further inside the wire. It sounded like a modern-day Alamo.

'Hey, man,' Ben said, 'we really need you guys to get down here and help out. We need a shitload of men and a shitload of ammo.'

'Sure mate, I'll see what I can do,' I told him. 'I'll get back to you ASAP.'

Word of the situation had made it to Brian and Dave, and soon we were gathering up all the extra ammo and heavy weapons we could find and loading it into our vehicles. I had been to the Najaf compound a couple of times, so I knew the layout and how to get there. The CPA was set back 200 metres from a main road, across open, undulating ground. To one side lay a multi-storey hospital, which offered perfect sniper positions, as it looked directly onto the CPA and the main road.

According to Brian, there were hundreds of Mahdi Army militia arriving by bus to join the fray. I knew the boys would be firing thousands of rounds just to keep those fuckers at bay. We gathered what spare boxes of ammo we had and even emptied some of our personal mags, taking spare rounds from whoever didn't need them. We loaded everything into the Chevys, by which time my team were kitted up and ready to make the hour-long drive to Najaf at warp speed. But just as we prepared to screech out of the gate we were stopped. According to Brian, news from State Dept was that there was no way we could get anywhere near the Najaf CPA, not without being hit ourselves.

Being smart buggers, the Mahdi Army had set up roadblocks to isolate the compound and prevent any reinforcements reaching it.

The only safe option left was to send the Blackwater Little Bird helicopters. So we did a rapid replan and set off to rendezvous with them. In the ten minutes it took us to drive our arsenal-on-wheels to LZ Washington at breakneck speed, Hacksaw and his Little Bird crews were cleared by state and good to go.

To save weight, and in order to get as much weaponry to our guys in Najaf as possible, the flight crew decided that they would use only the one pilot and one door gunner per helo, instead of the normal crew of four. We filled the Birds with as much weaponry as we could cram inside, after which I asked Hacksaw if there was room enough for me to go with him and get dropped off at Najaf. I had swapped out my MP5 for a Dragunov sniper rifle and gathered as many mags and rounds for it as I could find.

White Boy and Ben were my old team-buddies from Karbala, the contract we'd run with Jerry as my running mate. We'd lost Jerry to Fallujah, and I was shitting myself that we were about to lose these two to the siege at Najaf. I felt driven to ride to their rescue, do-or-die. But Hacksaw told me that, sadly, it was a no-go. All the room on the helo was taken up with guns and ammo and the one door gunner. I unslung the Dragunov and stacked it into the Bird, together with the mags and rounds. *But fuck me, I still really wanted to get there and help them out.*

White Boy had a great and very capable team of guys, but they were few in number and getting overrun by the hordes of militia was a real possibility. Another factor was sheer fatigue. Depending on how determined al-Sadr was to capture the compound, this could be a long siege. For sure, someone needed to get down there and charge over the ridge with bugles blowing. Unfortunately, the call was out of my hands. All we could do was watch as the Birds rose above the T walls, dipped south and disappeared in the direction of Najaf.

I called up Ben and told him to hang in there. Help was on the way.

The Mahdi Army fighters proved persistent and die-hard. They had taken to charging the compound from the road in coordinated waves. Our Blackwater guys and the small marine contingent were keeping them at a distance with their firepower, but the Colombians were also showing their true grit and value. They had taken up positions in the dead ground between the compound and the road, like the meat in the middle of a sandwich.

One very brave Colombian soldier found himself about to be overrun. As the militia closed in on him, he retreated under fire to a piece of dead ground, lying low out of sight of the advancing militia until they were almost on top of him, when he popped up and shot two of them dead. He then ran back to another piece of dead ground, and continued to do this, supported by the BW boys and marines from the roof, until he ran out of ammo. There were two militiamen still advancing on him. With still thirty metres to go before he was back with his team, his options were pretty limited, so he pulled out a pocketknife he had recently bought at the PX for $10, a lot of money for a young Colombian. (The PX is a US military grocery shop that sells all kinds of items from the US.)

Unfolding the small sharp blade, he lay as still as he could behind a small rise until he was sure the two pursuing militia were upon him. Then the little five-foot fucker jumped up right in front of them, catching the militiamen by surprise. The Colombian charged them with his PX knife held out horizontally at head height and scalped the nearest pursuer, who dropped to his knees with blood cascading down his face. The brave Colombian then swung his arm around and slashed the jugular of the second militia guy, before swivelling back, bringing the knife down through the top of the first guy's freshly exposed head. He then pulled it out and sprinted to the safety of the compound. Seeing this impressive display of lethal hand-to-hand combat, the boys on the roof of the CPA cheered him in and finished off the two attackers.

The fighting proved relentless, with very little time for sleep or rest. When the guys did get a break, they were busy reloading belt ammo for the SAW machine guns, tending the wounded or cleaning their overworked assault rifles and magazines. If they slept at all, it was while on their feet or sitting in a chair, still fully kitted out in body armour.

Throughout the siege the Little Bird crews – pilots, door gunners and mechanics – made numerous lifesaving supply runs with ammo, food and medical equipment. They also performed casualty evacuations, lifting out the wounded. One brave door gunner strapped an injured marine into the co-pilot's seat and, for the sake of saving weight, stayed behind to help the boys fight it out, offering additional firepower while Hacksaw flew the injured man back to the IZ.

This was ballsy stuff and it meant that if the pilot got hit, there was no one left to take over the controls. The bird would most certainly go down, but they accepted this risk with little thought of their own safety. I think it's fair to say the boys in Najaf owed their lives to those Little Bird pilots and crews. After three days of fighting, a detachment of US special forces commandos finally managed to reach Najaf, driving in under darkness using night-vision goggles (NVG) and riding in specialised SF gun-trucks. By then the boys had been at it for seventy-two hours straight.

Once the special forces and further military units arrived, al-Sadr could see the way the wind was blowing, and he called off the attack. The Battle of Najaf was over, but the number of killed and wounded militia was reported to be in the hundreds. The Spanish medics re-emerged from their hiding place and the Colombians re-established their positions, clearing out the bodies that littered the open ground.

White Boy, and the other Blackwater guys, plus the GC at Najaf, were so impressed by what they had witnessed from that brave Colombian soldier, they held a small ceremony out the front of the CPA and presented the Colombian hero with a special forces Gerber military knife. It was the least he deserved.

A week after the Najaf battle, White Boy and his team made it back to the team house in Baghdad. We caught up with them over a few beers and they gave us a bit of a verbal AAR. It was obvious to anyone with a military mind that, in the absence of any swift US military reinforcements, the small contingent of fatigued marines would have been overrun, had our boys not been there. But there seemed to be a dark cloud hanging over all that had happened at Najaf, and no one, not least the guys, knew why.

After a few days in Baghdad the team was recalled to Moyock. Apparently, the high-ups at BW HQ were concerned with the publicity the boys were getting, and especially with footage of the fighting surfacing on websites. Someone in Moyock seemed to think that the image of civilian security contractors fending off hundreds of fanatical attackers was not helpful. That was the military's job after all, they argued. We were just security contractors, there to protect and transport those doing the rebuilding.

We weren't 'mercenaries', they complained, and this could look bad, which completely ignored the fact that our boys had not gone there to do the military's job. They were there doing BW work and were forced to defend themselves as well as their client when they came under attack. But it seemed Moyock didn't get it. Protecting their ass, the lucrative contracts and the company image, was clearly more important. Shockingly, once they'd made it back to the US, the Najaf boys were unceremoniously fired.

Meanwhile, as the American public grew increasingly unhappy

at the sight of dead soldiers being shipped home in flag-draped coffins, the deaths of contractors went largely unreported. There wasn't even an official database recording the names of our dead brothers, while our body count too was steadily rising. The argument seemed to be that soldiers fought for their country, while we fought for money.

My answer to that was that we all fought for money. The contractors may have been earning more than the regular soldiers, but we all earned far less than the bosses of the companies making a killing from the conflict, and a hell of a lot less than the warmongering politicians who were profiting from the whole business on the side-lines. So, who were the real mercenaries?

The same week as the attack in Najaf, al-Sadr's Mahdi Army attacked the CPA compound in Al-Kut. As I'd seen for myself when conducting site recces the previous year, the compound sat alongside the river, and it had been reinforced with high T walls on most sides, but not all. The base security force was a mix of local Iraqis, plus a contingent of Ukrainian soldiers, while the personal security of the Kut GC was provided by Triple Canopy contractors.

During the recces, I had met one of the Triple Canopy commanders, a guy called JC. He was a legend among the special forces circles but, like so many of us contractors, he had taken a job in Iraq because life on Civvy Street was about as fulfilling as watching soft porn with your in-laws. And, just like Jerry and I had experienced in Karbala, JC had to deal with an idiot of a GC who thought he knew more about security than he did.

The GC was a British diplomat who believed he was wanted there by the Iraqi people, to make a difference. To my mind, those over-educated and naive GC idiots didn't have a clue about what the man on the street thought. They didn't seem to realise that they were seen as the figureheads of an occupying force that showed no sign of leaving. They were seen as being more of the problem than the solution.

Against the advice of JC and others, the GC had insisted that the four-metre-high protective T walls were not to be extended along the riverbank, because they would obstruct the view of the river from his office. That only made the job of keeping him and his staff safe so much harder for JC and his team, plus the Ukrainian soldiers based there.

Just like in Najaf, the attacks on the Kut CPA escalated to hundreds of heavily armed militiamen firing rockets, machine guns and mortars at the vulnerable areas of the camp. Unsurprisingly, they were quick to exploit the gap along the river where the T wall protection was missing. The lightly armed Ukrainians fought valiantly, but they soon began to run out of ammo, while the local Iraqi 'guard force' abandoned their positions.

As the battle raged, the Triple Canopy boys and the Ukrainians were forced to repel attack after attack, with all close to exhaustion. After three days of being under siege by small arms, rockets and mortars, and with ammo running desperately low, JC made the call to abandon the camp by vehicle, but the GC tried to order another vehicle to block their path, so no one could leave. Under intense fire, JC gave him a final ultimatum: *Get in the fucking vehicle or be left behind.* Under covering fire of a helicopter gunship, they managed to abandon the camp and drive to the nearest friendly location.

Once again, the defence of a CPA compound had been orchestrated by a private security company, in cooperation with a military force. Like our boys in Najaf, they had repelled a well-armed and coordinated attack. If the Ukrainians had been there on their own, it is very likely they would have been overrun. They were so low on ammo they had had to rely on a resupply from JC and his team. Unlike our boys in Najaf, however, the Triple Canopy guys didn't get fired for it.

It was against this frustrating backdrop that my three-month stint came to an end. I unloaded my magazines and gave all my weapons one final clean before disassembling them. I then packed them away in a steel trunk I had purchased the day before. Inside I also placed my work clothes, boots, pistol holster, vest, armour, bullets, med kit, go bag and any other shit I had lying around. Finally, I wrote my name on my M72 rocket launcher, HE and WP grenades, before lodging them in the armoury.

It felt nice, but weird, to be putting on the civilian clothes I had packed away three months earlier. I padlocked my steel trunk and wrote my name on it in permanent marker with the warning, 'Leave the shit in here alone, or else.'

The boys had staged the Blazers on the road outside the team house, ready for my drop off at BIAP. I said my goodbyes to Brian, Mo and whoever else was around. I gave Noodle a call via the Thuraya and bade my farewells. He was out doing a job at the time, something heroic so he could earn a better call sign, or so we all liked to joke.

'Hey, bro, I'm heading out now,' I told him. 'Keep your head down and be safe, OK. Oh, and another thing, do me a favour and keep away from that new haji market in the IZ. I have a feeling that thing is going to get hit soon.'

For some reason, some knucklehead in the State Department had given permission for a local bazaar to be set up *inside* the Green Zone, just down the road from the medical centre and one of the most popular bars inside the walls, the Green Zone cafe. The market was run by Iraqis and sold all sorts of knick-knacks and trinkets, but to me it was the perfect excuse for the insurgency to infiltrate the IZ. Or to coerce local market traders into doing something bad, such as planting a bomb, most often with the threat of death to them or their family.

With a few last words of caution to Noodle, I saw Yard Dog signal that they were ready. With my travel bag loaded in the back with Stumpy, who used it to prop up his SAW, Two Trays asked me one last time if I'd made sure to take all the ammo out of it. It was an easy enough thing to forget when heading home. Not a smart move.

I confirmed that I had, grabbed a set of borrowed body armour and cranked Yard Dog's AK to use while he was driving. I may have been heading out, but I was still C1. Yard Dog, as my 2IC, would swap in only once I was gone. Just as I was about to give the order to pull out, one of the other teams arrived to process some newbies they had just collected from BIAP. There was a tall guy whose face I thought I recognised. Then he spoke and I realised I was right. It was that Aussie fuck from Karbala.

'Hey, Goodie,' I yelled out. On hearing his name, Pete turned around with a bit of an uncertain look. 'Hey, mate, how's it going?'

'Hey, Baz,' he replied, once he saw who it was. 'I'm finally here, mate. I'm one of you bastards now. Thanks for putting me forward.'

'Welcome brother,' I said. 'I'm about to fuck off on leave, just on my way out. I'll be back in a month.'

'Good on you mate. Enjoy the break.'

While I was away, Goodie's new BW teammates would change his call sign to something very Aussie, in their view: 'Dingo.' *Fuck me, that's not even trying.*

It felt good to be heading home, but I wasn't there yet. There are plenty of stories of guys getting killed on their last day in-country or even on their way to BIAP. There was a story doing the rounds of a soldier getting killed on a C-130 military aircraft just as it was leaving the ground. He had taken his helmet off, thinking he was home and dry, and then been hit in the head by an insurgent's bullet coming through the side of the plane. *Now that's shit luck.*

As we left the gate, I radioed up: 'OK guys, safeties off, eyes open, here we go.'

The Prodigy's 'Breathe' was thumping out of the stereo. In a way, I would have preferred absolute silence, but I didn't want to show any sign of the anxiety or stress I was feeling, so I left it to blast out, giving the appearance of business as usual.

We made it up Route Irish without getting hit, pulled up outside the departures terminal and said our goodbyes. It was sad to see the boys turn around and head back into Baghdad. We had become a very tight team – the envy of many in the company. We kept to a very strict working standard but knew how to have fun too. If anyone had asked me to stay, I would have told them to fuck off, but watching them drive away, all I could think was this: *Make sure you're all here in one piece when I get back, you buggers.*

Once I got inside the terminal, I found myself watching the other outgoing passengers. The long, snaking lines of KBR employees were mostly Filipinos and Americans who looked like they had lived hard lives in minimum-wage jobs and for whom coming to Iraq was their big money shot. Those leaving seemed to have stocked up on 'Iraqi freedom' propaganda – T-shirts, ball caps and huge US flags from the PX. They looked 100 per cent convinced they had been here for the right reasons.

I wasn't.

The change in the calibre of the incoming security contractors was glaringly obvious. There were fewer of the Tier 1 types of the early days, keen to blend in rather than stand out. This latest batch looked like they were in competition with each other to see who could inject the most steroids, pump the most weight and wear the tightest T-shirt. Some even had their arms covered in ridiculous squiggly lines, which I supposed had to be someone's interpretation of a 'tribal tattoo'.

No doubt a lot of them claimed to be 'Māori tattoos', and we Māoris did have a long tradition of such body art. I had a few such traditional tattoos myself, each of which meant something personal and intimate to me, my family, clan or tribe. But to my mind these guys just looked ridiculous – like they'd let their kids have a bit of fun with indelible marker pens.

I noticed a few guys at the other end of the terminal, and right away it was obvious they were from New Zealand, or Aotearoa, to use the original Māori name. They had tanned skin and dark hair and I recognised their posture, which was warrior-proud, with a slight hint of 'don't fuck with me', but which could instantly change into hysterical laughter if they saw someone trip up or do something to arouse their dark humour.

The biggest giveaway, though, was that their arms were covered in genuine Māori tattoos: markings that denoted their individual tribal identities and allegiances. They also wore large *pounamu* – green stone or bone – necklaces. The designs of the necklaces were either the *koro* – a representation of the spiral frond of a fern's new-growth, symbolising eternal life – or the *toki* – an axe blade, symbolising strength. There are any number of other designs. They're worn by Māoris for many reasons – ceremonial, religious, or as a means of being in contact with the spirits of loved ones and the ancestors.

I felt a surge of pride. *Kapai* – 'everything is good; no worries' – I told myself. *Kapai boys.* I smiled to myself.

Soon enough I was through check-in and on the plane.

As it thundered down the runway, rapidly gaining speed, I'm sure we were all hoping that the insurgents had decided to take a day off from lobbing mortars and rockets into BIAP, at least until we had gone. As soon as we lifted off, there was an almost audible sigh of relief, but it was short lived, for the pilot soon started the high-speed corkscrew climb to altitude. I was lucky enough to be on the side of the plane that faced the ground, and I could see the distinctive shape of the BIAP terminals growing smaller and smaller.

As Baghdad disappeared behind me, my thoughts turned to the boys, hoping they had made it back to the team house safely. Then I thought of the millions of poor Iraqi civilians, and the thousands of soldiers down there who, unlike us contractors, didn't have the option of leaving every three months, or simply when they had had enough.

Those poor fucks were stuck there, with little sign of any resolution to the God-awful mess any time soon.

CHAPTER 9

For me, arriving back in Aotearoa is something I'm always in two minds about. I love coming home to that small but undeniably beautiful country, yet I enjoy leaving even more. We Kiwis have a lot of hang-ups, plus a bad habit of holding back people who are trying to get ahead. It's called tall poppy syndrome. Over the years, I'd adopted a habit of booking a first few nights on one of the top floors of a nice hotel, with a view of the ocean, to be alone with the waves and ease my way back into dealing with home.

Often, I'd lie awake all night staring into the dark. One night I stared at the ceiling until early in the morning. It was then that I heard the thumping rotors of a helicopter flying close over the roof of the hotel. It sounded so good, so familiar, and somehow so soothing, that it was all I needed to send me off to sleep. If only I could arrange a gunfight outside the hotel, maybe I would sleep like a baby for days.

Only after a few nights of gradual adjustment to 'normality' did I feel able to reach out and visit family and friends.

I have four fantastic children – two sets of twins, would you believe – from my first marriage: two boys, Zel and Shannon, or Chaz for short, and two girls, Keely and Arden. I clearly applied my SAS 'double tap' training to having children, but there was nothing Tier 1 about my parenting. If you look in the dictionary under 'Absent Father', you'll see I am the living definition. For various reasons I just wasn't there through most of their childhoods, and my greatest regret is not having spent more time with them. For that I am truly sorry.

Whenever I did feel ready to venture out of my hotel, catching up with family and friends would inevitably mean drinking and, as usual, getting beyond remembering anything, which, of course, meant a monster hangover for several days. That, among other things, had proved fatal for my relationships with my female better halves. I had also started to show signs of serious depression and would often wake up not knowing if I felt like talking to anyone. If I didn't, I would just be silent all day, which only made the situation worse.

What I couldn't explain was that, although I may not have been saying anything out loud, there were full-on conversations going on inside my head, ones that I couldn't shut off. It was totally exhausting, and when I returned from that first full stint with Blackwater, that internal dialogue was all about the messed-up shitstorm that was Iraq.

One night a few days after I'd come out of my hotel-by-the-beach purdah, I went on a drunken bender with my brother-in-law Dave, smashing back the beers and verbally killing every Linkin Park song to which we only knew the chorus. I must have been whining on about my failed relationships a bit too much for him, because he wacked me on the side of my head and reminded me that I'd already met the perfect woman and treated her abysmally.

Maybe he was right. Just before I'd headed for Iraq last time around, I'd met a woman called Jennifer – call sign 'Jen' for short.

Jen was beautiful, funny as hell and we'd got on incredibly well. By all indications she'd fallen for me, but I'd acted like a complete asshole. As Dave spoke, I realised that he was right. Sometimes, what you're searching for is right in front of you.

The next day, with just enough liquid courage still left in my system, I called Jen up, hoping the caller ID wouldn't reveal it was me, given how badly I'd treated her last time around. When she answered and recognised my voice, she was less than enthusiastic, but with a great deal of apologising and admitting what a dick I had been, we arranged to meet.

Not feeling totally in control, I went inside her place and tried to explain again why I had called, why I had treated her like I had and how sorry I was, just in case my previous fifty versions hadn't hit home. She listened intently and, although I still had a long way to go, I could see that this was going remarkably well. The more I talked with her the more I realised I genuinely had strong feelings for her.

Then my end game started coming into focus. *Fuck it*, I told myself, *you haven't felt like this in years. You have someone sitting right in front of you who actually loves you for who you are. Do it, I dare you.*

So, right there and then I asked Jen to marry me, obviously thinking she would say no and tell me to fuck off, or that she needed time to think about it. Typically, though, she called my bluff and said yes. She even came up with a date, on the spot, done and dusted. So, for my remaining time in New Zealand we spent our every hour together, and, given my mental state, I even found it easier to get to sleep without having to rely on alcohol. My dreams were another matter. They were taking a nasty turn, but I told myself I'd deal with them later.

Halfway through my time back home, I was chilling with Jen when Noodle called from Baghdad to let me know that two insurgents had infiltrated the Green Zone, carrying backpacks stuffed full of explosives. They'd done so posing as market traders, as if they were setting up their stalls in the 'local haji market'. The explosions were timed to detonate simultaneously; one had torn through the venue, killing a lot of the Iraqi stallholders and several Americans who had been trinket shopping, and one had blown up the Green Zone cafe we frequented.

'Holy fuck.' It was just as I'd feared, and immediately I was back with my boys in the heat and dust and the fear of Baghdad. 'Were any of the guys there? Was anyone hurt?'

'No, bro, none of our guys,' Noodle reassured me. 'After your warning to keep away I did just that and I told the others the same.'

To the displeasure of many in the IZ, Noodle explained, we now had to roll as heavily when escorting clients inside there as we did outside. If people were pissed off, then screw them. We couldn't trust anyone, anywhere, any more. Of course, the call from Noodle didn't do my nightmares a world of good. But Jen and I seemed to weather the storm, and we were still an item by the time it came around for me to head back to Baghdad.

I packed up my gear, saw my children one last time, then headed for the airport. I was really excited to be heading back and looking forward to seeing the guys. I had missed them and thought I really needed to be back at their side. I said farewell to my new fiancée – see you in three months' time – called my sisters and mother one last time, then boarded the first of several flights that would spirit me back to Iraq.

It felt good to have something positive to focus on, but just as soon as the plane took to the skies, I forced myself to pack all that away and get myself back into Iraq mode. Time to get my head back in the game.

Some forty-eight hours later, the BW CASA flight landed at BIAP, and I made my way to the arrivals terminal, followed by a group of Blackwater newbies. They seemed suitably impressed that I was returning for my third stint in Iraq, and even more so when I saved them from being scammed by some local Iraqi chancers, who had set themselves up as phoney customs officials at BIAP arrivals, to relieve unwitting new arrivals of their shiny, expensive kit.

Even better was seeing my guys, who had come to BIAP to welcome me 'home'.

'Damn, it's good to be back,' I told them, as we man-hugged. 'I missed you fuckers.'

I turned and bade farewell to the gaggle of BW newbies. 'Well, you guys, take care. I'll see you around most likely.'

They stared at me, surrounded by my gang of gunned-up mongrels, with a look that said: *Who the fuck was that masked man?*

Hey, a guy can enjoy the moment, can't he?

My boys walked me to where the vehicles were parked. It was good to see those ugly, up-armoured workhorses once again, and I got another welcome from Bullfrog and a new guy, Clutch. Clutch had replaced Noodle, who had gone to work with the BW team based in Mansour. It was sad not to have him with us, but I knew I'd still see him in and around Baghdad. After all, the Mansour team house was but a short drive away from our own. I also knew he'd do well over there because Noodle would do well no matter where he was sent.

Just before we mounted up, Peanut whispered that he needed to have a talk with me in private once we reached the team house.

'OK, bro,' I told him, intrigued as to what was up.

Reclaiming my position as C1, just before we rolled, I came up on the radio: 'OK guys. Safeties off, eyes open, let's go.'

And you know what, *it felt good*.

I was back in Baghdad, and it felt right leading a group of top guys with guns in one of the most dangerous places in the world right then; a group of guys who would fight and die for each other. My team.

There had clearly been a few changes in my absence. Checkpoint 1 (CP1), to exit BIAP, was looking more like a proper security post than the sack of shit it had previously resembled. They had apparently taken quite a few hits, so security had been beefed up, with man-and-dog teams now a part of the fixtures. It even had a tin roof to provide some shade for the poor fuckers working there.

While I had been away, a massive VBIED had managed to find its way into the middle of the crowded Iraqi waiting lane at CP1, before the driver blew himself up, killing a huge number of locals. The insurgents had really stepped up their game, and now didn't give a fuck how many of their own they killed, it seemed.

The drive back along Irish felt great. It was all so familiar and so comfortable, and all the guys were alive and so *on it*, which was a huge weight off my mind, though I sensed there was a bit of tension somehow concerning Yard Dog, who had been team leader during my absence. I gazed out of the open window at all the familiar sights and had this weird feeling that I was returning home.

Pulling up in front of the team house again was fucking awesome. The boys had dragged out my trunk and placed it beside my bunk.

'Hello, old friend,' I announced, as I opened the lid to see all my essential kit sitting there, just as I had left it. I half expected to hear angels harmonising.

I pulled everything out that I needed to reassemble: my MP5 parts, aim point and mags, Glock pistol, Glock mags, belt holster, ID card holder, Rhodesian vest, armour, sand goggles, carabiner, radio, handset, spare battery and Nokia earpiece. I checked my RPK mags and a shitload of bullets that would need to be reloaded, along with my go bag with extra ammo, medical kit and E&E supplies, and made sure my M72 and RPK, plus the HE and WP grenades, were still in the armoury.

As I changed from my civilian rig back into my war attire, the feeling of everything fitting just right felt... great. I slipped into my T-shirt, cargo pants, work socks, boots, green and black shemagh, air-crew gloves, sand-coloured ball cap with a sand-coloured US flag on the front, plus Maui Jim sunglasses. The feeling as I did so wasn't just physical, it was *emotional*. The civilian gear had felt uncomfortable and forced, while this felt natural; *like a second skin.*

I placed my body armour at the foot of my bunk, ready, and reassembled my MP5 in less than thirty seconds. 'Dang, you still got it,' I chuckled to myself.

I stood up and looked at my reflection in the mirror. *Now, that's better. That's the bugger.* I looked down at my civilian clothes. They would need to be washed and folded away – not needed for another three months. *Amen to all that.*

While the boys set up the white plastic garden table and chairs, plus the chilled beers and fired-up hookah, I called over Peanut, ostensibly so he could give me a hand reloading my magazines.

'What's up, mate?' I ventured, once we were sat together on my bunk loading up my thirteen mags of 9mm.

'Well, bro,' he said, 'it's like this: I don't trust Yard Dog.'

'Why's that?' I asked.

'Simple. He doesn't know what the fuck he's doing.'

'Do tell.'

'We went on a few runs and his briefs were shit, for one.'

'OK,' I said. 'What else?'

'We nearly drove into an ambush, but Two Trays spotted it and we got away before it all turned to ratshit.'

This was disturbing news, for sure. 'Explain it to me, bro,' I said.

'Well, we were driving down River Road to the Electoral Ministry, when we came to a fake IP checkpoint, and they tried to pull us over. It was obvious these guys were not IP. Two Trays in the back Blazer called Yard Dog and warned him not to stop but to bust through. Trouble is, Yard Dog was determined to stop, and in fact he got Bullfrog to slow right down.'

'Fuck, really?'

'Yeah. Seeing this could turn nasty, we all muzzled the IPs with every gun we had.'

'OK, then what?'

'Well, Two Trays drove right up behind Yard Dog's vehicle and nudged it hard, to let the fucker know to get out of there. Two Trays then screamed through the radio for Bullfrog to floor it, which he thankfully did, ignoring Yard Dog's commands to stop. Stumpy cracked off a few rounds at the IPs, which sent them scattering, as we busted out of Dodge. Sure enough, he could see other guys with guns hiding off to one side, so he let them have a few bursts as we got the fuck out of there.'

'And what did Yard Dog do?'

Peanut eyed me for a long second. 'You know what, he got on the radio and told us to pull over, 'cause we had just run through an IP checkpoint and he wanted to go see what they wanted.'

I shook my head in disbelief. 'You are fucking kidding me. He still didn't get that it was an ambush?'

'No, bro, not at all. He even chewed the shit out of Two Trays for it when we got to the ministry.

'OK, bro, that's not good. Can you ask Two Trays to come see me, but stay out there so it doesn't look suspicious to Yard Dog, OK?'

While Peanut was away, I thought about what he'd just said. How the hell hadn't Yard Dog recognised it as an ambush? Had he not learnt anything during his time in Iraq? The insurgents were renowned for impersonating IPs, and even the real IPs were known to be in with, or sympathetic to, the insurgency. It was one of the reasons why no one did a thing that they said, not unless they were partnered with the US military.

As ever, it was good to lay eyes on Two Trays. The big cheerful fuck always put a smile on my face.

Two Trays gave his signature grin. 'Hey, bud, good to have you back. Peanut said you wanted to see me. What's up?'

'Tell me about the IP ambush on River Road, bro.'

'Ah,' he said, with a knowing look. 'That. Yeah, well, we nearly got shot up by a bunch of fake IP types. I could see it was a bullshit checkpoint, but for some reason Yard Dog couldn't. I told him to bust through, but he still wanted to stop and chat with the fucks, so I got Brownie to hit him in the ass with our vehicle, so we could get the fuck out of there.'

'How did that go down?'

'Well mate, he freaked the fuck out until he heard Stumpy laying some rounds down on the fucks. Even then he still thought it was a real checkpoint. He even tried to chew me out at the ministry, but it was as plain as the massive dick in my pants it was an ambush. Yeah, he would have got us all killed if we had stopped.'

'OK, bro,' I said, pondering the situation. 'Why do you think he didn't see it, even after all the time he's been here with us?'

Two Trays glanced at me. 'Simple. Because you've been in charge. He's never had to make those kinds of decisions before.'

I sat there more than a little shocked, trying to take in all that Two Trays was saying. Had my guys really come that close to getting seriously fucked up while I was away? It was like all those nightmares I'd had in New Zealand coming to pass, all at once.

'And did Peanut tell you about the negligent discharge as well?' Two Trays added.

'You what?'

'Oh, you'll love this… Well, he took us to the crossed swords one Friday for training and started going on about weapon transitions: dropping his AK down and drawing his pistol, like we had never done that before. I asked him if he had unloaded his weapons, so he knelt down, going through the motions with the AK and then the pistol. Then he did the transition drill again while standing in front of us and, "Boom!" The fucker hadn't unloaded his pistol correctly, and there was still a round in the chamber.'

I shook my head in dismay. 'Anyone get hurt?'

'None of us, but who the fuck knows where the bullet ended up, as there were other teams out there training as well. He tried to shrug it off as if it was deliberate, but he was all red in the chops.'

Two Trays stood up and looked me directly in the face. 'Baz, he's not cut out to be C1, or in any command position at all, mate.'

'OK, thanks.' I glanced up at him, meeting his gaze. 'I hear you, bro. Seems I might have fucked up. Trust me, I read you loud and clear.' Then a thought struck me. 'Hey, d'you remember when we met in Jordan at the Bristol Hotel, and Yard Dog said his service was classified?'

'Yeah, I remember.'

'Didn't you think that was a bit strange? I mean, when I hear that old "classified" line, I tend to smell bullshit.'

'Unless it was genuinely classified, in which case you would never even hear about it,' Two Trays pointed out, cleverly.

'It's never really bothered me, as Yard Dog did everything that I asked him to do.'

'Yeah, but that doesn't make him a leader,' Two Trays said. 'So, what are you going to do?'

'I'm not sure yet. What do the rest of the boys think?'

'They were a bit freaked out but got on with the job. They did well.'

'OK, mate, I'll think about what's best to do.' I paused, before brightening. 'So, are the beers ready? Baz needs to get fucked up.'

The weather in Iraq was getting hotter, which made me very happy. The security situation was heating up, too, which also made me happy. It appeared the insurgents operated better in the sun, just like me. As the attacks increased, so did our excuses for getting out into the Red Zone. I wasn't looking for trouble, but I wasn't shying away from it either.

There were a lot more hits all across the country. On Route Irish and MSR Tampa the gun and IED attacks had hit an all-time high. The tricky bastards were hiding bombs in false rocks or filling empty soda cans with explosives and rolling them under cars. It was a bit hit and miss, but they sure were becoming innovative.

They were also filming most of the attacks. I sat down to watch the clips on online platforms like Ogrish and LiveLeak, not for the ghoulish pleasure, but because they were a great training aids. They provided an insight into the insurgents' evolving tactics and thinking, plus their methods, and their favourite strike points, which we might even recognise from the footage.

There was also a bigger surge of foreign fighters coming into the country. This was a development that needed to be taken seriously. If fighters had gone to all the trouble of getting to Iraq, then they were not only highly motivated but likely well-trained. It all meant we had to be even more vigilant. Speed and firepower were still our best friends, and if we thought we were being watched, we would let it be known we were ready and willing to fight. When we travelled anywhere, we had so many guns sticking out of our vehicles that we looked like motorised porcupines, ones that would seriously mess up anyone who dared try and mess with us.

The insurgents weren't singling out any of us in particular; they were just hoping to catch anyone unfortunate enough to swim their way. Any one of us could be in the wrong place at the wrong time when they chose to detonate an IED. Maybe we'd be driving down Irish, shopping at the haji market or drinking in the Green Zone cafe. It would just be our bad luck, and there was no point in taking it personally.

It worked both ways. If some Iraqi's behaviour matched our target-indicator sequence, and we thought our lives were at risk, they could expect to receive a burst of hot lead. The killing of our guys in Fallujah had erased any thought of fair play and manners.

As contractors, we were free to operate on a level playing field with our adversaries. The military had stringent Rules of Engagement (ROEs); we did not. Good old G. W. Bush and his boys had decided that we did not have to follow the same rules and we could therefore, technically, get away with murder. Why they decided that, I'm not sure. None of us would just murder some poor fuck for the sake of it. The truth is, none of the guys on my team wanted to be murderers, and we didn't figure any of the bad guys were particularly targeting us personally.

Of course, we'd all heard the rumours of the $250,000 bounty on the heads of Blackwater contractors, but the insurgents didn't know our names; they had no list.

Or so we thought. That was until Big Army assaulted an insurgency compound and found a laptop that had been taken from one of the boys from another team killed by a roadside IED. Why he had been travelling with his laptop no one seemed to know, but it contained details of loads of personnel, including many of us in Blackwater Commercial. So, it seems the insurgency *did* know our names after all. I would have preferred that they didn't.

Then, shortly after my return to Iraq, a story hit the airwaves that grabbed everyone's attention. There on the team house TV screen was a man in an orange jumpsuit, sat in front of a group of guys standing shoulder to shoulder, dressed all in black, before a large black banner with Arabic writing on it. The guy sat down looked to be European, maybe American. Then the black-clad fucker in the middle started reading off some scripted pages while jabbing a finger at the guy in orange, like he was blaming him personally for something.

After a couple of minutes ranting, the guy dropped the pages, reached into his vest and pulled out a massive Rambo-style hunting knife, while the others pounced on the orange-suited guy and rolled him onto his side. The ringleader with the big-ass knife knelt on the shoulders of his victim, and just as he brought the knife to the poor fucker's neck and started sawing, the TV cut back to the studio. The footage, the newscaster said, was too graphic for television viewing, but he explained that it showed the victim's head being cut off and placed on his lifeless torso, like a trophy.

Holy fuck, I thought, *that's a bit uncalled for.*

The perpetrator was thought to be one Abu Musab al-Zarqawi,

a Jordanian terrorist we had been hearing a lot about recently. The victim was an American by the name of Nick Berg.

'Hey, has anyone pulled it up on Ogrish yet?' I asked.

'Doing it now,' someone replied.

We were used to seeing the unedited propaganda clips on Ogrish and they were always unpleasant, but poor Nick Berg was a soft target, someone who was in Iraq believing he could help the population and make a difference. But now he was dead and, like our boys in Fallujah, his death served as another example of the brutality we could expect if we were ever unfortunate enough to be taken alive.

The orange jumpsuit, we gathered, was a reference to the abuse and torture suffered by Iraqi prisoners at Abu Ghraib prison, which had come to light the previous month. And how had this mistreatment leaked out? One of the American guards had posted the pictures of what they were subjecting the poor orange-clad prisoners to online. *Fuck knows why, the idiots.*

Those pictures quite rightly shocked the world, but why the architects of the war were shocked I had no idea. What did they think was happening while they turned a blind eye? America had changed the rules defining torture, so as to make some of it legal, and that had opened the door for all sorts of barbaric shit to take place. Water boarding, electric shock treatment, anal invasion, dogs and 24/7 loud music were just some of the methods allegedly used. The US also had an international programme for nabbing suspected terrorists. Dubbed 'Extraordinary Rendition', it was just another term for global kidnapping. And we were reaping the whirlwind.

As I watched the full uncut video of Nick Berg's beheading, it occurred to me that we would have to adjust our own policy now, as none of us ever wanted to star in a video like that or, worse still, have our families subjected to the torture of having it splashed across every channel on the endless 24-hour news cycle. This material would be out there and accessible for ever online, and I could not bear the thought of my kids, Jen or any of my family seeing it. The more I thought about it, the more I knew I would sooner kill myself than be captured by these fucks.

I figured it was time for a chat with the boys, who had set up the tables again for another lovely warm night of cold beers, hookah, cigars and song.

'Hey, shitheads,' I began. 'We all saw the beheading today, right? Well, I don't know about you, but I will not be starring in my own execution. So, what I propose is that we all wrap a strip of this red electrical tape around one of our pistol mags.' I held up the roll of red tape. 'If we get into a shit fight and it's pretty fucking obvious that we can't get out, and we are getting short on rounds, then this is to be our last pistol mag.'

I held up one of my pistol mags I had prepared earlier, like some TV chef showing the finished version of the dish he'd just started creating.

'If I get down to this mag, it means that I don't have anything left.' They could see where I was going with this. 'So, if shit comes to shove and there is absolutely no way out of the fight and I get down to this last mag, then I'm going to slot myself right in the fucking head, so I don't get captured.'

I threw the roll of red tape onto the table. 'It's up to you guys what you want to do, but that's my plan.'

Everyone was in agreement. As the tape was ripped off and passed around, I just hoped it would never come to that.

But in spite of the ever-increasing number of attacks, some things are worth risking life and limb for, right?

Sick to the balls of chicken and rice, we'd heard a rumour that a Burger King restaurant had just opened at BIAP. Just the thought of it made our mouths water, so we decided to pay a visit, hoping like hell it was true.

Of course, we would have to be on the lookout for attacks, both from the insurgents, but also so-called good guys. Big Army had decided that the best way to deal with anyone they weren't sure about was to open fire first and seek positive identification later. It didn't matter whether you were friend or foe; getting shot at by those fucks was becoming a regular bad habit. The chief problem was this: they were shit-scared of being obliterated by a VBIED, and when they saw our civilian vehicles, they weren't sure who the hell we were.

To make matters more confusing, some security companies deliberately 'dirtied up' their vehicles and dressed like the locals, in an attempt to blend in. That might have made them less at risk from the insurgents, but it was an open invitation to Big Army to obliterate them. It wasn't difficult to see the soldiers' dilemma.

Typically, when approaching a Big Army convoy, the lead or tail Humvee, depending on the direction of travel, would indicate they had seen us and would wave us through. To make doubly certain all was good, we would give and then receive a thumbs-up and proceed with our flag on the dashboard and our boxers clenched firmly up our asses. Unfortunately, they'd often forget or not bother to radio further up the line, and we would pass warily only to get shot at by some jerk-off in the middle or the far end of the convoy.

Much as we'd love to shoot back, it would be suicidal. These fuckers had very big guns and loved to use them, which was why, when we hit Route Irish with burgers on our minds, our hearts sank as we spied an entire convoy of Humvees parked on the side of the road. As we approached, we did the usual thing: slowing down, waving our US flag, while waiting for a positive reaction. Yard Dog was commanding the front vehicle with me in the rear. He reported back to me that we had been seen and were cleared to proceed past the convoy's tail-end Charlie. So far so good.

Being nice guys, we waved back and sped up a little to pass by as quickly as possible. We got about three vehicles along before we heard the crack of small-arms fire, followed by the deafening *thwack-thwack-thwack* of bullets tearing into steel as they tore into the side of our vehicle. I immediately got my head back behind the side pillar protection, while the guys in the back tried to make themselves as small as possible.

'What the fuck? Cut it out!' I yelled. 'Fuck me, here we go again, those stupid fucks are shooting at us.'

I told Peanut to slow down, grabbed the US flag from the dashboard and slung it out the window, screaming at them that we were friendlies. The guys who were firing just yelled right back and signalled with their arms for us to keep back. The trouble was that we were now halfway down the line, and I could see Yard Dog speeding away, leaving us further behind.

As we slowed right down, I radioed Yard Dog that we had taken fire and were stopping, and I waited for his acknowledgment. I heard nothing.

'OK, once more. Yard Dog this is Baz. We have taken fire. Shots fired, shots fired. Pull over. Over.' Again, no response.

As I continued to watch them draw further away from us, I tried a third time. 'Hey, Yard Dog, pull over, we have taken fire. Over.'

I wasn't sure why he wasn't responding. Maybe his radio had cut out or something. I called Brownie in Yard Dog's vehicle, and he confirmed they could hear me loud and clear.

'What the fuck is going on in there?' I demanded, breaking a wee bit of radio discipline.

To my consternation, Brownie replied that Yard Dog could hear us on everyone's open radio mikes but was frantically telling Bullfrog to ignore my call and carry on driving.

'Really?' I radioed back.

Everyone in my vehicle had heard what had been said, reaching the same conclusion that I had: Yard Dog was bailing on us.

Oh, you had better not be!

'Do you want me to pull over, Baz?' Bullfrog came back. Obviously, he had had enough of listening to Yard Dog's bullshit.

I thought about it for a second. 'No, bro. Keep going until he tells you to stop. I want to see what happens.'

I radioed again, but this time making a complete break with radio protocol. 'Hey, cunt. Pull the fuck over, we have just been hit.'

While this had been going on, the Big Army guys had finally got their shit together and waved us through. I waved back and smiled while thinking fuck you very much, as there was nothing else that I could do. There was no point in us making life any harder on ourselves by calling them out, and besides, relations between the military and security contractors were getting pretty tense, so it was best to play nice.

By this time I just hoped Yard Dog had a damn good explanation for ignoring my radio calls and abandoning us. About two miles down Irish I saw Bullfrog had finally pulled over. The boys were pulling security, while Yard Dog was standing by the vehicle with a shit-eating grin on his face. We pulled up behind, noticing that we had picked up a flat tyre, no doubt from one of the bullets Big Army had sent our way.

We got out and inspected the side of our vehicle, counting the bullet holes. One in the back right tyre; one in the front door where I sit; one in the right pillar arm where the doors close and where my head goes, and another in the rear right door. Considering we had been a moving target, we had to give it to the shooter; it wasn't a bad group, to be honest.

'That boy deserves a medal,' said Stumpy.

Had we been driving a fraction faster, a fraction slower, or had he aimed a little higher, we could well have had those babies come through the open window and into us.

Bullfrog and the guys from the front vehicle gathered around to inspect the holes. We all agreed that we had been very lucky indeed. The guys knew the shit was about to hit the fan, so they got busy changing the flat tyre, while I pulled Yard Dog off to one side.

'Did you hear me call you on the radio?' I asked, patiently.

'Yeah, I heard you,' he admitted, still grinning.

This was not the answer I wanted to hear, and my blood was starting to boil. 'You heard me tell you we had been hit and to pull over?'

'Yes,' he repeated.

'Then why the fuck didn't you answer my call and pull over?' I asked, trying to keep my voice calm but not doing a very good job at hiding the look of anger in my eyes. Yard Dog stared down at his feet as his grin left his face. He knew that I knew the answer, but he tried to laugh it off.

'I thought you were joking. I mean, I knew you were OK. I just wanted to get in front of the convoy.'

'You thought I was joking?' I repeated, very slowly and deliberately. 'You thought I was joking?' Once more, only louder. 'You motherfucker. You knew we were OK?' I repeated his excuse. 'How the fuck did you know we were OK from way the fuck ahead of us? Look at the vehicle,' I said, my eyes boring holes in him.

I gestured at the Blazer, not giving a fuck that I was vocal enough for all the boys to hear. 'Here, cunt, take a look and tell me how you knew we were OK.'

He looked at the side without moving any closer. 'Well, you guys are OK, so all good,' he said, fishing for an escape.

By now I was seething. After all these months running together, there was no way Yard Dog could possibly think I was joking.

'You know I do not fucking joke around when we are on runs. Not ever. Jokes are for the team house, never on the road. You fucking know that, don't you?'

'Yes, but—'

'No fucking "buts". The time for "buts" is over.' With that I just looked him over disgustedly, letting my eyes say more than my words ever could.

I could see him now as he really was: he was scared, and he was chicken shit. If we had been under an insurgent attack, he would most likely have run to save himself. I don't think he even realised what the rest of the boys in his wagon would have done if he had tried to run. I have absolutely no doubt they would have neutralised him and come back to help us out, even if it had meant shooting him in the head and dumping his ass out of the vehicle.

All that bullshit talk of 'classified service'; I figured the fucker had no service record at all; he was all shit. But why the secrecy? Why all the innuendo, instead of just coming clean? There would have been no shame in it. But now I could only look at him with the same distain I'd felt for Randy back in the early days of Blackwater Commercial. I gazed at Yard Dog as if I was looking at someone I hated; like someone I didn't know any more. The curtain had been ripped down, and he knew it. From that point on he was dead to me.

I do not have a problem with anyone who doesn't have military experience. However, Yard Dog seemed to know that without military experience he shouldn't have been there in the first place, which was correct. Iraq was not the place to start a new career, especially not in this business. Of course, there would always be learning and adapting in situ; hell, even I had had to go through that phase. We all did. But the least everyone should know is the basics of running a combat military PSD. But the worst thing for me was the feeling of having been lied to.

After the fizzing in my head had died down a little, I looked Yard Dog squarely in the eye and told him, 'You're done.'

I turned and left him standing there with the realisation that his time was now over. I wasn't going to fire him, but I didn't need to. Leaving would be the only way for him to save what little face he had left. He needed to fuck off and think about life and decide if he could actually do this job. It felt like a massive let-down for me personally, as it was me who had made him 2IC in the first place. He had managed to bullshit me this whole time, which was about the worst of all.

The guys had nearly finished the tyre change, so we killed time taking pics of each other and the near misses while standing like sitting ducks on Irish. We were still doing this when the Big Army convoy that had shot us up drove on by. We smiled and waved at them while mouthing 'you useless fucks' under our breath. To really put the icing on a shitty day, when we finally got to Burger King it was closed; they had sold out of burgers less than three hours after opening.

Hungry, but very grateful to be alive, we drove back to the team house. I had swapped Yard Dog out for Two Trays commanding the lead vehicle, and it was a very quiet drive. We arrived at the team house, and I pulled Yard Dog to one side, calmly telling him how I felt deceived and let down. The rest of the guys filed into the house for some chow, and as they passed him the looks on their faces revealed their own sense of betrayal.

'There's no excuse for what you did and I'm past wanting any,' I told him. 'Go pack your shit.' Yard Dog looked surprised. Maybe he'd hoped that during drive back I'd softened my stance about what had happened and how I felt. 'I'll go tell Brian you'll be on the next CASA flight out.'

Seeing that I wasn't joking, Yard Dog lowered his head. 'OK,' he replied. 'No hard feelings?'

'Nah, bro, no hard feelings. Take some time and get your shit sorted.'

We shook hands, but I held back from the man-hug.

As surprising as it may sound, I felt absolutely no animosity towards him. Yes, I boil really fast, but I cool down just as fast too. To his credit, Yard Dog had taken it as well as could be expected. I was certain the rest of the guys would be relieved to see him go, even if it was just to sort out his head and his priorities. They knew he wouldn't ever be in charge of them again, and that was a good thing. I gathered the guys, explained what was happening and told them to expect a BIAP run the next day.

While we were debriefing as normal, two armoured SUVs carrying the BW crew from Al-Hillah pitched up at the team house. We chewed the shit for a bit as they unloaded their vehicles. They told us that attacks between Baghdad and the Al-Hillah turn-off had mushroomed, and there were plenty more down Najaf way too. They seemed to think something big was brewing there again. *Round Two*, I thought. You couldn't fault the Mahdi Army for persistence.

Among the Hillah team was an African American dude I hadn't had the chance to meet before, name of Bruce. He was former US

Army and he seemed to talk with a bit of a stutter. I didn't think any more of it but went to tell Brian that Yard Dog would be heading out on the next CASA flight. Brian was cool with that, particularly after I explained what had happened and my concerns about Yard Dog's 'classified' record. He revealed there were others who suspected Yard Dog's story too, himself included.

Yard Dog was duly added to the next day's flight manifest. I could have put him on the Mambas' list for them to run him to BIAP, but I decided it was best to keep team business within the team. The Mamba guys didn't need to know.

Peanut seemed to have a new skip in his step and had gone as far as setting up the beers, table and chairs himself, without having made the shit list that earned that job. We gathered and cracked a few beers to toast another day of survival. Bruce and a couple of the Hillah boys came and sat with us, and we offered them a beer. We guessed they would decline, as they had to head back to base at Al-Hillah, but you have to at least offer, right? The last thing you want is to be known as the team that doesn't even offer a fucking beer.

While we chilled, I got talking to Bruce and a few of the others. Yard Dog had finished packing and come down to join us, but if he had been expecting a big send-off, he was to be sorely disappointed, for there was only Two Trays, Brownie, Bullfrog, Peanut and me from the team. Not even wanting to share a beer with him, Brownie got up and walked off. It was a move that was timed perfectly, and it left no room for interpretation as to how the guys felt. Yard Dog noticed the snub and a look of shame came back to his face.

'Where's Stumpy and the others?' he asked.

'I think Stumpy's gone to work out,' I replied. Not that Stumpy had ever worked out in his life, the little fat fuck. 'The rest are...' I stumbled, tiring of lying. 'Fuck, bro, work it out.'

He had put their lives – all our lives – at risk. Although they wouldn't hold grudges, this was their way of saying, 'Fuck you very much, now fuck off. Don't let the CASA ramp hit you in the ass on the way out.'

A couple more of the Hillah guys came over and joined us, and this actually helped lift the mood a little. Bruce had a nice friendly manner and wasn't privy to the beer-table rules governing conversation. Right off the bat he admitted he was there to make money for his family. He had a five-year plan that included saving every dollar he could to buy a nice house back in the US, sending his kids to good schools and retiring.

With what we were earning, this was all doable, and since the beer-table rules had been shit-canned, we went around explaining our personal five-year plans, which were all pretty similar to Bruce's. After an hour or so, their team leader emerged and they mounted up to head back to the Hillah team house, with a quick stop-over at the IZ PX on their way out of Baghdad. We said our goodbyes and they fucked off, leaving a big cloud of dust to waft over the yard and settle on our beers.

'Bruce was a nice guy,' I remarked. 'Was it just me or does he have a bit of a stutter?'

'Yeah, nice guy,' Two Trays agreed.

'No, man, that's just the way they talk,' Yard Dog cut in.

'What d'you mean?' I asked, not sure what he was on about and who he meant by 'they'.

'You know, black people. They talk like that.'

'Like what?' I asked, still confused.

'Black people,' he said again. 'They deliberately talk with a bit of a stutter to show they're from the street.'

'Fuck off,' I said. 'He had a real stutter.'

'No, I've seen it plenty of times: that's how they talk,' Yard Dog insisted.

I looked at Two Trays, who just rolled his eyes so far back in his head he could see his own ass. I wasn't sure if Yard Dog was on drugs or just being a racist dick, but I'd had enough either way. I could feel any pity I'd felt for the fuck transforming back into anger. I leant forward on my chair, making eye contact with him from the other side of the table.

'Dude, you're already in the shit, don't make it worse for yourself. Shut the fuck up.'

Two Trays was staring at him with a look of: *How fuckin' dumb are you, bro?*

I just couldn't get why this idiot couldn't read the situation.

Yard Dog sat back and cracked another beer, but any goodwill was gone. I hadn't had much experience working with African Americans. It still confused me why they weren't just called Americans. But I wasn't going to let Yard Dog shit on someone I thought was a nice guy. I'm half-Māori, and it made me wonder what shit Yard Dog said about the likes of us, behind our backs. Hell, he may even have been right, but I wasn't in the mood to let him have any victories, no matter how small.

An hour later, we saw the Little Birds heading out somewhere. They were always buzzing over us on some mission or another, and we soon found out what it was this time. It was not good news. The Hillah team guys had been hit on MSR Tampa by a massive roadside IED. Their first vehicle had made it past safely, but the second one caught the full brunt of the blast, somersaulting in the air before coming down on its wheels facing the opposite way to which it had been travelling.

Bruce and one other person riding in that vehicle had been

killed – instantly, I hoped. The surviving guys had called for the Little Birds to provide air-support and laid down some rounds. The insurgents waited until everyone was gone before moving in and filming the aftermath: the bloodied scene and the abandoned items the guys had just purchased at the PX, an hour before.

The footage showed not only the gloating insurgents but, once again, locals attacking the vehicle, hitting it with their footwear before picking it over for whatever items of value they could carry away. The video commentary claimed the insurgents had made a 'glorious attack on the CIA'. Fuck knows why they still believed this. Maybe they saw Blackwater as a CIA company because of some of our contracts? Or maybe they presumed all contractors were a front for the CIA? Either way, it was bad news for us.

The killing of Bruce and his buddy was a stark reminder of just how close death was for us all. It was one of the reasons we ran as hard as we did and celebrated in the evening after every day we survived. We were playing our own version of Russian Roulette, hoping we could dodge the bullet for at least one more day.

I had once thought there were good and bad Iraqis: those who didn't try to kill us were good, and those that did try to kill us were bad. By now, though, I didn't really differentiate. I preferred to think they were all bad until proven otherwise.

Later that night I made a call home to Jen, just to hear her voice. She was my rock and one I desperately needed and missed right now. She had never once questioned me being in Iraq, but she understandably didn't want to live her life permanently stressed out, and she had all her friends reminding her what a shitstorm Iraq was becoming.

The day we'd reconnected while I was back in NZ, she'd just got back from seeing her friends at a local cafe, and they had tried to convince her not to see me. To say they didn't like me was an understatement: they hated me for the way I had treated her in the past. But deep down, Jen knew we had some crazy connection and I'll be forever grateful that she didn't listen to them. Now, they were calling her with every story that made the news from Iraq, asking if I was OK or whether she had heard from me. Maybe they were secretly hoping I'd be the news.

No, that couldn't be it, right?

The next day we drove Yard Dog out to BIAP, and he said very little during the drive. There wasn't much of a fanfare from the guys either; just a few of them offered a 'later, bro'. But when all was said and done, he'd done a reasonable job, and I hoped to see him again but in a position he could handle. We said our goodbyes, but I still had one thing I needed to take care of. As a way of building a brotherhood, I had presented each of the guys with something to show they were now part of my team. It was a silver skull ring, a batch of which I had had made up in New Zealand. The centrepiece was a flaming skull's head with a cigar gripped in its teeth.

Just before he turned to walk away, I leant forward to Yard Dog. 'I'll take the ring until you get back, bro.'

He looked at me in disbelief. 'You're joking, right?'

'No bro, I'm not joking. Remember, I never joke on the road.'

He slowly took the ring off and placed it in my hand. The final act of being cast out.

'No hard feelings,' I said, then turned and walked away.

CHAPTER 10

As time wore on, we got busy running tasks all over the country, including trips north to Kurdish Iraq. I found the Kurds to be a completely different breed of people from their Arab countrymen. I'm not even sure if calling them 'countrymen' is right, as they don't tend to have a lot of love for each other. Their language is different, their flag is different, their religions and customs are different, and they sure as shit look different.

When I made my first trip to Kurdistan the thing that struck me most was that instead of black hair and Saddam moustaches everywhere, there were women with blonde tresses and men with bright red hair. Generally, the Kurds are stockier than Iraqi Arabs, with many of the men wearing the national dress: a drab olive military-style outfit. They have a very long and proud fighting history, and after the US invasion they jumped at the chance to establish their independence.

They'd had a shit time under Saddam, who played different Kurdish factions off against each other. He forced Kurds out of their homes in the city of Kirkuk and resettled the area with Arabs to control the oil fields. Then, in the final days of the eight-year

Iran–Iraq War, Saddam let his cousin, 'Chemical Ali', gas the shit out of the Kurdish border town of Halabja. The attack on 16 March 1988 wiped out between 3,000 to 5,000 people.

Driving north, the landscape changes from flat brown desert to rolling verdant terrain, complete with mountains, rivers and ravines. The temperature is cooler, and the winters can be downright miserable, unless you like rain and snow that is. It is like being in a completely different country, and the Kurds strictly enforced their borders, encouraging the Arabs to go only as far north as Mosul, Iraq's second-largest city.

This made Kurdistan more stable and somewhat safer than the rest of Iraq. The insurgents seemed to have accepted that Kurdistan was pretty much a 'no-go' area. The difference in looks and language made Iraqi Arabs stick out like dog's balls on a pigeon, so any attack would be harder to disguise and therefore easier to counter. But that didn't stop the insurgents from trying, and they would occasionally score a successful hit, like the one they carried out on the Kurdish Parliament in the city of Erbil. It was enough to keep the Kurds on their toes.

Erbil felt so much more like a normal city than Baghdad. There were plazas, shops, schools, functioning traffic lights and even road rules – well, kind of. Best of all, there were plenty of liquor stores and bars in the Christian area.

The gleaming form of the newly built, high-rise Sheraton Hotel was somewhat spoilt by the anti-blast T walls and Jersey walls that surrounded it, but this would be our base for a good few days while we ran our client to and from meetings at another hotel set higher up in the hills on the outskirts of the city.

The reception area was not unlike so many other smart international hotels the world over – that was, if the smart international hotels you used had armed guards, sniffer dogs, bag and ID checks and metal detectors. Unlike the rest of Iraq, the Erbil Sheraton didn't allow weapons inside.

This was a first for us and we didn't like the prospect of not being armed, but rules are rules, so we took off our war rigs. I escorted the client to check-in, while the guys squared away the vehicles in the hotel car park. I was still at reception sorting out the rooms when there was a noisy commotion at the entrance. Someone or something had set off the walk-through metal detectors and they began to beep like fuck.

Without looking up, I grabbed the client and moved him behind a solid concrete and marble pillar, so as to shield him from any blast or attack. I felt especially vulnerable without a weapon. After about ten seconds of nothing, I peeked around the corner and saw that the hotel guards were gathered around the bleeping offender and were giving him orders in Kurdish. I couldn't help but wonder what kind of idiot had tried to bring their weapon into the hotel.

Despite the language barrier, it was clearly signposted with simple diagrams that no weapons were allowed. Then, through a small gap in the crowd, I was finally able to see the identity of the culprit: *Stumpy. Who else?* The guards were pointing and waving their hands, instructing him to open his bag while the little shit wore his best 'I don't speak Kurdish' expression and tried to feign ignorance.

Eventually Stumpy gave up protesting and the guards took his bag off to one side, indicating for him to open it. He slowly unzipped it, and I saw one of the guards take a hesitant peek inside, before glancing up at Stumpy, then back inside the bag, then back at Stumpy, who was doing his best to avoid eye contact, pretending that he was unaware of anything in the bag that might interest the guards.

The guard reached inside and pulled out the little fucker's pistol. He showed it to Stumpy, who did his best to look astonished. Then the guard removed three 9mm pistol mags, which he placed next to the pistol. The guard delved inside for a third time and rummaged around before suddenly stopping. With his hand still inside the bag, he slowly raised his eyes to Stumpy, then, like a magician producing a rabbit from a hat, he dramatically pulled out two M67 high-explosive fragmentation grenades.

The other guards began jabbering away in Kurdish, which needed no translating: *Fuck me, this guy's insane.* As the guard continued, it was like watching a child play Lucky Dip; each time he reached his hand inside the bag, it would re-emerge with another banned piece of lethal ordnance.

When they finished, the total amount of contraband Stumpy had tried to sneak into the hotel amounted to one Glock pistol, three full Glock magazines, two M67 hand grenades, one AR-15 rifle bayonet, an assortment of loose 5.56mm rounds, one Gerber knife and about twenty rounds of linked 5.56mm SAW belt ammo.

After I had checked us in, I thought it prudent to go see the guard, who was busy telling Stumpy to go and lock away the pile of weaponry – apart from the Gerber knife, which, for some reason, he was allowed to keep. I felt I should explain that he was actually with me and not some little fat hairy insurgent with a Prince Albert, which, by the way, had also set off the metal detector.

I don't know if it was that or the large amount of weaponry he had tried to smuggle in, but Stumpy was guaranteed to receive special scrutiny every time he came into the hotel from then on.

With the first meeting not until the following afternoon, the client wanted to use the downtime to see the sights of Erbil, which meant I had to split the team into two groups: one to recce the meeting venue, and another to take him around town. Under normal circumstances, I would be reluctant to let a client go out and about like that or to split the team, but he was a typical, down-to-earth Aussie bloke called John, who I happened to like.

I made some calls, and it turned out that my old Unit buddy 'T', who we'd run into while lost in Nasiriyah and trying to navigate back to Baghdad with just a tea towel, was now based in Erbil. He confirmed that Erbil was about as safe as you could get in Iraq, but he said to remain vigilant. His client was going to be at the same meeting as mine, so he gave me directions and told me he'd see me there. Feeling reassured, I split the team in two: Two Trays and his crew would go off and recce the route and venue; my group would take the client to Erbil market.

The city centre market nestles below Erbil's very impressive hilltop citadel, a fortified mound dating back to around 5,000 BC. Finding it was not a problem, but getting a parking space was another matter and, since the people of Erbil followed the basic rules of the road, it did not seem appropriate to use the muzzle of a gun to persuade people to move out of our way, as we might have in Baghdad. This sucked.

I told Peanut to drop us off and to find a space as close as possible, staying in contact with me by phone or radio, depending on which one would work. Needless to say, the BW comms were no closer to being sorted, meaning we were still relying on line-of-sight radios and shit cell-phone service. I told Peanut I would send SITREPS (situation reports) every twenty-five minutes, as best as I could, but not to panic unless I missed a few or he got none at all. If he heard gunfire or an explosion, then he should make for our drop-off point, which would serve as the emergency rendezvous.

According to T, openly carrying weapons in public in Erbil was not acceptable and we really didn't want to attract any undue attention. Besides, this wasn't like Baghdad, where we would roll heavy to give the impression that fucking with us was not a good idea.

I instructed the guys to wear a jacket over their weapons, to hide them from view, but when Stumpy tried it the jacket hid fuck all; it still looked like a gun under a coat. Reluctantly, they opted to carry only pistols, leaving the long guns in the vehicle with Peanut. My MP5, on the other hand, and Bullfrog's folding-stock short-barrel AK were no problem, ensuring we had at least two forms of automatic fire if needed. Stumpy was reunited with his grenades, so he happily brought those along too.

The bustling market was a maze of alleys and walkways, all set under the cover of corrugated iron roofing. A tantalising array of smells, colours and sounds hit me, as eager stall owners vied for attention. There seemed to be every imaginable type of spice, herb and vegetable there, along with knockoff-brand running shoes, T-shirts, soccer jerseys and a shit-ton of cheap Chinese plastic toys.

It was noisy and cramped, with each stall jammed up next to its neighbour; the sort of environment where you needed to have your head on a swivel. The walkways between the stalls were worn smooth by centuries of foot traffic, and I could only wonder at the millions upon millions of feet that had trodden this way before. But at the same time, my security head told me it would be a great place for an insurgent to lurk.

The place was packed: children running all over the place, women bartering with the stall owners and everyone stopping without warning to chat with someone or other. It was a sensory overload, as I tried to scan hundreds of faces, hands and bags on the lookout for anything suspicious. Fuck me, it was all on.

I put Bullfrog in the lead to clear a passage while I walked with the client. Stumpy was doing his best to blend in, keeping a few metres behind us, hopefully far enough away that he would not be immediately linked to us, but close enough to spot if anyone paid us a little too much attention. In effect, he was a walking QRF. Given he was also a short, hairy little fuck who stood about the same height as most of the Kurds, hopefully they'd just think he was one of them, only uglier.

After twenty minutes I tried calling Peanut by phone and then on the radio but, predictably, had no luck. I'd just have to try again later when we were in a better area. I could sense eyes on us, and I was beginning to find it unnerving. I didn't necessarily feel we were in any immediate danger. The looks were more curious than hostile, but I didn't like being the focus of everyone's gaze, and it was safe to assume that word of us being there would go from stall to stall like a dose of the clap in a religious commune.

It also felt claustrophobic. I didn't like being surrounded by so many people, with everyone pushing to get past. I could see the vendors being pulled this way and that by whoever grabbed their attention, but I realised it was just the way they did business. I had to adjust and keep moving forward, ensuring that the client didn't get too engrossed.

When people tried to push past, I would move slightly closer to the client. If they came within my personal circle of comfort, I would move them out with an 'accidental' nudge. Most of the time this worked, but on more than one occasion I had to give the offender a stronger shove and a bit of a death stare to achieve the desired result.

The other problem was keeping track of where we all were. Bullfrog would turn a corner thinking we were behind him, only to find we had wandered off in another direction. It was impossible to yell out to him above the deafening noise of the place. Sometimes, even our line-of-sight comms didn't work here. It was a matter of constant head swivels, eye gestures and nods to get messages across.

Every so often the client would see something he liked and want to stop. It was usually some crappy souvenir: coloured stones, trinkets or the like. He would do his best to bargain with the vendor, but he always ended up paying more than he should. After a few stops, he was having trouble carrying it all. He turned, holding out a fist full of shopping bags. I looked at his hand, then at him, and gave him my best look of: *You got two shows of getting me to carry your shit, mate: no show and shitshow.*

'Can you carry these, please?' he asked, gesturing at the bags again.

'No, I can't,' I said, before returning to look for the bad guys.

He got the message that I had a job to do, which wasn't being his personal shopping assistant. He turned back, fumbling the bags higher onto his wrist and continued shopping. *Good. Now that we know our respective roles we can carry on.*

After an hour flopping around the market and me still having no luck sending Peanut a SITREP, I was glad when the client called it quits and we somehow found our way out of there. I was finally able to radio Peanut and twenty minutes later he pulled up in front of us, we got in the vehicle and made our way back to the hotel.

It had been a great learning experience for the guys, who hadn't ever faced that sort of situation in Baghdad; that feeling of being exposed in the confines of a crowd, when you're battling with problems of orientation, communication and more. During the debrief back at the hotel, the guys shared the discomfort and unease they'd felt in the market but appreciated that it was a useful experience. I told them they had handled it well.

Around 15:00, Two Trays radioed that he was back at the hotel with the other team, so we met in my room. He started by showing me what was what on a map, explaining the time it took them to drive to the rendezvous, the route and any obstacles along the way. He told us the meeting hotel was heavily guarded by the Asayish and the Peshmerga, the former being the Kurdish police intelligence unit, while the latter are the famed Kurdish military, who had gained a fearsome reputation fighting Saddam over the years. Both were top-tier and hardened outfits. They knew how to lock shit down, and both felt a burning hatred towards the insurgents, which made us feel pretty damn good. To add to that, the hotel's position perched on the hilltop meant that any hostile approach from whichever direction was sure to be spotted.

After Two Trays was finished, I told the guys we would be rolling out at 10:00 the next morning. They headed out to prepare the vehicles and to ensure all our kit was ready.

The drive the next day led us over some very steep, amazingly dramatic landscapes. Although we were in Kurdistan, the friendly north, we still rode like we were in Baghdad, leaving nothing to chance: *safeties off, eyes open, let's go.*

Once we arrived, we escorted the client inside. I could tell that the other attendees were people of some significance: the number of gleaming Land Cruisers pulling up with more guards than might be hired by a Hollywood star testified to that. It was going to be a long day, and once the meeting was close to getting underway, I found a place for me and the guys to chill out.

One of the last arrivals was escorted by a team that looked very familiar: it was made up of my former SAS mates from New Zealand. 'T' was among them, and I couldn't help but wonder if their client knew the calibre of the guys who were protecting him. New

Zealanders in general, and Māoris in particular, embody a fierce, warrior culture, which is perhaps why our national sport and religion is rugby. We love the physicality, teamwork and comradeship, and we have consistently been at the very top of that game for many years. We like a good fight and will give 100 per cent every time.

When the early British settlers had tried to do to the Māoris what they had done to other native cultures throughout the British Empire, we strongly resisted being enslaved, dehumanised and eradicated. Perhaps that was why I felt some innate sympathy for the Iraqi people, who mostly viewed the Coalition forces as Crusader invaders.

By now there were least 500 former New Zealand soldiers on the ground in Iraq, working with the various security companies, and we had earned a fearsome reputation. It wouldn't be until 2006 that we suffered our first casualty, which we all would take very hard. The death of a brother soldier and countryman was something we would take personally, even if we didn't know him. It's the bond of a small nation, I guess. Plus, coming from a tribal culture means that we tend to feel it harder still.

With the clients safely in the meeting, I had time to catch up with T and the rest of the boys. Apparently, there was another group of the New Zealand boys based in Kirkuk, and they were getting hit pretty hard, but like true professionals they were handling it well. He liked working for the British security company, but from what he could see they had a very different way of running things, and largely because they were lacking a lot of basic kit. It wasn't the first time I had heard that.

For some reason, they weren't allowed to carry long guns out of their vehicles, only their pistols, which mostly meant the antiquated Browning 9mm, which first came into service in 1903. Don't get me wrong, it's a great pistol, but there are much better ones out there now. Some of the guys also had a shortage of body armour with plates. As for getting promoted, that was near-impossible unless you were British, came from a certain regiment or public school or had friends in the right places.

A lot of the problems sounded familiar to me. Promotion was definitely not one of our issues, but what they did have that we didn't was good long-range communication. They could talk to each other from just about anywhere across the length and breadth of Iraq. That being said, we had addressed most of the other issues they raised. I told T that when I got back to Baghdad, I would put them in touch with one of our excellent fixers, who knew how to get a lot of the stuff they were lacking.

After several hours, the meeting ended with handshakes, kisses and a rush to get the fuck out of there. Everyone departed like the beginning of the Indy 500, with Land Cruisers and chase vehicles roaring down the hill at breakneck speed. Our guy wasn't that high on the totem pole and was a pretty chilled-out Aussie, so I decided to hang back.

On the drive back to Erbil, he didn't share too much about the meeting, but he did indicate that things weren't exactly going to plan for the Coalition. Apparently, the Kurds wanted independence quickly and had expected the US to bring a lot more to the table. They knew they held most of the cards – oil, air bases, tough fighting units – and they were only too aware of their value.

Of course, a big part of the trouble for the US was that the Kurds had been fighting a long-term guerrilla war with Turkey, and as Turkey was a NATO ally, the US couldn't be seen to be supporting the Kurds. Things weren't turning out to be quite as simple as the US had anticipated prior to invading Iraq. Things in the Middle East seldom are.

I settled the client back at the hotel and we headed for a few beers at the hotel bar. There were a couple of guys that Bullfrog and Two Trays knew from another company, so they came over and joined us. We made our introductions and soon they got talking about home. One of the guys, Wingnut, was telling us about his girlfriend back in the States and the problems he was having. He wanted to know whether it was normal, her doing the things she was doing.

'What things are those?' I asked, intrigued.

'Well,' he said, pausing to think and taking a gulp of his beer. 'We're earning damn good money here; $400 per day is not to be sneezed at, eh.'

'Too right,' we agreed, without telling him what we were on.

'Well,' he continued, 'every time I check my account, I can see she's almost maxed it out.'

'What do you mean?' I asked, kind of knowing what he meant but wanting to hear the meaty details.

'Well, every day I can see withdrawals of large sums from the account. So, at the end of every month when my pay goes in, I'm no better off than before.'

'That's bullshit,' Two Trays remarked.

We all looked at each other. It didn't take a rocket surgeon to figure out what this lady was up to. What *was* confusing was why Wingnut couldn't work it out for himself, but then, as they say, love is blind.

'You mean to tell me,' I said, 'that she is taking the money out as quick as it is going in?'

'Yeah. So it seems.'

'What's she doing with it?' Peanut asked.

'Fucked if I know. I can't see anything being used on the credit card, and the other bills like water and power are on an automatic payment.'

There was a pause to see if the penny would eventually drop. It didn't.

'Dude,' I said. 'It's obvious.' Someone had to let the poor fucker know.

'It is?' he asked.

'Yes, mate, she is taking cash out of your account and putting it into an escape fund.'

'An escape fund?' he asked.

'An escape fund, my dim-witted brother, is a hidden account in which she will accumulate your money like a fucking chipmunk storing nuts, ready for the day she leaves you.'

'You really think so?'

'Yeah, bro, I really think so.'

'Is there anything else?' Two Trays asked.

By now Wingnut was in too deep not to continue and, with us hanging on his every word, he told us how, on a holiday to the Bahamas, his girlfriend had got talking to another guy at the pool, gone back to his room and not returned until three in the morning. At least Wingnut didn't need us to spell out what she had been doing.

'Come here, mate,' I told him, 'you need a hug.'

By this time we were actually starting to feel sorry for the dumb fuck.

Wingnut seemed like an excellent guy. Dumb as fuck, but an excellent guy nevertheless. He would, in my opinion, be a great catch for any deserving woman, but, as it was, he had some serious problems. Soon, my evil mind was churning. I didn't want to let this go, especially as Wingnut was obviously screaming for help.

'Bro, I've got an idea,' I announced. 'Why don't you call her and clarify this right here and now? Not the fucking Bahamas part, that's done and dusted, but the bank account. That's something you can get under control immediately.'

'How?'

'Mate, just tell her you know about her bullshit and it's over.'

'Yeah,' the others chimed in for support.

'No, I can't,' he muttered.

'Why the hell not?' Stumpy asked.

'Well, she doesn't like it when I call her.'

There was a stunned silence from us all.

'Hang on, hang on, bro,' said Stumpy. 'She fucks around on you on holiday, empties your bank account as soon as your monthly money goes in, and, for the icing on the cake, doesn't like it when you call her? You got yourself a fuckin' keeper there, bro.'

We all burst out laughing. But I had to help the poor fuck, so I cut back in. 'Listen, Wingnut, I have a plan.'

'What's that?' he asked.

'Give me her number and I'll call her on my phone.'

'Why?'

'I'll pretend I'm from your company and ask her if she has heard from you recently. I'll say you have been kidnapped or something and I want to know if anyone has reached out to her, you know, for a ransom.'

'Then what?' he asked.

'Is she down as your next of kin in your company insurance?' I asked.

'Yeah.'

'Of course she is,' Two Trays added.

'I'll tell her that there might be a big pay-out for her if you wind up missing or dead.'

Eventually, Wingnut seemed convinced that the plan was sound. 'OK,' he said. 'Here's her number.'

'Hey, what the fuck is this princess's name?'

'Kate,' he said.

'OK, here we go.'

I composed myself as best I could and told the others to shut the fuck up. I put on my serious face before dialling the number.

'Ah, hello, is this Kate?' I asked, trying to sound really serious, as all the guys leant in to listen.

'Yes, this is Kate.'

'Hello Kate, my name is Baz. I'm calling you from Iraq.'

'Oh, yeah,' the voice on the other end said, without any noticeable sense of worry or concern.

'Yeah, I'm calling to ask you if you have heard from or had any contact with Greg lately?' Greg was Wingnut's real name.

'No, I haven't. Why?' There was still not a hint of any concern.

'Well, your name is down as his next of kin and beneficiary for his life insurance policy.' I paused to make sure she'd heard that. 'There was an incident involving his team and we haven't seen or heard from Greg in a few days. Now, I don't want to get you upset or alarmed, but we suspect he may have been kidnapped and is possibly being held hostage.'

'No, I haven't heard from him,' she repeated.

'OK,' I said, 'I'm his company manager, so I just need to check that there have been no calls, offering proof of life or anything?'

'No,' she said again, only this time I'd noticed a slight change in the inflection in her voice. The word 'no' seemed to have been dragged out just a split second too long.

'OK,' I said. 'It's really important that if he or someone connected to him does call you, you immediately call me on this number, OK?'

'Um, yeah, OK,' Kate replied, still without the slightest hint of any concern for Brother Wingnut. 'Um, so that... Um so...'

She wanted to ask me something, but I could tell she was struggling for the right words. 'Yes, go ahead,' I said.

We all moved in closer to the phone. 'So, you said I'm on his life insurance, right?'

'Yes, that's correct.'

'Well, just suppose...'

I waited.

'If he's been kidnapped and they kill him, or something stupid like that,' she said, followed by a giggle, 'I mean, how much is... you know. If they have, well, how much is his insurance worth, and how soon before I would get it?'

BOOM, trap slams shut. Do not pass go and mostly certainly do not collect 200 fucking dollars. *Holy fuck.* We all looked at the phone in astonishment, then at Wingnut.

'Well,' I started to say, trying to remain serious, but Wingnut lunged forward and grabbed the phone. He stood up and looked around, desperately trying to find somewhere private to talk. We were all so stunned we just sat there in silence.

Not finding anywhere to run and tired of bouncing off the walls trying, Wingnut just went for it right there and then. 'Hey, Kate! Kate, it's Greg. What the fuck do you mean, how long before you get the insurance? I'm here and alive. That was a test and you just failed!'

At that moment Greg finally managed to stomp off out of earshot. A pity, but finally, hopefully, the penny had dropped. We all agreed that Kate was not a nice person.

Several minutes later Wingnut was back, and we were all anxious to hear what had transpired. 'She's pissed off with me for fooling her,' he announced, morosely.

'*Fooling her*?' Stumpy repeated, not sure he had heard right.

'Bro, you've been getting right royally ass-fucked, *and she's pissed off*?' I queried. 'Wake up, bro. Wake up.'

Wingnut sat in silence for a bit, as the truth of the situation slowly sank in. 'Oh well, I'll change the accounts and kick her ass out of my house.'

'Yeah, bro,' we all agreed.

'Get it done and get it done now.'

'Let's have a beer.'

I felt no guilt at all over what I had done. If anything, I had saved a hard-working brother from impoverishment and ridicule. I decided to call Jen. It was about two in the morning back in New Zealand, but I knew she wouldn't mind. As I dialled the number, I signalled to Wingnut to listen in.

Within a couple of dial tones a sleepy voice answered.

'Hi, baby,' I said.

'Hello, baby,' she replied. 'Is everything OK?'

'Yes. I just wanted to tell you that I miss you and love you.'

'I miss and love you too.'

'OK baby, go back to sleep. Good night.'

'Good night,' she replied, and I hung up.

'There you go, bro, that's how a call home should go,' I told Wingnut.

'Yeah,' he said. 'You're a lucky guy.' He glanced around at us all. 'Hey, boys, thanks for that. I knew she was using me, but I didn't want to face it, I guess.'

'No sweat, brother. Glad we could help.'

The one thing we all needed, other than knowing that we were part of a great team who would do anything for each other, was to have someone at home who loved and cared for us. For most of us, that was why we were here doing what we did. We all had our five-year plans. Almost everyone was going to use the money to forge a better life; to save as much as we could and then retire or be set up to start something new.

Unfortunately, given the way we lived, working hard but playing harder, we kept slipping. The five-year plan became a six or seven-year plan. Even so, we still had a goal, and the love and support of someone back home was crucial. It helped us cope with the knowledge that it could all finish in a flash any time; a bloody mess on the side of some dirty Iraqi road. A brighter future and a better life was what it was all about, and if we had to make it on the backs of the poor Iraqis, so be it.

The following day, we mounted up as a two-vehicle convoy and headed back to Baghdad. I decided I would be in the lead vehicle with the client. I figured with our speed we would have a better chance of missing any IEDs. At the end of the day, our job was to get the client there and back unharmed. If that meant we needed to take a hit to ensure his safety, that's what we got paid for.

We were about three hours out of Erbil on a stretch of road that was potholed to hell, when I saw a battered old white sedan pull onto the highway from a side road and start driving towards us, in our lane. I mean directly towards us, on the same side of the road. *Eeew, this isn't good.*

I looked at the vehicle that was rapidly getting closer. I was waiting for him to pull over onto the correct side of the road, but he didn't. I radioed the second car to alert them, while telling Peanut to flash the lights. Peanut did just that, but to no avail. The sedan kept travelling directly at us. I reached down and braced my MP5 on the dashboard, with the barrel pointing directly at the oncoming vehicle through the windscreen. In my head I was counting down the distance, judging to myself at what point I would have to open up, because if it was a VBIED I would have to make a decision pretty damn quick, to keep us out of its blast zone.

Without turning my head I told Clutch in the rear to get the client down on the floor of the vehicle and to block his ears. We knew from experience that the sound of firing in a vehicle is very loud. Clutch managed to fold John into a very small bundle of Aussie joy and then lay over him. To reduce the risk of burns from the spent shell cases, I turned the MP5 to the right so the ejected brass would fall down to the floor and not bounce around the interior of the vehicle.

The distance between us and the oncoming vehicle was quickly decreasing. I rechecked the safety was on full auto and touched my vest, feeling for another full mag. By now the sedan must have been no more than 150 metres to our front. *Fuck, this is going to have to happen.*

I started to squeeze the trigger and felt the tension being taken up. It must have had no more than a micro-millimetre to go before spewing out fully automatic lead through our front windscreen and into the sedan. Just as I was poised to open fire, the fucker suddenly swung back onto his side of the road. *Holy fuck and thank fuck for that.*

As the sedan shot past, I looked over to see who the fuck I had come so close to annihilating. Sat behind the wheel was a wizened old guy who must have been at least eighty. He'd certainly never used moisturiser in his life. As my heart rate began to slow again, I could see what the crazy old boy had been trying to avoid: there, on his side of the road, was a series of huge, crater-like potholes. The silly bastard had decided to gamble his life – and ours – rather than bump the shit out of his dirty old vehicle.

As I collected my wits and tried to calm my breathing, I was quietly grateful that he had pulled it off and I hadn't ended up killing him. But had it been a VBIED, had I waited too long and let him get too close? I wasn't 100 per cent certain either way, but blowing apart that old man would have played right into the hands of those who were already comparing Blackwater contractors to a bunch of lawless killers. There was no right answer, but the incident had passed, and we were alive. I told myself I would have to come up with a drill to deal with this, for future runs.

Just north of Baghdad there are a couple of crucial turn-offs; miss them and you'll find yourself in some bad areas, likely to result in the end of your days. The infamous Sadr City is one. There had been hundreds of attacks, and we sure as shit didn't want to end up there. I knew we must be getting close to our turn-off, and we were starting to get the usual looks of blind hatred from the locals. Doubtless, our presence on the highway had been called ahead to the local militia, who were known to frequent a green mosque that sat right beside the road. We had to keep moving at all costs and get through as quickly as possible, meaning that my navigation had to be bang on.

The trick for me was to keep one eye looking out for key landmarks, while estimating the time we should be within sight of them dependent on our speed, and to check them off one by one. In navigation terms these are called 'waypoints'. Sometimes they would come up more slowly than I anticipated, which would introduce a bit of self-doubt, and there was always a nagging thought in the back of my mind that we could possibly be heading into the wrong place.

It was always an intense time: searching for the landmarks while keeping an eye out for attack indicators. Were the roads empty of people? Were the locals running? Had a hasty roadblock been erected? Were there pigeons, kites or kids? Fuck me, it was all burning through my head and no doubt the boys were having the same thoughts.

We also had to be on the lookout for IP roadblocks and check-points, real and fake. Sometimes these choke points were unavoidable, but we would always approach anything not manned by US military with maximum caution. Even if it was Big Army, given their stress levels and tendency to shoot first and ask questions later, there were no guarantees of safe passage. They would often close off the road to all but military vehicles, sending us around another route. Sometimes, we couldn't help but think they did it just because they didn't like contractors.

As we neared those crucial turn-offs on the approach to Baghdad, I spied a US military convoy on the roadside up ahead. We slowed to a dead crawl, approaching the rearmost vehicles with utmost caution. The soldiers were splayed out around their vehicles in what were meant to be all-round defence positions, without exposing any part to a possible sniper, although to me it looked like a bit of a gaggle of shit.

I radioed through what I was seeing and told Peanut to keep it dead slow, so the soldiers could get a good read on us and the US flag now lain on the dash. This seemed to do the trick, as we were waved forward by some very young and obviously low-ranking guy. We pulled up beside him and I asked what the problem was. Their convoy of about fifty vehicles had been on their way to Ramadi, in central Iraq, but one of their lead trucks had just been hit by an IED. Holy hell, that was one hell of lot of vehicles. No surprise that the militia knew they were coming and had had time to set up an ambush.

It was clear that we wouldn't be able to get past them for a while, and there was no way I wanted to seek out an alternative route. The road ahead was the only one I knew well, and by now we knew the local militia would have been alerted to our presence.

I asked the soldier how long they'd been stuck there and was told about forty minutes. Likewise, they weren't keen on staying for any length of time, as they were sitting ducks for mortar attacks or sniper fire. I asked if there had been any casualties and apparently there had been one injury. With nothing much more to say, we were just going to have to wait for a helo to evacuate the injured soldier, so we could all move the fuck on.

I looked around and weighed up our options. There weren't a lot to be honest. 'D'you mind if we hang here with you guys?' I asked. 'We can tuck in behind you and offer a bit of defence while we wait.'

'Who are you guys?' the soldier asked.

'Blackwater.'

'Blackwater?' he repeated. For some reason the soldier seemed impressed, and he began yelling into his comms. 'Hey, sergeant, we have some Blackwater guys here who want to tuck in with us until it's cleared.'

'Blackwater, you say?' the sergeant radioed back.

'Yeah, Blackwater.'

'Yeah, no problem,' came the response.

I'm not sure why us being Blackwater had furnished instant security clearance, but right now it sure was nice to hear. I radioed the guys to pull up and position our vehicles side by side, so we could use them as cover if there was an attack. That done, we all got out to stretch our legs, take a piss and wait. I walked around each of my guys, telling them to keep it professional. We must have been a bit of a novelty, for a few of the soldiers wandered over and started asking questions about life as a security contractor. Others came to goggle at Peanut's Beowulf .50-cal.

My impression was that a good number of US soldiers were planning to jump ship and become security contractors, just as soon as they could. Essentially, we were doing what they were doing, but without facing daily gun battles with a well-armed and determined enemy. Obviously, we weren't as well equipped, but we had better rotations and far better pay. It was an attractive proposition for the average grunt on a one-year rotation, earning shit money and facing a good chance of being shipped to Afghanistan next, to face yet another shitstorm the US government couldn't seem to finish.

I didn't envy those guys and girls one bit. Most of them, I figured, came from relatively poor backgrounds, where their future was either to take some shitty job at Walmart or face a life strung out on drugs. To them the US military looked like a great option, with its promises of cash lump sums and paid college tuition. To many, that had to seem a far better future than remaining in their home town. Pretty quickly, they got to hear that we in the security industry were earning four times what they were, and they wanted in. They saw it as a natural career move and a way to get ahead in life, just as we did.

For the more senior ranks, however, it wasn't such an easy choice. If those older guys left the military, they would lose their pensions and the privileges their rank and years of service conveyed and would have to start from the bottom again. Even so, the gap between the regular military and the contractors in terms of pay, lifestyle and the way we operated was still obvious. That, I figured, was the chief cause of the resentment we faced from many of the old fuckers.

Fuck dudes, it's not our fault that your rut has become your trench.

Plus, we didn't have it all our way. Yes, business was very good right now, but the regular soldiers had the protection of all their advanced military technology. If they were killed or wounded, they were rightly held in high esteem, with honours, flags, medals and ceremonies galore. With the Veterans Affairs (VA) system back in the States, they had access to zero-interest loans, top medical and psychological therapies, physiotherapy and service dogs. I hear they even had free Starbucks.

We security contractors had none of that. If we died, our names would only ever be remembered by friends and family. We were expendable. No one gave a fuck. Most of the guys in uniform assumed that the amount of money we were paid justified the lack of acknowledgement; our zero profile. The only reason the deaths of Jerry, Wes, Mike and Steve had become so widely known to the world public was because a media crew had filmed the event and broadcast it on TV.

Otherwise, no one would have known, and no one would have cared.

CHAPTER 11

A n hour after we'd 'joined' the Big Army convoy, a Black Hawk
helicopter swooped in to recover the injured soldier. Above, an
F-15 fighter jet made a series of low passes, keeping an eye open
for the enemy. Its presence alone served as a strong deterrent. It
was an awe-inspiring sight, and it underlined my point about the
differences between our two worlds. If it had been us sitting on the
side of the road, fucked up by an IED, we would very likely be left
to fight it out alone, or to wait for Hacksaw and the air boys to fly a
Little Bird to our aid.

And of course, that would all depend on whether we had the
means to make contact with anyone, which more often than not we
did not.

As the convoy began to move off, I thanked the soldiers who we
had bunkered down with and we said our goodbyes. I felt sure that
during our brief encounter a few of them had made up their minds
as to their next career move. Good on them. It would be good to
have them with us. Their experience was needed, as it was obvious
that the talent pool was fast becoming a muddy puddle. If fat Steve

and Jim were any indication, we needed all the former soldiers we could get.

As we were this close to Baghdad, I opted to tuck in and trail behind their last vehicle, keeping within sight and hopefully under the arc of the big .50-cal HMG (heavy machine gun) that the tail-end Charlie was swinging about menacingly.

As we crawled past the scene of the IED strike, I could see the damage the blast had caused. It looked as if the bomb had been placed up against one of the aluminium street lamps. Although the blast had been large, the force had been dissipated in every direction, due to the weakness of the material the pole was made from. To maximise the force of an explosion, the charge should be anchored to something very solid, which will push it out in the direction of least resistance.

As it was, some of the blast had hit the lead Humvee but not with enough force to kill the occupants. Still, the wounded soldier had been very lucky indeed, and I hoped his or her injuries weren't serious. As we left the scene behind us, I had that old self-preservation thought running through my mind: *better you than me.*

By now, we were all keen to get back to the team house. The IZ was only thirty minutes away, give or take, so we peeled off from the Big Army convoy and gunned the engines to get up a good head of speed, when Two Trays came up on the radio.

'Baz, Two Trays. I think we have some fuel issues here.'

This normally meant only one thing: the fuel was contaminated with water or some other nefarious liquid, which was now starting to get into the engine.

'OK, mate. How bad is it?'

'Well, we are still moving, but it's starting to skip every time we try to accelerate.'

That was a common symptom of water in the fuel. Eventually, the water would fill the carburettor and the engine would stop running altogether. Not a good scenario when out in enemy territory. Equally, I didn't want to pull over to fix the problem. This was neither the time nor the place for running repairs. Luckily, this was one of the many 'what if's?' we had planned for during team training. This however would be the first time we'd put it into practice.

'OK, mate, here's what we're going to do,' I announced. 'We'll pull off slightly to the right and slow down. You coast up and get in front of us, over.'

'Roger that,' Two Trays replied.

Peanut, hearing what was going on, gently pulled over to the right. I could see the client, John, was looking a bit anxious, so I told him what was what.

I gave him the usual: 'Don't worry... We've done this before... We're professionals... Blah blah blah,' not all of which was bullshit.

Two Trays's Blazer came spluttering up besides ours and I could see the frustration on his face; none of us wanted to break down in the middle of bandit country.

'OK, mate,' I radioed, 'we're going to pull in behind you. I want you to put the vehicle into neutral but leave the key turned on, OK?' I felt sure he'd know all this, but it was worth emphasising, because turning the ignition off would mean he couldn't steer or brake. 'We're going to push you the rest of the way back.'

'Roger that,' Two Trays confirmed.

Still travelling at over 70mph, Peanut moved in behind their vehicle.

'OK, mate, tell Bullfrog to take his foot off the accelerator,' I radioed.

'Roger that,' Two Trays responded.

As their vehicle started to slow, we gently came up behind it, until we matched its speed.

'Steady bro,' I told Peanut. 'Gently does it.'

I knew I didn't have to tell him this. Peanut was doing an excellent job, but my nerves were kicking in. I could see the concentration on his face as he lifted himself in his chair to get a better look at the ass-end of the vehicle in front.

Stumpy, who was sitting in the trunk monkey position, set his gun aside and began signalling to us the distance between the two vehicles, bringing his palms closer together like a slow-motion clap. I radioed Two Trays to let him know we were about to make contact, knowing Bullfrog could hear this too.

As the two vehicles touched, fender to fender, it was so gentle I barely felt the contact. At that speed, had we hit them hard, we could have spun them out of control. We were now in the perfect position to give them a ride home.

'Contact made,' I radioed. 'Keep your wheel straight and only gentle turns, and we will push you all the way.'

'Roger, mate,' Two Trays replied.

By now, the client's eyes were like watermelons, seeing the vehicle in front so close on our nose. I could tell he was nervous, but he clearly trusted us enough to say nothing.

For the next ten kilometres or so, we pushed them towards the IZ, moving at a ridiculous speed. Luckily, the road was mainly straight so we didn't have to worry about slowing for bends. To the locals, we must have looked like something out of *The Dukes of Hazzard* – that is, if they'd ever seen *The Dukes of Hazzard*. Maybe *The Sultans of Mecca*. Either way, the move seemed to be working and we were happy to be in motion.

One kilometre out from the IZ lies a slow left turn that takes you into Checkpoint 11 and the IZ proper. We gently crept right as one vehicle, to get into the correct lane. Everyone was doing their part: arms extended out of the windows, fingers up in the familiar – please wait, get out of the fucking way – pyramid, as we raced ever closer.

'Hey, Baz, I can see the checkpoint,' said Two Trays.

'Roger, mate, we are going to back off and let you drift in, OK?'

'Yeah, roger that. All good.'

With that, we backed off and let Two Trays's vehicle drift towards the checkpoint in a decidedly ghostly fashion… but we were not there yet.

The lead Blazer was now approaching a Big Army checkpoint. Being a freewheeling and largely silent civilian vehicle, it was likely that their truck would be seen as very suspicious by the already highly strung gate guards. I thought it best to remind Two Trays to turn on his hazard lights and throw up the flag.

The checkpoint ahead was divided into a series of lanes, a bit like a bowling alley, divided by three-foot-high concrete Jersey walls. You joined the applicable lane, depending on your nationality and clearance level. The Iraqis had a lane all for themselves, and the military had another, which we were cleared to use, so we slowly steered our way towards that one.

The guards who manned the lanes were also segregated, depending on nationality. The ones furthest out were usually Iraqi military. Those poor bastards were always getting blown up so, needless to say, they were hella jumpy. The next layer of gatekeepers were often from third-party countries, such as Chile or Georgia, those who had fallen for the 'you're either with us or against us' line. I'm pretty sure none of them had expected to be put out as bomb fodder by their US comrades. Finally, there came the American troops perched high up in steel-plated towers, watching over everything with sniper rifles and machine guns. Or they were to be found sitting in their Bradley Fighting Vehicles (BFVs), hunkered behind their .50-cal heavy machine guns.

As Two Trays approached the outer layer of security, he placed his flag on the dash where the snipers in the towers could see it, flashed his lights and put his hazards on. As we hung back and watched, we hoped they'd have an easy time getting through. But, as I've said, we still weren't there yet.

We kept scanning our arcs of fire. The insurgents had worked out this was as good a place as any to attack, while their targets were stuck in these slow lanes of death. Recognising that Two Trays was not a threat, the Iraqi guards waved the Blazer through, but as Bullfrog tried to fire up their vehicle engine again, it just coughed and spluttered and refused to start.

I radioed Two Trays, letting him know we would move forward to push them again, but this confused the hell out of the Iraqi guards. I could see Two Trays trying to explain by bumping his fists together, then pointing back to us, then pointing to his vehicle and repeating the pushing movement. The Iraqi guard looked like he was being given the international sign for two penises touching. *Good one, Two Trays; this is not the place.*

Eventually, the communications barrier seemed to be broken and the guard nodded his head and waved us all through. We crept forwards, flag out and hazards on. But, just for a change the signal had not been passed on. Our arrival was greeted with bullets pinging off the Jersey wall to our sides. How the moron of a sniper did not realise what was going on was beyond me. There was no way they couldn't see us through their optics.

I instructed Peanut to stop, as I was getting pretty fucked-off with always being shot at by these assholes. After all, they were meant to be on the same side as us.

'Fuck me,' I exploded, as we rolled to a halt, not worrying too much about the client hearing. Like I said, he was an Aussie, so this kind of language was common as dog-fuck to him.

Then the asshole in the tower shot at us *again*. The poor Iraqi guard dived over the Jersey wall, as the rounds zipped by at foot level. He got to his feet, very pissed off, and yelled at the tower in what I'm guessing translated as, 'Hey, fuck, your mother is a hairy goat, and your father is a donkey's butt hole.' After which he climbed back over the barrier, pointed to our vehicles and yelled, 'Ameraci! Ameraci!' He then gestured for us to move up, which we did, and we continued to push Two Trays forward.

'Shukran,' I said, as we crawled slowly past him. I did not envy that poor bastard one little bit.

Crawling ahead, we made our way to where the Americans lay. The guards looked about eighteen years old but were probably more like twenty-somethings. I was so pissed off at getting shot at all the time, I decided I was going to let them have an earful.

I leant out of my open window. 'Hey, you fuckers,' I yelled to the guys sitting on top of the BFV. 'What the fuck are you doing? Tell that cunt up there to use his target identification before shooting at anyone. Is he fucking retarded, the useless cunt?'

The guys in my vehicle started to chuckle, as did the client, John. At that point, a figure emerged from the tower and gazed down at the soldiers on the BFV. 'What's the problem?' he yelled.

I couldn't see him, but by then I was a long way past giving a fuck. I threw my door open and got out and gazed up at him.

'You are, fucker: *You're the problem!*' I yelled. 'What's the idea of shooting at us?'

I could tell he didn't like me yelling at him, but I could also tell he wasn't inclined to climb down and confront me head on.

'Fuck you,' he yelled back.

'No, fuck you, you fat useless cunt,' I retorted.

This must have scored big, as the guys on the BFV were looking on in trepidation but also chuckling fit to burst.

'Who the fuck are you?' he yelled down, trying to regain his God-in-the-sniper-tower dominance.

I reached for my CAC card, the State Department identification card all contractors carried. For some incomprehensible reason, mine had the equivalent rank of a full bird colonel.

'I'll tell you who we are, motherfucker, we're fucking Blackwater,' I yelled up at him. 'You heard of us?'

There was silence, as the look on his face suddenly changed. For some reason, and I'm not sure why, he stopped trying to look like the tough guy.

'Oh,' he said. 'Sorry about that.'

Sensing weakness and not wanting to relent now that I had him back-peddling, I redoubled the attack. 'Sorry? Fuck yeah, you'll be sorry,' I yelled back, waving around my CAC card some more. Even the guys on the BFV had stopped smiling.

'Hurry up and raise the barrier,' tower guy yelled to someone on the ground.

As if by magic the barrier rose, and I got back into the vehicle, keeping my eyes on the asshole in the tower for full effect and bending extra low to make sure I didn't hit my head on the door, thus ruining the victory I'd clearly won with the whole stare-down.

Once in, I radioed through. 'Let's go, boys.'

As we passed the gaggle of soldiers and made our way down the road to the team house, still pushing Two Trays's vehicle in front of us, I glanced over at Peanut. 'Any idea what that was all about?'

'No idea,' he said.

I was still perplexed as to why my announcing we were Blackwater should have had such an effect. Maybe he was thinking about getting into the same business as us and didn't want to fuck his pitch in Moyock. Either way, it had worked, and we were finally back. *What a day.*

We reached the team house, unloaded the vehicles and got ready for the debrief. Bullfrog had the hood up and was surveying the fuel problem in their vehicle.

Just then I heard a voice from behind me.

'Hey, Baz.' It was the client, John, and he was extending his hand towards me. 'Thanks for everything, mate. You guys are switched on and I appreciate it.'

We shook hands. 'Well thank you, John. Just doing our job.'

'No mate,' he said, in that unmistakable Aussie accent. 'I mean it, well done. Thank the boys for me too, OK.'

'Sure, John, any time. I'll let the boys know.'

I showered, before giving Brian a heads-up about the tower-guard incident at Checkpoint 11.

He glanced up from behind his desk. 'Yeah, not surprised. The company has been overloaded with applicants, even from the military guys serving here now.'

It seemed what had happened in Fallujah, plus the video footage from the Al-Hillah attack, was still fresh in a lot of people's minds.

'This could be a doubled-edged sword, mate,' I told Brian. 'For sure we need good guys, but we don't need guys out for revenge.'

'It's a concern,' Brian admitted. 'That's why we have to keep the vetting process real tight.'

They did, and I hoped to hell that they would keep it that way.

The vehicles were cleaned and refuelled, Bullfrog draining the water out of his engine and replacing all the petrol. Once all the *mahi* – Māori for 'work' – was done, it was well past fucking beer o'clock. And you know what? After the day we'd had, I figured we'd earned it.

Since the deaths of our guys in Fallujah, the pressure on the military to respond was building on all fronts. Not for the first time, it seemed that the decision makers were being influenced by public and media opinion, rather than proper strategic thinking. That was their problem. Ours was the surge in interest from people who wanted to come to Iraq to exact revenge. Moyock was getting hundreds of applications a day. The folks there had an awful lot of weeding out to do. That posed a real challenge, and I feared it was inevitable that some idiots would slip through.

The new guys I'd seen arriving recently were just not of the same calibre as the earliest batches. The BIAP PX had even taken to selling a range of idiotic patches that these guys seemed only too keen to plaster all over their kit, making them look like puffed-up billboards. They sported slogans like:

'Operation Iraqi get some.'

'Mercenaries don't die, they just regroup in hell.'

And the very worst: 'Kill 'em all. Let God sort 'em out.'

I likened it to The Prodigy track we played to pump ourselves up for the run on Irish. We hit play at the beginning to get ourselves into kill-mode, then hit stop at the end to get ourselves out of kill-mode. But to me, these patches were a way of keeping a bunch of dim-witted fucks in kill-mode 24/7. The mind and body can't function like that for long, not without some drastic mental consequences. Plus wearing a badge that read, 'Kill 'em all. Let God sort 'em out,' certainly wasn't going to win the hearts and minds of the Iraqis – not that that was ever the intention of those sorts.

For a short while my team and I went to live in the Red Zone, moving into the hotel adjacent to the Al-Hamra, the one where Tom and some of the guys had stayed when we'd first formed Blackwater Commercial and where we'd spotted Sean Penn. I got Noodle back on the team, which was fabulous, plus Cash, and a new guy, call sign Bird, so it was a full complement of knuckle-draggers who all knew my rules and operating procedures.

Based at the Al-Hamra complex were a bunch of new BW guys who'd taken over manning the ESS contract, the one Jerry and the guys had been on when they were killed. This new team were the younger breed of former SEALs, and many had worked together before in the Teams, or doing whatever came after on Civvy Street. To me it seemed a number of them still had that laid-back, 'too cool for school', 'let's work on our tans' mentality.

Their project manager (PM), Rich, struck me as being a perfect example. Rich dressed like he had just come from a Beach Boys cover band concert, with his mop-head of hair, baggy shorts, Hawaiian shirts and ugly-ass Teva 'trekking' sandals that you'd normally see ageing German tourists wear with long socks. I hated the sandals and, to be honest, I didn't take much of a liking to Rich either. Maybe it was all down to his attitude or the way he dressed like he was never going to leave the hotel, or maybe it was just me being a fussy fuck, thinking: *At least put some boots on, you fake fucker; you're here to do a job.*

The Teva-factor became my barometer as to whether Rich was ever going to do his job and lead his guys on runs, outside the pool bar. Whenever I saw his guys load up, I'd look to check what footwear Rich had on. Nine times out of ten it was those fucking Tevas, which meant he was going nowhere. What a fucking tosspot. Some of my dislike for Rich was due to the fact that he was here to take over from Tom, and for sure Tom had gone out on the runs. That was how you got to know the ground. This fucker had absolutely no intention of ever leaving the hotel, I was sure of it.

Rich had a shadow, Malcolm, his 2IC, or 'ops o' (operations officer), as he preferred to be called. I didn't know if he was a former SEAL or not, and, in all honestly, I didn't care. He occasionally ventured out on a run, maybe all the way into the IZ, which I guess he had to do to justify his presence. At the hotel, however, Malcolm always walked about four paces behind Rich, like some fucking lap dog.

My team and I soon came to realise that Rich confused the difference between being a leader of the guys and being one of the guys, and he didn't know how to do either properly. He allowed the guys that worked for him to blur the line between supervisor and subordinates. Now, I could be completely wrong. Maybe his guys really liked his free-rein way of doing things, but in my opinion the best way to get someone to follow you is to show you can do the job yourself and do it well. *Lead by example.* Rich needed to establish the rules and standards that he expected when out on the road before handing over to his men. Instead, he was the guy who just passed on the tasks.

It wasn't uncommon to hear Rich's team drinking around the pool, bragging about how they had shot the shit out of this vehicle, or had run that vehicle off the road, because they didn't get out of their way fast enough. Hopefully it was just beer-talk bravado, but, either way, it was bullshit. I'm not saying they never went out and trained, but if they did it was a rare thing. By contrast, I trained my guys every Friday, and we trained hard, because our lives depended on it.

Before you think I'm being unfairly hard on these new guys, remember I had been in-country for almost a year, and I had learnt what did and did not work the hard way. These guys had been in Iraq for two weeks and were acting as if they had already done the hard yards and knew all there was to know.

One day, Rich asked me if I had been to Kut, which I told him I had.

'Oh, that's cool, bra,' he said.

I ain't your fucking bra, bro. Why did the fuck always say 'bra'? I mean, I'd heard laid-back surfers using it in Hawaii as a bastardisation of 'bro', but we weren't in Hawaii, and unfortunately the only genuine Hawaiian I'd known out here was Brother Wes, and he was dead.

'Can you tell me a bit about it?' Rich continued. 'About Kut?'

'Sure thing. It's a shithole and a bitch of a place to get to with multiple ambush sites along the way. There's a shitty little single-lane pontoon bridge, which is the only passage over a deep river. The road is always backed up with traffic and it's a perfect place for the insurgents to hang out, spot targets and attack at will. As it's the only way into Kut, if they don't get you going out, they will wait and get you coming back. Oh, and there was a big shootout at the Kut compound a few months back, the very same one you're probably thinking about going to. Why d'you ask?'

Rich stood there with his eyes wide and head wobbling a bit. 'Well, um, well... It's like we have to get a client to Kut, then bring him back the same day, but none of my guys have been there.'

'Well, now is a good time for you to learn.'

You have maps, so go do some recces and find out all you can from someone, other than me, bra. Of course, I knew what he was fishing for. It was pretty fucking obvious. He wanted me to offer my help,

299

but I wasn't going to volunteer myself or my guys. Or at least, not without him doing a shit-ton of grovelling.

'Um, the thing is,' Rich continued, 'we are a bit thin on the ground.' I knew this was bullshit. He had plenty of guys, but none of them had a clue how to get there and I didn't believe he was intending to go himself. 'Ah, um, d'you think, um, mate, can we use a few of your guys?'

You chicken-shit fuck.

'So, you want my guys to help you out on this run?' I asked, wanting him to say it.

'Yes, mate, if that's OK.' He had used the term 'mate' twice now, no doubt in an effort to appeal to my kind-hearted New Zealand side.

'Dude,' I said, 'I have a contract and a client who has places he needs us to take him to.'

The truth was, we had moved out to the Red Zone chiefly to free up space in the team house. Our only runs right now were to drop the client off at the IZ in the morning and pick him up again in the evening, but still it was a paying contract, so we took it seriously. I actually did have the time to help Rich, but did I want to, that was the question.

'Dude,' I said again, 'why would I want to risk myself and my guys on a run that isn't even our contract? What happens if we get hit? That would be bad for our client and the company.'

I didn't mind going, and in truth I really liked the ESS guys, but I wanted a shitload more grovelling from Rich. Besides, they should have been able to handle the run themselves. That's how you learn. Fuck me, it ain't rocket science. What was his chief fear, I wondered? His team having to do the run without any help, or the possibility that he might even have to go himself?

'Tell you what, Rich,' I added, 'I'll ask my guys if they want to do it, then I'll get back to you. When is it?'

'The day after tomorrow and we will brief at 09:00.'

'OK, I'll let you know, but it's best that you keep planning as if we won't be there, so you don't get too disappointed, OK?'

I left him with that. Saying 'no' would have been easy, but 'yes' required the input of all my guys. As much as we had come to love looking for trouble, particularly when we were nursing hangovers, I needed their blessing if we were to help these fucks out, risking their lives when they really didn't have to.

I made a call on the radio. 'Meeting room, now.' This worked a treat and in no time we had gathered.

'Hey, shitheads,' I began, 'I've been asked by Mr Teva next door if we could help him out on a run, the day after tomorrow, to Kut. I told him I'd run it by you guys first, before letting him know. Think about it and let me know your thoughts.'

I could see from their looks that they weren't too fussed either way.

'What do you think?' Stumpy asked.

'Well, to be honest, I don't see why we should. We're not part of their contract. If we get hit, questions will be asked about why we weren't servicing the people who presently pay us. On the other hand, I'm not convinced that those guys are capable of doing the run, given their inexperience and lack of training.'

'Well, I've never been to Kut,' said Clutch.

'Me neither,' a couple of others chimed in.

'OK, then,' I said. 'Who wants to go to Kut for the day?' Like it was a special treat. The boys looked at each other and nodded.

Maybe they were thinking, as I was, that if someone had intervened with Jerry on that fateful day, he and his team might still be alive. I told the guys to pull out the maps and figure out the best primary and alternative routes, rally points and likely ambush sites, and then to get their kit together. It was already sorted, of course, but you can never give your gear too many checks.

I told them we would meet at Rich's ops room at 09:00 on the day of the run, once we had dropped our client off at the IZ. My plan was to listen in on their brief and determine from that if they had their shit together and were ready. I would also be looking to see how Rich was dressed, which would tell me if he was going as well.

'Those fucking Tevas,' I told my guys. 'They'll tell me all I need to know.'

After our deliberations, I telephoned Rich and told him we would come if nothing popped up in the meantime – thereby giving me an out – and that we would be there for his mission brief. Rich thanked me a little too enthusiastically – not a good sign – but he seemed genuinely pleased to have our offer of help.

'OK, dude, see you the day after tomorrow,' I said, just before adding, 'Oh, fuck, I forgot to mention…'

'Oh, what's that?' he asked.

'We have one condition.'

'Ooh,' he said a bit slower. 'What's that?'

I left a pause for effect. I love doing that. 'That you come on the run too.' This was met with silence, but I could sure hear him breathing. 'You there, mate?' I asked, feeling the giggles wanting to kick in.

'Ah yeah, mate, I'm here.'

'Well, are you in?'

'Um, I'll have to check, but I think I can make it, Baz, no problem.'

'Good. See you then.'

'Later, bra.'

I knew there was almost zero chance of him coming. I just wanted to put the shits up him, making him think about those who did go out every day and the stresses and mental preparation it all took. I knew he'd find an excuse, but I just wanted him to have a shit night's sleep too.

I set about getting my head around the run. Even with as much road-time as my guys and I had, I never treated any mission as mundane. My belief is that as soon as you treat a run as no big deal, you will likely slip up. The next day we pinned up the maps and went over the route, using my knowledge from my earlier visit. We had everything covered as best we could, except – as usual in Blackwater Commercial – for the lack of usable radio comms.

The BW State guys had it all, so why didn't we? We were making the company very good money, so there was absolutely no excuse. Any QRF is effective only if they know where to start looking for you, and for that you need comms.

I planned to have a set of orders for my guys and to integrate those into Rich's plan, while staying as separate from them as practicable. I would not split up my guys, and I was sure Rich wouldn't want to split his guys either, but I wanted to ensure that we were going to be utilised correctly, as one team. The glaring issue was the one I had pointed out to Rich: the single-lane bridge that separates Baghdad from Kut.

That bridge had been put in place after the original one was blown up, either in the invasion or by some other fucker. It was one of those steel-lattice Bailey bridge-type things, which engineers can throw up in a matter of hours. More importantly, it was the only crossing point for miles. I gathered Stumpy and Two Trays for a confab; the more ideas the better.

'Dudes, it's been a while since I've been over that single-lane bridge. I'm not 100 per cent happy about it,' I told them.

'Me neither,' Two Trays agreed.

'So, what do you want to do?' Stumpy asked. 'Head out and take a look?'

'Yeah. What say tomorrow, after we drop the client? We should be back in time for the brief, and it will be good to do a recce before we actually get out there and find out it's fucked.'

'Yeah, why not?'

'OK, tell the boys what's happening and see you later for a beer.'

An advance recce of the bridge wasn't something I should have to do. Rich should have done some form of look-see, or at least have put it in his orders. It's just basic close protection practice, but I didn't have a lot of faith in his skills, experience or man-management, so I wasn't holding my breath.

The morning of the Kut mission, we saddled up and took the client into the IZ early, stopping in at the military canteen for some chow: a good breakfast of biscuits and gravy. But we didn't stick around for long. We had a good few clicks to cover to get to the bridge, do the recce and get back for the brief, and there was always the chance of delays. Mornings were the chosen time for IEDs and VBIEDs, not to mention the suicide bombings that were becoming increasingly common in Baghdad. It seemed they preferred to make their one-way trip bright and early. I guess it was when they had plenty of energy, or maybe it was before the drugs and booze they'd been fed had worn off, following a long night of brainwashing by those too important to make the ultimate sacrifice themselves.

The traffic out was hectic, as usual. For the life of me, I still couldn't work out why there was always a morning rush, like it wasn't a war zone. It's not like many of the population even had a job or a school to attend. Maybe it was just force of habit and their way of trying to continue with a normal life, despite all the chaos.

We made our way out of town on a south-easterly route that none of us was hugely familiar with. The roads could change from one day to the next, so looking for something familiar as a reference point wasn't that easy, but after twenty minutes the traffic started to thin out, which was an indication we were possibly on the right track. Sure enough, a few minutes later we joined the queue to cross the bridge on the road to Kut.

I got on the radio and told Two Trays to mark it on the GPS as a waypoint. We drove a bit closer to get a look at the bridge, before we pulled off to one side. As expected, it was manned by Iraqi Police, which was never a good sign. They were acting as the 'stop/go' men, allowing the different directions of traffic to use the bridge in turns, which meant they got a good long look at whoever was passing, no doubt alerting the insurgents to anything juicy.

Up on the bank at the side of the bridge were a group of young boys, who were very likely another form of early warning for the bad guys. Because of the steep sides leading up to the bridge, there was no place to turn around. Once in the queue you were well and truly hemmed in, until you could find a place to turn around on the far side. You would then have to try to recross to get the hell out of there.

Having seen enough, I instructed the vehicles to turn around, one at a time, and slowly drive back about 200 metres. I didn't want to reveal to any hostile eyes that we were together. There would be plenty of time for that when we returned with the ESS guys. Once we had rendezvoused, I radioed that we should head back to the hotel for Rich's mission brief.

'What do you think, Bullfrog?' I ventured.

'Fuck me, it looks like the perfect place for a trap.'

'Yeah, agreed. But I'm not sure they would bother to ambush anyone on the bridge itself. They'd probably use it to ID someone crossing, then alert the shitheads further up to ready an ambush.'

'Maybe, but there's a perfect killing ground there at the bridge. Why not attack where you can have almost guaranteed success?'

'Possibly because of that, bro. If they were to attack at the bridge, can you imagine the heat that would bring on the IP from Big Army? The bridge would get closed, pissing off the locals, and every IP from here to Timbuktu would be shot. No one would ever obey their commands again, as they are the only fucks controlling the bridge. It would be obvious they were in on it. Well, that's my thinking, anyway.'

Bullfrog nodded. 'So, what d'you reckon they'll do when we roll through?'

'I think they'll let us cross, count the vehicles and the number of guys and see how well armed we are, then send that info up ahead. Then the shitbags will try to hit us somewhere between the bridge and Kut. I think we are in for a shit fight today, bro.'

'Roger that,' Bullfrog replied.

You had to think like an insurgent, get inside their minds – that was the only way to stay ahead in this game.

Once back at the Al-Hamra Hotel we headed for the briefing room. All of Rich's guys were there. Five minutes later, Rich himself walked in, with his 'ops o', Malcolm, trailing right up his ass. I nodded to Rich that we were all there, then casually glanced down at his feet. Fuck me dead, he was wearing those Tevas.

'I guess he isn't coming on the run today,' I remarked to Two Trays.

'I guess not, the useless cunt.'

I had a look around my guys, who shook their heads in disbelief. We found places to sit as Rich moved to the front, where there was a whiteboard with a map of Greater Baghdad.

'OK, guys,' he began. 'Well, ah, unfortunately, I can't make it on the run today. I, um, well, I have to get the manning in to Moyock this morning, otherwise I'd be there with you.' If he'd had the balls to look up, he'd have seen the looks of contempt on our faces. Peanut let out the old 'bullshit' cough loud enough for everyone to hear.

After a bit of giggling, and not just from my guys, Rich continued. 'I'd like to thank Baz and his guys for helping us out today. Thanks boys. They have been to Kut, so their assistance and knowledge is greatly appreciated. The TL for today will be Bam Bam. He will give you the brief on today's run, so pay attention.'

Fuck me, I thought, *he isn't even going to brief his guys. Dang, this boy has no scruples.*

Bam Bam was another former SEAL. He was a likeable-enough guy, about 5ft 8in. with beach-blond hair and a friendly manner.

'OK guys, today we have the run to Kut,' he said, then spent about thirty very long seconds trying to find it on the map. 'We will leave at 10:00, following this route, ah, where is it?' Ah here we go... this route, and we should be back about 15:30, all going well, so we'll be able to get a run into Burger King at BIAP on the way back. Are there any questions?'

He eyed his guys, looking for fuck knows what. I sat there, not too sure what I had just heard. Two Trays and the rest of my guys were equally bemused, thinking: *Come on, there must be more.* But, no, there didn't seem to be any more. *Are you shitting me?*

'No questions?' Bam Bam asked again. 'Good, OK then, see you at 10:00.' With that, he started to step through the guys who were sitting on the floor in front of him, as if to leave.

'Fuck me,' I said to my guys. 'This is not going to do. This is not going to do at all.'

I stood up before anyone could leave. 'Hang on,' I announced. 'No, no, no. Hang the fuck on,' I repeated, raising my voice above the chatter in the room. 'No, that's not it, so all of you – sit the fuck down.'

It was the turn of Rich's boys to look bemused. Rich, himself, who hadn't managed to quite slink away, looked at me and could see that I was far from happy.

'Ah, yeah, guys, sit down will you,' Rich muttered. 'Baz wants to say something.'

'Fuck, yeah I do,' I said, walking over to the whiteboard and turning to face the crowd. 'That was the worst set of mission orders I have ever heard, so sit the fuck down and listen in. This is how it's going to go.'

Stunned by the sudden hijacking of the brief and the bad language, they looked at me, then at Rich. Bam Bam tried to make his way back to the whiteboard, to give the impression that he was part of the new, upgraded floor-show, and to try to save some face.

'No, bro, you sit down too,' I told him, pointing to a space between two of his guys. 'That was the worst briefing I have ever heard,' I repeated. 'The fucking worst.' *Pause for effect.* 'Ever. I'm not sure how you guys briefed in the Teams, but I'm pretty fucking sure it wasn't like that. Correct?'

Most of the guys nodded their heads in agreement.

'Right, my guys and I have been asked to help you out on this run because we have been to Kut, but I'll be fucked if we are going to accept that as the mission brief.'

I eyed Bam Bam, who by now wanted to fall through the gaps in the floor.

'I'm going to brief you,' I told them. 'So, take out your notebooks and pay attention, OK?'

More nods of agreement from Rich's guys, and more dirty-ass grins from my guys.

'Before I begin going through the SMEAC format, I want everyone to get up and regroup themselves how they sit in their vehicles, with vehicle one in the front here, then two, then three, and I want every vehicle commander to get his fucking map out and follow me, as I explain things.'

For the next forty minutes, I talked, covering everything they needed to know. Rich's guys seemed blown away with the detail, the logic and the flow, as I went through the different subject headers, eventually arriving at the ground to be covered in more detail.

'Are there any questions so far?' I asked. There were none, but I waited for five seconds just to make sure everyone was listening.

'OK guys,' I said. 'The ground. I want you to know that, in all likelihood, *we will get hit today.*' I let that settle in a bit, as the guys stared at me and then at each other with startled expressions. To make sure they had heard me correctly I said it again. 'In all likelihood, we *will* get hit today.'

The guys all looked a lot more serious now.

'The bridge,' I explained, pointing to it on the map. 'This is like the checkout of a grocery store. There is only one way in and one way out. I believe that the IPs who man the bridge will ID us as we go over it. They'll get our vehicle numbers and types, men and possible client location. They will then call ahead and let the insurgents know.'

I looked around for a reaction, but you could have heard the pin from one of Stumpy's grenades drop.

'Unfortunately,' I continued. 'This is the only route to get to Kut and back in one day. The alternative,' which I pointed out on the map, 'would take us all day, which would mean we would return at night, so that's not happening. Now, I expect the likely ambush site to be within this stretch of road, around here. Has everyone found it on their maps?'

I was glad to see many nods of affirmation, like a bunch of kittens following a laser pointer on the wall.

'Good. This stretch of road seems to be the perfect place for an ambush because, from my way of thinking – and the lie of the land – if I was going to ambush someone, this is where I would do it. It's the most likely place, OK?'

Heads nodded again.

'At each end of this stretch of highway is a sharp elbow corner.' I pointed them out on the map. 'Each vehicle that makes the turn will be out of sight of the one behind or in front of it for a few seconds. Then there is this high ground to the left and a steep slope down to the river on the right. I figure they will attack from the high ground, with the river cutting off any chance for us to turn the vehicles around and get the fuck out of there.'

More than a few of the guys looked over at Bam Bam, as they realised that they had been seriously short-changed.

'Everyone got it?'

More nods.

'OK, here's what we are going to do. From here out I will have Two Trays lead in our blue Blazer. In his vehicle will be Bullfrog driving, Cash, Bird and Tank.' As I said their names, they all raised their hand for the others to see who they were. 'Why Two Trays in the lead? Because he knows the way to the bridge and because I said so, OK.' More nodding. 'You guys will then fit in as seated here or in the order Bam Bam wants you in, and we will take up the rear in our green Blazer. In that vehicle will be me, Peanut as driver, Noodle, Brownie and Stumpy.' Each in turn raised their hands.

'Before we actually cross the bridge, Two Trays will pull over. Bam Bam, your three vehicles will then take the lead.' They all looked a bit concerned at this news. 'I want you in the front because you have sedans, and we have Blazers that stick out like fuck. If Two Trays remains up front, we will be spotted as a convoy straight away. Don't worry, you won't get lost.'

Besides, I figured they needed to feel some discomfort at being first over the bridge, if only for a short time.

'After Two Trays has pulled over, he will drop in behind your last vehicle, so make sure you radio him when you're about to pass. I will then drop in behind him, so we will be the last two vehicles of this shitshow to cross.'

There was some hurried re-examining of their maps.

'Don't worry, once we have all crossed, Two Trays will take up the front position again and lead the rest of the way. OK everyone, are you all following so far?'

Everyone nodded a big yes. So far so good, I thought.

'Bam Bam, once your three vehicles get across, I want you to carry on up the road about two or three kilometres and find a place to pull over. Then you need to quickly swap your client into a different vehicle.' Bam Bam looked a bit confused. 'You have two armoured BMWs of different colours and one soft-skin, right?' I asked.

He nodded.

'I believe that if the IPs figure out that we are a PSD convoy, they will try to determine which vehicle is carrying the VIP and pass that information on to the shitheads up ahead, so you need to move him to another vehicle, OK?'

I saw the look of fear on the faces of the crew who would carry the client first, as they realised that they were the most likely to get targeted.

'Don't worry, it gets worse,' I continued. 'By this time Two Trays should have passed you guys to take the lead position again. He will radio his approach just like you did for him. Everyone with me so far?' I asked.

More affirmative nods.

'OK, as we get further along the route, Two Trays will radio everyone when he is approaching the likely ambush site. Everyone will acknowledge that they've heard him, OK? It's vital that we all stay within radio distance, but – and this is crucial – I want irregular spacing between vehicles; no running lights and no advertising our presence any more than we have just done on the bridge. Do not drive excessively fast, and do not run any blocking moves on local vehicles. I want us to blend in as much as possible, especially through this area,' I emphasised.

'You guys all have low-profile vehicles, so let's utilise that. Let the locals get in between us but maintain visual and stay at comms distance. Try not to look like an obvious close protection convoy. Let's try to confuse the bad guys a bit. If they are willing to kill their own people to get to us, then they really are a bunch of assholes, but let's not make it too easy for the pricks. Alternatively, if we enter the kill zone without any local cover, I want your soft car to have its windows down and weapons out and ready. In that situation, I want you to look like a gun-toting, pissed-off fucking porcupine.'

'If you see anything that is in any way suspect in this zone and are 80 per cent certain that we have been identified from this high ground, call it out, and then, if you think it warrants it, give it a burst. I really want to emphasise this point, guys. Hesitation can kill, OK?

Scan the high ground and scan ahead and, if need be, give it a burst. Do not expend all your ammo; I want controlled two to three rounds max. Keep calling it out over the comms and keep it controlled.'

'I want to make it clear to those fucks that we know they are there, and I want to make them keep their heads down.' I glanced around and could see the guys were enthused by the plan. 'As I've said, I figure the attack will come from the high ground to the left, but I want the guys on the right side of the vehicles to keep a keen eye on your side as well. If the ground is steep and totally wrong for an attack, then I want you to try to act as a spotter for the left side. Help them out with any mag changes and be prepared to jump in, in case of stoppages. You guys figure it out, OK?'

'OK, once we are through this area, go back to 100 per cent cover of your arcs of responsibility, as normal. Remember, this is where I think we could get hit because it is where I would hit someone, but always remember that anywhere and everywhere is a possible ambush site, so don't let your guard down at any stage, OK? Everyone got that? Now, are there any questions?'

I waited for a minute. I then saw Rich, in his fucking Tevas and Hawaiian shirt, make a move like he had to somehow add his two cents' worth and restore some credibility. As he was about to raise his hand, I cut him off.

'Yes, Rich. Can I help you?'

'Ah, this bridge,' he said, pointing at the map from the back of the room.

I pointed it out for him. 'This one, yes?'

'How do you know it's manned by the IPs and that it's where we will get made?'

It was a pathetic attempt to try to restore his credibility and only set him up for a bigger, deeper fall.

'How do I know?' I repeated, acting a bit goofy. 'Hmmm... How do I know?' I glanced at my crew of mongrels, who knew exactly what was about to happen.

'Yeah, how do you know?' Rich repeated, a bit cockier and louder so everyone could hear.

'Well, I know, mate, because I've read other mission briefs and incident reports, as anyone going on a run should do before they go,' I said, glancing across at Bam Bam. 'But more importantly, I know because we went out there, this morning, to have a look at the bridge. That's how I know. Me and the boys went out there after we dropped off our client and checked it out. It's called a recce, bro.'

This was the slam dunk with nothing but net; a hole in one on a par five. I watched him shrink in front of his guys. He had been made to look foolish and incapable, which is exactly what he was. He knew he should have been better prepared for this run. He should have carried out some sort of recce himself, instead of just handing it all over to some other poor fuck.

As for my guys, they were basking in the admiration they were getting from the other crew. Some of Rich's team even leant over and whispered, 'You guys were out there this morning? Holy fuck.'

'OK,' I interrupted. 'Let's get this shitshow on the road. See you in the car park in fifteen minutes. Let's go, boys.'

My guys and I got up and slowly walked out, leaving only the sound of our spurs ka-chinging in the air.

CHAPTER 12

I've said it before and I'll say it again: to me the job was no different from being in the military, except for the obvious and glorious difference in rates of pay. Everything we did still had to be thoroughly planned and practised, then planned and practised again.

As former SEALs, Rich and Bam Bam had absolutely no excuse for serving us that shit sandwich they'd tried to pass off as a mission brief. I'm sure if their SEAL Team bosses had heard it, they would have had them doing flutter kicks in the surf until their stomachs exploded.

Right now, this slackness was coming from guys who had clearly decided that the high tier they'd reached in the military was enough to get them through Iraq on reputation alone. Blackwater seemed to predominantly hire from within the former-SEAL community, and, in my experience, we were not experiencing this kind of problem with guys from other US military branches, such as army, rangers or marines, or even from some of our former police guys, like Stumpy.

The older generation of former SEALs, like Brian, George and even the owner, Erik, also seemed well squared away. Maybe it was a generational thing, but the way some of these guys were acting was dangerous, not to mention disrespectful to the hundreds of excellent operators who had come before them.

My guys and I might drink like there was no tomorrow, mainly because there was a high chance there would be no tomorrow, but we trained hard every week without exception. We would never leave off the training until I was happy that we had the drills squared away. As their team leader, I always went harder than the guys, to lead by example: *a beer earned tastes better than a beer stolen*. I even had plans in place in case I went down on a run, and I know my guys would have carried on and not lost their shit. We were a well-oiled team and the envy of many others in the company.

I would often get requests from guys who wanted to join us, and I would take some if they were up to our standard and the contract allowed. To me it was like the selection processes to get into Tier 1 units like the SAS and Delta Force: they never let the standard slip and I saw no reason to do so now. But from what I observed of the number of new companies being formed, they had to be way less stringent in their vetting procedures, that was if they had any at all. Most were being set up by former operators in-country, who saw an opportunity to make big bucks fast but didn't have the essential business know-how.

At the conclusion of the Kut brief, we went back to our rooms like a bunch of giggling schoolgirls.

'Fuck me, Baz,' Noodle announced, 'you showed those fucks. How embarrassing.'

'Yeah, bro. Right now, they are a liability to themselves. This run, hopefully, should fix that, but we are going to have to do the heavy lifting if the shit hits the fan, as I can't see them staying disciplined and keeping their shit together. I hope I'm wrong, because there are some excellent operators in that crowd, but leadership is a real issue. And while they are under Captain Teva, they aren't getting any better.'

The move out was surprisingly smooth. We were a five-vehicle convoy, which was huge in the private security world, but I didn't want to mix up men and machines. I just hoped that with the variation in distances between us, we wouldn't be too obvious.

One of Bam Bam's team in the soft sedan slid in behind Two Trays's Blazer, then came the two armoured BMWs, with me as tail-end Charlie-cum-mobile QRF. Peanut was driving, and we had Noodle and Brownie in the back seat, plus Stumpy in the ass. The trouble was that because Two Trays and I had the large Chevy Trailblazers, and you didn't see many of those in Iraq, it didn't take an avid reader of *Hot Rod* magazine to work out they weren't being crewed by locals.

The morning traffic rush was dying down, so we made pretty good time towards the bridge. Two Trays called it as we got close and the chatter on the radios increased, before Two Trays radioed that he would be pulling over and vehicle positions were swapped, exactly as briefed. *So far so good.*

As expected, there was a queue of vehicles waiting to get across the bridge and a steady stream crossing back towards us. This was a good sign, as it meant there would be plenty of local traffic on the road between us and the anticipated ambush zone. All the better for us to mingle with.

When it was our lane's turn to move, the line nudged forward slowly and I radioed for everyone to keep off the comms. I needed the channel clear, so Bam Bam in the lead vehicle could advise when they were past the IPs and what attention they had attracted. As the first BMW drew level with the policemen manning our side of the bridge, they didn't seem to pay any obvious attention. There were plenty of these 6 Series BMWs in Baghdad, with a lot being used by the insurgents, so our presence might not have registered at all. But no sooner had Bam Bam radioed that they were crossing the bridge, than the guys in the second BMW were on the air.

'Vehicle one, the IPs saw you and are paying you a lot of attention, over.'

Fuck me, here we go. 'Roger that,' we all acknowledged.

As each of our vehicles crawled past, the IPs eyeballed them, trying hard to look inside and scope out the occupants. As we pulled closer to one of the IPs, who had his attention fixed on the two BMWs, he reached into his pocket and pulled out a mobile phone.

'OK, there it is,' I announced. 'He's going to call our presence ahead and alert some fucker up the road. Fuck.'

By now the others should be about 500 metres ahead of us, looking for a secluded place to swap the client out.

'Hey, Two Trays, did you see that fucker pull his phone out?' I radioed the other Blazer.

'Yeah, I did, roger that, bro. Leave it to me.'

I wasn't sure what he had in mind, but if there was one thing I knew about Two Trays, it was that he could improvise real good. I mean, look how he got his call sign, right?

'Stumpy?' I radioed.

'Yeah, bro,' he answered, from his position behind me, manning the SAW. 'Shoulder that baby, will you, and make sure you point it right at that IP fucker when we pass, OK. And sweep the rest of them while you're at it.'

'Roger that, with pleasure.' Stumpy was one of the best guys in my team, as was Tank. During their time with me, the little fucks seldom saw where we were going, only where we had been. Facing backwards wasn't for everyone, but it was one hell of an important position. There were too many cases of insurgents racing up behind unsuspecting vehicles and unloading mag after mag into the back and sides, killing everyone too busy facing forward. Our boys in Fallujah were a tragic example.

Stumpy had set up his trunk-monkey nest like a little shop of horrors. His SAW was hooked in with bungee cords, giving him full range to swing the thing from side to side, without shooting up the vehicle. He'd also strung up a line of grenades on paracord, like a killer clothesline, with the HE (high-explosive) ones at the top and WP (white phosphorus) or thermite ones below. Damn, that little fucker loved his grenades.

To his side lay four 200-round boxes of 5.56mm ammo, laid out ready for a quick belt change. To his other side was his go bag jam-packed with all the additional ammo, extra grenades and 24hr survival equipment he might need, if we had to leg it on foot E&E – Escape and Evasion – style. Last but by no means least, propped up against the back of the rear seat, he had his AT4 anti-tank weapon. The little fucker was ready to spoil anyone's day. Stumpy had the option to wear a Kevlar helmet but, like the rest of us, decided not to, mainly because it looked goofy and really fucked up your hairdo. We all opted for ball caps. They were far more practical and besides, we would sooner get shot in the head and die quickly.

As we approached the crossing point, the IP who had been paying so much attention to the BMWs turned and suddenly spied Two Trays and the up-armoured Blazer right in front of him. Damn near shitting himself, he stepped out in front of the vehicle and gave him the pyramid 'wait' signal with one hand, while still holding his mobile phone in the other. There was, of course, no reason for us to stop.

'Keep going,' I radioed. 'It looks to me as if he's trying to separate us from the rest of the convoy.'

'Yeah, bro, my thoughts exactly.'

Two Trays told Bullfrog to step on the gas and to ram the IP off the bridge if he didn't get out of the way. With the Blazer picking up speed and barrelling towards him, the IP leapt to the right to avoid getting his legs squashed. Hopping around like he was standing on hot coals, he realised he still wasn't safe and resorted to trying to climb up the support cables running along the wall, clinging one-handed. As Bullfrog pulled alongside, Two Trays reached out of his window, grabbed the cell phone out of the horrified IP's hand and casually tossed it into the river below. Bullfrog then sped off and our vehicle followed, close enough to squash the IP fuck if he was stupid enough to try to climb down.

Once we were both past, he jumped down looking furious, and reached for his AK, bringing it to bear with his now very free and empty hands. Just as he was in the process of cocking it, however, he glanced up to see Stumpy's grinning face staring down the open sights of his 5.56mm belt-fed Bringer of Death. Had he gone as far as getting a round into his weapon, it would have been the last thing he would ever have done. His IP colleagues, realising what was happening, abandoned their posts and ran for cover.

'Two Trays, Baz here. Good move, mate, well done. Over.'

'Yeah thanks,' he answered. 'Whoever he was calling is going to have a hard time getting reception now.'

There was no doubt in my mind that the IP had been calling ahead, letting the insurgents know that there was a US convoy coming their way and telling them to get gunned-up and ready. I hoped he hadn't had time to give the full skinny before his phone met a watery grave. They had other phones, of course, but it was good to let them know that we knew exactly what they were up to.

We were all across the bridge, so we sped up to get back into radio range. Every 100 metres or so I did a radio check, until after about five kilometres I finally made comms with the rest of the crew. With some relief, I let them know that we were finally on their six, after which Two Trays roared past, taking up the lead again.

'Is the package swapped over?' I asked.

'Roger that,' someone replied.

'OK. Keep moving, I can see you now. Let's go.'

The music of choice for this run was something a bit less house. The Prodigy were excellent for Irish and really got the blood flowing, but this was going to be a longer trip, so I'd put together a list of my favourite Bowie tracks. First on the list was 'Sound and Vision', of course. And then, naturally, 'Under Pressure', which is undoubtedly one of the best songs ever in the history of songs.

Some crews liked really heavy metal shit, but you couldn't listen to that all day or you'd end up shooting yourself, and if we all did that, it would defeat the purpose of having an insurgency in the first place. Bowie had hundreds of great tracks and as long as I was C1, I was also head DJ.

The road was busy with traffic heading in the same direction as us, overtaking and cutting in and out of the convoy, and as we weren't in any great hurry this suited us just fine. Those fuckers would overtake and undertake in the most stupid of places: left side, right side, it didn't seem to matter. Oncoming traffic was just another game of chicken. They seemed to have no fear in their shitty-ass vehicles, more often than not overloaded with people and all their worldly possessions, as they thundered down the road oblivious to anyone or anything.

We were due to reach the suspected ambush area less than forty minutes after crossing the bridge, and the tension was cranking up in all the vehicles. As the minutes ticked by, I could imagine the guys counting down the clicks on their maps.

Soon enough we were approaching the X, along with four civilian clunkers interspersed among the convoy. As there was no oncoming traffic, I told Two Trays to be ready to move to the centre of the road. If the insurgents hadn't already worked out who was who, for sure the sight of the two US-made Trailblazers would identify us. My plan was that if they were going to attack, and we couldn't drive our way out of there, we would move up beside a local vehicle and use that to shield us from the bad guys.

OK, I know what you're thinking: that's some callous bullshit right there, and not very ethical. *Hey, them's the breaks.* My job was to protect the client and keep him alive and, in order to do that, I had to keep myself and my brothers alive. If it was going to happen, I would sooner it happened to someone else I didn't know and not us, and I'm sure most people would feel the same if they were honest.

At that moment, Two Trays radioed that he had spotted some males dressed in black on the high ground, to our left.

'Fuck,' I said aloud, feeling almost pissed off that this seemed to confirm my suspicions. I radioed all vehicles, reminding everyone to stay mixed in with the local traffic as much as possible and not to show any weapons. I could see a lone male up there, dressed head to toe in black, as Two Trays had said, standing up ballsy as fuck and making no effort to hide.

'Yep, got him, ten o'clock high,' I called on the comms. 'Lone male, ten o'clock, high ground.'

'Roger, seen,' everyone replied.

I was keeping a close eye on the figure, when all of a sudden I saw him turn tail and dart off the ridgeline, disappearing from sight. It was a classic attack indicator.

'All vehicles, I just saw that fucker on the hill run off.'

'Oh, that's not good,' someone said.

'All vehicles, this is Baz, bust it out of here. Go, go, go!'

I received four 'rogers' from the teams, followed by four puffs of shitty exhaust smoke as they punched their accelerators. Peanut hit the gas too, and we accelerated up beside the unsuspecting vehicle to our front. For a while we shadowed the poor fucker, who must have been a little surprised to see a big SUV sitting alongside him on the open highway. I looked over at the driver, giving him a smile and a wave. In the back was a female and three children. Next to the driver was a big suitcase sitting on the front seat. It looked like it contained all their worldly possessions. The driver gave a somewhat unsteady wave back, not really knowing what else to do.

I was starting to hope that the liquid in our tank was mostly petrol and not water, as the thought of the Blazer spluttering and losing speed at this moment was not a good one. Dodgy fuel in Iraq was a fact of life. Like street crack cocaine, it was cut with all sorts of shit like water, urine and any other liquid available to make it go further.

But we continued thundering down the road, engine roaring, gradually closing the distance between the killing ground we were in and the safety of the far bend, but we still had two more civilian vehicles to pass to catch the rest of the convoy. It was now that I could feel my stomach start to knot. That fucker on the hill must have been a spotter. If so, an attack should be coming from either our left flank or the front pretty soon.

Peanut was rocketing down the left lane, with only the two slow fuckers on our right, as we closed in for a very rapid overtaking move. Then, without even so much as a glance in his rear-view mirror – in which he would have seen us haring down on his ass like an angry Chevy tsunami – the nearest fucker suddenly pulled out right in front of us, in a piss-poor attempt to overtake the even slower fucker in front of him.

'Fuuuuccccckkkk!' we all yelled in unison, as Peanut slammed on the brakes causing all of us to wish we had put our seat belts on.

Our big heavy Blazer came screeching up to the ass of the sedan in front, and I saw Peanut straighten his arms to brace for the impact. I slammed my foot hard on the non-existent brake pedal and put my right hand on the dash, not wanting to let go of my MP5, knowing that if I did, it would turn into a knee-breaking missile. The screech from the front tyres was as loud as fuck, and blue smoke and the smell of burning rubber filled the vehicle. Through the smoke I saw the head of the idiot driver in front glance around in sheer panic, wondering where the fuck the deafening noise was coming from.

Just as we were about to make the inevitable contact, the driver swung his shitbox to the right, cutting off the vehicle he was trying to overtake. The driver of that car hit his brakes, to avoid being forced off the road, and by God knows what kind of miracle we roared past, missing the sedan by a layer of paint.

Peanut immediately moved his foot off the brake and back on the accelerator, causing the Blazer to buck and take off again like the space shuttle. As we pulled away, however, Two Trays came up with a call that sent cold sweats down our backs.

'Contact front! Contact front! Tracer twelve o'clock high.'

Through the open windows of the Blazer we could hear the distinctive CRACK-CRACK-CRACK of a large belt-fed machine gun opening up. I looked forward and up and, sure enough, I could see tracer arcing its way towards us from the hill directly to my front.

'Argh, fuck!' I yelled to everyone in the vehicle. 'Here we go!'

Even in broad daylight we could see the muzzle flash and the tracer rounds lancing in.

'Fuck me, do we have anything left in this, bro?' I asked Peanut, wishing we had something like a *Mad Max* nitro gas button to push.

'No, bro, foot's flat. This is all we got.'

'OK, bro, give it everything but maintain control.'

This wasn't a time to panic, so I kept my voice as calm as possible, even though I was shitting myself as I visualised the results of the incoming HMG rounds slamming into us. My only hope was that the fuckers wouldn't have compensated for our speed properly and would be aiming at where we were, not where we were going to be. With a shit bucket of luck, we would be able to outrun the shower of bullets that would soon be raining down upon us.

Come on you fucker, a voice yelled inside my head, as I willed the Blazer to kick into hyper-speed and get us the fuck out of there.

We were painfully aware that, despite having ten-millimetre plating on our sides and back, we had nothing over our heads. The roof of the vehicle was soft-skin, so rounds coming down on us would tear through it like tissue paper before ripping into us. We needed to get as close to the shooter's position as we could as fast as possible, to try to cut off his angle on us.

I'm sure I wasn't the only one in the vehicle starting to pucker up and hunch my shoulders, to make my head as small as possible, and suddenly wishing I'd worn one of those stupid Kevlar helmets. Any second now, we were going to get obliterated by hot, supersonic balls of full metal jacket, which would pulverise our soft bodies to mincemeat. I hoped like fuck it would be quick, and please, you know the rules, not the face.

The damn road seemed to go on for ever, but the longer we waited for the impacts, the closer we got to the base of the hill. If only we could make it to that bend, we'd be OK. *Come on you fucker*, I willed the Blazer. Every metre we travelled was a metre closer to survival.

The tension was horrible. I could feel my shirt sticking to my back and then, as I waited for the rounds to hit, my bloody leg started to shake. I got the cold sweats and the hairs all over my body were up on end. Thoughts of my soon-to-be fatherless – well, even more fatherless than they were used to – children flashed through my mind, and I thought of Jen, who would no longer have to worry about her friends being angry at her for wanting to marry me.

I felt sad and disappointed for fucking that up and a million other things in my life. I knew I wouldn't die old, but I didn't want to die this young, either. I held my breath but, as I waited to die, nothing seemed to happen. No bullets, no impact, no pain.

It was Stumpy's voice that broke the silence, coming in over the radio from his post in the rear. 'Holy shit, guys, look at that.'

'What?' I croaked, unable to see behind. My voice was still cracking with anxiety, as I cleared my throat. 'Stumpy, what is it?' I asked again.

'Those poor fuckers, the locals we just overtook, they are getting totally hammered; fucked up; I mean pulverised. Holy fuck,' he said, forgetting he was still transmitting. 'They… they're getting chopped to shit by the incoming.'

I leant forward, trying to get a look through my side mirror. I spotted one of the white sedans shoot uncontrollably across the road, like it had just been flicked by some invisible hand. Steam was billowing out of the hood, half-obscuring the windscreen, which had been smashed to pieces. The front tyres had burst, and the vehicle front had dropped to the road. There looked to be no one controlling it any more, and then I lost sight of it, as it skidded behind us.

'What's happening, Stumpy? Give us a commentary, will you?'

'The vehicles we just passed are dead, the people are dead. Shot to shit.' He was struggling to keep his voice controlled. 'It's horrific, bro. Both vehicles are getting pounded, and it looks like everyone inside is shredded.' He paused for a terrible beat. Then, 'Baz, this is total destruction. Both vehicles have stopped dead and there isn't any movement in them at all.'

'Why the fuck did they get hit?' I asked aloud to no one in particular.

'Hold on,' Stumpy came back over the comms.

'Yeah, mate,' I acknowledged.

'Hang on, there's a white SUV, further behind. It's getting some hits on it as well. Fuck me it's… oh, hang on… it looks like a PSD convoy.'

'How can you tell?' I asked.

'They all have their front headlights on, mate. It's the lead vehicle of a PSD convoy. Two white Land Cruisers have stopped, and a third vehicle is way behind. They look to be getting the incoming.'

Just as he finished, we reached the turn and roared around it at top speed, a short distance below where the shooting was actually coming from, but too close for the shooter to adjust his angle down onto us. For now, at least, we were through.

I tried to process what the hell was happening. Another PSD team must have been just a few clicks behind us crossing the bridge. Maybe they were identified because they'd made no attempt

327

to blend in, or maybe they had been mistaken for us. They weren't driving low-profile vehicles and they had their headlights on – a dead giveaway. It's a move I never understood in Iraq, the old 'hey, hey, here I am, come and get me' signal. Maybe they were just an easier target.

But if we were lucky, the poor PSD fuckers behind us were unfortunate, and the civilians even more so; those guys were just trying to get to where they needed to be. Two families completely wiped out, and who gave a damn about them? As much as I held to the belief 'better them than me', I felt shitty that they had got what had probably been meant for us.

There was nothing I could do about it, though. I don't really give a fuck about what men do to men, but as soon as innocent women and children are involved, I get very pissed off. Men are fuckin' dicks.

'You OK back there, bro?' I asked Noodle.

'Yeah, bro,' he said, his tone indicating how he was feeling. Like all of us, he was glad to be alive, but sad at the price others had paid.

'That was fuckin' brutal, bro,' he said. 'I think I'll call the wife and kids tonight, if we make it back.'

'Amen, brother.'

We rounded the corner and left the hill behind us, but I could still hear the bumping of the machine gun as it echoed through the valley. Soon, even that faded, the sound of Bowie drifting back to my ears. I turned the music down and radioed for Two Trays to keep punching it, while we caught up with the tail-end of the convoy.

I settled back to watch my arcs and slowly turned Bowie back up to listen to another of my favourites, 'Wild Is the Wind'. Apart from the music and the roar of the engine, there was a deafening silence in the vehicle. I was already visualising what I would do if I caught those fuckers on the hill. I would have them kneel in front of me, looking down the hill facing the burning vehicles full of dead civilians: husbands, wives, children. And then I would shoot them all in the back of their heads. Not directly on the centre line or right into the brain but just off to one side, so that half of their face and jaw would smash open and they wouldn't die immediately.

I wanted the last thing they saw, as their blood filled their eyes, to be the innocent families they had killed.

The rest of the drive was quiet, and we arrived in Kut in a subdued mood. The client was attending a meeting with the local tribal leaders, the military and CPA officials, to talk about the next steps to ensure a peaceful future. Basically, another bullshit meeting with sloppy handshakes, false promises and absolutely nothing achieved. Why the fuck did someone from a catering company need to be in on that? I had no idea.

We parked across from the town hall where the meeting was taking place and left the client to Bam Bam and his guys. They all looked so typically American, with their sand-coloured ball caps, Oakley sunglasses, war-kit vest and mag holders, shitty AR-15s and Glock sidearms hanging down their legs like John Wayne.

Yeah boys, that's it, I told myself. *Looking good, but you buggers wouldn't have got here if it wasn't for us, and now you're all puffed up doing your best to get seen.*

Just as Bam Bam and his boys disappeared, a whole group of Toyota flatbed trucks came roaring in with a Toyota Land Cruiser tucked into the centre, kicking up all sorts of shit and dust before stopping right in front of us. We slipped our safety catches off and gently moved behind the vehicles. More than a dozen armed Iraqi males jumped out of the trucks and rushed to encircle the Land Cruiser. They looked across at us with the same distaste and mistrust with which we looked at them.

After a short Mexican standoff, during which they convinced themselves – incorrectly – that we were not a threat they couldn't deal with, the passenger door opened and a short, bearded figure stepped out. Dressed completely in black, with a flowing robe wrapped around his shoulders and a large black turban, he strode towards the venue, surrounded by his posse.

I don't usually pay much attention to those who think they are important, but something about this guy was different. He carried his stocky frame with a certain authority and had a brooding air, with a thick black beard and deep-set dark eyes. I knew immediately who it was. It was the Iraqi Shia cleric, Muqtada al-Sadr.

The contractor side of me was saying: *That's the fucker who ordered the attacks on Najaf and here in Kut, just a few months back*. The side of me that thought the whole war was bullshit was saying: *Fuck me, that's Patrick Swayze, leader of the Wolverines, from* Red Dawn.

No wonder there was so much security. It had to be a big meeting all right. As al-Sadr headed towards the venue, the crowd of locals who had gathered were getting really excited, trying to reach out and touch him. He gave a slight wave, nothing more.

'Do you know who that is?' I asked Noodle.

'No. Didn't get to see him.'

'That was al-Sadr himself.'

'Really? Then those must be some of his Mahdi Army guys. So those are the fuckers who attacked Najaf?'

'Yep.'

'Well, at least there won't be any attacks on the meeting.' He paused. 'So, who were those fuckers who hit us on the road? You would think that today of all days it would be a bad idea to attack anything around here, in case they got the wrong target.'

'Yeah,' I said. 'I wonder who it could be.'

We slipped into our standard, 'hurry up and wait' routine: pulling sentry on the vehicles, napping in the vehicles, sitting on the vehicles, kicking the tyres on the vehicles, pissing on the vehicles, smoking cigars on the vehicles, chewing the fat with the guys in the vehicles, eyeballing Sadr's guys from the vehicles and being eyeballed back from their vehicles.

It was all on.

'Hey, bro,' I asked Noodle. 'You ever seen *Red Dawn*?' The two of us were standing off to one side, where we couldn't be overheard by the boys.

There was a long pause before he answered. 'Yeah, bro, I've seen it.' Then, without any prompting, 'So, what you're saying is that al-Sadr is the character that Patrick Swayze played, while fighting the invading Russians. And the Russians are the Americans in this case. And those fuckers over here, the Mahdi Army, they're the Wolverines; you know, a bunch of locals standing up to an invading force; fighting against oppression and enslavement to keep their traditions, customs and way of life safe; fighting for their freedom. Is that what you mean, bro?'

I looked at Noodle's smug grin and held his gaze long enough so he could see my *go fuck yourself, you over-educated fuck* expression. I tried to pretend that wasn't what I was going to suggest at all, but Noodle was ahead of me again.

'Nineteen eighty-four, bro,' he said before I even had a chance to ask if he knew when the movie was made.

'Oh, go fuck yourself,' I quipped. 'And hand me the cutter, you fuck, 'cause the Baz wants a Cohiba. Care to join me, you fuck?'

'Glad to,' he replied, still looking very pleased with himself.

Time dragged, as it tends to on PSD jobs, and between puffs on one of Fidel's finest, Noodle and I admitted to having a quiet dash of admiration for al-Sadr and his followers. Then we moved over to talk with the boys about the ambush.

'Who d'you think would attack along that route, today, if they knew this meeting was taking place?' ventured Cash. 'There would have been warnings put out by al-Sadr to stop the stupid shit for one day, don't you think?'

'Hey, do you remember that new player in town, Zarqawi?' I asked.

'That fucker's really starting to become a cock-sized thorn in everyone's ass,' said Cash. 'Is it possible it was him?'

'Makes sense,' Two Trays answered. 'I hear he and his following are loosely aligned to al-Qaeda, and he sure would benefit from peace talks like this breaking down.'

'Fuck me,' said Cash. 'That's all we need, another asshole to watch out for.'

There were also rumours of Iranian sniper teams and Chechen mercenaries making their presence felt in Baghdad. It would have been stupid not to take them seriously. We wouldn't train any differently, as a threat was a threat, but those fuckers would more than likely have military training and employ tactics and counter-measures similar to our own, rather than the haphazard shoot-and-scoot hits we were used to.

Hours later it was meeting end. At this point, everyone normally tried to prove their importance by leaving first, but, on this occasion, there was no doubting who was top dog. Sadr's boys stormed out brandishing their AKs in the air, yelling and pushing the star-struck locals aside. Surrounded by his circle of armed 'Wolverines',

Sadr jumped into the rear seat of the Land Cruiser, the guards sprinted to clamber on the backs of their flatbeds and the convoy raced off at 100mph.

Al-Sadr has left the building.

Next it was the turn of Big Army. Not wanting to be outdone by the Wolverines, they headed for their roaring Humvees, over-revved their engines and tore off in the opposite direction.

Last out were Bam Bam and his boys, surrounding their catering client, plus several other white-men VIPs and their CP teams, all trying to out-fearsome each other in their war outfits; all trying to look as if they had the answer to this unholy mess.

We mounted up and waited in the pre-positioned vehicles as they loaded the client back into the hard BMW. Bam Bam radioed that we were going to the Kut CPA, for chow, before heading back to Baghdad. Nice, I thought. We could do with a good meal, and this would give me time to brief him about the ambush.

We drove the short distance and parked up again. I looked around trying to envisage the shitfight of a siege that had occurred here earlier in the year, noticing that the T walls had now been placed along the riverside, which must have spoilt the GC's view from his office window. What a shame. Once the client had been ushered into the chow hall, we took our cue, removed our kit and made our way in to enjoy some good old KBR DEFAC (dining facility) prison food.

And there it all was, sitting in all its glory in shiny steel food trays: hamburgers, hot dogs, chilli, vegetables of different colours, salad and sodas. To be honest, it was absolutely beautiful, and we made complete pigs of ourselves, knowing that every meal for the foreseeable future would be chicken and fucking rice.

Afterwards, while the client and the Kut GC went to his office to admire the view of the T wall, I got the chance for a heads-up with

Bam Bam. He was understandably concerned about heading back along the same route. In any military or CP situation you always try to have a back-up route, but, as I had briefed earlier that morning, the alternative would not get us back before dark. And if we didn't get moving pronto, our primary route wouldn't get us back before dark either.

I looked at my watch, then at the sky to judge how much light we had left. 'OK,' we're going to have to gun it back flat-out all the way.'

'Yeah, good idea,' Bam Bam agreed.

'Make sure all the vehicles are refuelled, equipment checked, new batteries on the radios, radio checks done, and wash the vehicle windows free of bugs. Then tell me when you're ready to roll.' To my guys, this was usual pre-run practice, but to these guys it was all pretty new. Once everything was done, I briefed everyone on the route and the plan.

By the time we left the Kut CPA, we had three hours of decent light remaining. That was plenty of time, as long as we had no delays, but it was going to be a gumball rally to get back regardless. No one wanted to be outside the walls at night. As Two Trays led out, we radio-checked one last time before gaining speed like a very well-armed iron horse.

As we approached the ambush site, I dreaded what I would see. Instinctively, we all searched the high ground in case those fucks had hung around in the hope of extras, but they must have bugged out following the hit that morning.

We barrelled past the site of the attack and could hear the sound of broken glass crunching under our fast-moving tyres. The wreckage of the two civilian vehicles was still where they had ended up. One was nose-first in a ditch, the other right behind it. Both were burnt out, riddled with bullet holes and full of blood stains and shattered glass, but thankfully there were no bodies.

In that split second, I imagined seeing the ghosts of the families sitting in their sedans, totally unaware of what had happened, still enjoying the ride but with nowhere to go any more; never leaving this stretch of road and never arriving at their destination. But for an accident of fate, it could have been us.

That kind of thing can play on your mind; the split seconds that determine whether you live or you die. Maybe if I had taken a moment longer, or a moment less on the brief that morning, things might have been different. We might have been on another part of the road. We might never have seen those poor people and they might still be alive.

It was horrific, but what could you do? They were dead and we were alive. Would I have had it any other way? No fucking way. It was just one more thing to keep me from sleeping well. Place it on the pile, please.

We recrossed the dreaded bridge, but by now the duty IPs were a new shift. Perhaps the earlier lot had fucked off, fearing that any survivors from the ambush might return to kill them. As we were the last to make it across, I radioed Bam Bam that we would break off and head for the IZ, to collect our client, as they wanted to head to BIAP and hit Burger King.

To be honest, I was glad to see them head off, and for once I wouldn't conduct a debrief for the entire convoy. Instead, I'd do one just with my guys. Besides, the other team had a new mission: Mountain Dew, chewing tobacco and high-fives at BIAP Burger King on a job well done. On a positive note, they'd gained some valuable experience from us, our methods of briefing and time spent on the road. I hoped they would get their shit together and become an effective team.

Fuck it, I thought, *we all had to start somewhere.*

A couple of days later, we popped over to some new restaurant that had opened in the IZ. While we were there, we started talking again about the ambush on the road to Kut. By some bizarre coincidence, sitting at a table within hearing distance were two of the guys who had also been caught in the attack. It turned out they were a British security team, and they were riding in the convoy of white SUVs, which had hit the ambush lights full-on.

We were more than a little curious to hear their side of the story. 'Did you see us in front of you?' I asked.

The TL shook his head. 'Not at all. All we saw were these two shitty-looking white sedans. Then all of a sudden, we saw them skidding and bouncing all over the place and wondered what the fuck they were doing.'

'Didn't you hear the gunfire?' Two Trays asked.

'No, mate, we had the windows up and the music blasting, and we heard fuck all.'

'Then what?' Stumpy asked.

'Well about a fucking nanosecond after seeing the sedans getting destroyed, bullets starting slamming into the front and roof of our vehicle, a soft-skin Land Cruiser. We knew we were under attack but had no idea where from. It took a few seconds for us to slow down enough to try to throw in a U-turn and get out of there.'

'And what about your second vehicle?' Noodle asked.

'Well, that drove into a hail of shit big time. While we were able to turn around, they got riddled.'

'Did anyone get hit?' Cash asked.

'Yeah, mate. Unfortunately, the driver got two in the legs and two through his vest, he's fucked up, but he survived.' We glanced at each other with a *fuck me that was close* look. 'And our tail gunner got two in his back and one in the back of his head and died instantly.'

'Fuck, that's not good.'

'No, mate,' he said, glancing down at the floor. 'He was a good mate of mine. We were in the same regiment.'

'Fuck, bro, sorry to hear that,' we said in a lame effort to console him. But I mean, what the fuck *do* you say?

'Hey, them's the risks, eh, guys,' he added, weakly.

The second guy then took up the story. 'We pulled back as far as we could, but our vehicle was seriously damaged and really starting to shit the bed. The second vehicle managed to reverse out pretty much alongside us. I could see the look of sheer terror on the driver's face, but despite his injuries he did a great job getting them out of there. Our third vehicle was further back and was able to stop without any damage.'

'I didn't see your vehicles on the side of the road when we came back through,' I remarked.

'No, mate, we crossed over into the second vehicle, as ours had died. It had fluid spewing out of it and two flat tyres, so we cross-decked the injured and dead into the third vehicle and they fucked off back to Camp Victory Medical Centre, while we towed our vehicle back to the bridge and left it there. And you know what?'

'What?' Two Trays asked.

'Those fucking IPs promised our vehicle would be safe with them, but when we went back to pick it up, it had been completely rat-fucked. I mean stripped of *everything*. They would have taken the paint job if they could have, the dirty fucks.'

Listening to their story of death and mayhem, I didn't have the heart to tell them that they had advertised their presence, driving with their lights on like some dumbass presidential convoy, or that the IPs would have made them the minute they crossed the bridge. They had enough on their plates, without me pointing out all the obvious mistakes they'd made. I just didn't think it would make them feel any better, and it sure as shit wouldn't change the outcome either way.

'So, what are you guys up to now?' I asked.

'We're out of here. Going home. The guy that was injured – the driver – he's already in hospital back in the UK. This shit just ain't worth getting killed for. Sure, the $350 per day is good, but I can find a cheapskate job back home and just be grateful I'm alive.'

We were a little surprised that they were only getting $350 per day. We presumed everyone was on about the same as us by then, that the days of shitty Custer Battles pay were gone. But, as we discovered, they were working for one of the new companies that were starting to pop up. It seemed to me that whoever they worked for had spent fuck-all money on the essentials, like armoured vehicles and proper training, and the guys running the roads had paid the price. Same-old, same-old.

'Well, I guess your company is screwed, once you guys leave,' I remarked.

'No, mate, there are plenty of guys willing to fill our boots. In fact, the twats running it are now talking about manning the positions with Iraqis and having only Brits as team leaders. Well, they can stick that right up their arse.'

'Fuck yeah, bro,' I said. 'You two are making exactly the right decision.'

With that we stood up and shook hands and said our goodbyes.

What we had just heard was deeply sobering. But truth be told, our company really wasn't that different. Although we were making millions of dollars for Blackwater, like those guys, we were running without essential gear – namely, proper comms. There was no fucking excuse for it, none at all.

And sooner or later, it was bound to come back and bite us on the ass.

7

CHAPTER 13

The heat in Iraq can be a problem for some, but I loved it. Rich's crew seemed to be enjoying the sunny times too. Their pool parties were becoming a regular fixture, just like our gatherings for evening beers, except that we called it a night no later than 22:00. They seemed to be out there long into the mornings. How they were doing their runs while carrying those kinds of hangovers beat me.

I had gone out a few times sporting the mother of all hangovers, and I had been a lot less than 100 per cent sharp. I always made sure that I wasn't in the same vehicle as the client, not before the sun and several bottles of water got me back to fighting-fit. Plus, we all made sure to cover for one another. If someone wasn't feeling good, we would adjust the vehicle manning, but I never allowed anyone to go on a run still shit-faced. Maybe Rich's crew had a magic remedy we didn't possess.

Wednesday 2 June 2004 dawned like any other day in Iraq. We were out doing our normal early-morning run when we decided to pop into the team house for a water resupply and to see what we could scrounge. A new pizza joint had opened nearby, and we hoped there would be some leftovers in the fridge.

As I dropped my kit in the TV room, I noticed Rich was in the ops room. *Fuck me*, I thought, *what's brought you out of your cave in the Al-Hamra?* Even more surprising, he wasn't in shorts and Tevas, though his war-gear still looked and smelt brand new. I sat myself down in the ops room, pretending to check through the mail, fully intending to give him some shit as soon as the opportunity arose, but it quickly became apparent this was not a morning for that.

It turned out that Bam Bam and his team had been travelling back to the IZ along Tampa, and their driver hadn't seen a massive hole in the road caused by an earlier IED. He'd lost control of their vehicle, which rolled several times. As loose items were catapulted around the interior, one of those guys, Kato, was hit on the head by the fire extinguisher or some other hard object and killed.

No one in particular was to blame. It was just one of those freak accidents, and Rich and his crew were devastated, as were we all. Kato was one of the top guys in their team, and he and Bam Bam had been close, having come up together through the Basic Underwater Demolition course that all SEALs do.

I went outside to find my guys doing their best to console Rich's team. It was always hard when someone got killed. It was the nature of the business, so we kind of accepted the risks, but we always thought we'd die in a gunfight, an IED or some other battle-related incident. None of us foresaw dying in a road traffic accident (RTA), though at the speeds we were forced to drive it was one of the greatest dangers.

A few days later, Bam Bam escorted Kato's body back to the US, to deliver it to his wife and family. A couple more of the team were also sporting minor injuries, but however much they might not have felt physically or emotionally ready to get back into the saddle, the show had to go on. They just had to put any thoughts of grief out of their heads, so it didn't cloud their judgement out on the road.

With Bam Bam out of the country, it was up to a couple of the other senior guys to take control. Chris, call sign 'Lurch', was another former SEAL and a big, easy-going, likeable fucker. At 6ft 2in. with chiselled good looks, he reminded me of Jerry. Chris could easily have slipped into the Hollywood scene as a military adviser, and with looks like that maybe forged an acting career. Instead, he was here with the rest of us mixing it in Iraq.

Ever since the Kut run, Lurch and I had gelled. He respected the way I ran my guys and the mission brief I'd given that day. He was due to rotate out on leave, but the team numbers were depleted due to the accident. Despite nursing his own injuries, he decided to stay on for a few days to help assimilate some new operators – four Polish former-GROM guys that Blackwater had just hired, Adam, Krzysztof, Artur and Paul.

The Polish guys had only just arrived in-country, so they hadn't earned any call signs yet. Chris rightly felt they shouldn't be running missions without an experienced operator to lead. After that, he could leave and properly mourn the loss of Kato, back home.

Three days after Kato's death, Chris, plus two guys, JC and Rat, set out in two vehicles for BIAP, together with the Poles. Rat led with two of the Poles in an armoured SUV, while Chris, JC and the other two Poles brought up the rear in a soft-skin SUV. The run along Irish wasn't anything the team hadn't done many times before, but it would be good training.

At around 10:00 they'd just passed under the first of three over-bridges and were moving out to overtake cars coming onto Irish from the side ramp. This kind of traffic was nothing out of the ordinary and they could usually rely on their speed to get clear of it. Suddenly, the rear, soft-skin vehicle exploded into a fiery ball, as it was struck by a rocket-propelled grenade (RPG) fired from behind.

The missile hit around the back passenger door, blasting a cone of molten shrapnel inside, through the occupants and into the engine, causing the vehicle to roll to a stop in flames. Hearing the explosion and seeing his buddies' vehicle now in flames through his side mirror, Rat yelled at his driver to reverse back as fast as possible. His aim was to pull up next to the burning hulk, using their armour as protection, while they cross-loaded the guys out and into their vehicle.

As they shot backwards, two vehicles sped past and screeched to a halt about 100 metres ahead, cutting off their escape forward. The well-drilled attackers got out, formed up in a line and opened fire with small arms and PKM belt-fed machine guns. Rat's SUV and Chris's stricken soft-skin, by then side by side, were being sprayed with bullets. The protection afforded by the armour was limited, for the SUV was being hammered with armour-piercing and incendiary rounds, which were bouncing off the road into the vehicle's under-belly and slowly eating their way through the reinforced windshield.

Round after round slammed into the glass, and with each hit the windscreen began to spider and splinter. It was only a matter of seconds before it would fail. At the same time, hot tracer tipped with phosphorus was being fired directly into the engine compartment. Finally, it penetrated the fuel tank and ignited the leaking fuel and oil.

With both vehicles immobilised, those not already killed by the RPG had no choice but to get out before they burnt to death. Under a hail of bullets, they needed to fight their way out, but their only form of cover was the SUVs, which would soon be blazing infernos.

The guys were under attack from at least a dozen well-trained insurgents, who began moving in for the kill. As the survivors desperately returned fire to the front, a second group of attackers drove up alongside them and opened fire at close range, from the other side of the two burning wrecks.

Fighting like demons, the guys were having to spray rounds and lob grenades to the front and their flank in a desperate effort to keep the murderous fucks at bay. Every time the attackers tried to advance on their cornered prey, they were driven back by a hail of bullet and grenade blasts.

There was no way the guys were going down easily, and they were determined to take as many of the fucks as they could, but, boxed in and slowly being roasted by the heat from the burning vehicles, they were starting to run out of ammo. They realised their only chance was to take the fight to their attackers and go on the offensive.

Adam, one of the former GROM guys, led the way, charging the attackers to their flank, blasting any who came into his AR's sights and throwing grenades into their vehicles as he rampaged through them. Blanking his mind to the pain of a broken clavicle and three bullet wounds sustained during his one-man assault, he broke their line.

Adam's incredible heroism effectively turned the tide of the battle, forcing the insurgents onto the back foot. Rat had been shot in the head and legs, and he'd taken several grenade fragments to his face, but he too continued to fight. Having used up all his AR ammo, he resorted to throwing high-explosive grenades, killing and wounding several of the attackers.

The surviving BW guys regrouped. Redistributing their few remaining mags, they returned to the battle in one last heroic push. Lobbing their remaining grenades at the retreating attackers, they fired off all their rounds until finally their guns were empty.

Seeing the attackers retreat, laden down with their dead and wounded, the guys seized their chance. They were unable to take any of their fallen comrades with them because of the inferno that had engulfed the vehicles. They ran to the central barrier, crossed to the opposite carriageway and stopped a startled local. Paying him cash to commandeer his vehicle, they drove off, seeking medical treatment for their innumerable wounds.

Out of the team of seven, only three made it out alive. Two had gunshot and shrapnel wounds, while the other had hardly a scratch on him despite having had dozens of grenades and hundreds of bullets fired at them. Chris, JC and two of the Poles – Krzysztof and Artur – in the rear vehicle were killed instantly by the initial RPG into their soft-skin vehicle.

The ESS contract had now claimed nine lives: the Fallujah four, Jerry, Wes, Mike and Scott; Kato, who'd died in the RTA; and now Chris, JC, Krzysztof and Artur. The loss of them was hard to bear. It felt somehow as if we were losing the battle in Iraq; as if the scales had somehow tipped in the insurgents' favour. These latest deaths really made me think personally about the dark realities of being here.

A QRF might have saved some of Chris and his team, but none had been stood-up. This had become standard practice within BW teams, as there just weren't enough guys to be kept on standby. Even if there had been, there would have been no way for anyone to know what was happening due to the lack of any usable comms system. None of us had had any idea what was happening to our brothers out on Irish, who were no more than ten clicks away, not until it was way too late.

In my view, it was criminal.

The news of the attack came in only by word of mouth, as another security company had driven past, seen the results of the carnage and realised it was a BW team that had got hit.

Equally disturbing were the slick, military-style tactics used by the attackers. Never before had the insurgency taken the fight to any security company like this. Usually, they would either shoot-and-scoot, attack from a distance with indirect HMG fire, mortars or rockets, or rely on IEDs. It was obvious to us that highly trained 'foreign fighters' were in town, ready to mix it up.

For a while now we had all heard reports of 'foreign fighters' flocking into Iraq from Iran, Syria, Chechnya and even across Europe. We were convinced the attack on Irish was the work of a well-trained 'foreign fighter' unit because of their willingness to withdraw, taking their dead and wounded with them so they could not be identified.

At about this time, we also started seeing the use of a new and fearsome type of bomb: not so much an improvised device using old artillery shells wired together, but a purposely made rocket-forming projectile (RFP). This fucker was a game-changer, as it used the principles of employing a shaped charge – common in the military world – to cut through steel, armour, metal bridges and even large concrete structures.

An RFP contains explosives with a high velocity of detonation, packed behind a concave housing. When the charge is detonated, the concave metal, normally copper, instantly inverts, transforming into a molten slab that travels so fast and so powerfully that it cuts through its target like a laser. RFPs would prove extremely effective and absolutely deadly.

With all of that in mind, it was more important than ever that my New Zealand mate, T, and his Kiwi teammates in Baghdad had the right equipment to face this deadly threat. We moved back into the team house, and I put a call through to Jim, one of the Kiwis based in Baghdad, asking what hardware they were deficient in. What he told me was shocking: they were suffering from a shortage of the most basic tools of the trade – automatic weapons, mags and ammo.

Jim was one of my old Unit buddies. He'd joined the SAS a couple of cycles before me. He was a solid operator, but he did look like he was about to have a heart attack whenever he went for a run, despite having been in Air Troop – although, to be fair, Air is the least physical troop within the Unit. Let's be honest – if you could swim, master boats and tame the mighty oceans like Neptune himself, you would be in the hardest-working troop in the Unit: Amphib Troop. *My old troop.*

I mean, any fucker can flop out of the ass-end of a plane and let gravity do the work, right?

Anyway, Jim was grateful for any help, so I took their order and asked our fixer, Mo, to make some calls. It took Mo a few days to work his magic, and once I had all the merchandise, I called Jim and we arranged for him to come and pick it up. He and his boys were excited to finally get something sensible in their hot hands, as all requests to their (British) company for automatic weapons seemed to have fallen upon deaf ears. Just like our comms request had at Blackwater.

If the company won't supply it, we'll go get it ourselves, they'd decided. Damn right. Who gave a fuck what the company bosses sitting pretty in London thought? They weren't the ones risking their asses running the streets of Iraq on a daily fucking basis.

Just as my boys and I gathered around the garden furniture to start our nightly life-appreciation class, Jim pulled into the parking area, accompanied by another Kiwi buddy of mine, Walter. Unlike us, Walter hadn't been in the Unit. He was a military physical training instructor (PTI), and if you were to hear him tell it, you'd think that the PTI selection course made SAS selection look like a Sunday picnic with the Girl Guides. He would go on about how it was the hardest thing you could do in the NZ military, while we would just laugh and let him carry on, the cheeky fucker.

Walter and I had met some years back on a promotion course. We were known as 'Double Trouble' because of some of the shit we'd done together, but that's another story. My buddies and I greeted each other with the Māori Hongi, after which I introduced them to my guys. Two Trays was quick to stand up and show the others how the Hongi was done, but, as Jim and Walter made their way around the table, I was cracking up at the looks on the other boys' faces. They were hoping to fuck they'd seen it right, so they could imitate the actions without making an ass of themselves, although I think Stumpy was actually applying a new layer of lip gloss. Once that was done, we cracked some more beers.

Their company, Control Risks Group (CRG), had gone to New Zealand in early 2003 and had cleaned the place out of all the best guys. It was a smart move because at that time 'the circuit', as private security work was called by the British, was being manned by British-based guys, from forces like 22 SAS, the Parachute Regiment, the Royal Marines and so on. CRG saw New Zealand as an untapped source of top-notch guys. I reckoned that the standard of soldier throughout the entire New Zealand Defence Force (NZDF) was equal to a lot of the 'elite' British regiments, but I would say that, wouldn't I?

Consequently, there were a lot of former NZDF guys working with CRG all across Iraq. To Jim and Walter, it was almost like they had never left the NZDF, but I was happy to not be a part of that. I liked being the odd man out in a US company, and Blackwater in particular. I figured it showed a certain individuality and an ability to get on in life after leaving the military, which, believe me, some guys struggle to do.

Once we'd chewed the fat a while, we turned to the business at hand.

'On the menu tonight,' I announced, in my best maître d' voice, 'we have ten AK assault rifles, all in good working order. And, yes, we have already inspected them for serviceability, and they are all good to go. Next, we have fifty AK mags, as, without them, Sirs will find that the guns will be, as we say in the business, well-fucking fucked. Next, we have 1,000 rounds of Ukrainian – yes, the good stuff – 7.62x39mm, still encased in their green shipping tins. Then we have two ammo-can openers. I'm sure Sirs will appreciate that these are just as important as the bullets, as there is nothing worse than trying to cut open a tin of fucking bullets with your mate's fancy new Gerber knife.'

Jim and Walter looked mesmerised.

'Bro, this is excellent.'

'No, this is awesome.'

We loaded the booty into their vehicle before throwing a blanket over it, so people who didn't need to see it, didn't see it.

'How much do we owe you, bro?' Jim asked.

'Nothing, brother. It's on the house,' I told him. 'You guys need it, and we can get this shit any time.'

The looks on their faces were easily worth the cost. I had, in fact, paid for the shipment myself and made sure Mo was well covered for risking his ass. It was a small price to pay to ensure the brothers were properly taken care of, and I knew for a fact that they would have done the same for me if needed, so it was all good.

'Nah, bro, come on, what's the damage?' Jim insisted.

'No bro, nothing. It's all good. *Kapai*. Oh, and one other thing: I also have a box of leftover grenades, as even Stumpy can only carry so many. Plus, there are claymore mines, detonators and a lot of other shit that goes boom if you want it.'

'Hell yeah, bro,' Jim said. 'If you don't want it, we will take it.'

So, we loaded this into their vehicle as well, realising we needed a bigger blanket. That done, we exchanged Hongi and man-hug farewells, and they departed very happy campers.

Later that night, I received a call from Jim to pass on that all the guys in his crew wanted to thank me, Mo and my guys. Jim also told me that the money they had collected to spend on the weapons – the money that we didn't want – would be used to buy a shit-ton of booze, and that they would be back in a week to deliver it. Now, that was an offer I couldn't refuse. I told him that we would look forward to it, if we all survived the next seven days.

For us, Thursday was always the best night to let our hair down, as the Iraqis didn't work on a Friday, which is the Muslim holy day, and our client liked to relax with a beer himself around the pool in the CPA. We could kill our hangovers on the Friday by doing some training at the crossed swords and downing buckets of water in the hot sun until the fog in our heads cleared.

Bang on the nail, Jim and Walter pulled up outside the team house the following Thursday, and the back of their wagon was chocka with cartons of beer. It was an emotional sight and there may even have been a few tears. We unloaded the vehicle and stacked every cooler box and bucket we could find with beers and ice. Needless to say, it was going to be a big night.

Walter had brought his guitar, and as the beers flowed the tunes started. We sang all the US classics and a few from New Zealand, both in English and our native tongue. My guys were well impressed with the bond between us New Zealanders and our quirky sense of humour, and it gave them just a peek into our tribal heritage, which is strong. They wanted to see the Haka, the Māori challenge used as a means of preparing for combat, or to send off a fallen brother, which we are taught to perform from an early age. It was with the Haka that the New Zealand rugby team would face their opponents, prior to the match commencing.

But, with the beers flowing, we stuck to the oldies and goodies, accompanied by Walter's three chords. It was well into the early hours before the guys headed out. For us it had been a great night, and my guys were honoured to have seen a bit of our Māori culture. I figured it had given them a better understanding of me, as well. We cleaned up and hit the sack, hoping to snatch a few hours of sleep before struggling our way through a few hours of training.

We did just that, before heading back to the team house for a well-deserved afternoon nap. Our work-hard, play-hard ethic was maybe why some in Big Army didn't like us and some wanted to be us.

A few days later, I was out front enjoying a beer with the boys, when who should roll up but the BW team from Al-Hillah. They'd been to BIAP to pick up Dingo – 'Goodie' of old, the guy I'd originally persuaded to join the BW teams. Dingo had just rotated back in, after a month in Australia. The flight had been delayed, so they figured it was safer to stay the night with us, rather than risk driving in the dark and possibly interrupting some bad bastards digging IEDs into the side of the road.

After they'd dropped their kit, and some had fucked off to the pool and girls in the CPA, Dingo came and sat with us and cracked a beer. I couldn't help but notice that he looked different from how I had seen him before. He had a faraway gaze in his eyes that didn't bode well.

'How's it going, mate?' I asked. 'How was home?'

'Ah, not so good, mate,' he replied.

'You OK, bro?' I asked, not wanting to pry, but concerned.

'Nah, mate, not a good trip,' he repeated.

I knew he'd recently got engaged, so I tried that. 'How's the fiancée, mate? She glad to see you?'

'Er, mate, look, sorry, I'm just a bit tired.'

This was not good. This was not the happy-go-lucky Aussie fuck I had got to know in Karbala when he'd been flying solo. I leant in close, so the others couldn't hear: 'Dingo, you all right?'

'Mate,' he said, 'do you have anything stronger than beer?'

'Sure, bro. Hang on a sec, I'll be right back.' I went inside and fetched an 'in case of emergency' bottle of Glenfiddich whisky. 'Here you go, bro. If you need to talk, let me know, or I can just leave you the fuck alone if you want.'

'Yeah, bro, thanks. I just need a bit of space. Hey, I'm going to go on the roof, if that's cool, and drink this up there.'

'Sure, mate.' I told him I'd check on him when I crashed in a couple of hours and left him to it.

I was more than a little worried. Sometimes, guys put pressure on themselves to return to Iraq, even though they didn't want to. Then friends and family back home expected us to return to them, but they didn't see the personal demons we kept hidden deep inside.

They had no idea what we did and what we saw on a daily basis. We got pretty good at keeping that stuff locked away.

Maybe Dingo had returned to Iraq when he really didn't want to, not wanting to appear somehow weak. Whatever was eating him, he sure as shit wasn't a happy camper. A couple of beers later I was ready to hit the sack, but first I went to the roof to check on my mate. There were no lights up there, so it was as dark as fuck. I called out for Dingo, but there was no answer.

The roof of our team house doubled as an outdoor gym. We had weight machines, a treadmill and free weights spread out all over, plus that fucking big Russian Dushka anti-aircraft gun. I knew the layout by heart, but, after thirty seconds floundering around and tripping over stray weights, I still hadn't found him. *Fuck this*, I thought, and turned on the light on my phone. It was then I spied Dingo, slumped against the side of the parapet wall with the almost empty bottle of whisky by his side.

Holy fuck. He'd very nearly downed a whole bottle of Glenfiddich in just forty minutes. That's not normal, not in anyone's book. I leant down and checked for a pulse. After a few seconds, I detected the reassuring beats.

'Hey, bro, you there?' I asked. Dingo was breathing, but he seemed completely out for the count. 'Bro, you're going to feel this tomorrow,' I said, as I rolled him onto his side on an exercise mat, then rolled up another to form a makeshift pillow. The night was warm, but I got him a blanket and left him a bottle of water for good measure before fucking off to bed.

The next morning, I headed back to the roof and, as expected, Dingo was still out cold. I gave him a shake, knowing his guys would want to head back to Al-Hillah soon, and I wanted to give him time to freshen up.

'Hey, bro, you good?' It was kind of a silly question, but what else are you going to ask. 'Hey, Dingo, you Aussie fuck. Wake the fuck up.'

I had brought a couple more bottles of water, to add to the unopened one I had left the night before, and slowly poured a little over his mouth. This got him stirring, but not much. Eventually, with the addition of a little more water, he rolled over and gave a groan; the kind of groan that indicated he was going to feel like shit for a very long time.

'Holy fuck,' he said, 'I'm still drunk.' Well, at least he was still alive.

'Bro, go get in the shower. Your boys will be heading out soon.'

'OK, mate.' Still very groggy. 'Give me a minute will you.' Which is drunk talk for, *I'm going back to sleep.*

'No, bro, let's go. Been there, done that. I know that old trick. Here, I'll help you up.'

I put his arm over my shoulder and lifted the heavy fuck up. It took a bit for his brain to regain control of his legs, but eventually he was on his feet, and we wobbled downstairs to the shower.

'Here, bro, get in there,' I gestured, and ran the cold water for him.

After about fifteen minutes, I checked on him again, and to my surprise he was a lot more coherent, even though he still looked like a pile of camel shit.

'Hey, bro, I'm heading into the IZ with my guys for breakfast. You going to be OK?'

He gave a nod, but I was hoping he wouldn't just collapse back onto the shower floor for a few more Zs. Before I left, I let him know that his guys were getting their vehicles ready to head back to Al-Hillah.

'Hey, bro, you take it easy OK? I'll see you in a few.'

'Yeah, mate, thanks a lot,' he groaned back. 'I'll see you soon.'

With that we shook hands and I gathered up my guys. When we got back an hour or so later, the Hillah guys and Dingo were gone.

Four days later we were cleaning out the vehicles from a run into town, when I noticed a figure sitting in the front yard all by himself. *It was Dingo.* I left the guys to finish off and went over.

'Hey, mate, what the fuck are you doing here?' I said, trying to keep it light.

'Hey, mate, I'm heading home. I've had enough.'

Wow, whatever had made him pull the pin, it must have been pretty fucking serious. He looked hollow; his eyes sunken and glassed over.

'OK, bro. How are you getting to BIAP?'

'Mambas, I think,' he answered. 'They'll be taking me in about twenty minutes.'

Soon enough, the Mambas staged up, and I helped Dingo load his bags and watched as he climbed into the back of one of the big white beasts.

'You take care, brother,' I told him, before shaking his hand, really hoping he would look after himself.

'Yeah, mate, you too,' he replied.

And then off they went to BIAP, so Dingo could catch the first of several flights that would take him back to Australia to face whatever he needed to there.

A week later we got word that Dingo's body had been found in his vehicle out in the Aussie bush, with a gunshot through his head.

There were rumours as to why he had killed himself, but the one that seemed most likely was that his fiancée had terminal cancer. While he'd been back home, she had sadly passed away. If that was true, then I can't even begin to imagine the pain he must have been going through. To come back to Iraq after a terrible event like that – it was, obviously, the wrong thing to do.

Maybe he'd thought he could lose himself in the work, but not even Iraq would help bury that kind of shit. I guess I'll never know for sure, but I lost a good mate, and he is missed.

Hasta Luego, Dingo. Later, my brother.

Rest in peace.

As tragic as it was, I couldn't dwell on it, so I packed the trauma away and filed it with all the other bad stuff, under 'open at another time'. Iraq was getting more fucked up by the day and was definitely not the place to try to sort out your demons. Nor was it a retirement home, but for some reason Moyock seemed to think their new contracts were just right for some of the more 'former' operators from the seniors' homes somewhere. They arrived and would be tasked to run the daily operations and administration for the rest of us.

Some of these old fucks hadn't been in the field for twenty years or more. Most had been out of the operational loop for so long they didn't even know how to run a bath, let alone a team house full of 'A' types in a combat zone. A few had come and tried – and promptly left – having not had any luck on Civvy Street, or in their marriages, for that matter. They needed the cash more than they wanted to do the job. They figured this was their last bite of the cherry, not realising they'd bitten off more than they could chew.

One day one of the oldies arrived, as part of a contingent of fresh recruits, and me and my guys were tasked to drive them down to Al-Diwaniyah, a town lying about halfway between Baghdad and Basra. This guy had served with the rangers in Iraq, during the first Gulf War, and for all I know he had done a fine job back in 1991.

But that was then, and this was now. He still seemed to believe that he was a fit young ranger and was continually banging on about his previous time in Iraq.

To get them to Al-Diwaniyah, I'd organised a minibus for them, plus a bongo truck for their luggage. Depending on the time we got there, we thought we might have to stay the night. But we set out bright and early, hoping to make it there and back in a oner, and I had my Blazer lead, the minibus behind, followed by the bongo truck, and Two Trays's Blazer taking up the rear.

Each vehicle had hand-held comms, and I had the radio sitting with the driver in the minibus on open mike, so everyone could hear. No sooner had we got underway than the former ranger guy began banging on about some big battle he had personally won in the Gulf War, saving everyone's lives. It was getting increasingly annoying, with the old dog clogging up the airways, spinning shit like it was a Sunday drive tour through the Little Bighorn. It got to the point where we were laughing each time he piped up, and any respect we might have for the old geezer was rapidly dying.

Normally, I would just jump on the radio and tell him to shut the fuck up, as we needed the comms open for real live events. But each time he claimed a ranger victory the strong smell of bullshit was wafting through the air, and sometimes I can be a bit of an immature fuck. No, honestly, it's true. So, instead of shutting him down, I started to egg him on by asking things like, so, what about this bridge? What about that tree over there? Was it a sniper's nest and did he leopard-crawl up to it and take out the shooter with his boot laces?

It amused me for a while, but eventually I told the driver of the minibus to get a hold of the radio and tell Ranger McDanger to can it. We arrived at our destination and unloaded the new guys who, like me, were sick to death of hearing make-believe war stories. It was getting a bit late, and when running Route Tampa there was always the risk of IEDs, VBIEDs and ambushes, but we were so done with Ranger McStranger that we refuelled and turned right around for Baghdad and got the fuck out of there.

We made it back OK, but a few days later Ranger McGranger started sending in contact reports. It sounded like they were fighting off hordes of insurgents hell-bent on breaching the walls. He even sent requests for more ammo and more body bags, as they were apparently filling them at an alarming rate. Not that anyone had any body bags.

The last thing we needed was another Najaf-type siege, so I put a call through to one of the guys we knew down there, to see if any of this was legit. After a few unanswered dial tones, we presumed they were too busy fighting off the bad guys to take the call, but then a sleepy voice came on.

'Hey, bro, what's going on down there?' I asked.

The guy with the sleepy voice seemed confused.

'I hear you guys are under attack,' I explained.

'Who told you that?' he asked, sleepily.

'Your PM, Ranger McPainger. He's been sending in reports that you guys are getting hit each night and need ammo and body bags.'

'Body bags? Fuck, we don't even have tea bags. Nah bro, we're good here, thanks.'

There were no nightly attacks and never had been, not since the day they had arrived. In fact, the guy I spoke to asked if he could come up to Baghdad, as he was being driven insane with the boredom and all Ranger McNutsack's wacko bullshit. Needless to say, after a short while Ranger McBullshit was given two options by the company: aisle or window seat, on the plane home.

Since our return to the team house, my guys and I had been occupying one of the upstairs rooms, in between running all over the
country delivering new guys and equipment to the widely scattered
Blackwater teams. In recent weeks I'd been taking my instructions from Brian, who'd moved over to the Greystone team house
in Mansour, which I had no trouble doing, as he was in Iraq and
always had been. But I was also getting bugged shitless by some
faceless project manager based in Moyock, who somehow seemed
to think my guys and I worked for him.

He must have been very young, very dumb or a former military
officer – or maybe all three. He would email details of a new task
or instructions on how he wanted me to do this or that like he was
issuing orders to some underling. It had pissed me off no end. I was
reaching the limits of my tolerance and was starting to push back
big time. So, when we got news early September 2004 that we were
to get a new guy to run the team house, I hoped this might get the
fucker from Moyock off my back at last.

There are several things I judge a man on when I first meet him:
one is his handshake, the second is whether he looks you in the
eye as he does it, and the third is his shoes; not the brand or style,
but whether they are properly looked after. If they are unkept and
dirty, I immediately conclude he's a slob. If you can't get those three
things squared away, then you likely can't get anything squared
away. There's a very old saying my father taught me: *shoes make the
man.*

The new guy arrived to take over both the running of the team
house and the Mambas, so he was right in the hotseat. He looked
to be in his mid-forties, with the body of someone who took pride
in himself. He struck me as being a man's man, with a handlebar moustache and he looked me in the eye as he offered a firm

handshake. Most importantly, his boots were top notch. Right off the bat I liked him. His name was Guy and went by the call sign 'G2'. G2 was clearly someone who would not put up with any bullshit, which was exactly what we needed right then.

Shortly after his arrival, I received an email from my faceless project manager in Moyock – let's call him Stephanie – directing me and the guys to drive across the length and breadth of Iraq to retrieve all the AR suppressors, like the one Jerry had way back when, that had been distributed to the BW teams. The email informed me that these were actually meant for someone else completely, some other contract, and someone back in the US had just realised this.

I showed the email to G2 who agreed that it was utter bullshit. The questions it raised were legion – like, where the fuck were those damn suppressors now? How did we know if they were still in the location or with the person they'd originally been sent to? And even if they were, why would they give them up, just because I asked?

But what really pissed me off about the email was what it revealed about just how out of touch the Monday-to-Friday ass-jockeys were in the US. We were on the ground risking life and limb, following their dumbass instructions, while they were planning the next company BBQ before heading home to their not-so-perfect families, patting themselves on the back for a job well done.

Getting in the Blazers and driving around war-ravaged Iraq to search for supposedly missing suppressors was simply not going to happen. I figured it was high time I told whoever it was back there that I was not going to do it – but in a manner that was not so in his face that it got me the sack.

I emailed back:

Dear Stephanie,

Upon looking over your request, I have come to the conclusion that the chances of successfully collecting these black steel tubes are very low, without a high risk to life and, as I'm sure you are aware, some very expensive equipment.

However, if you can send me a current list of where these items are definitely located, plus an alternative method of collection, my team and I would be glad to look into the matter for you.

I look forward to your solution, blah fucking blah, blah, blah.
I pressed 'send', and sure enough I got a reply back pretty damn quick.
'Hey, G2, it's arrived,' I announced.
I read it out to him:

Dear Baz,

Thanks for your reply, and obvious concern for your team's safety. I have heard very good things about you, and you are spoken of very highly back here in Moyock...

'Well,' I remarked to G2, 'I like that. That's a nice start.'
A good old bit of bullshit, oh, I mean flattery.
I carried on reading it aloud:

However, it is very important that we retrieve these objects as soon as possible. Unfortunately, we cannot find any updated list of their precise location at present but hope you may be able to come up with a working solution. Thank you for your understanding. You and your team are doing a great job.

Please let me know when you have them all in your possession.

Yours, Stephanie.

G2 grinned, knowing that I was not about to accept what was clearly now an order.

I replied:

Dear Stephanie,

I am sorry to hear you have no records of where these black steel tubes are now located. Maybe this is a reflection on whoever was in charge of issuing the items in the first place, and I am at a loss to understand why anyone in the company thinks my team and I should risk our lives fixing this blatant incompetence.

I cannot, and will not, risk my life and the lives of my guys driving around Iraq to try to locate items that were issued incorrectly, and for which no one has any records. Since their issuing was a long time ago, no one will know where they are likely to be now.

I am sorry, I cannot fix your problem for you.

Yours, Baz.

G2 read it over and gave his seal of approval. 'Mate, this is bullshit. I don't see how you can be expected to find them with no list or guidance as to where they all are. Do you want me to send an email and let them know it's a waste of time?'

'No thanks, mate,' I told him, 'I've got it covered.'

I explained to him my cunning plan and let him know I was prepared for the response. As expected, the keyboard warrior in Moyock couldn't help but spring the trap with his next email. Basically, Stephanie was demanding that I load my guys up and go find the suppressors. He demanded we visit every Blackwater outpost and collect them, despite the fact that he had no idea where the fuck they were. For a real kicker, he even asked me, 'How hard can it be?' The fuck expected me to get back to him with them all in my possession within the next fourteen days, no excuses.

I showed G2. He shook his head in despair. It was clearly time to take the gloves off. *OK*, I thought, *here we go*. But before I sent my reply, I covered my ass with the old 'BCC' to Brian, just so he could see the bullshit being dumped on our heads.

Dear Stephanie,

As you may, or may not be aware, there is a war here in Iraq, and the roads are far from safe. In fact, it is estimated that there are, on average, fifteen attacks per day here in Baghdad alone, with a casualty rate over 70 per cent, not to mention the loss of vehicles, weapons and other items that are all worth a lot of money.

I appreciate that you have faith in me to complete the task due to my experience and time on the roads. My team and I now fully realise the seriousness of these items and are willing to scour the country to locate them, as directed.

But just as you have made demands on me, I have a requirement for you. Before my team and I leave on what may be a one-way trip, I ask that you come to Iraq to accompany us on the mission. As you clearly have all the information on these worthless pieces of shit, then surely you are the best person to ride with us to every Blackwater site in Iraq and Kurdistan, to collect them.

In fact, I insist you join us, and I am certain that you are the kind of man who would jump at this chance to get a bit of time in Iraq, and to see a mission, that you yourself planned, fully completed, no matter how long it takes.

If you can please clear your calendar with Erik, or whoever you report to, then send me your arrival date. I will pick you up from BIAP myself. We will then immediately drive around the country to all the BW bases, in any order that you decide, and go and get these fucking things together.

Kindest Regards,

Baz.

It's all well and good sending guys off to their deaths from a safe distance. Fuck that, I wasn't having any part of it. Anyway, I had laid down the challenge. Now all I had to do was wait and see if he had the balls to accept.

I shut down the office and joined my guys outside for a beer. I had advised them what was going on, and they were waiting to hear the latest. I gave them the long and short of it, and they gave their nods of approval.

A while later Brian called. 'Hey, mate, how's it?' he asked. 'So tell me, who is that idiot you're dealing with back in Moyock?'

'I'm not sure, mate,' I replied. 'But, as you can see, we'll do the job but only if that fuck comes with us.'

'Yeah. Good move, that should shut him up. But let me know how this plays out. I'll let you deal with it for now, but, either way, I'm going to make sure this doesn't happen again. I don't know what's going on back there, but no one is risking lives for an administrative screw up. Oh, and by the way, I have a new contract for you, starting November. You can take your guys, but you'll be getting another ten from Moyock.'

Damn, a fifteen-man team.

'What is it?' I asked.

'You'll be running the International Republican Institute contract. I'll brief you more tomorrow. Go have a beer – it sounds like you need it.'

'OK mate, I'll keep you posted.'

The International Republican Institute (IRI) was a Washington-based group whose self-proclaimed mission was to 'advance democracy worldwide'. Hmmmm... I wondered if they had been over to ask the Iraqi people if that's what they wanted before the war had kicked off and their country had been propelled into chaos and Armageddon? Still, a contract was a contract, and a fifteen-man team sounded good to me.

The next day, there was one more email from Stephanie. As expected, it informed me that, on further consideration, it had been decided that the suppressors would be collected by other means. 'Stephanie' thanked me for the invitation to ride with us but, due to many important tasks in the US, he would have to respectfully decline. Finally – and I'm sure this was double-edged – Stephanie said he looked forward to meeting me in person and expected to be in-country before the end of the year. *Blah fucking blah, fucking blah*. Victory was mine. He shoots – he scores.

Most importantly, my guys were happy. They'd had faith that I'd sort this out and I had. But dealing with such idiots just made a tough job even harder, and I was in need of a break myself by then, so my rotation out was timely.

Little did I know that I'd be returning to face the mother of all battles.

CHAPTER 14

My time home passed all too quickly. Seemingly in the blink of an eye, I was back in Baghdad.

Soon after, we got word that there was going to be a Vietnam Tet Offensive-style attack in and around the IZ. Hordes of insurgents were going to try to breach the walls of America's citadel and kill us all. *Good luck with that*, I told myself. Where, when and after taking what narcotics had the insurgents dreamt up that little gem? One could only imagine.

The team house already had a sandbag battlement added to the roof, with pre-planned fire lanes and defensive positions. Plus, we had the very large DShK up there ready to let rip. There was absolutely no way we could test-fire the fucker in the middle of Baghdad, and the only time we ever manned it was for selfies to send home. But there was always a first time, and maybe the insurgent's Vietnam moment was going to be it.

With nightfall on the day of the supposed mass assault, to my horror I noticed that Rich had arrived at the team house, complete with his Teva sandals. Perhaps he was heading out on rotation, or maybe someone in Moyock had finally woken up to the fact that his leadership abilities were zero. Either way, it was the last thing we needed, on tonight of all nights.

While we set up the tables for a few beers, to toast yet another successful day avoiding death, he leant over the sandbag parapet on the roof and yelled down to me. I completely ignored him, until I realised he just wasn't about to give up.

'What do you want?' I yelled back, with undisguised disdain.

'Hey, I'm going to have to get you guys to wrap up the drinks for tonight and come up to the roof, so I can designate some firing positions.'

'Did I hear that right?' I asked my guys. 'What the fuck did I just hear?' *Is he fucking insane?*

After sharing a laugh with the boys, I stood up and held Teva boy with my stare. 'Hey, Rich,' I yelled.

For a moment he stopped preparing for the Alamo and glanced down. 'Yeah?'

I locked eyes with the fuck and paused for a few seconds. 'Go fuck yourself. You don't tell me or any of my guys what to do, OK?'

Then, for dramatic effect, I cracked another Amstel, took a big swig, let out a big sigh of contentment and sat back down. After a few seconds of silence, I glanced at Two Trays.

'Hey, is he still looking at me?'

'Yeah,' he said. 'And he ain't happy.'

'Good, that's what I wanted to hear. Fuck him. That useless shit isn't fit to give anyone orders, let alone us.'

'Yeah, damn right,' the guys chimed in. Clank, drink, dead marines.

As any dipshit who knew the layout of that area would tell you, there was no chance of a ground assault. To organise the number of suicidal die-hards necessary to accomplish such a mission would have been nigh-on impossible for the insurgency and, in any case, it would have been a dumb move in anyone's book. And the insurgents were far from stupid.

Of course, there was no massive ground attack that night, or any other night for that matter. We drank and laughed, while the sad conscripts Rich had managed to corral on the roof gradually drifted away to bed, or to other more productive things, like stabbing themselves. The only noise we heard was soothing thumps of big guns on the outskirts of Sadr City. We had become so used to that it would have sounded wrong without it.

That got me thinking of my last break, in New Zealand. This time, I'd really struggled with the quiet. I needed the sounds of battle to put me at ease and send me to sleep. The lack of noise stressed me out. When I'd got together with my kids, the peace and quiet had put me constantly on edge and I found it hard to focus. One evening I'd gone out for dinner with Jen and the kids. My boys couldn't decide what they wanted from the menu, and they were doing what every normal kid does – picking this and that, then changing to something they thought was better.

After a short while of them doing that, I could feel my stress levels rising, and all of a sudden I snapped at them to fucking hurry up and choose something. I growled that there were kids in Iraq who didn't have any such choices and would be lucky to get one dead pigeon, if they could find it in the rubble and dust of what had once been their home.

Jen had placed her hand on my arm, giving it a gentle squeeze, which brought me crashing back to reality, but the damage was done, and I could see from the looks on my boys' faces the grim truth: that they were frightened of their father. I instantly felt like such a piece of shit.

They weren't to know – and why should they? – about the situation in Iraq. I had brought it all home with me and made them feel bad about something completely out of their hands. I did my best to apologise, but it was too late, and for the rest of the meal they sat in silence, waiting for me to erupt at them again. It took a lot of explaining and making up before they could enjoy coming out with me again.

Another time, I was driving with Jen to look at a house we were thinking of buying. The one we had our eye on was tucked away in the bush, with no one around and only the sound of the birds to break the silence. We decided it was perfect. As we drove back it was dark and I was tired. All of a sudden there was a bright flash of light on the left side of the road, that startled the living shit out of me. I hit the accelerator to get off the X and as far away from the ambush as possible. My heart rate jumped and the hairs on my arms and neck were up, and I could feel the sweat on my forehead.

'Are you OK?' I yelled to Jen. 'Are you OK? What was that?'

She gazed at me, horrified, as I accelerated faster and faster, and she began yelling at me to slow down. I snapped out of it after I began to see the streetlights and the trees, realising that I was in New Zealand, not on Route Irish. I gathered my emotions and slowed to a normal speed.

'What was that?' I asked, feeling my surprise turn to anger.

'It was a speed camera,' she said.

'A what?' I yelled.

'A speed camera. There's a cop sitting back there with a road-mounted camera.'

'A what? A fucking cop?' Now I was fuming, and I slowed down to pull over.

'What are you doing?' she asked.

'I'm going to go back to kill him.'

'What? You can't do that!' she said, looking at me.

'Fuck him. I thought it was an IED.'

'What's an IED?'

'A fucking roadside bomb! You idiot, haven't you learnt any-thing after all this time?' My rage was back in full swing, and for a moment I was back in the Blazer with my team, but I soon began to calm down again, as it dawned on me where I was. 'It's a bomb, baby,' I said more quietly. 'A bomb. A roadside bomb. I thought that was the flash from a roadside bomb.'

Instead of turning around, I pulled back onto the road. But inside, I was still very tense and angry. We continued to drive, but, as you'd expect, it was one quiet journey. It took a long time for me to completely calm down. All I could think of was going back to ram that camera up the cop's ass, so every time he farted, he took a picture of his colon. I never really calmed down enough to forget about him, and just like all the other incidents, I buried it, piling it on the heap to be processed later, or maybe not at all.

Another morning, I woke up feeling just as tired as when I went to bed.

'Are you OK?' Jen asked.

'Yeah. Just a bit fatigued, I guess.'

'Well, you were having bad dreams.'

'Really? I don't remember.'

'You were yelling, and you jumped up onto the bed, standing with your hands spread on the wall, yelling for me to hurry up and get more ammo.'

'Holy fuck. I don't remember any of that. Sorry if I scared you.'

'It's OK,' she said. 'You stopped and went back to sleep, but you carried on talking all night, telling someone to shoot someone over there, and to get another one over there, like you were in some kind of battle.'

'Oh, Jesus,' I said. 'Sorry.'

Nothing more was said about it, but that was one of many nights of yelling and bad dreams. A lot of that shit was rooted in Fallujah, and as it happened that dark chapter was very far from being closed.

Seven months after Jerry, Wes, Mike and Scott had been killed, the full might of the US military was sent in to steamroll Fallujah once and for all. There had been a marked increase in attacks and bombings in Iraq, many of which were thought to have originated from Fallujah. It was hardly surprising. In theory, the city was run by a local militia – the Fallujah Brigade – which had been backed and armed by the US military, with orders to keep the insurgents out. But by September 2004, the insurgents had seized control of the city, plus most of that US-supplied weaponry. Fallujah had become the epicentre for the insurgency and its proxy capital.

There were now so many different types of bombings that whoever was in charge of giving them acronyms had to be having a hard time keeping up. There were ones for vehicle-borne bombs, bicycle-borne, animal-borne and body-borne, launched bombs and static bombs. I even heard of a Homicide Improvised Explosive Device (HIED), which supposedly supplanted the Suicide Improvised Explosive Device (SIED) in a legalistic nuance that was somehow meant to deter those hell-bent on killing us and themselves. Clearly, they wouldn't want a US criminal record, having blown themselves to pieces. After all, it might stop them getting a Green Card.

The Second Battle of Fallujah, as it became known, would see some of the most brutal fighting since the invasion in 2003. The aim was to push the insurgents into a small quarter, where the might of the heavy artillery and airpower could finish them. But it meant the US marines and ground forces had first to clear almost every building, so as not to leave their backs exposed as they advanced. A lot of the marines even had to fight hand-to-hand to drive the insurgents from buildings and streets.

The insurgents had spent months rigging Fallujah as a death trap. Blocking streets and alleyways, they tried to channel the troops into killing grounds, hiding weapons and ammo caches across the city. Using guerrilla shoot-and-scoot tactics, they left booby traps at every turn to seriously hinder the troops. The casualty numbers mounted, and the skies over Baghdad became thick with grey Chinooks ferrying reinforcements in and the dead and wounded out.

No matter how fortified Fallujah might be, it was never going to end well for the insurgents. The big advantage the military had was technology and raw firepower. The thing the insurgents had that no Western force possessed, however, was the hunger to die for their cause. After several weeks of intense fighting, the US military encircled the remaining insurgents and tightened the noose. The cover of darkness was no protection either, as Big Army utilised advanced night-vision and thermal technology to unleash bombs, bullets, missiles and artillery with pinpoint precision. The insurgents had nowhere left to run, and they could no longer hide.

The US military also hammered in thousands of munitions tipped with deadly depleted uranium (DU). In fact, they threw so many radioactive DU rounds over that city that Fallujah wouldn't need street lights once the war was over. The entire place, and those who went back to live there, would be glowing with radioactivity for a very long time to come. It was a really shitty thing to do, and no one gave a fuck.

There are two things I hate above all else: incompetence and hypocrisy. The US military was by no means incompetent when it came to waging war, but from where I stood, they were full-on hypocrites. Can you imagine the shitstorm if any other country, or the insurgency for that matter, had used DU on American soil or against American soldiers? Holy shit, there would be all shades of hell to pay, as politicians complained about the evil use of chemical weapons and demanded a response to 'war crimes'.

I mean, weren't bogus claims about weapons of mass destruction (WMDs) the excuse for invading Iraq in the first place? Isn't DU a WMD? The Iraqi Ministry of Health would later report 'damning evidence' of higher-than-normal rates of birth defects and cancers in areas of heavy fighting, where the US used DU extensively. Wasn't that a war crime? Or was the crime defined by the nationality of the perpetrator?

When I looked at what the Iraqi insurgency was doing in the cold light of day, I'd asked myself this: isn't that what you would be doing, if your country was invaded and occupied for no justifiable reason? And, as much as sending in the marines might have satisfied those on their sofas back at home, demanding blood in revenge for the death of our boys, did anyone pause to consider the effect this was going to have on countless lives in Iraq, and on both sides of the wire?

It wasn't just the immediate trauma, but the much longer-lasting psychological effect; the hatred stored up for generations, and the post-traumatic stress disorder suffered by all. PTSD is like depleted uranium – it hangs around unnoticed for years, but just the slightest kick of the sand, or the flash of a police speed camera, can be enough to stir up nightmares, cold sweats, paranoia, domestic violence, drug and alcohol abuse, physical abuse, suicide, murder, filicide and homelessness, and the knock-on effects for the offspring of those who suffer.

So, listen in, all you armchair generals: be damn fucking careful before you scream from the rooftops to send in the troops, unless you're prepared to go into battle and fight shoulder to shoulder with them yourself, or to send in your own children; unless you're prepared to go and look after a wounded veteran and spend quality time with their families who need support; unless you're prepared to house them when they are homeless, hungry and living on the street; unless you're prepared to hold them when they want to scream, cry, hurt others or kill themselves because they did what you wanted. Unless you're fully prepared to deal with the consequences of your screams for bloody revenge, I strongly suggest you shut the fuck up and sit the fuck down.

As the heavy thump of the Chinooks thundered overhead, shuttling to and from Fallujah, I decided to make a call to Jen in New Zealand. It was a nice hot day in Baghdad, so I went to stand outside the team house, partly for the sun, partly for better reception on the Thuraya, and partly because I didn't know if I could keep it together in the house, where eyes would be upon me.

We talked about the usual light stuff first; how's this and that person? Do your friends still hate me? Oh, they do, good. Then I slowly started to talk about my deepest, darkest thoughts; about what was going on here and how the situation was changing. I found myself talking about stuff I couldn't expect Jen to comprehend, but she listened patiently, and when I was finished, she asked me how I was feeling and why I didn't just come home. I wondered what to say, but all I could think of was that I couldn't leave the boys, knowing that I would feel like I was abandoning them.

On top of that, I was thinking there was no fucking way I could earn $600 per day in New Zealand, so what about the money? I think she knew what I would say but just wanted me to say it, to let a bit of the water out of the bath before it overflowed. It was nice to have someone to talk to about things I wasn't able to say to the boys. Maybe that was all I really needed.

As we talked, there was an almighty explosion from the direction of Gate 11, no more than 400 metres away. It was so big that even the dust where I was standing was kicked up by the pressure wave. The wall I was leaning on shook violently, and as I glanced up in the direction of the blast, I heard Jen screaming down the phone, in panic and fear.

'Are you OK? What was that?'

'Yeah,' I said, calmly. 'I'm OK.'

'That was so loud. It sounded really close. What was it?'

'Oh, just someone dying,' I replied. There was no stress in my voice. I had become desensitised to the danger.

'You don't sound very worried about it,' she said.

'Nah, I'm OK. Well, better than how that fuck is feeling, anyways.'

I wasn't worried, but she certainly was.

'Oh, OK then, you be careful, OK?' she said.

But she had picked up on the fact that I was no longer shocked by death, or maybe I just no longer cared.

'Yeah, I'll be careful,' I lied. 'God knows how many people just died, but it wasn't me, right, so why should I worry? Look, babe, I'd better get inside before something falls on my head from the blast.'

'OK,' she said. 'Be careful. I love you.'

We hung up. I stood there staring at the massive dust cloud fisting into the sky. My only real thought was, 'Wow, that was crazy'. Someone halfway around the world had just heard the sound of death as it happened, just a few hundred metres away, but this was the new normal for me. I felt numb; jaded. As long as it wasn't my death, I was OK with it. Just something else to file away, to deal with later.

As the battle for Fallujah raged, I realised I had been in Iraq for one whole year, during which time the place had deteriorated into a living hell for the locals and a very dangerous place for anyone else. I was awaiting the arrival of the new guys from the US to man up the new International Republican Institute (IRI) contract. We were going to be housed out in Karrada, just a stone's throw from the 14th of July Bridge and the IZ but still formally in the Red Zone.

Larry had been brought over to be my project manager. It was good to see him again, so long after G-Man and I had helped him carry out those early recces of the CPAs the previous December.

In Karrada, IRI had rented a row of houses on a street close to the Tigris River, with the busy River Road separating them from the Al-Hamra Hotel. Our big-ass American presence wasn't exactly welcomed by the remaining Iraqi residents and, to fuck them off even further, we blocked off all access roads with T walls and installed barrier-arms and checkpoints. Complain all they liked, that wouldn't change a thing. Like Big Army, we were here, and they just had to live with it. Of course, their main concern was that our presence made the area – and them – a nice juicy insurgent target.

The IRI office and our new team house were at one end of the street, with our furthest house 120 metres further down. At the far end of the street was an old high-rise apartment block, which had once housed Saddam's Republican Guards but had been looted by the locals once the Americans had rolled into Baghdad. It had been completely fucking gutted, and the concrete shell was occupied by an Australian Army infantry company, who were using it as an observation post with views across the city.

Since we were going to be neighbours, I thought it prudent to go and introduce myself and let them know that we were moving in down below. Also, I hoped that, with our shared ANZAC history and fierce rugby rivalry, they might be willing to provide us with any intel they picked up regarding trouble in the area.

The new guys flew into BIAP, were picked up in the Mambas and driven to the team house for a few days of briefings and training by me and my guys. Chatting with them I learnt that most had served in the military, after which they'd struggled to find decent civilian work, concluding that Iraq was the place to use their skills and earn good money. Virtually all had applied exclusively to work for Blackwater, and they had done so after seeing what had happened to our boys in Fallujah.

As long as it wasn't for bad reasons like revenge, I was cool with that.

Americans are the most patriotic, God-fearing, flag-waving, hand-on-heart, anthem-singing people I have ever met. These guys were no different. Their love of country had been drilled into them from an early age, and they really did believe that the US of A was by far the best country on earth and that they had to do their bit to keep it that way. Having witnessed the Fallujah deaths, they somehow felt they should try to make it better. It was like comforting a bereaved family at a time of loss. Although none of them had ever met Jerry, Wes, Mike or Scott, they somehow felt they too had lost brothers in the attack. I admired them for that, but I would keep a sharp eye on them nonetheless, just in case there were some who weren't quite so selfless.

There was also a surprise – an old face – among the new arrivals. Yard Dog had rotated back. He'd returned with a new attitude, a new outlook on life and a new set of hair plugs – transplants – sprouting from his head. I was happy to take him back but not in any leadership role, and I reunited him with his skull ring. To his credit, he had no problem with that. To augment our security, Blackwater had also hired twenty static security guards, all from Jordan. Their commander was a likeable but shifty-eyed little fucker called Omar, who was straight out of central casting for a bad guy in an *Indiana Jones* movie.

Omar's job was to organise the Jordanian guard rotations and to report directly to me. But from the get-go I had a feeling that he was not the one really in charge, just the one nominated as guard commander, because he was the only fucker who could speak any English. As long as the system worked, I didn't give a damn.

Rose from the team house also came to join us. She had been away for a while, getting over the loss of 'her Jerry'. Plus, there was also one other Iraqi lady hired to help Rose with the cooking and cleaning.

A small alleyway connected our team house with the main IRI office, and I set up my ops room in the lower-level garage of their house. All five of the IRI houses were constructed of solid stone and mortar, with steel gates and eight-foot-high outer walls. We felt very secure once we were inside, but if the bad guys hadn't known we were in the neighbourhood before, they sure as shit did now that we'd fortified the place.

The IRI staff consisted of around a dozen highly educated young Iraqi men and women who had been hired from Washington. Their security was to be overseen by a young American guy, who had not yet arrived in-country. There would also be five other expat staff: three more Americans, plus a young couple from the Balkans who had run another IRI office in Erbil, in the north of Iraq.

The IRI's core principle, as it was explained to me, was to spread

US republican-style democracy throughout the world – an oxymoron, if ever I heard one. To my mind, a better mission statement would have been, 'We come in peace, but shoot to kill.'

For the next few days, I took the new guys training over at the crossed swords. As there were a lot of them, it took a while to get to know who was who, but several were starting to stand out. Thankfully, I hadn't had to kick anyone out on day one, as I had done before because of issues with fitness, or fatness for that matter.

There were guys from the marines, the army, the green berets and SEALs; there was a guy who had been in the Los Angeles Police Department (LAPD), and somehow a bloody Scotsman had been thrown in for good measure. The Scotsman immediately got the call sign Haggis. He'd been hired from another company, and, since he had experience in Iraq, I used him to assist me in training the new guys. So, between my New Zealand accent, Stumpy's Chicago twang, Two Trays's incessant belly-laughs and Haggis's broad Scottish brogue, the new guys were not having an easy time of it. In fact, I spent one morning just letting them hear me speak on the radio, so they could get their heads around my accent.

I watched the guys closely for any indiscretion or screw-up that would help me call sign them. The first on my radar was a former marine who, to me, had a typical South Carolina drawl. To him a vehicle was a vee-hic-cal, with each syllable dragged out. A big solid guy, like a bear, he always had a smile on his friendly face, so he got 'Yogi'. Always keen to learn, Yogi really loved America or, as he would call it at 100 decibels, 'Merica.

Next was a former marine captain who knew his shit and was always eager to help get the guys into line. Surprisingly his music of choice was the band Hooverphonic, a band I liked who reminded me of Portishead, and he was covered in tattoos, which was something I think he did once he was out of the service as a rebel-lious middle-finger salute. I warmed to him, especially as he was forever telling these stories of sick but funny sexual encounters, 'hammering' this chick or 'hammering' that one. So, I call signed him 'Hammer'.

There was a black guy who was former army. He struck me as being lighter skinned than your average black American, so he earned the call sign 'Shadow'. The former LAPD cop got 'Dodger' after the baseball team. He put me in mind of a younger version of Two Trays: always friendly as fuck with a big chuckling laugh. Then there was this huge black guy, and I mean *huge*. He stood about 6ft 6in. and was as muscular as hell. He was so ripped he probably had muscles on his morning shit. He already had a call sign that he wanted to be keep, and because he was so huge and so ripped, I was cool with that. He was 'Zen', and, what do you know, that's exactly what I would have called him anyway. Wow, isn't that weird?

The final guy to catch my attention was another solid-as-fuck fucker. Not as solid as Zen, as no one was. Zen was in a solid cate-gory of his own. This guy was the same height as me, but he looked as if he could bend concrete, so I called him Rock. The remain-ing guys still had to make some impression on me, but, for now, Haggis, Yogi, Hammer, Shadow, Dodger, Zen and Rock were my go-to new guys.

These guys would be team leaders, with the others slotting in as team members. Each would look after their client and their team in their allocated house along our street, and they would report to me in the operations room in the garage basement of the IRI office house.

We were allocated a fleet of low-profile vehicles with blacked-out windows: two armoured 7 Series BMWs, one S500 Mercedes and another BMW, both of which were soft-skin. I was not able to bring the Blazers, but they were pretty damn shot by then anyway. Returned to the guy we had hired them from, the look of horror on his face was apparently priceless. The months of hard-running, bullet holes and dents had messed them up pretty badly. He tried to argue for a pay-out, but it wasn't happening. And that, boys and girls, is why you should always get the full-insurance option.

BW was in the process of purchasing some armoured SUVs from Triple Canopy, but, until we received them, we would have to make do with the four vehicles we had been allocated. They came with the usual pros of not being easily identifiable to the insurgents and the usual cons of not being easily distinguishable from insurgents' cars by Big Army.

At the end of day six at the crossed swords, I decided it was time to put all our training into practice. I gathered the teams and let them know that I was happy with their progress and that they were almost ready to get on with the contract. Before they did, however, I needed to see how they would operate on the mean streets of Baghdad.

I gave them a warning order that we would be hitting the road the next morning, which was met with both excitement and apprehension. I reiterated that there was only one way to know what it's like to be shot at, and that's to get shot at for real. There were a few looks of disbelief, but it's exactly like training for a boxing fight. If you hit the bag all day but never get in the ring with someone, how do you know if your training was any good?

I told them to get all their kit and ammo ready, to have their go bags loaded and to give their weapons a very light clean but not to strip them down. I told them to make sure the vehicles were fuelled, watered and ready to roll, with medical packs in each vehicle. The briefing would be at 09:30. The reason for giving the weapons only a light outside clean, or 'field clean' as it is known in the military, is that we'd just been on the ranges and everyone's weapon was working 100 per cent. To strip it apart for a deeper clean would remove that certainty, as something could change when they were reassembled.

That night, my old crew and I sat out having a beer, while the newbies did their final checks and gear preparation for the twentieth time: the usual nerves, I guess. I felt sure we'd be OK, as the guys had performed well, but I had an attack of nerves myself, wondering if what we were doing was actually a good idea. Maybe it was tempting fate. There were on average more than seven attacks a day in Baghdad, and at least four rolling VBIEDs every morning, so just slightly fewer than there had been before the marines flattened Fallujah.

My plan was to take the new guys close to Sadr City and the ministries, which were still places to be avoided. *Ah fuck it, you don't know until you try.*

The next morning we gathered in the briefing room. I'd hung up some maps of Baghdad, with an overlay of the ministries and other points of interest such as the Palestine Hotel, Sadr City, the Monument to the Unknown Soldier, Haifa Street and the route I intended to take us on, plus an alternative route in case we hit trouble. Our primary route was marked in green, the alternative in red. All things going well, the trip should take us about three hours.

I'd planned a stop at the Greystone team house, so they knew where it was, before looping back onto Irish and into Camp Victory for a PX shop as their reward. Just for good measure, I'd briefed Hacksaw the night before, and he'd promised to provide some air cover with the Little Birds, should we need it. I fucking loved those

Little Bird guys: pilots, mechanics, door gunners, the lot. They were always willing to risk their asses to provide any kind of assistance, and there are many guys alive today who have them to thank.

As the guys gathered in their vehicle configurations, I went through the SMEAC orders format. A good set of 'orders', as it is called, will normally take about an hour. Of course, the 'What ifs' are included, just in case the plan should get fucked up. We have another saying in the NZ military called the '7 Ps': Prior Planning and Preparation Prevents a Piss Poor Performance. In keeping with the 7Ps, I had drilled the guys hard over the past week and I was confident that they would perform well.

There were some obvious nerves, but no one was going to say they didn't want to come. I finished up with a bit of reassurance that the Little Birds would be on standby, if needed. In truth, they weren't sure if they could do much as a QRF, especially as our comms were so useless, but at least it made the new guys feel a bit better. If I did need the Little Birds, then I would just have to hope like fuck my cell phone would get through.

So, my biggest concern for the umpteenth time was our lack of proper comms. Every Blackwater team leader had begged Moyock to provide a decent comms system. It was top of our lists, whenever Erik and his sled-dog guys came to pay us a visit. It felt like someone, somewhere was preventing us from getting it. Maybe they didn't think we were worth it, but it wasn't like we didn't generate enough income for the company.

As we set out, everyone's nerves were taut. I had spread my veteran guys around the teams, to add some reassurance. Just before we passed out the gate, I came over the radio with my routine drill: 'OK guys, safeties off, eyes open, here we go.' Now the shit was real.

The talking between vehicles was good and to the point, as guys used the clock-ray method to indicate the ins and outs of round-abouts and corners, plus possible threats. About three minutes into the drive, I came up on the comms again, for an all-vehicles announcement, with a little test I had planned to see just how switched on the guys were.

'All vehicles, Baz,' I said, receiving the chorus of acknowledge-ments in the right order. 'Keep your eyes peeled and, for those that haven't already done so, load your weapons.'

I knew there would be a few who, due to nervous excitement, would have forgotten to cock a round into the breach. That can prove fatal, as the middle of a firefight is not the time to find out you have forgotten to load your weapon. I heard a few 'oh shits' come back over the comms, as those who had forgotten fixed their mistake.

'All TL's,' I continued, 'you guys ensure all of your guys are locked and loaded before ever getting in a vehicle again.'

Driving in Baghdad is like bumper cars at the funfair. First in, first served, and it doesn't pay to get all bent out of shape about it. The local population, like us, also had places to be. My rule was to blend in and avoid any unnecessarily aggressive techniques. Sure, block a lane to enable your vehicles to pull out and shield the prin-cipal vehicle, but drive like a local wherever possible. It took the drivers a few kilometres to get used to it, and now and then I had to get on the comms to tell one or another to relax.

As we approached the main roundabout at Nisour Square, leading onto the Monument to the Unknown Soldier, there was a sudden burst of gunfire. For this area it was nothing unusual; the Palestine and Sheraton Hotels were nearby and always under attack. Three pickups came charging through the roundabout, with two guys on the back of each dressed all in black uniforms. They had some shoulder patch I couldn't recognise and they were firing their AKs into the air, waving the muzzles at the local cars to get them to move out of their way.

It was a typical Iraqi government CP move, but something the newbies had never seen before. I radioed for all vehicles to slow down, keep calm, but keep alert, but, before I was even finished, I heard the unmistakable sound of an AR being fired by someone in our convoy.

'Who the fuck was that?' I radioed.

No answer.

'Who was that?' I repeated.

'Um, it was Piper,' came back the reply.

'What are you firing at?' I demanded.

'The flatbeds,' he replied, in a tone that showed he was not sure if he had done the right thing or not.

'Why?' I asked.

'They were firing their weapons.'

'Were they firing at you?'

'Um, no.'

'Were they firing them anywhere near us?'

'Um, no.'

'So why did you fire at them?'

There was silence, and I could tell the rest of the new guys were unsure whether Piper had done the right thing.

'OK, listen in. Remember what I told you in training. Do not fire at anyone unless you or any of us are being fired on, or unless you are certain that you have to prevent someone from firing at us, and you believe 100 per cent that by doing so you will prevent harm from coming to you or any of us. From what I just saw, we were not under any threat, agreed?'

'Yeah,' came back a chorus of replies.

'Er, one thing,' Piper interjected.

'Yes,' I answered.

'I, um, shot the wing mirror off the vehicle.'

Quite aside from Piper's unnecessary use of force, which could have drawn unwanted attention, he had shot off one of the most important items for helping with rearwards observation. We relied heavily on the wing mirrors to see who the fuck was behind. The more eyes-on, the better. We now had a blind spot.

I was starting to rack up a few debrief points, one of which was for Piper to repair the mirror before I'd let him or the vehicle out on the road again. Oh well, that was the aim of the exercise.

The rest of the drive went well, and the guys settled into the hustle and bustle of Baghdad pretty good. It would take many trips before they fully got the hang of it, if anyone ever did, but we had broken the ice. We turned into the Mansour district, and I pointed out the tall telecom tower, as a key waypoint. As we made our way to the Greystone team house, I told them to watch for the reaction of the Iraqi guards, who were manning some of the more affluent properties in the neighbourhood.

'Read their faces and the way they act. That can tell you a lot about us being here, and you may see a few attack indicators from those fucks.'

We rounded the corner and pulled into the Greystone house. I was glad to see the drivers stage the vehicles properly, turning them to face the way out. Piper had located a roll of duct tape and was repairing the hanging mirror. He had fortunately missed the glass, so it was a simple-enough fix. Shit was getting done and I could see this was mostly going to be a good team.

While they were so engaged, I caught up with Noodle, who was based back at Greystone now. He'd just returned from training the Iraqi National Intelligence Service (NIS), teaching them how to use their CZ 75 Czech-made pistols, plus some AK drills. According to Noodle, the whole thing had been a joke. One day he'd have a full complement of guys, the next only half would turn up. Some guys turned up and registered by their name, only to have someone completely different attend the next day, under the exact same name. Even though it was clear from the ID photos Noodle had that this fucker looked nothing like the previous one, he'd try to palm himself off as the genuine article.

I told Noodle to watch his back and never get out in front of them, unless he had someone with a loaded gun standing behind them too. You just couldn't trust them. Noodle reassured me he'd be careful. As we said our goodbyes, I walked past the front door and did a double-take. There, right inside the entrance, stood a tripod-mounted PK belt-fed machine gun, with the barrel facing the gate and some extra boxes of belt ammo close by.

'What the fuck is that?' I asked Noodle. 'And whose idea?'

'Have a guess.'

'George.'

'Damn right.'

By now, George had become something of a legend within the Blackwater community. One night, some dickheads further down the street were having a shootout, which was keeping George awake. Only concerned that the noise was interfering with his sleep, he got out of bed, put his cowboy boots on and climbed up to the roof, stark naked. At the top of his voice, he screamed for everyone to shut the fuck up, after which they promptly did. No bullshit. All fire immediately ceased and not another peep was heard all night.

The crusty old fuck went everywhere in his cowboy boots and

talked like he had been chewing rocks since childhood. He was a fit and tough old bird, and I could see his way of thinking: the PK, being behind the tinted glass of the front door, could be seen only from the inside. Any guys trying to storm the walls were going to receive a nasty surprise and get cut to mincemeat trying to figure out why no one had noticed the fucking-great machine gun.

I man-hugged Noodle and we went our separate ways. I told everyone to mount up, as we would depart in ten mikes (military for 'minute'). Piper had done a reasonable job on the mirror but received a shitload of ribbing for his first 'kill' in Iraq. Someone had cut out the shape of a wing mirror in duct tape and stuck it to his vehicle door, just like the decals indicating kills on a fighter plane.

We made our way back through Mansour and, as usual, we got some looks from the property guards. A lot of the embassies had been based in Mansour, and there were very well-off Iraqis still living in the area. It wasn't known whose side they were on at any particular time of the day. I radioed the guys to tell them to return the hard stares, giving the impression that to fuck with us would mean the end of life as they knew it. Later, I'd teach them the smile-and-wave technique, but the death stare would do for now.

If you made yourself a daunting target, the shitheads would think twice before having a go at you. While the insurgents wanted to give the impression that they were happy to go to the afterlife, in truth not so many were in any great hurry to get there. They preferred to leave that to the growing number of drugged-up, brainwashed orphans, war widows and angry young men who they had at their disposal.

The smart ones did the brainwashing and sent the weak ones off to meet Allah. It wasn't so dissimilar, I thought, to the rich, white, bible-thumping, all-American politicians who seemed so eager to send disadvantaged kids and minority communities to fight their wars.

A short distance from the Greystone house, I noticed a group of families had set up a small, tented city; just a bunch of people trying to make enough money to get through each day. No doubt they'd lost their homes in the war and decided to erect their tents in what was a very up-market location. And why the fuck not?

The families lived communally, sharing whatever they had, and their kids were playing in the street, doing what children do, in spite of the crass stupidity going on all around them. They were playing soccer or tag, rolling wheel rims or throwing big-ass rocks at each other. No joke. I admired the Iraqis' resilient nature, and the children were no exception. Compared to Western kids, these guys were tough as fuck, and while they ran around bashing the crap out of each other, their mothers would just carry on doing whatever they were doing: cooking, washing clothes or gathering firewood. The families' tents were big, black, Bedouin-type dwellings, each of which provided a home for about twenty people. I couldn't help but admire them.

After the new guys had got their PX treat, we arrived back at our team house and slowed for the Jordanians to let us in. We had set up a daily password and licence-plate system. That way, the gate guards wouldn't get confused and let any old convoy into our inner sanctum. At this stage, I wanted them to stop everyone, every time. While our vehicles were stationary, the guys got out and deployed in all-around defence, looking for anyone who was looking for us.

With the exercise completed, I wanted to practise perimeter security and client evacuation drills. After the debrief, I instructed the team leaders to look over their properties and find the best overwatch and sniper positions, covering every house we owned all down the street. I also wanted them to establish safe rooms within their houses and alternative evacuation routes back to the main house. Additionally, each house was issued with a long gun – either a Dragunov sniper or a Belgian FN FAL – to be held in their arsenal.

Hammer had painted distance markers along the street every twenty metres, giving an indication of range and allowing sights to be adjusted accordingly. Unfortunately, the silly fuck had done the markers in day-glow spray on any lamp post, fence post or mailbox that happened to be to hand. The locals were less than pleased to see fluorescent graffiti all over their nice white perimeter walls and street furniture, but that was Hammer in a nutshell.

To prevent his paint job from causing any further animosity, I told Vincent van Hammer to clean the paint off and find some alternative method. He did just that, after which range cards were taped on the roof of the designated sniper position. Now, whoever took that post had all the information they would need to hand.

Next, I wanted to practise fire-and-manoeuvre and rapid evacuation from each house, starting with Hammer's. His was the furthest away from the main house. Next was Yogi's, followed by Dodger's on the opposite side of the road. Finally, we'd get all the way back to the main house. This plan was the last-ditch, 'we gotta get the fuck outta here' scenario.

My immediate action plan (IA) was this: all house members, including the clients, would make their way by foot to us in the main house. Those from Hammer's house would make their way to Yogi's, under cover from Yogi's team and the other two houses. The occupants of Hammer and Yogi's houses would then move towards Dodger's, covered by firepower from Dodger's team and the main house. Finally, all of them would move to the solid garage of the main house and my ops room. There, we would defend ourselves until we had defeated the attackers or help arrived. We had set up a safe room with food, water, toilet paper and porn mags. Only joking about the toilet paper.

My deliberate action plan (DA) was this: the team leader and driver would bundle the client into their vehicle and roar down to the main house, under cover of fire from the teams in the other houses, in the same order. Clear as mud. What could possibly go wrong, right?

To practise the IA plan, I had everyone kit up with everything they wanted to carry: war vests, mag holders, weapons and go bags. They were free to carry a fucking piano if they wanted, as long as they could still function. Once we had assembled outside the office house, I explained what we were about to do.

'OK dudes,' I began. 'We will now conduct some fire-and-manoeuvre, starting from Hammer's house, all the way back to here.'

They looked at the distance we had to cover and there were more than a few *oh fucks*.

'Yep,' I repeated. 'All the way from Hammer's house. Lookie-lookie, all the way down there, right to where we are standing now. And as we go past each house, we collect each team as we go.'

They looked at the distance and automatically calculated how much this was going to hurt.

'To do that, I want each team to go to their respective house. Snipers and spotters on roofs and everyone else in fire positions. Then, starting from Hammer's house, he and his guys will make their way down the road towards this location.'

Once every team was back at the main house, we would get the Jordanians back there too and lock the place down.

'Everyone got it?' They all confirmed that they had.

'Omar, you got it?'

'Yes, boss.'

'Right,' I said. 'Before we do anything, I want to conduct a little test. I want you all to get in lines of five.'

After a few quizzical looks, they got into rows with everyone lined up like at the start of a track and field race.

'OK, looks good. Now, gents, if you look ahead, you'll see that lamp post, ten o'clock, about twenty-five metres away.'

More puzzled expressions.

'Right then, on the command "go", I want the first row of five to sprint to the post. Run as fast as you can and once you get to the post, move off to the side to give room for the next guys, and so on, until we are all there.'

I could see the penny had dropped for a few of the more clued-up guys, and they started to readjust their pouch covers and straps.

'Right, first row, ready, GO!'

Like racehorses at the Kentucky Derby, the first lot took off sprinting in full war rig towards the finish post. It was not a pretty sight, as shit dropped out of people's pouches and holdalls and slammed all over the ground. There were magazines, knives and a host of other crap that started clanging off the tarmac.

Then, as if in slow motion, we saw the familiar round shape of a high-explosive grenade lift out of someone's unsecured pouch and gently make its way through the air and down towards the hard road. Together we turned our asses and covered our ears, in what was the best defensive posture we could muster. With eyes and ass-holes clenched tight, we waited for the familiar *crump* and the ball of fury to explode, sending splintered metal into our fleshy bits, but… nothing. To our relief, the grenade bounced off the road and rolled to a stop in the gutter.

'OK, guys,' I said, 'that's what I was testing for. Whose is that?'

The guys at the finish line all looked at each other, until the perpetrator finally raised his hand. *Piper.*

'Well, there you go, Mr Mirror-killer himself. Go pick it up and put the fucking thing somewhere secure.'

As Piper set off, mercilessly ribbed by his teammates, I reminded them all what this was about.

'It's no use being fully kitted-up if you have all your pouches undone and lose your shit before you get to use it. So, fasten everything. Second group, line up, ready, GO!'

And off they went. This time only one item fell out of someone's rig: a GPS. It didn't like hitting the hard ground one bit, as it cracked open and spilled batteries all over the road.

We did this until everyone had run the distance. Finally, I did the same. Despite Piper's best Jedi mind control, nothing of mine fell out. This was a good lesson, and to be honest a very basic one. I also noticed that there were more than a few of the boys puffing like they had just run the Boston Marathon.

'Fitness, gentlemen,' I announced. 'Get the fitness up. No good having gym muscles if you don't have the fuel in the tank to feed them. Plus, one last thing before we get on with the exercise. I want all those who lost kit to move forward and face front.'

Four guys did the walk of shame, heads bowed.

'As punishment, I want ten push-ups for every item that fell out, and I believe I counted six items, so that's going to be sixty push-ups.'

A couple of them started to unclip their vests and put their weapons on the ground. 'Oh no. Full kit. Sling your weapons over your backs.'

The rest of the guys began to chuckle, as they relished the

humiliating ritual that was coming. The four accused stood ready at my command.

'Oh no, you're not going to be the ones to do the push-ups,' I announced, as I turned away from the four. '*We will*, and you four will count them out for us.' There was a definite expression of surprise on everyone's faces; a collective look of 'what the fuck?'

At the four accused's count, we commenced to bust out sixty push-ups under the hot Baghdad sun. By the time we hit thirty-five, there were more than a few guys struggling and, as expected, a few started to curse the accused, who were counting the punishment out feeling like shit, which was exactly my plan. If there is one thing guys want to avoid more than a beasting, it's resentment from their teammates.

I believe in self-policing, and this would help everyone ensure they were ship-shape and ready to go at all times. Although we were civilians, combat close protection must be treated like a military operation to succeed. It was also a good way to bond the guys, and any loners would soon reveal themselves. In fact, I figured that was happening already. I'd noted, with a bit of concern, that the same player had made some basic mistakes. I would have to keep a very close eye on Piper.

The guys could see that I took what I did very seriously, and it showed my leadership style. I never asked anyone to do something I wouldn't do myself, and I let people make mistakes so that we could learn from them, provided they weren't the kind that got people killed. I hoped it also showed that I had some tolerance and was reasonable but that I knew what I was doing and wasn't to be fucked with.

I insisted that whenever anyone was outside and in the open, they were to be fully kitted-up: armour, vest and gun. I told them

I wanted them to be like firemen and to never have their kit out of arm's reach. You never knew when an attack might happen, and I didn't want anyone caught unprepared. This rule applied even when doing a workout: dress in your PT kit, but take your armour, vest and gun too.

Drills honed, we settled into a good routine, with the occasional trip to the IZ or BIAP. Whoever I tasked to do the runs was briefed prior to going and debriefed as soon as they got back by the TL who was on the run. For entry into our compound, we set up daily pass-words. Any incoming or outgoing team would call once they got within radio range, so we could check they weren't being followed.

December was a busy month, as we prepared for the Christmas wind-down. The IRI clients were looking forward to it, but I was already looking way beyond Christmas. I'd decided that I would do a five-month rotation this time, which would take me through to early April 2005. My reasoning was that it would enable me to save up as much money as possible for my upcoming wedding.

It was going to prove a long stretch, and I wasn't too sure if I had made the right decision. Even after the regular three-month stints, I'd found that I was burnt out and that my focus and energy were low, but I had asked for it and got it, so I had to crack on.

One by one the expat clients began to depart for their Christ-mas break. The last to leave was the young American guy who had arrived after the others, the IRI Ops O. We had given him the call sign Orange, due to the bright orange shirt he was wearing when we'd picked him up from BIAP. The guy had asked that we didn't hold a sign with his name on it when he first landed in-country at arrivals. Maybe he'd thought there would be a bunch of drivers in suits and hats with name boards waiting to collect their rides.

Orange and I had worked together well. On more than one

occasion I'd had to tell him that we would not do some unscheduled run or other, especially when they had dropped it on us at short notice, after dark to some bar they had heard was open at the Sheraton or out in the Red Zone. This was because of the obvious risk of driving at night. The IRI business might be theirs, but security was ours. Orange was good with it, every time.

With Christmas Day squared away, I figured it was time to reflect on the year almost done. With all the clients gone, I decided to plan a New Year's party. We made several trips to a certain house in the Red Zone, which was known to sell alcohol. The owner tried to keep it under wraps, with his stash of booze hidden away in a back room, so as not to alert the ultra-religious zealots, who would not have approved of him selling infidel alcohol, especially to the enemy, but in truth the place was the worst-kept secret in Baghdad.

There was always a shitload of security company vehicles parked up outside, loading up with cartons of beer, or whatever he had that kicked a bit harder. The owner must have been making a fortune to risk being blown up by the radical party-poopers. New Year's Eve arrived, and I had invited Noodle to join our festivities. He left the Greystone house with Mo but reached us at last light looking a bit pale.

'What's up, bro?' I asked.

'Frig me, as Mo and I were heading out of the neighbourhood I was getting a lot of dirty looks from the local guards. I suddenly realised that I stood out as a lone white guy in a black BMW, with only Mo for company, and we were passing a lot of nasty buggers who could have smoked us if they'd felt like it. I figured they must have either thought I was a one-man Rambo, and didn't want to tangle with me, or that I was a complete muppet, and they were too stunned by my stupidity to act in time.'

'So why didn't you loop back home?' I asked.

'What, and miss the party? You've got to be kidding.'

'Fair enough,' I said, as I cracked a beer and handed it to him. 'Drop your shit in the top room, bro. There's a spare bunk there. I'll meet you on the roof.'

Despite trying to be on our 'A' game all the time, sometimes we slipped up, and it wasn't until we were far from the safety of our castles that the reality of the situation dawned.

I'd already reached the point where gunfire wasn't phasing me. If I thought I was being lined up by some distant sniper when out in the open, I wouldn't even look for cover. It was a dangerous attitude and too often I would just think 'fuck it'. I was starting to believe I was bulletproof. As the weeks of my extended stint rolled on, this would only get worse. But right now, there was partying to be done.

As darkness fell, we gathered on the roof of our IRI team house. I had briefed Omar to tell the Jordanian nightshift not to be surprised by anything coming from up on the roof, as we were going to have a big night and it could get a bit messy. By 19:00 it was dark but warmer than usual for a December night. For whatever reason I decided that we didn't have enough booze and needed to do an emergency beer run.

This was a totally dumb idea, but, through the cloud of alcohol, I reckoned it made perfect sense. Sure, there were 400 beers in the cooler boxes, I reasoned, but there were *only 400 beers*, and what happened if we ran out? I rallied a group of equally drunk volunteers, and we kitted up for a gumball run to the beer house. Yes, the very house that would make a great target for the insurgents.

As the six of us drunk fucks crammed into the black soft-skin BMW, it was apparent that there wasn't enough room, and no one wanted to stay behind.

'Fuck it,' I said, 'pop the trunk and one of you can sit in there acting as the tail-end Charlie.'

Once we had finished loading up, we went roaring off in pursuit of the golden nectar, with guns poking out of every opening like a drunken hedgehog on wheels, spoiling for a fight. We pulled up outside the beer house, to the horror of the owner, who had closed shop for the day. In spite of his pleas for us to fuck right off, I wasn't taking no for an answer. With the flashing of several $100 bills, I managed to persuade him to open up again. Within ten minutes we had bought as many cartons of beer as we could possibly fit in the remaining space on the vehicle and roared out of there like the Dukes of Baghdad.

I cannot emphasise enough what a dumb idea it was. So many things could have gone wrong, and we would have been yet another group of names on the list of dead contractors that no one outside Iraq gave a fuck about. Nevertheless, we made it back and, apart from some shaken-up beer, the run was declared a great success. So, as midnight approached, I decided to implement my next stupid plan.

'Hey, Yogi,' I called. 'Come here, mate.' Yogi, the former marine with the deep Southern drawl, was another guy who had proved to be a totally solid operator.

'Hey, brother,' he replied, 'what's happening? What you want?'

Like everyone, I was still wearing my pistol, and as Yogi got within about one foot of me I drew the weapon and, at head height between the two of us, I let off a shot straight up into the air.

'Yee-hah!' I yelled, and bang on cue figures started to pull their pistols and do the same.

Before I knew it, everyone was blasting 9mm into the Baghdad night. The noise was deafening, and we were definitely well out of order. Any Big Army patrol might have thought we were under sustained attack, or that they were.

'OK, OK,' I yelled, fighting back the laughter. 'That's enough.' But it was too late for that, as a few of the guys hadn't finished unloading their mags. When it finally died down, we chimed in the New Year: 2005.

By around 01:00 I had drunk enough beer and Chivas Regal whisky and smoked enough cigars to kill ten men. I slipped off to bed leaving a handful of die-hards still at it. There was the occasional pop of 9mm coming from the roof, though nothing too serious, but some time after falling asleep I was woken by an almighty great *kaboom-kaboom-kaboom* coming from directly above me. It was so loud that the whole house was shaking.

Holy fuck, we must be under fire.

I grabbed some clothes and raced up to see who the hell was attacking us. I reached the roof and saw this one guy firing off bursts from the belt-fed Heckler & Koch MG43 machine gun high into the air. The tracer was shooting up and out in a beautiful arc and hopefully falling into the Tigris River. Holy fuck it looked nice, but it was just a little bit too much.

I decided to wait until he had finished before yelling out over the cheering and the deafness in my ears: 'Hey, numb nuts. Put that fucking thing away and get to bed.'

To my amazement, he dutifully put the big-ass gun down and headed for some shuteye. Well done that man.

The next morning I was the first to rise and, unlike the big gun on the roof, I was not firing on all cylinders. Somehow, I still had the ability to rise early after a night of hell-drinking, and it wasn't long before I began to recollect the previous night's crass stupidity. As I made my way to the roof to survey the carnage, my head was thumping like a belt-fed machine gun, and for the thousandth time I made the promise that I wouldn't do *that* again.

As I stepped onto the roof, the sight that greeted me sent a cold shiver down my spine. *Oh no, we're fucked.* From end to end it was plastered in empty beer cans, bullet cases and belt link. I had to get it cleaned up quickly so I could convince myself this had never happened. It could get me fired, and justifiably so. Even though it had been a collective effort, I was the one who had instigated the madness, and I was supposed to be in charge.

I'd almost finished tidying up when I was joined by Noodle and Yard Dog.

'Fuck, bro, what a night,' said a still-sleepy Yard Dog.

'Yes indeed, bro,' I groaned, not too proud of myself.

'That will go down in celebration history,' Noodle declared.

'Yeah, bro, I think it will, but I feel like a dick for letting it happen,' I confessed.

'Nah, bro,' he said. 'We all could have said no and, besides, no one threw a high explosive, so it could have been worse.'

Noodle always had this great ability to rationalise things. He was an old soul in a young body, and it is why I liked to refer to him as my Prozac. However, he usually managed to stop me from doing something utterly fucking stupid when I was drinking, but this time I'd caught him by surprise. It didn't matter that no one had been forced to join in with the gun-fest. I still felt guilty and that I had let myself and everybody down.

Once the place was a bit tidier, Noodle and I made some breakfast and watched the movie *Hero* with Jet Li. I love the colours and cinematography in that film. A bit later, Hammer came over from his house.

'Hey, bro, what a night.'

'Yeah, bro,' I muttered, though the last thing I needed was any more congratulations on the screw-up I had allowed on my watch. I've always been a 'regretful and depressed' day-after drinker. A heavy night's beers was invariably followed by a heavy day of apologies. Generally, if I'm having a good time, it means someone else isn't, and the last thing I need to hear are reminders of the stupid shit I've done.

We watched *Team America* together and, as funny as it was, I couldn't enjoy it. Once it was finished, Noodle said his goodbyes and headed back to Mansour. But it would take me a few days to get my head straight, and I decided that I really needed to get my shit straight, as well. I had let my guard down and felt as if I had lost my standing as the leader of this team. This may or may not have been true, but I still felt the need to redeem myself. The question was, how?

A few days later, I went to meet the new CO of the Australian company based in the vacant high-rise block. He told me that he and his guys had seen all the New Year's shooting and initially they had stood-to, thinking we were under attack. But when they looked through their night-vision scopes, they realised we were just doing dumb drunk shit and went back to bed. I apologised and when I left, I felt even more like shit.

A week later, the IRI clients flew back into country and work resumed as normal. It was good to get back into the swing of things, and it allowed me to put as much distance as I could between myself and that night. I desperately hoped I could erase it altogether and give myself some deniability.

This is how it works when you're drinking too much: time, you hope, will be the great eraser.

CHAPTER 15

A number of the guys who'd been assigned to my contract were slated to join Blackwater State, just as soon as they got their security clearance. Zen's had just come through, which meant that man-mountain would soon be leaving us. So, when Orange came to the ops room to tell me we had a run to Tikrit coming up, it seemed a good opportunity for Zen to get some leadership experience, under my oversight.

There was going to be a big meeting between local tribal leaders and officials from the Electoral Ministry, and IRI was sending a representative. A run to Tikrit would mean a long day and, as Tikrit was Saddam's former home town, it was squarely in bad-boy country. We'd heard that Big Army were being hit every day in Tikrit, and reports from other Blackwater teams in the area weren't a lot better. This would also be the team's first major trip outside Baghdad.

As we were only taking the one client, we had to split the guys, so the other IRI staff could go about their daily business in and around Baghdad. Zen and I worked out a plan we were both happy with, and although he was a little resistant at first, I'd convinced him to add top-cover on the buildings around the meeting place, so we would have eyes-on.

The meeting was scheduled for an old compound, lying a few kilometres out of Tikrit. But first we had to head for a US military base that had been set up in one of Saddam's old palaces and follow their Humvee convoy to the venue. Even though we were traveling in low-profile vehicles, any hope of slipping in unnoticed was gone once we joined up with the military. Bad guys would easily make us, and all they had to do was pass on our vehicle types to any waiting in ambush.

Generally, getting to the meeting wasn't the problem, because the insurgents wouldn't know when and where you'd be coming from. It was during the meeting, or on your way out, that shit tended to get funky.

Zen briefed the guys using the SMEAC format I'd taught them. Each group was seated in their vehicle configurations, and the roles and responsibilities of each team member had been given out the day before. That way they had time to prep their kit and for drivers to ensure they had filled their vehicles with good petrol from the IZ.

The top-cover guys were equipped with long guns and binoculars. I got Yogi to grab the infamous HK MG43 party gun – don't remind me – and a shitload of belt ammo. As I had been to Tikrit several months back, I would take the lead vehicle with Yard Dog driving. He'd decided to wear a shemagh over his new hair plugs, to blend in. I'm not sure why, since to me he just looked like a pale fucker wearing a shemagh.

Zen did a good job presenting the orders, but, just as we were about to mount up, who should raise an issue but Piper. He'd decided he wanted to travel in a different vehicle, along with a buddy of his from way back. That guy had been kicked off a BW contract down country for being a dipshit who no one could work with. Why he'd been sent to me I had no fucking idea, but shit like that had started to happen a lot recently. As much as we had resisted taking him, Moyock insisted: we just had to make it work.

He was a young, tall, string-bean of a guy, call signed Stretch. Piper had listened to Zen's brief, and it was only afterwards that he had decided he wanted to ride with Stretch. Zen made the mistake of asking Piper why he wanted to change vehicle, but, before he could answer, I cut in with a firm 'no'. He wasn't changing the line-up and that was all there was to it.

Zen looked relieved; Piper looked unhappy. I asked if he had a problem, but I didn't let him answer before telling everyone to mount up. Everyone could see the anger building inside me. This fuck was becoming more than just a problem child. As much as I would have liked to cut him from the run, we needed him, if for nothing else than to take a bullet to the face to shield one of the good guys.

The drive to Tikrit would take us through areas that were still seeing heavy combat. There were several dodgy bridges known for frequent ambushes, and the burnt and twisted steel barriers were evidence that some unfortunates had paid the ultimate price. Where the road ran close to the river, tight groves of trees obscured the open desert beyond, making it impossible to see the source of an attack if the insurgents used the dead ground and long-range weapons.

We set off, everyone sounding tense as they called out potential threats over the comms. Finally, a change in scenery indicated that we were approaching Tikrit itself. Though there were still plenty of trees and fields, the place had changed dramatically since I had first travelled through it, back in 2003. Tikrit had then been a bustling town, with thronging marketplaces. Now the streets were bombed and empty. It looked like daily life had just stopped.

We found the RV spot and linked up with the military. With them leading the way, we drove out of Tikrit and across a dusty patch of land that doubled as a soccer field. The military didn't seem to appreciate or care that we were in sedans with very low ground clearance, and, while their massive vehicles just bounced over the bumps and hollows, we had to crawl and angle our approach to avoid the grounding. After three kilometres of doing that bullshit, a walled compound came into view. We drove inside and were ushered to a parking spot by an IP, who clearly wasn't overjoyed to be there.

As Zen and his crew escorted the client inside, I noticed that the IPs had stopped staring at us, jumped to their feet, straightened their berets and started trying to look as sharp as possible. Clearly someone of importance was about to arrive. I used the distraction to move the vehicles out of the walled compound and into the open. Meanwhile, Shadow and some of the boys conducted a sweep of the compound and the inside of the hall, while Yogi and his crew did the same to the exterior before taking up positions on the roofs of the tallest structures.

Although there were plenty of Humvees, all bristling with .50-cals and MK19 40mm grenade launchers, there were hardly any soldiers to be seen, except for the occasional glimpse of their helmet tops bobbing up out of a turret. I guess these fucks had better things to do than be worried about what was going on outside.

I wasn't particularly interested in the meeting. My main concern was the possibility of an attack using mortars, rockets or a long-range belt-fed machine gun. It would be simple to lob some high explosives into the compound and let the shrapnel work its magic, ricocheting off the hard walls, tearing our flesh like razor-edged pinballs.

I strolled over to the building we'd selected as our overwatch position and climbed up to the roof to take a look. Haggis and Yogi had already lugged the MG43 up there. They'd worked out a one-on one-off shift routine, and Yogi was lying flat on his back enjoying the sunshine. I took the binoculars from Haggis and scanned the area to the front: low, flat, with scattered buildings and tree cover.

'Hell, bro, you could strike from anywhere out there,' I remarked, 'and we wouldn't have a clue where it came from.'

'Yeah, man,' Yogi drawled, in that thick South Carolina twang that always made me smile.

'I was talking to Haggis, you retard,' I joked.

'Ah hell, brother, no need to be like that,' he retorted, without shifting the ball cap that was covering his face.

Between Haggis's Scottish burr and Yogi's southern drawl, I'd kind of messed up partnering them together, especially if they needed to call it over the radio. But, hell, what was done was done, and they made a good pair of operators.

'OK, don't burn yourselves out here, we still have a long drive back. Get plenty of rest and water.'

After an hour on overwatch, Haggis and Yogi were swapped out by Piper and Stretch. How those fucks had managed to buddy up was anyone's guess, and just the sight of them together was pissing me off. Oh yeah, Beavis and Butt-Head were really grinding my gears.

When their time on the roof was coming to an end, I found out who was slated to replace them and tasked them to do something else. It wasn't as if we wouldn't be bugging out shortly, so I climbed the ladder and poked my head over the parapet. The first thing I spied was Piper and Stretch lain in the prone position, their feet towards me.

'Hey,' I called out, just above a whisper. There was no response. 'Hey,' I said, a bit louder. Still nothing. *How deaf are these fuckers?* 'HEY,' I yelled, and, I'll be honest, a slight tingle of glee went through me. 'If you two are sleeping, then it's goodbye pork pie. Don't pass go; don't collect $200 and don't let the CASA ramp door hit you in the ass on the way out.'

Still nothing.

I climbed onto the roof, doing my best cat burglar impersonation, and tippy-toed until I was standing right over them. I looked down and both were snoring up a storm. Piper was even drooling out of the corner of his mouth. *Yep, I got ya now.* I quietly crept back to the top of the ladder and whispered in the radio for Zen to join me. I motioned for him to quietly climb the ladder, and, as he poked his head over the top, he spied the two sleeping beauties. His immediate reaction was not quite like mine.

'Fuck me,' he declared, and without any prompting he clambered up the final few rungs, sprung onto the roof and covered the distance between him and Piper and Stretch in just a few giant strides. Then, with a big swing from his muscular leg, he brought a size 16 boot down hard on both of their asses.

'Wake the fuck up you two,' he rasped, like a very pissed-off Darth Vader.

Zen's loud whisper might as well have been a scream. The two idiots jumped up and tried to compose themselves, but it was too late for that. Piper, showing just how much of a douchebag he was, even tried to offer an excuse and blame the lack of water.

'That's no excuse,' Zen growled. 'That's something you should have been prepared for, before starting your shift.'

To say I was laughing on the inside is an understatement. I had all I needed to get rid of Piper and his mate, the useless fucks.

The meeting was getting ready to wrap up, and a crowd started moving out of the hall like a human tsunami. At the same time, of course, the Iraqi security guys decided they needed to bust through, thereby jamming up the doors and the whole exit procedure. Our client, like us, was eager to get the hell out of there, but, as usual, everyone had the same idea – to be the first to leave in a cloud of dust.

I leant over to Shadow and whispered that now would be a good time for the insurgents to attack. We mounted up and waited for an opportunity to join the rush, which was a bit of a catch-22 proposition. If we moved out with everyone else, we would be joining a target-rich environment, but if we waited until everyone had left, we would lose the advantage of combined firepower. In the end, we were second last to leave.

'Where to?' I radioed Zen, who was with the client.

'Back to Baggers,' he replied.

It would have been nice to know that before we departed, but it was no big deal. Flexibility is a big part of the PSD game, and there's no need to get your balls in a twist over the small stuff.

The attack we had feared had not happened, or at least not where we had expected it. We left Tikrit behind, settling in for the three-hour drive to Baghdad. Twenty minutes down the road, there was a narrow bridge lying over a wide wadi, which was known to be one of the insurgents' favourite killing grounds. A few clicks out from the bridge we came up to the end of a long traffic jam.

Zen radioed for a SITREP, but the front vehicle couldn't offer much info. 'Can't see anything further up than 100 metres, without having to get out,' they radioed back.

'OK,' Zen announced. 'Everyone keep your eyes peeled and don't get out unless I tell you to.'

He was right. We were better sitting in the traffic incognito, not exposing or isolating ourselves, but as the minutes ticked by the tension and the heat in the vehicles kept rising. Even in the sedans and with our tinted windows, it felt like everyone could see us as plain as day. Five minutes turned to ten, then twenty, before Zen came up on the radio.

'Hey, Baz, the client needs to pee.'

I was waiting for that. It's a normal human function and we all do it, but there are good times and not so good times, and this was not a good time. It would have been a bit harsh to demand he pee in a bottle in the back seat of an armoured BMW, but as soon as he got out any anonymity we had enjoyed would be blown.

'OK, what d'you want to do?' I said, putting the question back to Zen, so he could figure out a solution. He was here to learn, after all.

'Umm, OK,' he said, 'when I give the word, I want everyone to dismount into all-around defence around the vehicles. Once this is established, I will let the client out and he can go piss.'

Zen was starting to get affirmative replies from the other vehicles, so, I waited for a gap in the comms, then cut in.

'No, bro,' I said. 'Why not consider this option. Why don't you and your team get out of your vehicle and secure your area, and the rest of us will provide as much visual cover from inside our vehicles as we can without revealing ourselves. Once we have given you the all-clear, you can let the client out to take a piss and then get him back inside pronto.'

'Yeah, roger that,' Zen confirmed. 'I'll let you know when we are ready, and you let me know when it's clear.'

'Roger that,' I replied.

'All call signs, you got that, over?' Zen asked. Within seconds, he received a full set of acknowledgements.

Zen and his crew, minus the driver and client, cracked their doors and made their hairy-assed Blackwater presence known. Standing with their backs to the vehicle, Zen moved to the client's door and did one final check, before I confirmed it all looked good. Zen opened the car door and used his very large frame to block anyone's view, as the client got out.

It was obvious that the client wanted to move into the bushes for some privacy. The road ran along a bank covered in tall grass, about four metres above what looked like a plantation of date trees. The ground between the trees was usually kept clear of any under-growth, but here the grass lay thick and high between the rows. It offered ideal cover for anyone wanting to move in on us without being seen.

Zen let the client take a few steps into the grass, as not everyone likes an audience when flopping their dick out. He stepped forward and started going through the motions, while everyone was doing as instructed and watching their arcs.

So far, so good.

Then, over the radio, someone piped up from one of the vehicles. 'Hey, we have a guy here who needs to pee as well.'

I waited for Zen's reply, and it was the correct one. 'Let him go in a bottle. I don't want anyone out of the vehicles unless I say.'

We already had guys staging defence around one vehicle. It wouldn't take a genius to work out that if a white guy stepped out of another vehicle, followed by others in the vehicle behind, then there were security vehicles in convoy and, in all likelihood, a dozen or more men.

The caller in the vehicle where the guy needed a pee radioed that their guy *really* wanted to get out and pee. He held his thumb over the send button of his radio for a few seconds, and I could hear some sort of commotion in the vehicle, with someone saying, 'I'm not pissing in a bottle, I'm getting out. Fuck 'em.'

Whether the thumb on the mic was a deliberate thing, I'm not sure, but it sure as shit let us know we had problems. I saw Zen's head spin and fix the offending vehicle with burning eyes, but before he could reach for his radio switch to lay down the law, a further call came over the comms.

'We are getting out, Goddamn it.' With that, the occupants of the vehicle at the rear did just that, while one of the team made a dash for the treeline. There was no way he could provide cover for himself, with both hands working his zipper and fumbling for his appendage, so his teammates were forced to expose themselves because this asshole needed to expose himself.

By now, Zen's client had finished, and, once Zen had got him back inside the vehicle, he marched down the line with a look like murder on his face. Every local waiting in line was now watching this very pissed-off man-mountain like a hawk. *Fuck, everyone was going to figure out exactly who we were.* Basically, one little shit's actions had exposed us all, and I wasn't the only one to work this out.

'What we do now?' Yogi came up on the comms. Zen didn't answer.

'Hold on, buddy,' I replied.

I scanned the line, looking for any attention we might be getting, and then I saw it – a young guy opened his door and stepped half-out. He first looked at Zen, then at our last vehicle, whose occupants had all got out, then at the client's vehicle. *Fuck it.* That was all I needed to see.

'OK,' I radioed. 'Everyone out, we have been made.'

No sooner had I taken my thumb off the radio than every vehicle door opened and a mass of ball-capped, Oakley-wearing, gun-toting Americans stood head and shoulders above the level of the vehicle roofs, hands on pistol grips, fingers outside trigger guards and dicks swinging. To be honest, it looked quite cinematic, and had it played in slow motion it would have been really cool.

Zen had by then reached the last vehicle, and I could see his big black muscular index finger waving in the face of the phantom pisser. Everyone else had now taken up defensive positions. I made my way to the rear vehicle, but as I got closer Zen's massive frame completely eclipsed piss-boy, who by now was getting a full serving of whoop-ass. When I finally got to see past the big fucker's gargantuan biceps, who did I see but... Piper. *Who fucking else?*

The little shit was staring at his feet, shoulders hunched, as Zen laid down the law, and the scary thing was that Zen was being very Zen-like. In fact, he was as calm as fuck.

'If you ever disobey me again, I'll tear your arms off and beat you to death with them. Then I'll shove the soggy end up your white ass and post you home to your Momma, you got that?'

Now that we were out, every fucker was eyeballing us, but the guys were doing their job: scanning for threats and looking menacing. While Zen was busy with dribble-dick, I looked around for likely attack points, and my gaze kept returning to the date plantation. That was the place I would attack from, if I was a Wolverine. I figured we had to get a sentry out that way pronto.

'Yogi, Baz, over.'

'Yeah, buddy,' he drawled.

'Where you at, bro?'

'Second to last vehicle, over.'

'OK, I'll come to you, bro, stay there.' I walked to his location, keeping my eyes on the date trees, but there was too much growth between the rows to see if there was anyone lurking there.

'Hey, bro, you got that big gun handy?'

'Sure do, buddy.'

'OK, take it forward about ten metres into the treeline and take a seat there. Make sure someone from up here has eyes on you and take someone with you to watch your flank.'

'Sure thing, buddy. You worried about bad guys in the treeline?' he asked.

'You got it, bro. It's a great place to advance on us from.'

Yogi walked to the back of his vehicle and banged on the trunk so their driver would pop the latch. He reached inside and pulled out the German-made machine gun like a proud father holding a newborn for the first time. He pulled out a long belt of 7.62mm link, roughly 300 rounds, slung them over his shoulder, grabbed his go bag and strode off down the bank with two guys in tow.

Yogi was now our forward lookout, who could give us warning if some asshole tried to creep up on us. I hoped that any shooters would need to get within visual range before launching an attack. At ground level, Yogi would have a better view down the rows than us up on the road.

A bomb attack was less likely, as the insurgents couldn't have known where we would be forced to stop. Between Yogi and the guys pulling security by the vehicles, we should be able to see down through the trees, and down the line of vehicles, if any shit tried to hit us. On his own initiative, Shadow had taken up the overwatch position for Yogi. Good thinking that man. I felt I had done all that I could.

Zen had finished chewing out Piper and was making his way back to his vehicle. I told him where I had placed Yogi and Shadow and why. I'd already made up my mind that Piper had to go. I would make a call and get the fuck kicked off the contract as soon as we got back to Baghdad. But, as we'd been waiting for close to an hour in the traffic jam, there was no way we'd get there before last light.

I pointed it out to Zen but told him that, with low-pro (low-profile) vehicles, we had a good chance of sneaking under the radar, provided we didn't look too much like a PSD convoy. Zen radioed the vehicle commanders and gave them the news. It would be their first night-move and as good a time as any to learn how to run in the dark.

I explained that they should drive with irregular spacing and that the only two vehicles that should run fairly close together would be the lead and client vehicle. The rest of us would be as close or as far apart as dictated by traffic, but we should stay within radio range. The only time I wanted us to bunch back together was if there were any further stops, or when we were close to the IZ. My final warning was to drive carefully, with no risky moves or overtaking off the hard surface. The last thing we needed was a flat tyre.

Just then I got a call from Yogi down in the treeline. 'Baz, Yogi,' he whispered.

'Yeah, bro, what is it?'

'I've got some movement.' His voice was real quiet, which told me that any threat must have been close.

'Roger that. How far out and what numbers, over?'

'I'd say about fifty metres out and more than one person.'

'OK, bro, keep eyes-on and report as needed. I'll make my way to Shadow and check it out.' I walked over to Shadow. 'Hey, bro, can you see anything from up here?'

'No, mate,' he answered. The bush was too thick to see anything further away than Yogi, squatted ten metres in front.

'OK,' I said. 'Keep your eyes peeled.' I got on the radio: 'All call signs, Baz. Those of you on the tree side of the vehicles, have a look into the treeline and see if you can spot any activity. Everyone on the road side, keep your eyes on your arcs. I don't want anyone becoming distracted by what could be a decoy to get us looking the wrong way.'

Yogi came up again, still whispering and with a bit more urgency. 'Hey, buddy, I got movement here for sure. Someone is moving through the trees parallel to us. I can see only one person, but there could be more. Shall I open up on them, over?'

'No, bro,' I came back, not meaning to take over from Zen but, given I had more experience, thinking it best I be the one to make this kind of call. 'Hold your fire. We don't know if it's a bad guy or a farmer. Just watch and report, but if you see a weapon and feel you have to, then go for it.'

I wanted Yogi to positively ID whoever was out there, but, at the same time, I had no problems with him smoking someone if he felt he had to.

I walked over to Zen. 'Hey, mate, I want one person from each vehicle on the tree side to slowly move down into the treeline. That way we can maintain security up here and have enough firepower where they'll have a better view of what's out there. It could be just one guy doing some work in his field, or it could be a bunch of guys trying to slip into an ambush position.'

Zen got on the case, making sure that one guy from each vehicle moved down the slope and, as they set off, it was just like being back on patrol in the military: sneaky and slow as fuck, which was exactly how I wanted it. I didn't want to give away that we were moving into counter-ambush positions and have anyone attack us mid-move.

They looked pretty impressive moving down together, each with their weapons in the shoulder. Once they had reached a place where they could see better, they radioed that they were in position. This wasn't something I had asked them to do, but they took the initiative and did it themselves. It showed they were switched on and working as a team, which was great.

'Dodger in position, over.'

'Haggis ready, over.'

'Hammer ready.'

'All call signs, roger that,' I replied. 'Let me know if you see anything.'

Now, if there was someone trying to do a nasty on us, they were in for a very big surprise. Ten minutes went by with no more comms from anyone. I was thinking of asking for a SITREP, when two of the guys stepped on each other, trying to get a radio message over, pressing send at the same time. This was another problem with the comms; you could only transmit one person at a time, or you'd cancel each other out.

'Baz, Dodger,' came a whispered call, after the necessary pause.

'Yeah, bro,' I answered.

'I see four guys with AKs about thirty metres to my twelve, over.'

Dodger was riding in the first vehicle, so this didn't make a great deal of sense. Whoever the bad guys were, if they had any clue on how to set up an ambush, they would have approached from a long way out, then moved in on our centre in single file, before spreading out parallel to our vehicles. Just then Haggis came up in his unmistakable Scottish brogue.

'Hey, bro, someone to my twelve.'

Before I could acknowledge his call, Yogi came up from the far end again.

'Baz, twelve o'clock to me, same, over.'

That confirmed it: whoever was out in the treeline had spread out the full length of our convoy, which to me could signal only an imminent ambush. I hoped they'd have to creep a bit closer to us before attacking, to get eyes-on. I glanced at Zen, who was waiting for me to give instructions.

'Make sure the client is lying on the floor and secure in the vehicle, bro. Brief him that we may have to engage something soon, so not to panic if we do.'

'Yeah, roger that, mate.'

'And let me know when you've done it please, bro.'

'Roger that.'

Zen moved to his vehicle and slightly cracked the road-side door. By doing so he hadn't exposed the client to the direction from which we were expecting the shit to come. Again, good skills.

'All call signs in the treeline, watch your front and if you feel you need to engage, you have my permission. Everyone up here on the road – find good cover and make sure you have a clear shot above the heads of the guys down there, but do not fire unless I say, because we can't see what they can.'

Ahead on the road, I could see the traffic was starting to move. Whatever had caused the jam must have been cleared away. If anyone wanted to have a go at us, it would have to happen very soon. I knew we would have to get back in our vehicles and get moving soon, but I didn't want whoever was down there to hit us while the guys were in the process of coming back up the rise and vulnerable.

'Baz, Yard Dog. Looks like things are moving,' he radioed.

'Roger that mate, out.'

I glanced at the line of guys up on the road with me, and then down where the guys in the treeline were. I didn't want to sit here all day waiting for some asshole who might or might not be trying to have a go at us. I had a choice to make, and I had to make it quickly.

'All call signs in the treeline, we have to get moving. Does anyone see anything, over?'

'Roger that,' Yogi came back. 'Someone with a gun is out there buddy and moving very quietly.'

That was all I needed to hear. They were carrying weapons and that justified any action I needed to take.

'All call signs in the treeline, and only in the treeline – listen up.' I repeated myself just to make sure there was no mistake. 'On my command of "three", I want you all to fire a burst of four to five rounds at the targets to your front.' This was going to be a mini version of 'the mad minute', the tactic US troops employed in Vietnam, where a section or platoon of guys would spread out in a line and shoot on full auto into the bush to their immediate front. They wouldn't be aiming at anything specific but if there was anyone out there, they would think twice about coming any closer. 'Everyone understand what I want, over?'

'Dodger, roger.'

'Haggis, roger.'

'Yogi, roger.'

'Hammer, roger.'

'OK,' I said. 'Once you have finished, stay there, stay silent and keep an eye to your front in case of a counterattack. On my command: one, two, three.'

No sooner had the word left my mouth than the entire bush line erupted into a cacophony of noise and dust, with all four of their weapons unleashed in concert. It was thunderous, with Yogi's belt-fed MG43 out-thundering everyone else's weapons. That big-ass beauty of a gun sounded like Thor's hammer as the trees to our front jumped and thrashed and the rounds kicked up a shit-ton of dust. For a second, branches and brush splintered as bullets tore through them. Then, just as quickly, it stopped. The echo of the volley rolled across the terrain, and then came the smell.

Wow – the smell of cordite is powerful and addictive. To paraphrase *Apocalypse Now*, I love the smell of cordite in the morning.

As the dust settled, I waited, straining to hear anything over the sound of the local vehicles doing their best to get the fuck out of our vicinity. The sudden heavy fire had startled the shit out of them, and they were scrambling to get away from any return fire that might be coming our way. But it was totally silent. I needed to know if there was an actual threat, in no small part to confirm in my head that we weren't leaving some poor farm workers bleeding to death in their field.

'Shadow, Baz, over.'

'Yeah, mate.'

'Hey, move down to where Dodger is in the treeline will you?'

'Roger that.' Shadow ran past the line of vehicles and made his way down to Dodger.

'I want you two to move out and conduct a clearing patrol from your position back to Yogi's end of the line. Don't venture out past visual range of the guys, over.'

They came back in the affirmative.

'All call signs in the trees, I'm sending Dodger and Shadow out to clear the line. Do not, I say again, do *not* shoot them, OK?'

By that time the line of vehicles was starting to crawl past. Despite the fact that the traffic was barely moving at 10mph, I had the remainder of the guys keep a close eye out for any possible drive-by attack.

Dodger and Shadow slowly made their way along the frontage of the guys, keeping within sight as much as they could. I didn't want to interrupt their focus with any extra radio calls, but a couple of the guys came up on the comms to advise that they could see Dodger and Shadow at their twelve and they had them covered.

'Roger bro, thanks,' Shadow replied.

A minute later, Dodger came up. 'Hey, we got something here.'

'Yeah, what it is, over?'

'It's a body.'

'Roger that,' I replied. 'Do you see a weapon?'

'Roger that, he's got an AK and he's dressed in a chest rig with AK mags. He's a baddy all right.'

'OK, do you have a camera with you?'

'Yeah,' Shadow replied.

'Take a pic and confirm he's dead, then finish the check along the line.'

'OK, roger that.'

I looked at Zen, who was processing what he had just heard.

'Hey, mate, go tell the client will you. He needs to know what's going on and that we'll be moving as soon as we can.'

'Roger that,' replied Zen, and he walked back to the client vehicle.

'Haggis, Baz. Were the insurgents out in front of you, over?'

'Yes mate. Well, one was,' Haggis replied. He had rightly already taken the credit for that kill.

I turned to see what the rest of the guys were doing. They were glancing at each other with a couple of thumbs-up being passed along. There was a feeling of achievement throughout the team, which was a good thing. They had all just been blooded, as it were: one person's kill in the team was everyone's kill.

'Baz, Dodger. We have reached the end of the line and there's more blood on the ground here but no body. The signs are they must have dragged themselves out and gapped it.'

'Roger that,' I said. 'Who are you out from?'

'That's me,' Yogi came up. 'I can see the guys to my front now.'

'Roger. OK, all call signs, Dodger and Shadow will walk in now. Once they get to you guys, make your way back to your vehicles. I want to be moving and out in five mikes.'

Shortly we were on our way. We had been in a static position for nearly two hours, but our defences had held good. As we reached the bridge, we could see the reason for the stop. The side guard rail, charred and twisted, had been peeled back like a banana skin. It looked like an IED must have been rigged on the opposite side of the road, shooting its deadly blast in the direction of its chosen target – a Toyota Landcruiser. It lay like a burnt and gutted carcass on the dry wadi bed below. The roof had folded in, and the whole vehicle was just a twisted mash of metal. *Fuck me, whoever was in that is no longer on this planet.*

'Baz, Zen. You think those shitbags we bagged back there were responsible for this mess?'

'I have no doubt, bro,' I replied.

I was sure it made us all feel better, not that we had any reason to feel bad. Except for one person, the team had worked as one. All as trained and as expected.

All for one and one for all.

CHAPTER 16

A few days later, I was returning from a run down south to Basra, where IRI was looking to set up a new office. I'd asked Noodle if he wanted to come with us, but he was knee-deep in training the IP – or future insurgents, depending on how you looked at it – and hadn't been able to get away. I'd figured I should catch up with him for a beer and a cigar, but I didn't give it much thought as I had a lot on my plate at that time.

For one thing, I still had Piper to endure. I'd reported the Tikrit incidents to Larry, but he figured moving him to another contract would be better than firing him. The problem was that he couldn't find anyone to dump him on, like some shit had dumped Stretch on me. Maybe it was due to manning shortages, but binning Piper would take far longer than I had hoped.

'What's new, bro?' I asked Rock, one of my team leaders, as we settled back into the team house.

'Well mate, there's been a couple of changes that you're not going to be happy about.'

'Oh, do go on.'

'Zen has been moved over to the Mambas and we have one of their guys as his replacement, call sign Shaky.'

'What the fuck? Who arranged that and why?' I was not happy, especially when I discovered the decision had been made by Larry.

'Well, Zen went over to the HQ house with his team a few days ago,' Rock explained, 'and he got into a bit of a pissing competition with someone in the Mamba team.'

'Who? What's the prick's name?'

'Well, actually, it was the entire Mamba team, and it almost got physical, and by physical, I mean Zen was about to beat the shit out of every single one of them and his boys had to drag him away.'

I knew Zen was a big strong fucker, but he was also one of the gentlest guys around. To get him so riled must have taken a hell of a lot.

'Any idea what it was about?'

'Yeah. You know how Zen always sends his wife a bunch of flowers on their anniversary, no matter where he is?'

'Yeah.'

'Well, someone in the Mambas tried to give him some ribbing about it, and it didn't go down too well. Before they knew it, he was chasing the Mamba fuckers around the HQ with the intent of snapping the first one he got hold of in half.'

'So, what's the problem? Why is he there and not here?'

'Well, it got into the "who does the most dangerous job" bullshit from the Mambas, and Zen challenged every single one of them to come and try what we do, which of course they all declined. It got pretty heavy, bro, and the Mamba IC wanted Zen shipped out.'

'What, for that? Are you fucking kidding me? Who the hell do those fucks think they are?'

'Yeah, well, Larry had to calm things down and, to make custard out of shit and so no one got sent home, he implemented a swap of roles for a couple of weeks so they could cool the fuck down and see what each contract did.'

'OK, well that's fucked up,' I told Rock. 'So, who's this guy Shaky? Was he the one Zen was trying to kill?'

'No mate, he was just the unlucky fucker who drew the short straw to come over here.'

This was the kind of shit that was starting to creep into company ops – people in Moyock who were forcing us to hang on to pieces of shit like Piper, who were putting people's lives in danger, but ready to fire Zen's ass over nothing. Although Larry had found a workable compromise, it pissed me off mightily. And what really lay behind it? Hard cash. The fact that every man on a contract was someone who could be billed to the client.

Shaky turned out to be a nice-enough guy, but I was beginning to find it hard to keep my energy and enthusiasm up. The two weeks passed, and we finally got Zen back in the fold again, but he didn't escape the ribbing. It seemed like a stupid thing to get into a shit-fight over, but someone must have really pushed his big buttons for him to go off like that. Just like my Aussie buddy, Dingo – RIP – you can never be sure what a guy is going through.

A few days after getting Zen back, I got a call from Larry that a deal had been reached with Triple Canopy for the purchase of their old hard wagons. He'd scored two hard Cherokee Jeeps and one Mercedes S600 with level-7 armour – the highest. That would give us an entire fleet of armoured vehicles.

I tasked Zen – 'The Black Mamba' as we now ribbed him – to get a few of the guys ready to go collect them. Triple Canopy had their compound just inside the IZ, so it should take them about an hour to get there and back. Well, an hour went by, and then another. I asked Rock where the fuck they were. He called Zen and I could see by the look on his face it was bad news.

'Hang on, you tell him,' he said, as he handed me the phone.

'Yeah, bro, what's the news?'

'Well, there's been a slight accident,' said Zen.

'What do you mean, a slight accident?'

'Well, er, we've rolled one of the vehicles.'

'What?'

'We rolled the Merc.'

'Rolled it, how?' I asked.

'It hit a Jersey wall and rolled.'

'How is that possible?' I asked. 'Triple Canopy is in the IZ, and all you had to do was drive back through the IZ over the bridge and back to here. Task complete, right? It's not like you can fuck that up, is it?'

I was getting more and more angry, as Zen explained how they had pulled out of Triple Canopy's place and about 500 metres down the road the Merc had hit the Jersey wall and rolled. I still could not work out how this was possible.

'The IZ has a strict speed policy and in order to roll a level-7 Merc you would have to be driving at well over that. How fast were you driving?'

'It wasn't me but one of the other guys.'

'Who?' I demanded.

'Piper.'

Instantly I felt the rage roar up inside me like a volcano. 'Piper!' I yelled down the phone. 'Please tell me he's dead, because that's the only thing I want to hear right now.'

'No, he isn't, but he's pretty banged up.'

'Fuck me,' I said. 'Where are you guys now?'

'We're at the HQ house and Larry is mad as hell.'

'I don't blame him. So am I. OK, get your asses back here as soon as Larry has finished with you guys.'

I dialled Larry's number and instantly, he answered. 'What the fuck, Baz? These fucks have totalled a brand-new Merc.'

Technically the Merc wasn't brand new. New to us, maybe, but I didn't want to split hairs.

'How did it happen?' I countered.

'I don't know. I'm not getting a straight answer from them, either. I'm going to sack every fucking one of them. This is unacceptable and Moyock are going to have my balls for this.'

'OK,' I said, 'let me see what I can find out, and I'll get back to you.'

I killed the call, had a quick chat to Rock about the long list of Piper's past fuck-ups then called Larry straight back. I reminded him that I'd wanted Piper fired long ago and did a run-through of his greatest hits. Larry agreed that I should do it when the guys reached the house, and he would sort it out from his end.

Half an hour later the guys were back, and I yelled at them to get their asses into the ops office. As they stood in front of me with their heads down, even Zen didn't look so big any more. I looked over at Piper, who was all cut up and bruised, then back at Zen.

'OK, tell me what happened.'

'Well,' Zen began, 'we left the Triple Canopy compound and made our way back towards the IZ team house and bridge. Then I got a call that Piper's vehicle had rolled, so we turned around and went back to see what had happened.'

'Bro,' I said looking him square in the face, 'I'm not interested in *what* happened, I need to know *how* it happened.'

'Piper, tell him how it happened,' said Zen.

Piper said he was driving at about 40mph when he tried to avoid a pothole in the road, rode up on a Jersey wall he didn't see, and the vehicle just rolled. I left a few seconds for the stink of bullshit to leave the room.

'How is it possible that a vehicle travelling at 40mph can ride up a three-foot Jersey wall and roll?' Jersey walls are straight sided; they aren't ramped at the ends.

I looked back at Zen. 'Is this how it happened?'

'Yeah. I didn't see the actual incident, but that's how it looked to me.'

I looked along the line and, to my deepening sadness, none was offering anything to confirm or deny this story. They either genuinely didn't know or had closed ranks around Piper.

'OK,' I said. 'I want AARs from everyone.'

'Larry has already asked for those,' Piper said.

'Then I want them too, you fucks.'

I was furious, not only because of the accident – which I didn't believe it was – but also because of the group closing ranks. I was gutted that they would do it. I felt they had turned on me.

'Fuck off and clean yourselves up. I'll see you tomorrow for the daily brief.'

I stormed out. I was devastated. *You backstabbing cunts.*

I could hear Rock having a go at them from behind the closed door. He too was disgusted. Perhaps I was wrong, and this was exactly how things had happened, but I just wasn't buying it. And neither was anyone else.

I went to the roof with Yard Dog, Haggis and Yogi, who weren't on the run but had heard what had happened and likewise thought it was bullshit.

'You know what?' I said. 'I've had it with this lot. I'm done. The company has changed a lot since I got here, and I'm not liking it one bit. If this is the character of the guys coming in, then I'm heading out.'

The guys were shocked to hear this but could understand where I was coming from, especially Yard Dog who, like me, had been with Blackwater Commercial from the very beginning.

'I don't know what to tell you, brother,' Yard Dog said. 'You're right though, this would never have happened in the old days. If you fucked up you admitted it, took what was coming and then got on with the job. For fuck's sake, I did.'

'Yes you did, bro, yes you did. And I did too, when I rolled the truck with my little J-turn experiment.'

This was the moment when I decided that I was going to quit Blackwater. I had been with them for more than a year and the company was changing, in all the wrong ways. Besides, there was a rumour that all BW contracts were soon to be manned only by US citizens.

My energy, which was already low, felt like it was draining out of me. Maybe I shouldn't have asked to do a five-month rotation, or maybe I had just let my own standards slip and I couldn't be fucked trying to bring them back into line. It seemed like the good days had gone, and right then I decided I needed to go with them. The next day in the briefing room, I gathered everyone who had been on the vehicle pick-up and laid down the law.

Just as I finished, I looked up at Piper. 'Oh, just before I go and Rock takes over, I have one last thing to say, Piper.'

'What?' he said, like some defiant cunt who had just got away with something he shouldn't have.

'You're fired. Go pack your shit and be ready to go to the IZ in one hour.' I saw the look of defiance drain from his face. 'Got it? One hour. Get your shit and get out of here.'

I left, and for the few seconds it took me to walk out I could have heard a pin drop. Five minutes later, Haggis walked into the ops room with Rock behind him.

'What's up, mate?' I asked.

'You can add Stretch to that ride with Piper,' Haggis said.

'Why's that?' I asked, intrigued.

'He just tried to have a go at you,' he said, in his thick Scottish accent.

'What do you mean?'

'Well, just as you left, he tried to run out after you, to attack you.'

'Did he? Where is the cunt now?' I asked. I was so fucked off I was ready for a good old bit of fisticuffs.

'No need, bro, I got to him first,' Haggis replied.

'Do tell.'

'He took off after you, so I tackled him and pinned him down while Rock gave him a solid clip around the ear.'

'What did the others do?'

'They jumped on him to stop him from getting a proper hurting.'

This was good news, and it slightly – just slightly – restored my confidence in the allegiance of the team.

'Where is he now?' I asked.

'Like Piper, bruised and packing his shit.'

'Roger, thanks, guys.'

Piper and Stretch were driven to the IZ an hour later, and I never saw them again. Two days later, we got word that Stretch had been arrested in Amman. He got so fucked up at some bar that he decided to rip up a framed picture of the much-loved King of Jordan. Bad idea. After the bar crowd had finished with Stretch, the local police had had their turn. Good riddance.

Another day brought another report of murder and mayhem, but this time thankfully not on our doorstep. It was 14 February 2005, and a massive bomb in Beirut had killed the former Prime Minister of Lebanon, Rafik Hariri, along with twenty-one others. The blast was so big it left a crater ten metres wide. Whoever wanted him dead really wanted him dead, and they weren't fucking around.

Lebanon had always had a tense (and sometimes bloody) relationship with neighbouring Syria, and, since Hariri had been highly critical of Syria's interventions in Lebanese politics, there were strong suspicions that Syrian leaders had been behind the assassination. As tragic as the assassination was to the people of Lebanon, however, it was the size of the bomb that piqued my interest. It was absolutely massive. Initial reports estimated it had contained up to 1,000lbs of explosives and had been hidden in a truck (it was later established that it had in fact consisted of 2,200lbs of explosive). My concern was that some shithead would be thinking he could use a similarly huge IED here in Iraq and get himself on the front cover of *Insurgents Weekly* in the process.

There was an abundance of military hardware, explosives and artillery shells knocking around Iraq. The country was Bombs 'R' Us for the bad guys, which explained the growing number of IEDs and VBIEDs. It was also why so many properties were surrounded first by a layer of twelve-feet concrete T walls and then with a layer of concrete blocks further out: to prevent VBIEDs ramming the gates and blowing a hole big enough for a second bomb-laden vehicle to get through.

A short while after the Lebanon bombing, I settled down to another Baghdad evening on the roof of the team house, looking forward to raising a beer to another day of staying alive. Thankfully, nothing much had happened during the day to piss me off. In fact, it had been far better than average, considering the increasing levels of *I-can't-give-a-fuck*ness that I was experiencing. Just as the big orange sun was close to down, heralding that beautiful stillness that fills the air, there was the biggest fucking explosion I had heard in all my time in Iraq. It was so unbelievably loud that we grabbed our beers and sank down below the parapet for cover.

After a few seconds, we jumped up and gazed in the direction of the blast, which was rumbling across the cityscape like thunder.

'Holy fuck that was big,' someone remarked. 'What do you think it was?'

We had developed an uncanny ability to work out what had just been blown up by the noise it made. We heard vehicles that had been packed with mortar and artillery shells go up all the time, and they were always very loud. With suicide bombers the noise was obviously less, due to the fact that they couldn't carry as much explosive on them, not without looking like those fat fucks Steve and Jim. But this was something entirely new.

'Fuck me,' I said, looking at where the noise and flash had come from. 'That's Mansour.'

Everyone agreed it was the most likely location, and I was instantly concerned for Noodle and the Greystone guys. I tried to call, but there was no cell service. Although that wasn't unusual, it sure was worrying. I tried again, but still nothing.

'I can't get through,' I said.

'Here, let me try on my Thuraya,' Rock offered. 'What's the number?'

I read it out to him, and he dialled it as soon as he had satellite hook-up, but, after a few minutes' trying, he shook his head.

Fuck me, what am I going to tell Noodle's wife and kids?

I recalled my initial apprehension about getting Noodle to come over and how I'd discussed the risks with him before he left NZ.

Although he had accepted that death was a possibility, as we all did, none of us ever really thought we would have to make the terrible call to someone's family. The reality, of course, was that there had already been far too many of those calls, but this was my best mate.

I looked at the huge pall of smoke rising above Mansour and tried one more time on my mobile. Still no service. I could feel the anger tightening my chest.

Then Yard Dog piped up: 'Hey, call the HQ house. Maybe they've heard something.'

I dialled Larry and in less than two rings he answered. 'Hey, bro, did you guys hear that blast, and have you heard from the Greystone boys?' I asked.

'Yeah. George is just on the other line with them.' I could feel the anger drift back to wherever I kept it buried, along with all the other demons. *See you next time.* 'They're OK, but there are a lot of broken windows. Apart from the house shaking like shit, there are no injuries.'

'So, it was close?'

'Yeah, just two blocks away. They think it's one of the embassies.'

'OK, roger, mate, that's all I needed to know.' I passed on the news to the others. We decided to have one more beer to celebrate and then called it a night.

The next day was quiet, so I wangled some time to go visit Mansour and take a look at the result of the previous night's blast. As we rounded the corner by the Telecom tower, the first things I noticed were the burnt date palms a good fifty metres from what would have been the epicentre of the explosion. The trees that faced towards the blast had all been burnt, giving a clear indication of the direction of the blast.

As we drew closer, the trees were more scorched, with tops

completely burnt off, and close to the epicentre they were just black-ened stumps. Sitting next to the entrance to the Libyan Embassy was the burnt-out hulk of a petrol tanker. Anything non-metal had been vaporised, and the wire rims lay on the ground where the tyres would have been. One side of the petrol tanker was complete-ly blown out, in the direction of the embassy, and the blast wall was blackened and pushed back a few metres, though remarkably still standing. The T walls had done their job, directing the force of the explosion over the top of the building. But still, the horrific heat from the blast must have been like an inescapable tidal wave of flame and death.

'Hey, let's park up there in the open ground and take a better look,' I said.

We pulled over opposite the wreck and got out. As I walked closer to the tanker, I was mentally re-enacting the events as best I could, given the evidence at the scene. I had been a tracking in-structor back in the Unit, so had had to piece together evidence like this and try to work out what had happened many a time. This was not greatly different, and once I thought I had worked the most likely scenario, I asked the others what they thought had happened. Shadow figured it looked as if the tanker had been packed with high explosives and that it had either been a suicide driver, or a remote-detonated bomb aimed at destroying the Libyan Embassy.

'Well fuck me, Captain Obvious,' Yogi cut in. 'It's parked directly outside the embassy, so that part is a given.'

'OK, here's what I think,' I said. 'I think the tanker was partly full of petrol, maybe halfway or a little bit more but not completely full. It was detonated with explosives, but they were not the primary blast, the fuel was.'

'How do you figure that?' Yogi asked.

'Well, look at the way the tanker's ripped open. See how it's mainly just the one side, and how much it's torn back. There's only a small tear in the opposite side of the tank, so it's likely that was where the charges were placed. The initiation device was either a timer or a remote detonation, and the initiation charges were used to direct the blast out that way.'

'How can you be so sure it wasn't explosives?' Dodger asked.

'Look here,' I said, pointing to the ground. 'There's no crater, none. Explosives would have blown the shit out of everything and torn the whole tanker to kingdom come. The blast was directed to blow in that direction, towards the embassy. Sure, there's a lot of damage around the tanker, but nowhere near as much as where the full brunt of the blast was directed. Plus, the tanker is still pretty much in one piece.'

As I glanced back to where our vehicles were parked, and then back to the tanker, I sensed I'd missed something. I looked around left and right, and then back to where the vehicles were. Then it dawned on me.

Holy shit. The Bedouin tents housing those Iraqi families – they were gone. Completely and utterly gone. We had parked on top of where their tents once were; where they had made their simple homes, and now they were gone. Everyone in that tented community must have been obliterated by the blast; at least twenty-five people incinerated along with everything they owned. A sudden sadness washed over me, and, when I mentioned the tents to the guys, the same horror dawned on them.

As we mounted up again, there was a heavy silence. I felt bad that we had accidentally parked our vehicles on top of where they had spent their last moment alive on this earth. It felt like a grave, which it was, and we should not have parked there.

Iraq and all its horrors were really getting to me now and time was dragging. Although I was here to ensure I had as much cash in the bank as possible before marrying Jen, I wasn't enjoying my time any more. Each day blurred into the next, and I felt like I was living with a full-time hangover, even when I wasn't drinking. Plus, the company was changing ever more rapidly. The rumours that Blackwater would let go all non-US personnel were hardening up. None of this news was good for the likes of me, Haggis or Noodle.

Plus, I was noticing more and more how the dregs from other contracts were being dumped on me. Clearly, they were purging themselves of their ineffective operators, dumping them on Baz, meaning they already saw the writing on the wall for me. I couldn't work up the righteous indignation to fight against it. Yes, I was disappointed, especially as some of the guys hunting for my ass were people who I had thought were friends, but to be honest I was toast; a dead man walking.

I just wanted them to hurry up and get it done.

I also understood that this was just business. I wasn't American, so my head was on the chopping block, and it didn't matter that I had been one of the founding members of Blackwater Commercial. They had unceremoniously chopped Tom, the actual founder of BW Commercial, after Fallujah, so why should I be surprised? But until it actually happened, and as jaded as I was, there was still a job to be done.

The evening after we'd inspected the burnt-out tanker in Mansour, Orange told me he wanted all the IRI clients brought over to the main office at 06:30 the next day, as they had a conference call with the States. I told him we would have them there by 06:15, no problem. The following morning a sleepy bunch of IRI clients were duly delivered. Hammer went back to his house to collect something they'd forgotten, so while he was doing that, I gathered the rest of my team leaders in the ops room for the daily briefing.

As I stood before the whiteboard, going over some basic shit and the new password for the day, there was a sudden massive explosion that shook the entire house from top to bottom. The ops room filled with a fine brown dust, and for a second it felt like the whole building was going to fall on top of us. We dashed out into the driveway area, the dust rolling off us like the contrail from an airliner as we ran.

'Everyone OK?' I yelled. I heard a 'roger' from all. 'OK, evacuation drill of the houses! Go! Go! Go!'

Everyone knew what to do. Those designated to the IRI office ran inside to secure the clients, moving them into the safe room. Figures sprinted for their houses, gathering their teams, while the rest of us spread out in defensive positions. Hammer was in charge of the furthest house, from where I figured the blast had come, so he would be the first we'd bring in.

'Hammer, Baz; radio check.'

'Roger, mate,' he replied. 'Ready here.'

'Yogi, Baz; radio check.'

'Roger, buddy, ready here.'

'Dodger, Baz; radio check.'

'Roger, mate, ready to go.'

The guys looked at me. 'OK,' I yelled. 'Let's go!'

We thundered down to Hammer's house, weapons up, scanning everything as we made our way along the street. Those in Yogi's, Dodger's and the IRI house had their snipers in place, just like we drilled for, and were giving us a running commentary.

We were scanning for anyone trying to break into our compound, or any secondary attack, whether by vehicle or on foot. As we passed each house and access street, we made sure to clear it as quickly as possible.

'All clear from here to Hammer's,' came the call from Yogi's sniper.

'Roger that,' I radioed back, while holding my position.

The guy behind me could now move past me, before he too dropped to his knee and called clear. I could then move past him in the same manner. After about 100 metres we were coming up on Hammer's house and we all stopped.

'Hammer, Baz. We are approaching you now, bro,' I radioed. With all the confusion and the thick cloud of dust still clouding his end of the street, I didn't want him to think we were insurgents.

'Roger that, bro,' he replied. 'We can see you. Clear to come in.'

As we neared the house, I was shocked to see that half of the building had caved in. The concrete pillars were bent and warped and were only being held together by the reinforcing steel rods. The vehicle port had collapsed and was now lying half on the ground. The windows were blown in and glass was everywhere. As we entered the house, the guys took up positions looking down the street, where a section of T wall had once stood. That was obviously where the blast had come from, and whatever had caused it must have been real big.

I didn't want the gap left unguarded, in case that was where the bad guys planned to surge in. Hammer had brought his guys down from the roof, and we were ready to move back to the IRI office.

'OK, guys,' I yelled. 'Change of plan. Hammer, are you and your guys OK?'

'Yeah,' he said. 'A bit shaken and dusty, but all good.'

'OK, you and your team hold here. Shadow and Stumpy stay with Hammer and give fire support. *Watch that gap in the T wall.*

The rest of us will pull back and pick up Yogi and his crew. Once we're done, I will head back here, and we'll see what the hell just happened.'

'Roger that,' they replied, and away we went.

As we approached Yogi's place, I could see he had brought his guys to street level. We blow-piped past them and made our way through Dodger's guys and back to the main house. We needed to secure the office and get the hard vehicles ready for an evacuation. We had practised this over and over, and everyone and everything was going right to plan.

I headed into the IRI office and made sure all the clients were alive and accounted for. Several of them were very shaken and utterly shitting themselves. Rock and Orange had taken charge of them, and I reassured them that we had everything under control. Although my adrenaline was flowing, it did indeed feel like we were in total control and doing what we were there for.

In fact, I was actually really enjoying it. *This is when I come alive.*

I asked Orange if the clients wanted to be evacuated. I could have made the call myself, but I wanted him to feel he was part of the team. After a few seconds, he put it back to me and asked me what I thought. I told him I wanted us to stay where we were, as we would likely expose ourselves if we tried to make a vehicle move. Besides, we were in a safe and secure location with plenty of firepower. If we chose to drive out and there was a follow-up attack, we would run the risk of driving right into it. Orange agreed, and I left him to it.

'OK, Rock, look after the clients – and keep them calm, bro,' I added.

I got on the radio, checking everyone was in their positions, and told them I was heading back to Hammer's house. Everyone else should stand by for further instructions. I told Omar to bring his

Jordanian guards back inside, then Omar, Haggis and I headed back down the street. Once we reached Hammer's place, I left the guys to find suitable fire positions, while Hammer and I went to take a look-see.

'I'm not 100 per cent sure what happened,' Hammer told me. 'I'd just got back from dropping the client at the office, when I saw this huge orange and yellow ball shoot right up in front of me. There was no noise, just this big ball of light. I dived back into the vehicle and lay as flat as I could on the seats, and there was this fucking huge blast. It shook the entire house to its foundations. Shit and concrete came raining down on the roof of the vehicle with glass flying everywhere. I was stunned for a few seconds, then I realised it was a bomb and ran inside to check on the guys.'

Considering how close the blast was to Hammer, he was in pretty good shape. We made our way inside the house, and everything was a mess. The furniture was smashed to shit, the contents of each room having been flung from one side to the other by the force of the explosion.

'Hey, check this out,' Hammer called from the bathroom inside the client's quarters. The bed was covered in long shards of mirror and window glass, with more shards stuck in the headboard and walls like darts. The top blanket of the bed had been shredded and the mattress was flipped up and torn.

'Wow-wee,' I said, as the realisation slowly dawned on me. Had the client not been on that early-morning call, they'd have been sliced to pieces in their bed.

The house was a complete write-off. The outside was little better, with the gardens covered in concrete and metal debris. Hammer and I peered into the pool, and there at the bottom was the front axle of a vehicle, with one of the front wheels still attached.

'Well, there's your problem,' Hammer remarked. It had become our go-to saying.

The explosion must have been a VBIED, some of the remains of which had ended up in the swimming pool. I gazed up at the big high-rise block where the Aussies were based.

'Hey, check that out,' I said, drawing Hammer's attention to the trees at the rear of the property.

Hanging in one of the highest branches was a human leg, pelvis still attached. The bone was exposed, and meat hung from it in strips. There was no clothing on it, but the leg still had a foot attached, and the foot was wearing a black dress shoe.

'Wow,' I said. 'I wonder what size that is and why he picked those shoes to blow himself up in. They look pretty nice. I wonder where the other one is, bro? We might get a new pair of shoes out of this.'

We both laughed.

'Maybe he wanted to wear his Sunday best when he went wherever the fuck he thought he was going,' Hammer remarked.

'Yeah, maybe, bro.'

We made our way over to the gap in the wall to check out where the four-metre reinforced concrete barrier had once been. Shadow was there standing guard, along with a few of the others.

'I wonder why he was aiming for the wall?' I ventured, to no one in particular.

'Maybe we weren't the target,' Shadow said, as he pointed to the Aussies' high-rise base, twenty metres away from us.

'Yeah, maybe,' Stumpy agreed. 'But why didn't he go for their main entrance?'

'Perhaps the dumb shit got lost and didn't know where it was, so just went for an area as close as he could get,' said Hammer.

I shook my head in disbelief. 'What a dumb fuck. OK, I'll call the

IZ team house and get them to arrange a new section of wall. We can't leave that gap, so we'll need around-the-clock security on it. Omar? You guys got this covered?'

Omar nodded, while looking up and down the gap like he was the foreman on a construction site. 'We got it covered, boss.'

Omar stepped outside the gap, then came back in with his head down.

'What's up, mate?' I asked.

'It's a shame,' Omar volunteered, now with real sadness in his voice.

'What's that, bro?' Dodger asked.

'There were families there,' he said, pointing towards the outside of the wall. We stepped through to see what he meant.

'There?' Dodger asked, looking at a mound of rubble. Slowly, we recognised the shape of something that had once been a small house.

'Yes, there,' Omar said. 'They had a large family, many children.'

We stared at the shattered heap in shock. *Fuck me, not again,* I thought.

I hoped that maybe the kids were at school, but I knew I was kidding myself. They had no school and were always home. I thought back to the families in the tents in Mansour, and the family of the boy in the collapsed apartment building at the Al-Hamra complex, the kid who'd lost his mind and ate dead pigeons. All of them were always home. They had nowhere else to go.

I felt the anger rise in me again. *What a fucked-up, shitty world.*

Omar stationed a few men in the gap, while Hammer's team escorted their client back to the house to retrieve anything worth saving, which was not much. Orange had put a call through to IRI in Washington DC, to inform them that they would not be attending the online meeting. I called Larry in the IZ team house to let know him what had happened.

Two days later, a flatbed lorry with four new sections of T wall arrived. Instead of putting a new section of wall in to replace the old one, I opted to wall off that end of the street entirely, cutting off Hammer's wrecked house and relegating it to the outside of our compound.

The vehicle parts in the pool and the body parts in the trees were no longer our problem.

CHAPTER 17

Come April, it was finally confirmed that non-US personnel would be phased out of all BW contracts. Noodle moved to the Mambas, which was the one remaining option, but I saw this as my ticket out. I would be kept on at IRI until I rotated out, but I had effectively handed control to Rock, since I was running on fumes and anger.

It was a shame. I had put a lot into Blackwater Commercial. But at the same time, in all honesty, I was done. Jen was planning the wedding, so all I had to do was keep myself alive for another week, and then I'd be out of there for good. As much as I tried to stay engaged, it was just a matter of counting down the days before I was like a bald man's head: *outta hair.*

I took a call from Noodle, who had just got back from BIAP on a Mamba run. They had apparently driven into the tail-end of a security convoy ambush on Irish. The Mamba ICs, Tool and Miyagi, had decided they should press on, as they'd hoped they could offer some assistance. After all, what the Mambas lacked in speed and stealth they more than made up for in firepower. As they had approached, one of the crew in the lead Mamba, a typically funny-as-hell Aussie guy called Manny, decided to announce their arrival by lobbing a 40mm M203 CS tear-gas grenade into the furore.

It sounded like a solid-enough plan, I thought, if not a bit unusual, particularly if friendlies were still on the ground. Noodle agreed, but the main problem was that Manny hadn't taken into consideration the direction of the wind. As they came roaring in at 30mph ramming speed, they drove smack into their own cloud of tear-gas.

'So, you were gulping the gas meant for the bad guys?' I sniggered.

'Yeah, but what bad guys?' Noodle continued. 'They'd all frigged off, just as soon as they saw our big white whales plodding towards them. The tear-gas filled the interiors of the Mambas like some fucker had popped smoke, and of course all our eyes and noses immediately started pouring tears. We were choking, vomiting and snotting all over ourselves like a bad German bukkake party.'

'Holy fuck,' I said, my sniggers turning to laughter. 'That's hilarious. And you couldn't see a thing, eh?'

'Hang on, bro, you haven't heard the worst of it. There I was on the M240 Bravo gun all pumped and prepped to open up on the bad guys when the friggin' cloud hit me and, like the rest, I started to cry, vomit, piss, shit – you name it, I did it – but like the true professional Kiwi soldier that I am, I stayed up in the turret trying to wipe away the facial fluids, ready to unleash hell. Then all of a sudden, "whack", I felt an almighty stinging smack to the side of my face. I thought I must have caught a bullet.'

'Well, clearly not or you wouldn't be speaking to me now,' I said.

'It was so hard I dropped into the interior of the Mamba,' Noodle went on. 'So, there I am, bro, down in the interior of the Mamba rolling around on the floor, with my face burning while I'm frantically feeling for the blood, my face burning like a mofo.'

'What the fuck was it?'

'I finally rolled onto my back in the vehicle and I could feel death's cold hand on me, bro, so I rubbed my face again, ready to bid goodbye to the world. Then, through watery, snot-filled eyes, I tried to look at my hand for the expected brains and blood that must have been pouring out. And then it hit me – pun intended.'

'What?' I demanded.

'The friggin' bungee cord, bro. Yes, the friggin' bungee that held the 240 in place in the turret had snapped when I pushed the gun forward to bring it up to my shoulder and it came shooting back at about a thousand miles an hour.'

By this time, I was killing myself laughing.

'Can you believe it? I thought I was a goner, bro, and by the time I got back to my feet with my teary eyes, snotty nose and stinging face, we had driven through the attack site and everyone had fucked off. I missed the whole thing.'

I was now bent double, and my ribs were hurting from laughing. 'Oh no, you poor fuck,' I howled.

'The trauma, bro, you have no idea. I'll likely have PTSD now, but I knew you'd be understanding,' he said, listening to me laughing fit to burst. 'Anyway, I gotta go clean snot off my vest. I'll catch you later, bro.'

I was grateful for Noodle lifting my mood. I had to survive only a few more days, but in Iraq it was never a given that anyone would, and, as it happened, there would be more than enough to feel shit about.

The British company Edinburgh Risk and Security Management (ERSM) had set up across the drive from our Blackwater HQ in the IZ. On 20 April their guys were on a run to BIAP to pick up some of their crew. Their modus operandi was to run low-profile vehicles, as a lot of companies tended to do, including ourselves. There were both good and bad points to these vehicles, but, if used correctly, the pros outweighed the cons. Some individuals in ERSM would even go as far as dressing up like the locals, which again had its pros and cons, but it seldom did much more than make you look like a Westerner trying to dress up like a local.

There were a few hard and fast rules about rolling low profile that we all adopted. They could sometimes make the hairs on your balls stand up a little, but they generally worked: first, never isolate yourself from the pack; secondly, don't expose yourself unless absolutely necessary; and thirdly, never stay stationary for long periods, always keep moving and stay off the 'X'.

For whatever reason, the ERSM team chose not to follow any of these basic rules. They set off for BIAP close to noon in their standard three-vehicle move. They had a soft-skin BMW as lead, with a driver, one person in the front seat and a third person in the rear acting as the shooter, covering three o'clock, six o'clock, nine o'clock and all points in between. Their second vehicle was an armoured B6 Mercedes sedan with a driver and a vehicle commander in the front seats and no more. Their third vehicle was a soft-skin BMW with a driver, the team commander in the front seat and a shooter in the rear. The team carried the typical assortment of weapons expected for such a security detail.

Why the team commander decided to travel in the rear vehicle, instead of the front as usual, was a puzzle. As they moved down Irish, he was too far back to be calling out threats and obstacles, and they had already compromised their low-profile advantage by conducting aggressive blocking moves.

About 350 metres from Camp Victory, Big Army had set up a

roadblock, due to an earlier IED that they were still dealing with. The Edinburgh Risk team had already revealed themselves by their aggressive actions and, to antagonise the locals even further, they had fired warning shots near some of the civilian cars. Now their route ahead was blocked. It was highly likely that some of the pissed-off locals had informed their insurgent buddies that there was a security team out on Irish ripe for the picking.

Edinburgh Risk's vehicles were stationary for more than thirty minutes. As time passed, the driver in the lead vehicle got tired of holding the car in gear with his foot on the clutch, so he put the vehicle in neutral and applied the handbrake while they waited for the road ahead to clear.

About forty minutes from the time they first stopped, one of the team noticed a white Suburban on a side road running parallel to Irish but decided it was not important enough to bring to the attention of the others. It was not called out as a possible threat and no one was made aware that it was acting very fucking suspiciously and had done a U-turn, obviously to get into a firing position.

Suburbans were mostly used by security companies. They were not a vehicle of choice for your average Iraqi. However, a shipment of Suburbans had been hijacked some time back, so the insurgents did have them. Whoever saw the vehicle may have thought it was from another security company, but it was a lone vehicle, and security companies didn't tend to drive around like that any more.

Inside the white Suburban was a group of insurgents armed with heavy belt-fed machine guns. They'd been alerted to the isolated and exposed ERSM team. With the three vehicles spaced no more than thirty metres from first to the last, they were sitting ducks. The insurgents opened fire, the first burst spraying all three vehicles.

The driver in the rear vehicle was killed instantly, while the guy in the rear seat was critically injured, with rounds severing the femoral arteries in his legs.

The second vehicle was also hit and immediately started leaking engine fluids all over the road, but, as it was armoured, the occupants were uninjured. The vehicle commander in the lead car was also killed instantly in that first volley.

With bullets raking his vehicle, the driver of the lead car tried to accelerate off the X, but, in his panic, he'd forgotten he'd put the vehicle in neutral and applied the hand brake, so when he hit the accelerator all the vehicle did was rev like fuck. Thinking the vehicle engine had been taken out, he decided to bail out and run to the middle of the road to take cover. But no one else in the team realised he had bailed, and they remained where they were, trying to lay down some effective return fire.

The armoured (and still drivable) vehicle moved up beside the first to provide cover, but as the two occupants got out to help lay down fire one left his door open – the door on the same side the rounds were coming from. That allowed rounds to enter the armoured cab, destroying some of the important working parts of the vehicle and removing any hope of using it for an evacuation. The team were under machine-gun fire for almost a full minute, which is a long fucking time when you're not sure where it's coming from and have lost command and control. The team commander was too busy dealing with the wounded in the last vehicle.

The final person left alive in the lead vehicle threw a smoke grenade to try to hide their movements from their attackers, but the damage was done by then. Only when the firing had stopped was the team able to limp with two badly damaged vehicles to Camp Victory for medical treatment. Edinburgh Risk lost three brothers in the attack. As harsh as this may sound, it didn't have to happen that way. To me it highlighted the importance of training, training and training some more.

Over the next day or so, the body count continued to rise. Throughout the time BW had used the Mambas, it was accepted that they were good only for BIAP runs. To go any further afield with those slow, hulking beasts was inviting an attack. However, some dipshit sitting in Moyock decided it would be a good idea to use them on some runs out of the city, carrying guys to stand up some new contracts. This would be another example of faceless, dickless assholes who were far removed from the shit we faced not understanding the limitations of the equipment, especially the lack of any decent, wait for it... *comms.*

Miyagi and Tool ran a very tight ship, despite the ship being more holed than the fucking Titanic. As always, they were having mechanical issues with the Mambas, despite Tool doing his best to keep them operational. This was a serious problem, but the brass sitting on their asses weren't interested in hearing that and ordered them to get on with it. The sooner the new sites could be stood up, the sooner the money would start flowing into the company coffers, eh?

It was 23:00 on the same day that the ERSM team had been shot up, when one of the Moyock sled-dog team awoke Tool and Miyagi to inform them that they would start a move to Ramadi, a city set around 100 clicks west of Baghdad, at 05:00 the next morning. On the way they were to drop off twelve guys at two locations in and around BIAP. From there they would carry on to Ramadi, before they were supposed to hightail it back to Baghdad to do their standard airport runs that day.

As this was a State Department contract, Tool and Miyagi went to the Little Bird guys asking for help. The pilots wanted to help, but they couldn't get approval to do so from those in charge. Tool and Miyagi had never been to Ramadi before, so they decided to stay up the rest of the night planning the mission. They concluded they were willing to give it a go but warned that they were unlikely even to get to Ramadi, due to the shit state of the vehicles. They asked if they could speak with another BW team, who had left for Ramadi earlier, to get some intel on what they might face on the way. James, the Moyock sled dog, told them what they already suspected: there were no usable comms to talk to the other team.

Prior to leaving the team house, Miyagi was approached by two guys, Sparky and Snowman, who asked if they could help. They had heard that five of Miyagi's guys had rotated out and knew that he might be short. Sparky and Snowman had been working on the Al-Hillah contract. In fact, Sparky was rotating home later that day. He had already packed his bags, but he figured it made sense to make himself useful in the meantime. Miyagi wasn't keen to use him when he was so close to going home, but Sparky talked him into it.

As Sparky had a drum magazine on his AK, Miyagi placed him in the right-rear gunner position, where he would normally position himself. Snowman, who, like Miyagi, had only an AR, went in the bongo truck that carried all the luggage of the teams they were running to Ramadi. Everything seemed to be going well until they passed Fallujah, whereupon Miyagi spotted two cars pulled over to the side of the road. He saw another two cars leave a dirt road further up and turn towards them. One was a white sedan with four males inside; the other, a maroon-coloured car carrying a family.

As the convoy slowed to assess the situation, so did the white sedan. The maroon car tried to overtake, but the white car cut it off and wouldn't let it pass. Miyagi fired two three-round bursts on the left side of the white sedan to get them to move out of the way, but only the maroon car pulled over. All of a sudden, Miyagi's Mamba came to an abrupt stop. He said he didn't hear anything, but he suddenly felt disorientated. He could see that the hood on the Mamba had popped open and was covered in white spots. His initial thought was that Tool must have forgotten to attach the pins that hold the hood closed, but, in the confusion, he remembered asking himself where the white spots had come from.

When the dust settled, Miyagi still didn't know what had happened, but he could see that Sparky was in a bad way. They had been so close to the VBIED that the shrapnel had penetrated the Mamba's armour, and Sparky, who had been closest to it, had been hit in the femoral artery. While his face and body looked fine, he was fast bleeding out. As Miyagi tried to comfort him, he recalled Sparky had a smile on his face.

As Sparky died, Miyagi quietly whispered into his ear, 'Thank you, and I'm sorry.'

Miyagi himself had several injuries, including a shrapnel wound in his upper right thigh, which had severed the artery. A teammate applied a tourniquet, which saved his life, while another treated a wound to his right shoulder. Tool, who had been driving, was extremely fortunate that the blast did not penetrate the thick Plexiglas window. Had it done so he would almost certainly have been decapitated.

Their team then executed a textbook move, crossing over their dead and wounded into the remaining Mambas, and within ten minutes they were back on the move, destroying the downed Mamba before they left for medical treatment; because they had no comms, they could not call for any.

Despite having just been bombed and having lost Sparky, the guys were ready for a secondary attack, with Miyagi himself manning the 240 Bravo in the lead gun spot. The guys spied two Suburban vehicles packed with shooters, who simply eyeballed them, but Miyagi was convinced they had been planning a follow-up attack, and had it not been for the fact that the Mambas were back on their feet and ready to rumble they would have certainly followed through.

The same day as the Mamba attack, a Mi-8 transport helicopter flown by Bulgarian pilots and carrying six BW guys, plus two Fijian guards from Al-Hillah, was shot down by the insurgents with an RPG. Footage of the burning helo, as it plummeted to earth, was posted on the internet, together with a video of the burnt bodies. I just hoped they had died instantly and had not been alive as they fell to the ground.

One of the pilots survived, but the fear on his face in the insurgents' video betrayed how he most probably wished he hadn't. As they dragged him to his feet, they could be heard asking him in Arabic if he had any weapons, before telling him to go. Then, as he tried to hobble away, his hands raised, one of the fucks unloaded his AK into the guy, who fell back and died on the ground.

My last night in Iraq rolled around, but I really didn't feel like doing anything at all. Everything was different for me, and I no longer wanted to be there. I just wanted to lie on my bed and be alone, but Yard Dog, Two Trays, Stumpy, Yogi, Shadow, Dodger, Hammer, Zen and some of the others were waiting up on the roof for a few farewell beers. We were amigos, and together we had been through a hell of a lot.

I had done my best to get them prepared for operating in Iraq. They were a good crew and I felt sure they would continue to do a bloody good job without me. We smoked a few cigars and sipped a few beers, but I just couldn't get into the groove. The beers no longer tasted as good as they once had.

Sensing this, Yogi produced a bottle of Chivas Regal. 'Here, bro, try this,' he said, handing me the bottle.

'No thanks, bro. I'm just not in the mood for a big one,' I told him. But after a while I looked at the bottle full of the lovely golden nectar and could feel it pulling me in. 'OK, I'll try one shot.'

I shouldn't have opened it, but, like a dumbass, I did. The next day I was up early as usual, but I had a hangover that would have killed ten men.

'Damn, buddy,' Yogi remarked, as I loaded my bags into the vehicle for the flight out, 'you were fucked up last night. I've never seen you like that.'

'What d'you mean?' I groaned. I had absolutely no recollection of the night before at all.

'Bro, you downed over half of that Regal in one gulp. It was like you were trying to kill yourself.'

I hadn't told Yogi or anyone about the depression I had been going through, and the Chivas was downed to drown it all.

'Oh shit,' I said. 'Did I hurt anyone?' It was a bit of a stupid question, but I didn't know what else to ask.

'No buddy, nothing like that, but you lobbed the empty bottle over your shoulder, and it flew off the roof and smashed the windscreen of the neighbour's vehicle to fuck.'

'Oh shit,' I groaned. 'That's not good. Can I do anything to calm him?'

'No, bro, I gave him a couple of hundred dollars last night and he's all cool.'

'Argh, sorry, bro.'

I looked at him with the one eye I could focus. 'Argh fuck, it's not how I wanted my last night to go.'

'No, bro, but you haven't been 100 per cent these past few weeks. You need a break.'

'You know what?' I said. 'This is it for me. I'm done. The non-US manning will fuck me anyway, and I won't go on the Mamba teams. Fuck that.'

'Well, I'm with you, brother,' Yogi assured me. 'We all are.'

'Thanks. Hey, my guns and kit are in my trunk in the storage room. Can you keep it with you? I might be back one day with some other outfit – you never know.'

Yogi assured me that he and the brothers would watch out for it.

It was hard to pinpoint what my biggest problem was, as I didn't really know myself. I would have found a ton of obvious shit if I had bothered to stop and think about it. I had been having plenty of sleepless nights; even the normally soothing sounds of war hadn't been helping much. But I put it all down to the fatigue, the five-month stint, the stress of the upcoming wedding and the fact that I knew that this was the end of the Blackwater road for me.

I felt a bit betrayed. We had been there when they first asked anybody and everybody from the special forces world to rush to Iraq to man the contracts. Now, we were all being tossed from the cot. It seemed that only US personnel were good enough to protect US interests. Well fuck you very much. But whatever had caused me to get so out of control was something I had yet to deal with. It would get a lot worse before it got any better.

After saying my goodbyes at BIAP, I went through the boarding and emigration process for what I knew would be the last time for a very long while. As the plane lifted off the ground, I had that familiar feeling of my life being in someone else's hands. *If we get shot down now, then inshallah.*

The plane spiralled upwards, and I gazed down at a shrinking Baghdad. I already missed the place, but my time with Blackwater was over and I knew it. It wasn't how I wanted to leave, but I had done what I considered to be a very good job, in a very difficult place.

In any case, for now – maybe for ever – it was *hasta la vista,* Baghdad.

AFTERWORD

En route back to New Zealand, Larry caught me in my room at the Bristol Hotel in Jordan. He'd called my Thuraya, and he sounded genuinely sad to see me go. But in the same breath he confirmed what I already suspected: I was not going to be invited back to Blackwater.

He said everyone in Moyock and in Baghdad were very happy with me and my time with the company, particularly as I had been there from the very beginning. But the times were changing, and it was only going to get more confusing before it got clearer, and he expected that a lot of the guys were going to move on. I told Larry that there were no hard feelings, but I thought it was a pity the gutless shits from Moyock didn't have the balls to tell me to my face, while I was in-country.

In fact, Blackwater had a dirty habit of informing someone they were no longer required only once they had left the country. That was fine if you'd managed to store your kit somewhere safe, while you made arrangements to find a new contract with another company. But not everyone did, and that meant they had just left all their expensive equipment behind, in the belief that they would be coming back to BW. The gear was often rat-fucked by some of the more unscrupulous company employees, and there were now a lot more of them among the ranks.

In due course I would return to Iraq, though not with Black-water, of course. During all my time, which would eventually be seven years in total, I did not lose one member of any of my teams. No one was killed or seriously injured. Everyone who was with me lived to fight another day and go home. The contracts we were in-volved with produced good outcomes. None of my guys or I ever did anything that I believe could be deemed excessive or warrant labelling us as criminals. We worked hard and played hard, while maintaining the highest standard, and I was proud of that.

I would often hear war stories – mostly bullshit – from guys who would love to recount the incidents and contacts they had been in-volved in, but our brand of close protection was, and always should be, about *conflict avoidance* – getting a client safely from one place to another – and we had done just that, every time.

Sure enough, most of the guys who had worked with me started leaving Blackwater as well. The place just wasn't the same. There were too many backstabbers sucking up to headquarters and jock-eying for the senior positions in the contracts.

In the meantime, Blackwater's reputation was being slammed at every turn. It didn't matter that, over the years and thousands of runs protecting clients and State Department CPAs and other fa-cilities, Blackwater never once lost a client, despite losing dozens of our brothers. Blackwater had become the scapegoat for everything bad happening in Iraq. I had experienced it first hand, when an Aussie company's security team had wanted to hide in our com-pound in Karrada after shooting some poor civilian on Irish. They had done a runner from the scene, after telling Big Army that they were from Blackwater.

I know this because I was the person who they told this to when I was called to the gate by Omar, to see if they were allowed inside. I let everyone know that none of our guys had been involved, having told the guilty team to fuck off.

Even the US media were jumping on the bandwagon, vilifying Blackwater without finding out the facts. It was, of course, a useful distraction, as the invasion turned pear-shaped and became an unstoppable civil war.

The final nail in the coffin for Blackwater came in September 2007, when seventeen Iraqi civilians were shot dead at the Nisour Square roundabout in Baghdad by, as we were led to believe, several trigger-happy assholes working the State Department contract. The rumour among those in the know was that at least one of those guys had known exactly what he was doing during the massacre. All he wanted to do was kill Iraqis and appear like some kind of hero, instead of the murdering asshole that he really was.

It also went to show how the 'American-citizens-only' manning procedure and the supposed security clearances and vetting processes weren't worth a pinch of shit.

Blackwater Commercial unjustly copped a lot of flak for the incident, even though they had absolutely nothing to do with it. Hardly anyone cared to find out that Blackwater had at least two entities running security teams on the ground in Iraq; everyone in Blackwater was simply tarred with the same brush.

Years later after an 'investigation' and several trials, by both the DOJ and the media, four members of the BW State contract were sentenced to very lengthy terms in prison for the actions of Nisour

Square. To me this verdict, at the time, seemed to be the correct outcome for the crimes the world was told they had perpetrated. Innocent until proven guilty right?

Then in 2021 President Trump pardoned the accused, to the outrage of the ill-informed. Even I was a bit sceptical as to why, until I was able to watch some in-depth interviews with the guys themselves. These are conducted by Shawn Ryan and can be seen on YouTube. Shawn does a great job of letting each of the guys explain the incident and its fallout from their perspectives, and listening to what they had to say certainly changed my mind. I strongly suggest you watch them.

I won't be able to do justice to their stories by attempting to retell them here, so, long story short, I would now say, 'If they want you, they will get you.' My belief now is that the boys were the sacrificial lambs, the low-hanging fruit, sent to the slaughter to appease the conscience of the screaming left-wing media, anti-Blackwater crowd and Iraqi citizens. The real war criminals however, the ones who started the whole invasion under bogus pretences, never faced justice. They were left to become incredibly wealthy 'elderly statesmen'.

The Nisour incident came not long after the devastating loss of five heroic brothers from the Little Bird team, in January 2007. They were bravely doing what they always did, which was providing a QRF to anyone who needed it. The Birds had responded when the BW State guys were involved in an attack out in a Sunni district of Baghdad.

As the first Little Bird flew in, their door gunner was shot and killed by automatic gunfire from the ground. That bird was forced to return to LZ Washington. Then a second Little Bird was hit and crashed into some power cables as it tried to land safely. Sadly, all four crew members were killed.

Although every Blackwater operator who died in Iraq should be remembered and honoured, I believe there should be a special place reserved for those Little Bird crews, who paid the ultimate price while bravely supporting us on the ground. Thank you, brothers.

As the rot really set in at Blackwater, we heard Moyock had hired lawyers to try to sue the families of Jerry, Wes and the other boys killed in Fallujah, to stop them claiming compensation. Like they hadn't suffered enough already. That was unforgivable. It wasn't like the company hadn't made enough money out of Iraq. They could have easily afforded to compensate the families properly for their losses and not even batted an eyelid and remained honourable. Instead, they dragged those families through a hellish court battle paying huge sums in lawyers' fees before an out-of-court settlement was reached.

Not right, not right at all, and they know it.

The one consolation from the Fallujah killings was that, years later, a SEAL Team captured the alleged mastermind of the ambush before handing him over to the Iraqi courts. At his trial he was found guilty and hanged by his neck.

After leaving Blackwater, I was fortunate enough to find a contract in the Kurdistan region of Iraq with Shadow as my new boss. By fortunate, I mean that the security situation was much better there than in the south of the country. I even managed to convince Noodle to come up and work with me. I then did the occasional job in Syria, Lebanon, Africa and Egypt, before Jen and I moved to Amman, Jordan, to live. At first we absolutely loved it, but by 2010 I was completely done with the Middle East.

I was tired and needed a change.

Although I would still work security contracts here and there, I have not been with a company like Blackwater since, and I don't think I ever will again. From what I hear from friends in the big security company game, it's even more than ever about the big money now, while the guys on the ground get the scraps, and their daily rates have been slashed to a fraction of what we were earning. The company's attitude is that if people don't like it, there are always other former military guys to take their place.

Iraq was the great security contractor experiment, where the owners of companies like Blackwater tried to showcase the viability of private operators alongside, or in place of, the military. Did it work? It did take some pressure off the military, but, as security companies moved more into combat roles, the casualties started to mount. Private security became a hard pill for left-leaning politicians to swallow, and it would really only be acceptable while there was a Republican President in Washington. Under Barack Obama, such companies slid back into the shadows, trying to operate unseen and out of sight of prying eyes.

To me and many others, the invasion of Iraq was a war crime. After a long period of reflection, the key question for me remains this: did I willingly participate in that war crime, and am I guilty by association for the pain and suffering of the Iraqi people? I think the answer can only be 'yes'. *Yes, I did willingly participate, and therefore yes, I am guilty.*

When I finally left Iraq, I would accept a training contract in Africa, one that would finally give me the opportunity to change my life in ways that I had been avoiding for so long. Jen moved to Canada, while I headed off to Juba, South Sudan, teaching close protection drills to the Sudan People's Liberation Army Presidential Guard. To my frustration, and like Noodle's contract with Greystone, every day was a Monday, teaching and reteaching the same stuff.

My drinking habits hadn't changed much, and during that contract I was drinking as much as everyone else on the training team, which was too much. I had a great bunch of old hands as my work colleagues, and all but two of them had worked in Iraq.

We trained hard all week, and partied harder all weekend, but I wasn't getting the happy kick I used to get in Iraq. I was also becoming more testy with Jen back in Canada. My occasional phone calls and emails were very dark, and, if I had been drinking, they were verbally abusive and out of line. Maybe it was the malaria meds I was on, which were known to kick the shit out of you and give you psychotic dreams. Hell, I sure didn't need pills to give me nightmares. I decided to stop taking the meds, preferring to risk getting malaria.

That didn't seem to be the answer at all. One day I woke to an email from her that said she was done with me, and, if I wanted to remain married, I had to stop drinking. It was a real kick in the balls, but, in all honesty, I kind of knew it was coming. I had continued to push my luck with stupid emails, almost goading her, and Jen had finally had enough. With yet another bad hangover, I read over what I had sent her the night before and cringed at the badly written and abusive accusations. I had accused her of having an affair and spending all the money I was earning. Really dumb shit.

Not taking the ultimatum as seriously as I should have, I continued to drink for the duration of the Sudan contract, blaming her and anyone but myself. When the contract finally finished and everyone flew out of Nairobi, in Kenya, for final goodbyes, it finally hit me: I was the only mug left alone. I had no home and I had no one. *Wow, what the fuck am I going to do?*

The owner of the hotel in Juba knew where I could rent a villa for a few months at a reasonable price, in the Nairobi suburb of Karen

– named after *Out of Africa* author, Karen Blixen. I settled in, but for how long I had no idea.

I used my time in Karen to reassess my life and my priorities and to try to rid myself of the true cause of most of my unhappiness. I found a gym and worked out regularly, getting my body in shape, then one day while I was looking for something new to read, I found hidden in the very back of a cupboard a book called *Shantaram*, written by Gregory David Roberts. At first, the size of the book was a bit daunting, but what else did I have to do, right? I started reading and was immediately hooked. I couldn't put it down.

Everything about Roberts's story resonated with me, and I could closely relate to the characters and their situation; Roberts was running away from his past, alone in an unfamiliar country, but was eventually able to find purpose and direction in the most unlikely of places. That was my life.

To say it changed me is an understatement. I felt like the book had come to me just when I needed it most, and I was ready to accept the magic in its message, which to me was: when life gives you the opportunity to change the shitty situation you put yourself in, be smart enough to recognise it, be smart enough to take it and be smart enough to action it to its fullest. You may not get another chance.

I guess it was the spiritual slap to the head I needed, similar to the one Dave had given me back in New Zealand when he reminded me of Jen, and what I was missing.

Apart from having my amazing children, there were three things I was very proud to have accomplished in life. First was joining the New Zealand SAS. Those three letters, 'SAS', hold a magic that opens doors. The second achievement I am proud of was working for Blackwater in Iraq. When I tell people, I never try to justify or explain what I did. I don't need to, but I love to look at people's facial expressions while they wonder what it was like.

But the third achievement I am so very proud of is giving up alcohol. Usually when I tell people, I am met with a mix of sympathy and admiration. Sympathy, because they have images of a drunken wife-beater or a raging alcoholic. A binge drinker for sure; a wife-beater, no. Admiration, because whoever I tell often wishes they could give up themselves.

Hey, I don't judge. You give up when you give up. When I did, like the plane leaving BIAP, I spiralled up above the danger and headed off to a place of peace and safety, not just for me but for everyone, as the world is a safer place now that I have stopped drinking.

It's been thirteen years since I've had a drop of alcohol, and I haven't missed it one little bit. It's only been during that time that I have started making decisions in my life that are fruitful and beneficial to me and those around me. It's amazing when I think about how many years and thousands of dollars I have squandered between hangovers. Jen and I are still together and very happy, living high on a mountain, with no neighbours, no noise and just our dogs. I also have a fantastic relationship with my children. We communicate almost every day, and I believe I am no longer the Shit Dad of the Century. And if I ever think about wanting to have a drink, which I don't, all I need to do is think about the hangovers, memory blanks and post-booze depression. To give up something as destructive as excessive drinking is hard, and it happens only when it's meant to happen. I am fortunate that it did when it did, and now, because of it, life is good.

Although my bad dreams still come and go, I have a better handle on them now. Every so often Dingo or Jerry will pop into my head unexpectedly, and I'll mist up and internally curse that my warnings about him were ignored. I still believe that if they had been heeded, Jerry and his team would not have been killed that day in Fallujah.

The BW boys have all moved on. I keep in irregular contact with a few of them since the years in Iraq. Noodle lives back in New Zealand and hits the waves on his long board as often as he can. So does T, who I believe reluctantly hung up the rugby boots only a year or so ago. Yogi bounces around between different contracts in the States. Stumpy returned to the Chicago PD, Mark is happily married and working his little ass off and Lish is sipping whiskey in Texas. Every so often I will get a message of catch-up from G2, Miyagi, Cash, Haggis, Tank, Rock or Shadow. It's always good to hear the boys are doing well and are healthy and alive.

I've lost touch with Two Trays, Yard Dog, G-Man and the original crew since I left Iraq, but I hope they are all happy and well. Sadly, Bullfrog died following an accident on his Harley and Tool from cancer. Before Tool passed several of the guys paid him and his family a visit and shared a few steaks, beers and stories. I'm told even the story of me rolling the hard car at the crossed swords came up. Good times.

Blackwater still gets a bad rap, and I guess it always will. But to us who worked for Blackwater USA in Iraq, we are all proud of what we did and achieved, no matter what the armchair quarterbacks say about us. And all I say to anyone who wants to put shade on us, or private military contracting in general, is that if you weren't there, you have no fuckin' idea.

We were Blackwater, and, like it or not, we always will be.

ACKNOWLEDGEMENTS

Special thanks to:

Damien Lewis
Jennifer Rice
Mark Boal
Hugo Lingren
Angela Chapman
Karen Soich LLB, LLM, Lawyer
Robert Amsterdam

CAST IN ORDER OF APPEARANCE

Rose: Baghdad Team and IRI housekeeper

Mark: BW administrator, Baghdad

Mr Custer: Custer Battles co-founder

Mr Battles: Custer Battles co-founder

Bobby/G-Man: Custer Battles, Edinburgh Risk and Security
Management

Chris/Yard Dog: Custer Battles, BW Commercial

Bill/Two Trays: Custer Battles, BW Commercial

Pappy: Custer Battles, BW Commercial

Muqtada al-Sadr: Leader of Sadr City and the Mahdi Army

Canadian team leader: Custer Battles

Nepalese team member: Sleeping Custer Battles member

Matt: Former Delta Force, Custer Battles project manager

Tom: Custer Battles, originator of BW Commercial

Paul Bremer: US de facto Head of State of Iraq

Randy: Custer Battles, BW Commercial before being fired after
Basra run

Mohamoud/Mo: Original BW Commercial driver and fixer

Frank: BW Commercial team member with bargaining 'skills'

Frank: BW State Dept project manager, Bremer detail, Green Zone
Larry: BW State Dept team member, Bremer detail, CPA recons
Mike: BW State Dept team member, Bremer detail, CPA recons
T: Former NZSAS/the Unit, CRG team member
Sean Penn: American actor and activist
JP: BW Commercial, BW ESS Kuwait project manager
White Boy: BW Commercial, Karbala and Najaf CP TL
Ben: BW Commercial, Karbala and Najaf
Jerry: BW Commercial, N1 team leader killed in Fallujah
Brian: BW Commercial and Greystone manager, Baghdad
Mark: BW Commercial finance administrator, Baghdad
Dave: BW Commercial administrator, Baghdad
Rich: BW Commercial project manager, Baghdad and Al-Hillah
Omar: BW Iraqi fixer, Baghdad
Mohammad: BW Iraqi fixer, Baghdad
GC: State Department official
Pete Goodie/Dingo: Custer Battles, BW Commercial
Cash: BW borrowed from time to time to supplement my team
George: BW and Greystone team member
Phil: BW and Greystone team member
John: BW team house administrator
Peanut: BW Commercial team member
Wes: BW Commercial N1 team member killed in Fallujah
Jason: BW Commercial B2 team leader
Scott: BW Commercial N1 team member killed in Fallujah
Mike: BW Commercial N1 team member killed in Fallujah
Oscar: BW Commercial team member
Lt General Sanchez: US military commander in charge of Iraq Ops
Erik Prince: Blackwater owner
Bullfrog: BW

Stumpy: BW

Tank: BW

Lish: BW

Brownie: BW

Randy: BW (New Randy)

James: BW Moyock sled dog

Alex: BW Moyock sled dog

Harry: BW Mamba team IC

Miyagi: BW Mamba team, later IC

T-Boy: BW Mamba team

Lionel/Noodle: BW and best friend

Carol: Sister

Bomber: Ex-SAS buddy

Pug: Ex-SAS buddy

Steve: BW fat guy 1

Jim: BW fat guy 2

Hacksaw: BW State Dept Little Bird pilot

Hollywood: BW team member, Najaf

Goldberg: BW team member, Najaf

Colombian military: Najaf CPA

JC: Triple Canopy Al-Kut IC

Zel: Son

Shannon/Chaz: Son

Keely: Daughter

Arden: Daughter

Dave: Brother-in-law

Jen: Fiancée/wife

Clutch: BW team member

G. W. Bush: US President

Musab al-Zarqawi: Terrorist leader

Nick Berg: US citizen beheaded by Zarqawi

Bruce: BW Al-Hillah member killed by IED

John: Australian client

Greg/Wingnut: Erbil hotel

Kate: Wingnut's girlfriend

Bird: BW member

Rich: BW project manager ESS

Malcolm: BW Ops O ESS

Bam Bam: BW ESS TL (Al-Kut run)

Kato: BW ESS killed in vehicle accident

Chris/Lurch: BW ESS killed on Irish

Adam: BW Polish

Krzysztof: BW Polish killed on Irish

Artur: BW Polish killed on Irish

Paul: BW Polish

JC: BW ESS killed on Irish

Rat: BW ESS

Jim: CRG ex-SAS buddy (weapon for booze swap)

Walter: CRG ex-mil PTI buddy (weapon for booze swap)

Ranger: BW Al-Diwaniyah (big stories)

Guy/G2: Team house IC

Stephanie: Faceless Moyock PM

Omar: Jordanian guard IC, IRI contract

Haggis: IRI contract

Yogi: IRI contract

Hammer: IRI contract

Shadow: IRI contract

Dodger: IRI contract

Zen: IRI contract

Rock: IRI contract

Piper: IRI contract

Orange: IRI security manager

Stretch: IRI contract

Shaky: Mamba swap to IRI

Tool: Mamba 2IC

Manny: BW Mambas

Sparky: Killed in Mamba attack

Snowman: Mamba incident